Cross Mountain Books

engaging books that inform, educate, and inspire

www.crossmountainbooks.com

Learn more about Sawbones
and the Pecks of Mossy Creek Series

Praise for Sawbones

"I have waited a long time to read Sawbones. Now I see why. The Author tells the story of Dr. Isham Talbot Peck, son, husband, father, landowner in Tennessee and Louisiana. He was a medical doctor but was unable to avoid tragedy in his own family. "Sawbones" articles were both entertaining and informative. Peck's thorough research into the backgrounds of these articles and the places and personalities mentioned brought them to life. Once again, Andy Peck has given us a glimpse into the triumphs and tragedies in the lives of the Peck Family."

■ LINDA GASS, Archives Assistant, Carson-Newman University, Jefferson City, Tennessee

"In his newest book – *Sawbones: The Life and Times of Dr. Isham Talbot Peck*, Andy Peck asks the question: how is it possible to know your ancestors in a meaningful way? The answer is found in the book itself. Dr. Peck was not only educated but also well-travelled and inquisitive. Subscribing to newspapers, he did not hesitate to share his opinions and observations with the editors. His great-great-great-grandson has taken these comments and has annotated them as to the people, events and locations mentioned. In so doing, he has discovered the persona of his ancestors. This is a gift not only to the Peck descendants but also to the heritage of Cocke County."

■ E. R. WALKER III, Cocke County Historian, Newport, Tennessee

"Students who want to know more of the times of the Civil War can search through Sawbones Peck's 60+ articles; giving readers insider experiences of military, family, and one's spiritual life during that period. Mr. Peck did a lot of homework to give students like me an easy way to understand the times of 19th Century Tennessee, America."

■ JUSTICE BRATTON, 13 years old, homeschooler in Kathmandu, Nepal

"Wow! If the study of history is the re-telling of stories, Andy Peck is a master. With painstaking, in depth research, he has produced not just a regional history but a book for all history enthusiasts. Using interactive QR codes, in addition to loads of photos and illustrations, Dr. Isham Talbot "Sawbones" Peck and his family's life and times are beautifully restored, allowing readers to agonize and celebrate with them from the cradle to the grave.

Utilizing biography, genealogy, and extensively annotated newspaper columns, readers are provided with a telescoping history covering considerable 19th century ground with reflections on events happening on the local, regional, and national stages including three wars, Reconstruction, and issues related to Native Americans.

Sawbones is a "must add" to our collection, not only for its biographical and genealogical information documenting hundreds of names and places but also as a reference tool for local history research and 19th century studies. It is a wonderful example for students and researchers alike of how thorough research can make history fascinating!"

■ ALBERT A. LANG, Special Collections Librarian & Archivist, Mildred L. Iddins Special Collections, Stephens-Burnett Memorial Library, Carson-Newman University, Jefferson City, Tennessee

"As students of American History, the journey into our collective past is never finished and our knowledge never complete. Author Andy Peck's latest effort, *Sawbones*, captivates the imagination and skillfully transforms the reader into an active participant immersed in southern 19th century American culture. Using QR codes, related websites, and extensive footnotes the reader is effortlessly able to further explore related events and subjects that are of interest, enhancing one's knowledge. *Sawbones* is an important contribution to understanding the 1800's era lifestyle, travel, politics and news of the day. This marvelous book chronicles Dr. Isham Peck's life and times, sorrows and opinions, while revealing his true character and wit. "Sawbones" is a must have for all history lovers."

■ ROB BEUCH, President, Jefferson County Historical Society, Tennessee

The Pecks of Mossy Creek

The Pecks of Mossy Creek series editor, Andy Peck, seeks to bring the Peck Family together through books, information sharing, and family gatherings. If you descend from the Pecks of Mossy Creek, please email andy@crossmountainbooks.com for more info and updates. The photos above were taken in July 2021 at Mossy Creek Station, Jefferson City, Tennessee. Special thanks to Linda Gass, Teresa Collins, Kim Stapleton, Downtown Mayor Frank Brown, and the Mossy Creek Foundation.

The Pecks of Mossy Creek

The Pecks of Mossy Creek series highlights the founding family of Mossy Creek (now Jefferson City), Tennessee and their ancestors and descendants. Adam Peck, Sr. and his wife Elizabeth (Sharkey) Peck pioneered west from their home in Fincastle, VA and floated down the Holston River on a flatboat. They settled Mossy Creek using a land grant of 5,000 acres Adam earned for his service in the Revolutionary War. As one of the Overmountain Men, he helped win the Battle of Kings Mountain in 1780, and eight years later founded Mossy Creek. Adam and Elizabeth initially moved into an abandoned fort, and then built their own log cabin. He built a grist mill, which was the first mill in the area. At his wife's request, they built the first church in Mossy Creek and named it Elizabeth's Chapel in 1790. The Pecks had a number of slaves, and Elizabeth taught them to read and write along with their 12 children. One of these slaves was named Uncle John, and they installed him as the first preacher. Rev. John Peck was called "the best human being there ever was," and the old log chapel became the foundation for the Methodist and Presbyterian churches in Jefferson City. In addition to the monument that says "Adam and Elizabeth Peck: Pioneers to the west from Virginia in 1788," the family burial plot in the Old Westview Cemetery in Jefferson City features a plaque that reads, "Pioneers of 19th Century Methodism at Mossy Creek."

The Pecks of Mossy Creek series seeks to highlight notable Peck family members and their stories and writings through the years. Some notable Peck family members are:

- ❖ Jacob Peck, Sr. (1723-1801) – Adam Peck, Sr.'s father and Revolutionary War Veteran
- ❖ Lydia (Borden) Peck (1728-1800) – Adam Peck, Sr.'s mother and daughter of Benjamin Borden II and Zeruriah Winter
- ❖ Judge Jacob Franklin Peck (1779-1869) – Adam Peck, Sr.'s son, TN Supreme Court Judge, State Senator and Geologist
- ❖ Judge James Hawkins Peck (1790-1836) – Adam Peck Sr.'s son, War of 1812 Veteran, U.S. District Judge for Missouri

Pecks of Mossy Creek Series Books

Ada's Journal and Emma's Letters: The Civil War Era Journal of Emma Peck
Charley's Novel: Mary Anderson and Peacock the Mineralogist, The Bad Luck of a Young Southern Girl

Cross Mountain Books is a proud supporter of the **Mossy Creek Foundation**. A portion of the proceeds from each book sold will be donated to the Mossy Creek Foundation in its efforts to revitalize the Historic Mossy Creek District in Jefferson City, TN. Learn more about this great project by visiting **mossycreekfoundation.org**.

Sawbones: The Life and Times of Dr. Isham Talbot Peck (1811-1887)

THE VOLCANO.—We have nothing new concerning the volcanic symptoms published about Bald mountain. Mr. Russell, of Newport, informed us on Saturday that he had read a letter, written by a reliable gentleman residing in close proximity to the embryo crater, to a relative in Newport, in which the writer spoke of the trem orousness of the earth to the extent of jarring the cubbard ware in his house, of a continual rumbling noise in the mountain and smoke constantly arising from its summit. The writer stated that the people of the locality were alarmed and making preparations to leave. But all of this has already been published, and until some better proof of its volcanic nature is exhibited the theory of our friend "Sawbones" should allay undue excitement.

Figure 1 - 1 Apr 1874 "The Volcano," *The Morristown Gazette*, Morristown, Tennessee

Volume I

Biography
Life and Times Timeline
Mossy Creek Beginnings
Vicksburg, Mississippi
Military Service and the Civil War
First 23 Sawbones Articles 1874-1878

Dr. Isham Talbot Peck
23 Feb 1811 – 28 Nov 1887

Dr. Peck, the inimitable "Sawbones," of Wolf Creek, came over on the Buncombe and took a western bound train Saturday night.

Figure 2 - 3 Dec 1879 "Personal", *The Morristown Gazette*, 2.

Sawbones

The Life and Times of Dr. Isham Talbot Peck (1811-1887)

Volume I

Written by
Andy Peck

The Pecks of Mossy Creek
Andy Peck, Series Editor

Cross Mountain Books

Valdosta, Georgia
www.crossmountainbooks.com

Published by
Cross Mountain Books in Valdosta, Georgia

Manufactured in the United States of America.

First Edition.

Cover Photo: Photograph originally by Samuel Anderson, circa 1863, New Orleans, LA, AI enhanced using Remini, then professionally colourised.
Frontispiece: Original photograph by Samuel Anderson, circa 1863, New Orleans, LA.
Back Cover Photos: Original photography by Andy Peck, 15 Jun 2023 in Vicksburg, Mississippi, Andy Peck with dad Drew, sons Justice (red shirt) and Hudson (black shirt) with cousin Jan Hyland Daigre (Warrant County Circuit Clerk) [left] and Vicksburg looking north from 10 South Rooftop Bar & Grill [right], news clipping from *The Morristown Gazette*, 3 Dec 1879, "Personal", 2.

Signed copies available. Books also available in quantity for promotional or premium use. For information, email info@crossmountainbooks.com.

www.crossmountainbooks.com
Facebook: fb.me/crossmountainbooks

Publisher's Cataloging-in-Publication Data

Names: Peck, Andy (Thomas Andrew), 1981- , author. | Peck, Isham Talbot, 1811-1887, author.
Title: Sawbones : the life and times of Dr. Isham Talbot Peck (1811-1887) / Andy Peck ; Isham Talbot Peck.
Description: Valdosta, GA : Cross Mountain Books, 2023. | Series: The Pecks of Mossy Creek. | Includes photographs, paintings, maps, and charts. | Includes bibliographical references and index. | 2 vols. | Summary: Biography of Dr. Isham Peck, pre-Civil War Army surgeon, life-long physician, Vicksburg cotton plantation owner, Mossy Creek/Jefferson City farmer, Wolf Creek fisherman, sportsman, and prolific writer to Morristown Gazette and Spirit of the Times newspapers under pen name Sawbones. Includes analysis of 41 Sawbones articles written from 1874-1886.
Identifiers: LCCN 2023914750 | ISBN 9781955121088 (pbk, vol. 1) | ISBN 9781955121125 (pbk, vol. 2) | ISBN 9781955121095 (hardcover, vol. 1) | ISBN 9781955121132 (hardcover, vol. 2) | ISBN 9781955121101 (ebook, vol. 1) | ISBN 9781955121149 (ebook, vol. 2)
Subjects: LCSH: Peck, Isham Talbot, 1811-1887—Biography. | Talbot, Cordelia M., 1808–1860. | Peck, Emma Elizabeth Henderson, 1833-1899. | Peck, Helen D. Rapalje Glass. | Peck, Jacob, 1779-1869. | Yoe, Pryor F. | Peck, Benjamin, Jr., 1829-1902. | Moody, D. L., 1837-1899. | Sankey, Ira, 1840-1908. | East Tennessee and Virginia Railroad Company. | Peck family. | Allen family. | Newspapers—Tennessee—History. | Physicians—Biography. | Dueling—History. | Methodist Church—United States—History. | United States—History—Civil War, 1861-1865. | Slavery—Louisiana. | Tennessee, East—History. | North Carolina—History. | Mississippi—History. | Louisiana—History. | Mossy Creek (Tenn.)—History. | Wolf Creek (Tenn.)—History. | Vicksburg (Miss.)—History. | Hot Springs (N.C.)—History. | BISAC: BIOGRAPHY & AUTOBIOGRAPHY / Medical. | HISTORY / United States / 19th Century. | HISTORY / United States / State & Local / South (AL, AR, FL, GA, KY, LA, MS, NC, SC, TN, VA, WV).
Classification: LCC F442.1 S28 2023 | DDC 975 P--dc23
LC record available at https://lccn.loc.gov/2023914750

For my mom,
MaryAnn

Thank you for always believing in me,
supporting me, and working hard
to provide for us.
I love you.

TABLE OF CONTENTS

FOREWORD

When beginning my research on Mossy Creek in the 1800s, my goal was to see it through the eyes of the contemporaries of the time period. Through reading newspapers, diaries, letters, books, and journals I fortuitously stumbled across the writer "Sawbones" writings for the Morristown Gazette. This writer added such a personal element to the history of the time with fresh and insightful commentary.

Through his writings in March of 1881, we can see his appreciation for the local hotel owned by Pryor Yoe, but additionally (and if he was writing for the chamber of commerce) "Sawbones" lays out a vivid description of the town with an account of the places of primary importance in this small town. We see suburbs of places still known and others long forgotten. We are given an account of what has stirred the local economy which brought publicity to local merchants and like so many small-town writers of his day the comings and goings of visitors. And if this wasn't enough, he includes gossip and controversy too.

Before long I affectionately called his observations "The Time Capsule" for Mossy Creek. I did this because "Sawbones" in a few short penned paragraphs was so thorough in his description but also so full of life. As I perused *The Morristown Gazette*, I knew any commentary written by "Sawbones" was going to be worth the read. Through research and a friendship with Andy Peck, I was made aware that this writer was Dr. Isham Peck, somebody of incredible significance to the history of this area. This gave his insights and writings extra meaning because Dr. Peck was truly a man of his century.

As Andy Peck has done with his series of books about the Pecks of Mossy Creek, he not only gives the facts but also gives us the personality behind the person. With his thorough research, Andy shows a man who lived enough for several lifetimes, and through incredible highs and incredible lows, he left a mark on his time and his community. Andy does not conceal or hurry by terrible moments in the history of his family but instead shows us

OUR MOSSY CREEK LETTER

Mossy Creek, March 22, '81.

To the Editor of The Morristown Gazette:

MOSSY CREEK

is, as I have already said, a thriving little railroad town. We have here five churches, nine dry goods, grocery and drug stores, a good flouring mill, tan yard, and last but not least, we have a first-class hotel for the accommodation of the weary traveler, and uncle Pryor is always ready to make his guests comfortable. In addition to all this, Mossy Creek has several sub-towns, viz: Collegeville, where Carson College is situate. There they have two stores. Then we have Jay Bird, Needmore, Old Field, Hell's Kitchen and Hayti—all of which are in close proximity to Mossy Creek, and all densely populated. We have here also a semi-monthly newspaper, known as the *Columbian Echo*. As to its whereabouts I am unable to inform you.

CRAMMED AND JAMMED

is J. W. Godwin & Bro.'s store with new goods just from the East and still they are receiving goods daily.

A CAR LOAD

of horses and mules was shipped from this place to Augusta, Ga., by Messrs. Bettis & Malcom on the 21st.

PERSONAL.

Dr. J. P. Legg & Son, of Grainger county, were in town a few days ago on their way home from the South, where they have been dealing in stock.

Mr. J. C. Richberg, proprietor of the Clinton Lime Co., was in town last week examining and prospecting our zinc ore. He pronounces it a very fine quality.

Esq. Ben Peck, of Rutledge was in town yesterday. Don't know his business, but he is a mighty bad man after calves.

SQUABBLE.

The Baptists of this section are getting into a squabble about where to build their church, and I fear that they are fixing for a law suit, which is about as expensive as building. SAWBONES.

Figure 3 - 30 Mar 1881 "Our Mossy Creek Letter", *The Morristown Gazette*, Morristown, Tennessee

how real these moments are with real commentary. In this book we are given a real look at the words and ideas of Dr. Peck with Andy's gift of bringing additional information and an introduction to the importance of the moment, not just to Dr. Peck but to everyone.

As a Civil War Historian, I would recommend this book as it brings to light the sense of obligation that families like the Pecks had in the moments after secession, the sense of civic obligation to their community and state. Here, many southerners of means rose up to "do their part". They raised the light dragoons to contend for the Mossy Creek Community as they "sought to fight off the tyranny of Abraham Lincoln." The call to serve was enhanced by Isham's gift of $1,000 to Benjamin Branner. Here we also see in a community naïve to horrors of war caught up in the pageantry of leaving for war. Through his account, we also see a community that gets to see and experience war in Mossy Creek. We see a population that gets to experience occupation and the Pecks are no stranger to this, either. Andy Peck includes many important reports from the actual battlefield writings of the time.

Just like his ancestors, Andy Peck makes this time period come alive, not just with the words of Dr. Peck, but also through his research and the sharing of valuable accompanying information. Andy has again made a significant contribution, not just to the Peck family, but also to Mossy Creek, Jefferson County, Tennessee and our Country. Please enjoy and treasure these volumes as I have.

David Needs
City Historian
Jefferson City (Mossy Creek), Tennessee
President of the Lakeway Civil War Preservation Association
(Photo courtesy of Carson-Newman University)

ACKNOWLEDGEMENTS

Sawbones would not have been possible without the courageous patience of my wife Sasha. First and foremost, I would like to thank her for bearing with me over the past seven years as I researched family history. I have spent literally hundreds upon hundreds of hours transcribing documents, scouring newspapers, interviewing historians, and traveling to the areas where Isham Peck lived. My wife has endured every early morning, every late night, and every trip, whether she joined me or stayed home with our three amazing boys. Thank you, Sasha! I love you and greatly appreciate your support!

I want to thank my sons, Justice, Hudson, and Noble. You have listened to me share stories about Isham, traveled with me to graveyards, libraries, courthouses, and stood next to me…helping share with others about the Pecks and the world of the 1800s. I will always treasure our one-on-one and family trips to Tennessee, North Carolina, Georgia, Florida, Alabama, Louisiana, and Mississippi, as we sought out every possible nugget about Isham and the Pecks' lives. I pray that you treasure Sawbones and every book I write about our family's rich history. I hope your children and their children are blessed by the books as well. These books are a significant part of your inheritance.

Despite my fear of neglecting someone, I would like to thank the following people who have helped me tremendously on this journey of family research, and with Sawbones specifically. Linda Gass, you are a treasure, and this book would not have been possible without you. Thank you for the Jefferson City tour, the phone conversations, emails, book reviews, Facebook "likes", and your countless contributions to your community. Coach and Historian David Needs, thank you for everything…for the history, for your friendship, for the foreword, and for your faith in Jesus and example you set for your family and your student athletes. Teresa Collins, thank you for your consistent support, your leadership with the Mossy Creek Foundation, and the encouragement you have been to me. Betty and Albert Walker, thank you for your friendship and hospitality, and for welcoming me into your Wolf Creek home so many times. Your contribution to Wolf Creek and Cocke County History is significant, and my books would not have been possible without you. Ann (Kirkpatrick) Peck, the wife of my 2nd cousin 2x removed, "Cousin Ann", you are beautiful. Your love of history, of all things Peck, of Wolf Creek, and your efforts to learn and preserve history will never be forgotten. I've loved our breakfasts each October in Black Mountain, NC, and my visits to your Montreat and Decatur homes. Thank you for Emma's Songbook, it is my oldest and one of my most prized possessions. Eddie Walker, thank you for your friendship and efforts to preserve Cocke County history. Justice Bratton, thank you for reviewing my books! Albert Lang, thank you for your friendship, reviews, and for your help with Mossy Creek and Carson-Newman history. Rob Beuch, thank you for your friendship, for your dedication to Jefferson County history, and for your selfless service to those who visit Glenmore Mansion. Dede Rehkdopf, thank you! Additionally, thank you to Jordon Rushing, Charles Pendleton, Jan (Hyland) Daigre, Dee Hyland, Jacque Painter, and Ike Lassiter. Thank you to my dad Drew Peck, for your support and joining me on some of my history expeditions. Thank you to every Peck and Peck cousin who helped with the genealogies found here. Thank you to my great-aunt Carolyn Arnette "Nette" (Peck) King, you have encouraged me this entire journey. To everyone who has contributed a photo, a story, a clipping, or a note, THANK YOU!   ~Andy

EDITORIAL POLICY

I love to connect people with stories and first-hand accounts that help open a window to our shared history. I am devoted to preserving stories and writings in their original form, so readers can engage, study, and learn from historical texts. Though not always possible due to space considerations, in addition to transcribing all the articles written to and from Sawbones, many are shown here as newspaper clippings. There is something significant, I believe, to experiencing writings in their original form. I am forever indebted to websites such as newspapers.com, the Library of Congress, and the National Endowment for the Humanities "Chronicling America" project. Their archiving, OCR, and powerful search engines allowed me to find each of the Sawbones articles.

Notes, references, and citations have been placed as footnotes, allowing the reader to quickly see where the information was gathered, and move on. This eliminates the need to constantly "flip to the back of the chapter/book" to find out more information. In general, the book is organized chronologically. The reader will notice that Isham visits certain topics multiple times. These topics are typically discussed most fully at their first mention, but occasionally longer explanations come later in the timeline.

When I began this project, I knew relatively little about Isham. You will see in some of my writing the element of "the unknown" and my process of discovery. Later, once I completed the manuscript, I returned to the beginning for editing and realized how much I had learned in the process. I have attempted to correct all errors, but also left in some of the "we'll have to wait and see" verbiage, allowing the reader to join me in the exciting process of discovery.

As I embarked on my journey of discovering family history, a few people cautioned me (in general, not specifically about the Pecks), "You may not be pleased about what you discover." My view is that history is history, we cannot change it, but we can learn from it. If you are considering researching your/our family history, my encouragement is to go for it. Every nugget we discover about our family's past, helps us better understand how we got here, and how to best move forward.

I, as the author, and Cross Mountain Books, as publisher, have sought to present here an accurate transcription, and explanation, of original source documents, seeking to place each text in its context. All references to slavery, and words used to refer to black people, are presented in their original form for historical purposes. No offense is intended. We believe that all men are created equal, and at the outset of this book, we publicly condemn any form of racism. We believe that accurately viewing the past can help inform us today, and inspire us towards a better future.

Very Respectfully,

Andy Peck
Author
Editor - The Pecks of Mossy Creek series
Cross Mountain Books

INTRODUCTION

Dr. Isham Talbot Peck didn't just live IN the 19th century, he LIVED the 19th century. His life was shaped and intertwined with the War of 1812, military operations with Native Americans and the Cherokee Removal, the Mexican-American War, the Civil War, and Reconstruction. He had some family members fighting for the abolition of slavery, and many others fighting for the Confederacy. He witnessed duels between the newspapermen of Vicksburg, Mississippi, and he owned both farms and plantations. He spent time in big cities around the world, but made his final abode nestled among the majestic and rustling creeks of East Tennessee and Western North Carolina along the French Broad River in Wolf Creek, Tennessee. He traveled by horse, stage coach, railroad, and steamboat. He was well-educated, and surrounded himself with newspapers from all over the country. He was leaned on by his church family to settle disputes, and he talked former slaves out of committing murder in the weeks after the signing of the emancipation proclamation. He wrestled a buck that left one of his arms disabled, and he suffered from neuralgia in his face.

He married three women, the first of whom was his cousin. He had nine children, lost five of them before his death, lost three of them to suicide, and was buried on the same day as his son Ashby. Two of his sons started newspapers, and both he, his dad, and his wife were prolific writers. His dad and multiple relatives were senators and governors of Tennessee, Kentucky, and Mississippi. For a period, his dad was a supreme court justice for Tennessee, his uncle was the judge for the U.S. District Court for the entire District of Missouri, and his cousin was the Chief Justice for the Mississippi Supreme Court…all at the same time. He and his father wrote articles for the famous *Spirit of the Times* by Bill Porter, which is said to have influenced the writing of Mark Twain. He published numerous articles in *The Morristown Gazette* under the pen name Sawbones, and people from around the country wrote responses to him. He was a physician, and his son Ed also served as a doctor, and railway surgeon. He and his family had their hand in geology, zoology, mineralogy, law, medicine, farming, planting, travel, literature, and the military throughout the 1800s.

This book is the fruit of years of investigating, digging, and trail chasing…and has benefited greatly from the digitized world we now live in. Where possible, I have included entire primary sources, giving you the pleasure of enjoying history in its original form. As you read about Isham, and his life and times, please take a moment when you are able to follow the links, click on the QR codes, and walk with me as I travel to many of these places personally. I hope that you enjoy the journey as much as I have.

~Andybones

Figure 4 – "Sawbones" by Pattie Peck Harrelson
Painting commissioned by author, includes features representing Dr. Isham Talbot Peck's life.
Cross Mountain, Wolf Creek, and Billy Buck from Henderson Plantation, 2020.

BIOGRAPHY OVERVIEW

Figure 5 - Dr. Isham Talbot Peck - Peck Family Collection - Digitized by the Author at home of Arnette (Peck) King 2017 Colorized 2022 by Michael Williams

What characterized the 19th century in Tennessee and America? I would submit to you, that by studying the life of Dr. Isham Talbot Peck, you get a fairly comprehensive answer. From 1811-1887, he lived 76 years that nearly spanned the entire century. His grandfather fought in the Revolutionary War and lived in Tennessee when it was still the State of Franklin, helping form the state constitution during the first two general assemblies. His father and numerous uncles fought in the War of 1812 under Andrew Jackson, receiving significant land holdings as a result. He moved to Vicksburg, Mississippi as a young man with his brother William Raine Peck, and became acquainted with plantations and steamboats.

His uncle, James Hawkins Peck, became the first Judge for the District of Missouri in 1822, just after Missouri became a state. His father, Jacob Clayton Peck, served as a Tennessee State Senator and eventually became a Tennessee Supreme Court judge, serving from 1822-1834. He attended Greenville College (now Tusculum University) starting in 1826, gaining a liberal arts education, and then received medical training. At age 19, his uncle James H. Peck became the 4th person in American history to be impeached by the U.S. House of Representatives. Even though he was acquitted (by one vote), this year-long trial made national news for him and the family.

Isham married his Kentucky cousin Cordelia M. Talbot in 1832, but immediately left to serve as a physician with the military in Mexico. We know from his passport application that he was 6' 3", light complexion, with blue eyes and an aquiline nose. Having land inherited from his grandfather Adam, and being given land from his father, by 1834 he owned 5,000 acres "on the waters of Paint Creek" in East Tennessee/Western North Carolina. By 1835 he was divorced and his ex-wife admitted to a mental institution. During the 1830s/1840s he served as a military surgeon at Ft. Des Moines (Iowa) and Ft. Dearborn (Chicago) on the frontier, and also did extensive travelling around the world. On 18 May 1837 he married a wealthy widow named Helen D. (Rapalje) Glass near Vicksburg and became a slave owner. He owned 52 slaves according to the 1840 Warren, Mississippi Census. We do not know what happened to his second wife Helen, but on 12 Oct 1848 he married Emma Elizabeth Henderson, and remained married to her for the rest of his life.

In 1853, Emma gave birth to their first child, Ada Louise Peck. Ada's life is a beautiful picture of the extreme joys and sorrows that are to come for Isham and Emma. She came with such joy, and her life ended with much sorrow. During the 1850s/1860s, Isham and his family made numerous trips between their plantation in East Carroll Parish, Louisiana and the Peck family homestead in Mossy Creek (Jefferson City, Tennessee) that they called Oakland. Fortunately, many of their adventures were chronicled by Emma, and can be found in *Ada's Journal and Emma's Letters: The Civil War Era Journal and Letters of Emma Peck*, by Cross Mountain Books, 2021. Isham and his family came face to face with the effects of disease and death during these years. They lost family members to yellow fever, scarlet fever, and eventually numerous family members to the Civil War.

Prior to the War Between the States, things were going well for the Pecks. Planting was profitable in Mississippi and Louisiana, the family had considerable legal and political influence in numerous states, and travel was accessible to them. They picked out a spot in Wolf Creek, TN and named it Glen Ada (after their daughter), then built a white mountain home on the land to spend their summers. They became close friends with the Allen family, and their relationship has persisted to this day. In 1859, though, tragedy entered their lives like a flood.

First, their beloved Ada died from cholera while they were in Louisiana. This devastated the family emotionally. In 1861, his brother William became a signatory to the Louisiana Ordinance of Secession as the Civil War broke out. The Peck family had considerable involvement in the war. Brother William enlisted as a private in the 9th Louisiana Infantry in Jul 1861, and eventually rose to the rank of Brigadier General, seeing combat at Gettysburg, and finishing his military career as the commander of the Louisiana Tigers. Their brother Adam C. Peck joined the Confederacy as well, was stationed for a time at Strawberry Plains, TN, and was eventually killed in the Battle of Piedmont in 1864. Isham was 50 years old when the war kicked off and he donated $1000 to outfit "The Peck Light Dragoons," a light cavalry unit organized under Capt. Benjamin M. Branner of Mossy Creek. Isham's cousin, Lafayette Peck, a West Point Graduate, was killed during the Battle of Tuscaloosa in 1863. Isham's uncle, Adam Peck, Jr., enlisted in the 11th Battalion, Georgia State Guards, at the age of 72. He had been a prisoner of war during the War of 1812, but nothing could stop him from getting in the fight. Isham's cousin, Jacob Young Peck (Adam Peck, Jr.'s son), died as a Confederate soldier in Atlanta while it was under siege in 1863. His sister Juliet died of unknown causes in 1864. The same year, his cousin Mary Catherine Peck died of cholera. His brother Wiley Hawkins Peck died in 1866 while visiting their brother William at his plantation in Madison Parish, Louisiana. Then his uncle, Adam Peck, Jr., died at the age of 75 in Dahlonega, GA. His father-in-law, William Henderson, died in 1867, just a couple years after the Civil War ended. The war may have been over, but the struggle for the Pecks, and their fellow Southerners, was not.

Conditions in the South were rough during this time. There was a cholera epidemic and many of the former slaves who still lived on their Louisiana Plantation died, along with 83 others on a nearby plantation. Many of the neighbors left, somtimes fleeing to other countries like Honduras. General Grant's Union Army had raided the Henderson Plantation (owned by his wife's parents) during the Battle of Milliken's Bend, taking an estimated $32,040 worth of grain, food, and other supplies. Many of the homes in the area were destroyed and burned by the Union Army. Isham lived on the

Henderson Plantation off and on, but was there in the aftermath of the War. In his letters to the editor of *The Morristown Gazzette*, he wrote about his interactions with the former slaves. His sister Eliza "Jane" Talbot (Peck) McEffee died in 1868 at the age of 56. Then his dad Judge Jacob died in 1869 at the age of 89. Just two years later, his brother William (the former Confederate General) died at the age of 52. In 1870, his mom Sophia died and his son Willie committed suicide. In the 12-year period from 1859 to 1871, when Isham was 48-60 years old, 17 of his close family members died including two children and his mom and dad, the nation began and ended the Civil War, and he saw hundreds of people dying around him on the plantations in East Carroll Parrish, Louisiana. During the same period, 4 of his children were born. Joy tempered by extreme sorrow marked the life of this man.

The last 16 years of his life, from 1871-1887, were marked by continued travel, time invested in his children, and settling down in Wolf Creek, TN on his 30,000 acres. He wrote extensively to *The Morristown Gazzette* under the penname Sawbones during these years, which made this book possible. Out of his 9 children, 3 sons committed suicide, 1 daughter died at age 5 (Ada), and his only other daughter (Helen, likely named after his second wife), died within a few months of them sending her away to boarding school. His four other boys lived to adulthood and married, three of them having children. In 1887, his son Ashby, distraught from being apart from his forbidden love with Matilda Emeline "Emily" Henderson, and apart from his daughter Ada Elizabeth Peck, killed himself in Jacksonville, FL where he worked as a night clerk and telegraph operator for the F. R. & N. R. R. (Florida Railway and Navigation Company's Railroad). When Helen died, Isham planted a huge white cross at the top of the mountain opposite Glen Ada. Six months later, when Ashby took his life, and they delivered the news to Isham the next day, he fell dead on the spot. They conducted a double funeral for Isham and Ashby. The grief of losing so many family members, especially children, and multiple sons to suicide, was too much to bear for this old doctor's heart. The cross he planted at the top of what became known as Cross Mountain, marked the border of Tennessee and North Carolina for over one hundred years, and stood as a testament to a father's love for his children, and his grief when they died before him. Cross Mountain Books exists as a testament to the power of this love, and the love of God which endures forever.

FAMILY

Dr. Isham Talbot Peck
Born: 23 Feb 1811 (Mossy Creek, modern-day Jefferson City, Tennessee)
Died: 28 Nov 1887 (age 76 years old, Wolf Creek, Cocke County, Tennessee)

Parents
Father: Judge Jacob Franklin Clayton Peck (12 Sep 1779 – 10 Jun 1869) Tennessee Supreme Court / Senator / Geologist
Mother: Saphronia "Sophia" Westener Talbott (14 Jun 1788 – 4 Jun 1871)

Siblings

Eliza Jane Talbot Peck (Born 1812 Mossy Creek, TN, Died 1868 Sneedville, Hancock, TN)

Adam Clayton Peck (12 Mar 1814 – 5 Jun 1864) – 1 Lieutenant, died in Civil War at the Battle of Piedmont, also a Methodist preacher

Wiley Hawkins Peck (10 Jan 1814 – 14 Jan 1866) – Famous for killing Charles Harris in New Orleans, died while visiting his brother William in Louisiana, see *Ada's Journal* Appendix 6 for more info

Juliet Nicholson Peck (31 Mar 1816 – 1864) – Married Dr. John F. "Rhoton" 15 Feb 1834, see 1897 *Southwestern Reporter* for land lawsuit

William Raine Peck (1818-1871) – Tallest/Biggest Civil War General "Big Peck", celebrated final commander of the Louisiana Tigers. Obituary and more can be found in *Ada's Journal and Emma's Letters: The Civil War Era Journal and Letters of Emma Peck*, Cross Mountain Books, 2021.

Martha Ann Featherstone Peck (26 Aug 1819 – 10 Aug 1882) – Nickname "Matt"

Cordelia Sophia Peck (1825-1825) – See the *Sawbones: Volume II* Appendix: Family Gravestones for more info and poem written for her

John Henry "Jack" L. Peck (1826 – 1894) – Private in the Civil War (CSA)

Extended Family
Dad's Side (Judge Jacob Peck)

Grandpa (Jacob's Dad): Adam Peck, Sr. (13 Feb 1753 – 13 Feb 1817)

Grandma (Jacob's Mom): Elizabeth Sharkey Peck (16 Feb 1757 – 11 June 1831)

Great Grandpa (Adam Peck, Sr.'s Dad): Jacob Peck, Sr. (7 Jul 1723 – Oct 1801)

Great Grandma (Adam Peck, Sr.'s Mom): Lydia Borden (1723 – 1800) Father is Benjamin Borden (who married Zeruiah Winter – his first cousin). Descendent of Richard Borden who settled in Rhode Island c.1638. Benjamin (1675-1743) received a grant from King George II of England of 92,100 acres in what later became Rockbridge Co, VA).[1]

Great Grandpa (Elizabeth Sharkey's Dad): Patrick Sharkey (1720 Ireland – 30 Jan 1786 Fincastle, VA), married Ann in Ireland. In 1742 he was an Ensign in Capt. George Robinson's company of militia.[2]

Great Grandma (Elizabeth Sharkey's Mom): Ann Looney (1725 Virginia – 30 Jan 1786 Botetourt, VA)

Mom's Side (Sophia Westerner Talbot)

Grandpa (Sophia's Dad): Isham M[oile?] Talbot (3 Nov 1759 VA – 30 Jul 1839 Louisville, KY) – Revolutionary War Veteran (fought at Brandywine, Germantown, and Battle of Blue Licks, KY)[3]

Grandma (Sophia's Mom): Jane Clayton Talbot [Isham Talbot's Cousin] (married 26 Dec 1786 in Mercer County, KY)

Great Grandpa (Jane Talbot's Dad): Isham Talbot, Sr. (3 Nov 1738 VA – c. 1832 KY?) – Revolutionary War Veteran and noted lawyer in KY, married Elizabeth Davis 29 Apr 1765 in Bedford Co.

---

[1] See *The Peck Clan In America* for more complete details. Author Susan Moore Teller, 2014, by Lulu Press, 28-35.
[2] *Adam the Younger, 1791-1866 in the War of 1812, The Second American Revolution* by Susan Moore Teller, 2016, Addendum
[3] *The Talbots: Centuries of Service* by Virgil Talbot, Colcord, OK 1983, 124.

Great Grandpa (Isham M. Talbot's Dad): James Talbot (13 Nov 1732 Prince George Co, VA and died 27 Mar 1777 in Bedford County. He was a wagon master during the Revolutionary War. Married Elizabeth Smith in 1759. She was the daughter of Phillip Smith and Mary Matthews.[4] Mary Matthews was the daughter of Baldwin Mathews of York Co., VA and Mary Digges, and Great Granddaughter of Governor Samuel Matthews of VA (1658-1670) and his wife Mary Hinton.[5] [6]

Marriages

1st Wife: Cordelia M. Talbot (8 Aug 1808 – 9 Jun 1860)

    Marriage Date: 19 Nov 1832[7]

    Marriage Location: Franklin County, KY

        Divorced: Petition presented on 4 Feb 1835 in the Senate of the Commonwealth of Kentucky "praying a divorce" by her father Isham Talbot on her behalf[8]

        Buried: Frankfort Cemetery, Frankfort, Franklin County, KY, Sec. H, Lot 330, Grave 3

2nd Wife: Helen D. (Rapalje) Glass

    Marriage Date: 18 May 1837

    Marriage Location: Vicksburg, MS

    Divorced/Died: Unknown

3rd Wife: Emma Elizabeth Henderson (1833 in Mississippi – 16 Sep 1899 in Lake City, FL)

    Marriage Date: 12 Oct 1848 (Isham was 36, Emma was 15)

    Marriage Location: East Carroll, Louisiana

Emma Elizabeth Henderson's Parents:

Father: William Henderson (1798 – c. 1867)

Mother: Louise Donohue (4 Mar 1813 in St. Genevieve, Missouri – 13 Feb 1897 in Lake City, FL), 84 years old. Notably, Emma's mom Louise was two years YOUNGER than Emma's Isham.[9]

Children of Isham and Emma:

1) Ada Louise Peck (25 Jul 1853 – 27 Mar 1859) – Emma wrote a journal from Ada's perspective starting when she was born. Ada died at a very young age and was buried in a glass top coffin in their front yard. See *Ada's Journal and Emma's Letters*.

2) William "Willie" Henderson Peck (30 Nov 1855 – 1 May 1871) – Committed suicide by laudanum at age 15

---

[4] Ibid, p112

[5] Ibid, p121

[6] For more info see: https://en.wikipedia.org/wiki/Samuel_Mathews, accessed 19 Apr 2020

[7] https://www.oocities.org/fww64/ishamtalbot.html

[8] Journal of the Senate of the Commonwealth of Kentucky, https://play.google.com/books/reader?id=Nmda AAAAYAAJ&pg=GBS.PP1, pg 223

[9] See obituary in *Ada's Journal and Emma's Letters: The Civil War Era Journal and Letters of Emma Peck*, 113-114.

3) Charles "Charley" Talbot Peck (16 Nov 1857 – 27 Feb 1882) – Died in Cincinnati at age 24, presumed by suicide by some newspaper articles. He started his own newspaper called the *Mossy Creek Independent* and travelled to Europe and South America. In April 1879, he wrote an epic southern novel called *Mary Anderson and Peacock the Mineralogist: The Bad Luck of a Young Southern Girl*. He also lived in New Orleans, LA for a time. An extended biography for Charley and his entire novel can be found in *Charley's Novel* (2021) by Cross Mountain Books.

4) DR. EDWARD JEROME PECK (14 Oct 1859 – 7 Jun 1927) – Beloved by his community where he served as community doctor for 40 years. Monument erected to him in Hot Springs, NC next to Fairview United Methodist Church. Divorced from his wife Cora Ward in 1900. Mostly estranged from his children after the divorce. See *He Loved the Folks: Dr. Edward Jerome Peck of Hot Springs, North Carolina*, Cross Mountain Books, for a full biography on Edward.

5) Ashby Henderson Peck (1862 – 27 Nov 1887) – Named after Gen. Turner Ashby (CSA), Telegraph Operator in Nashville, committed suicide at the age of 25 in Jacksonville, FL. Had a relationship with Matilda Emeline Henderson (1857-1920) and had one biological daughter named Ada Elizabeth Peck. Ada had 13 children and has hundreds of descendants.

6) Louis Sharkey Peck (15 May 1865 – 29 Jun 1937) – Trainmaster for the Seaboard Air Line, married Fannie Gibbens, died in Jacksonville, FL.

7) Paul Eve Peck (23 Mar 1869 – 22 Nov 1922) – Ship Chandler who moved to Jacksonville, FL. He married Ella King on 7 Jan 1891 in Lake City, FL. He died after a nervous breakdown at the age of 53.

8) Helen Emma Peck (21 Nov 1871 – 27 May 1887) – Born at Glen Ada, Wolf Creek. Died at 15 years old at Salem College. Cross erected in her memory at the top of the mountain.

9) Robert Lee Peck (29 Apr 1875 – 10 Jan 1938) – Born at Glen Ada, Wolf Creek. Worked for the railroad. Married Elizabeth "May" Purden on 9 Jan 1901. He became a train inspector and by 1910 they lived in Sanford, FL, with their children Helen and Lee. Died from appendicitis in 1938 in Sanford, FL. He was the Chief Dispatcher for the Atlanta Coast Line Railroad for 20 years and worked for the railroad for a total of 40 years.

More info about all of Isham's children can be found in *Ada's Journal and Emma's Letters: The Civil War Era Journal and Letters of Emma Peck* (2021), and extended biographies of each child can be found in *He Loved the Folks: Dr. Edward Jerome Peck of Hot Springs, NC*.

See the *Sawbones: Volume II* Appendix for an outline descendant report for each of Isham's children. It seeks to list out every descendant, living or dead, for Isham and Emma Peck. If you have information you would like included, or an update is needed to the information listed, please email the author at info@crossmountainbooks.com. Every effort has been made to include up to date and accurate information in all publications. Corrections will be listed on the Sawbones Resources webpage: www.crossmountainbooks.com/sawbones-resources.

Dr. Isham T. Peck House

MOSSY CREEK BEGINNINGS

Isham grew up as the son of a very prominent Judge in Tennessee. His grandfather, Adam Peck, Sr. (13 Feb 1753 – 13 Feb 1817) was a recognized veteran of the Revolutionary War, and had been given a land grant of 5,000 acres by George Washington. He floated down the Holston River with his wife

26	164	166	Peck Isham T	59	M	W	Farm Labor	2000	1000	Tennessee
27			— Emma	37	F	W	Keeps House			Mississippi
28			— William	14	M	W	Farm Labor			Louisianna
29			— Charles	12	M	W	Farm Labor			Louisianna
30			— Edward	10	M	W	Farm Labor			Tennessee
31			— Ashby	8	M	W				Tennessee
32			— Lewis S	6	M	W				Tennessee
33			— Paul	1	M	W				Tennessee

Figure 7 - 1870 Census from New Market, TN for Isham Talbot Peck family

Elizabeth Sharkey and settled the area that became known as Mossy Creek. His grandpa Adam founded the first church in that area, after living in the remnants of an old fort left on the edge of Mossy Creek. The church became known as "Elizabeth Chapel" and Adam and Elizabeth established one of their slaves, "Uncle John Peck" as its pastor. Elizabeth had taught him to read and write, and this chapel became the center of Methodism in the area. When Adam settled Mossy Creek in 1788, Tennessee was not a state yet. At the time, it was known as the "State of Franklin."[10] Adam had fought alongside John Sevier (who was the only Governor of the State of Franklin) who became the first governor of the new State of Tennessee in 1796.[11] This author theorizes that Adam and John Sevier became fairly close friends. Sevier had family in Madison Parish, Louisiana, and that is where Isham's brother Bill later had his mansion "The Mountain." John Sevier may have also been the person who encouraged Adam to settle in the "overmountain" region after the Great War.[12] Adam was appointed by Governor Sevier as the "Justice of Jefferson County" in 1796, and in the same year Adam Peck along with Alexander Outlaw represented Jefferson County in the first Tennessee Legislature. The next year (1797), Adam Peck returned as representative, but this time was joined by William Lillard. These are referred to as the 1st and 2nd General Assemblies.[13]

Adam and Elizabeth (daughter of Patrick and Ann Sharkey, of Botetourt County, Virginia) had 12 children (two girls and ten boys). Many of the children became notable figures in American history. Author Susan Moore Teller chronicles several of their accounts in her two books *"The Peck Clan in America"* and *"Adam the Younger: 1791-1866 in the War of 1812, The Second American Revolution."* To highlight a few, their son James Hawkins Peck, became Judge James Hawkins Peck, the first Judge for the District of Missouri.[14] Notably, he is only the 4th person to ever be impeached by the U.S. House of Representatives. He weathered the storm of impeachment and was eventually acquitted. If you want a long, dry, but interesting historical book, check out *Report of the Trial of James H. Peck: Judge of the United States District Court for the District of Missouri, Before the Senate of the United States … Against Him for High Misdemeanors in Office.* Available on Amazon and other websites as a reprint of the original work.[15] Judge James Peck (Isham's uncle) was impeached in 1830, when Isham was 19 years old. James had gone to Missouri to live in 1817, before Missouri was even a state (admitted to the union in 1821). Nicholas Sharkey Peck, Adam Peck, Jr., and Patrick all fought in the War of 1812, and there are accounts of their lives in the books written by Susan Moore Teller already mentioned.

Isham's dad is worth extended treatment, as he was a very prominent man in the history of Tennessee.

---

[10] https://en.wikipedia.org/wiki/State_of_Franklin
[11] https://en.wikipedia.org/wiki/John_Sevier
[12] https://en.wikipedia.org/wiki/Overmountain_Men
[13] According to "Families of Jeff County, TN – 200 Years" by Genealogical Society 1992
[14] https://en.wikipedia.org/wiki/James_H._Peck
[15] https://www.amazon.com/Report-Trial-James-Peck-Misdemeanors/dp/1345517483

JUDGE JACOB FRANKLIN CLAYTON PECK

(12 Sep 1779 – 10 Jun 1869) Tennessee Supreme Court / Geologist (Isham's Dad)
Isham's dad was 32 years old when he was born in Mossy Creek, TN in 1811. His mom Sophia was 23 years old. Isham was the oldest of their 10 children. Jacob made it into the Tennessee Centennial Poem and it paints a good picture of his life and impact.[16]

Tennessee Centennial Poem

by Mary A. A. Fry
"Jacob Peck was elected to the high position
Of Supreme court judge, which he held till the new constitution.
Born in Virginia, his father, Adam Peck, moved here
As soon as the roads were opened, he was a pioneer;
Was a member of the first Assembly of the State,
A man of learning and ability in debate.
Judge Peck was one of eight brothers, all brave, knightly men,
Of such height and build as we will rarely see again.
Several of them gained prominence in the Western States,
But it is of Judge Peck my history relates.
Educated in Virginia in Eighteen hundred,
He returned home a lawyer; it is not to be wondered
That with such advantages he should in time attain
Position as State senator, and from there to gain
Admittance into the highest court known to the State.
He filled the position with dignity, was sedate,
Cultured, studied music, painting, and was devoted
To zoology and geology, and was noted
For his cabinet of minerals he collected;
With these diverse attainments humor was detected,
Often in his opinions, though forcibly rendered,
Being original his dissent was often tendered.
Before an official was appointed to report
He published a volume of the decisions of the court.
After twelve years of service he retired to enjoy

[Supreme Court Judge Jacob Peck]
Ralph E. W. Earl, oil on fabric, c. 1830

Jacob Peck (1779-1869), a state senator from Greene and Jefferson counties and a justice of the Tennessee Supreme Court, was an amateur geologist who was fond of the chemistry and physical properties of minerals and mineralized artifacts.

East Tennessee Historical Society Collection, gift of Martha Rogers Withers

Figure 8 - Oil Painting by Ralph E. W. Earl, c. 1830, displayed at East TN History Center (Photo of painting taken by Author)

---

[16] Tennessee Centennial Poem by Mary A.A. Fry is available as a free download on google books, https://play.google.com/store/books/details?id=kozUAAAAMAAJ&rdid=book-kozUAAAAMAAJ&rdot=1, 82-83.

His home in Jefferson county, where, without annoy,
He pursued his favorite studies until the great age
Of ninety years he ended his earthly pilgrimage.”

There are many resources available online regarding Judge Jacob's life and history on the court. You can even find a free copy of the book printed on Jan 1, 1871 that includes a 3-year summary of cases argued before him. It's called *Reports of Cases Argued and Determined in the Supreme Court of Tennessee: Volumes 7-8* by William Wilcox Cooke.[17]

Isham and Jacob seemed to stay fairly close through the years, and Jacob and Isham are both mentioned in a book about Abolitionism in the South. In the book, *An Abolitionist in the Appalachian South, Ezekiel Birdseye on Slavery, Capitalism, and Separate Statehood in East Tennessee, 1841-1846,* author/compiler Durwood Dunn publishes a series of letters between Ezekiel Birdseye and Gerrit Smith, among others.[18] Here are some of the excerpts that help tell the story of who Isham was and what his dad, Judge Jacob, cared about.

On page 142, in a letter to Gerrit Smith, dated March 22, 1841, Ezekiel writes from Newport in Cocke County in East TN, “My Dear Sir – A few days since I met with Doctor Isham T Peck of Vicksburg Mississippi son of Hon[orable] Jacob Peck of New Market E[ast Ten[nessee]. Doctor Peck says he is acquainted with the Mr. Worthington whose residence you wish to ascertain. He states that his Post Office is Princeton Washington County Miss[issippi] which is about 100 miles above Vicksburg near the river. He says he came there from K[entuck]y [and] is confident he is the same man for whom you inquire.” […] *now [page 144 continues]* “My good friend Judge Peck says in a few years all will be made free [*referring to slavery*]. When I saw him last week I loaned him your reply to Mr. [Henry] Clay. He assured me it was his intention to write you. This unimportant as it may appear is worthy of some regard as it will do much to show that the most intelligent men at the South have much respect for the abolitionists.” […] *[continuing on page 145]*, “My hasty letter has so much that is personal that it would be probably imprudent to publish it. Should anything be selected I request that it should be such as could not easily be traced back. Judge Peck and myself are anxious to get up a free labor community or settlement where slave labor will be entirely excluded. There are great natural resources here for such a location. I am anxious to have an active correspondence between the antislavery portion of the North and South. Steady patient efforts with the blessing will eventually succeed. Sincerely your friend E Birdseye.”

In another letter to Gerrit Smith dated August 7, 1841, Ezekiel writes a long letter, even including an interaction between Judge Peck and a freed slave who had a legal dispute. For purposes here, I will just quote the final paragraph which reads, “Judge Peck remarked that he had been much occupied with professional engagements with some indisposition, that he should write you soon. I have feared

---

[17] http://tinyurl.com/tnsupremecourtcases
[18] *An Abolitionist in the Appalachian South*, Durwood Dunn, google book: https://tinyurl.com/bdcs7cmp

the influence of his son Dr. I. T. Peck who married a wealthy lady near Vicksburg some months since. Judge Peck and myself were conversing with him about our intention of settling our lands with free persons only. He replied that K[entuck]y and Tenn[essee] ought to be free states. I flatter myself that it will not be long before I can return to the North. Judge Peck says he is interested to accompany me. Sincerely yours Ezekiel Birdseye". This is informative as it gives us a glimpse into Judge Peck's social interactions and feelings on slavery, as well as Isham's. Also, it reveals that around 1841, Isham married a "wealthy lady near Vicksburg."

Figure 10 - Twenty Dollar Bill from Vicksburg Water Works Bank, 1838. Isham owned the building where the bank and Sentinel and Expositor for the Country newspaper was located. http://www.waterworkshistory.us/MS/Vicksburg/

Figure 9 – Vicksburg, MS and the Rebel Batteries 1863. Shows the western theater of the war, focusing on Vicksburg. The Vicksburg and Jackson, and Vicksburg and Texas railroads are indicated. Sneden, Robert Knox. *Vicksburg Missp. and the Rebel batteries.* [to 1865, 1863] Map. https://www.loc.gov/item/gvhs01.vhs00231/.

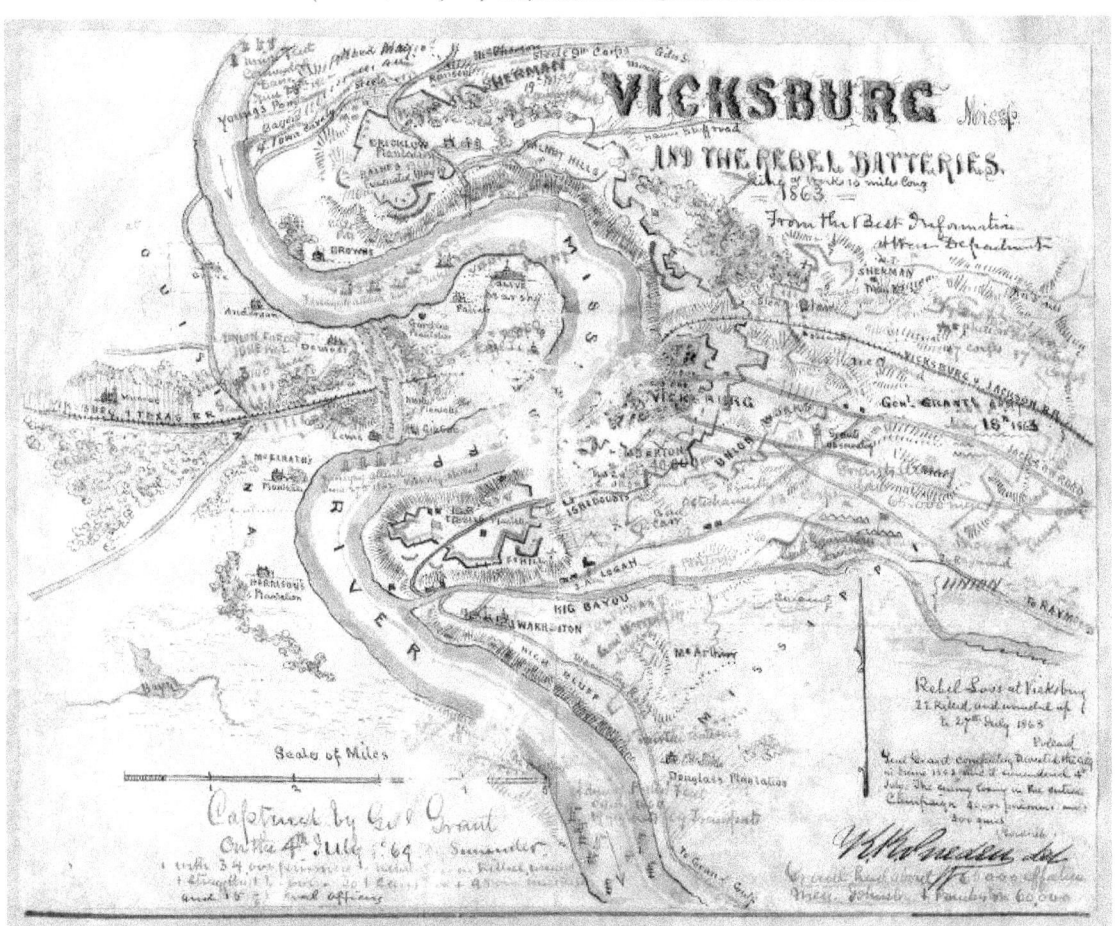

VICKSBURG, MISSISSIPPI

The obituary for Isham's brother, William Raine Peck, reveals that the two of them spent "their boyhood" in Vicksburg, Mississippi.[19] From numerous newspaper and Warren County records, we know that Isham lived and/or owned land in Vicksburg from roughly 1837-1857, when Isham was 26-46 years old. But if the statement is accurate, what took Isham and his brother William to Vicksburg when they were "young"? One theory is that they went there to live with their second cousin 1x removed William Lewis Sharkey and his wife Minerva. William Lewis Sharkey (1797-1873) was the son of Isham's great uncle (also called granduncle) Patrick Sharkey, Jr. (1760-1813). Patrick Sharkey, Jr.'s sister was Elizabeth Sharkey (who married Adam Peck, Sr), Isham's grandma (Judge Jacob's mom). This made William L. Sharkey, Isham's second cousin 1x removed (the grandson of Isham's great uncle Patrick Sharkey, Jr.).

Stated alternately, William Sharkey's grandpa was Patrick Sharkey III (1720-1786), and Isham's grandma, Elizabeth Sharkey (who married Adam Peck, Sr), was also the daughter of Patrick Sharkey III, they were brother and sister. So, William Sharkey was the son of his Isham's great uncle Patrick Sharkey, Jr. But William Sharkey was born in 1797, and Isham was born in 1811, so though they were one generation apart (1x removed), Isham was only 14 years Sharkey's younger. Add to this the fact that William Sharkey's parents (Patrick Sharkey, Jr. and Polly Rhodes) both died around 1813.

Here is an excerpt giving connections to Tennessee, Irish heritage, and more… "Among the first settlers in Tennessee was Patrick Sharkey, a native of the West of Ireland, some of whose descendants still remain in Tennessee, while a more distinguished branch descend[s] from Patrick Sharkey, junior, a soldier of the Revolution, who, about the beginning of this century [19th], removed into the State of Mississippi, then belonging to Spain. William Louis Sharkey, one of the sons of this emigrant, was born August 12th, 1798, and, at the age of fifteen, lost both his parents. He spent the first years of his orphanage picking cotton in the fields in the busy season, and obtaining instruction with the proceeds in the intervals. In 1821, he was enabled to enter a law-office at Natchez, and in 1825, we find him established as a lawyer at Vicksburg. In 1827, he was elected to the State Legislature, and in the two following years was its speaker."[20]

Isham was 10 years old when William Sharkey entered the Natchez law-office, and 14 when he became a lawyer in Vicksburg. At what age did he and his brother go live in Vicksburg? Why did Judge Jacob and his wife Sophia send their two sons to stay in Vicksburg when they were young? Was there an adult family member who looked after them all? Was the newspaper obituary inaccurate when it said that they spent their "boyhood" in Vicksburg?

More will be said in the pages to come regarding William Sharkey, but for now, know that he eventually owned a plantation just south of Isham and William on the banks of the Mississippi, he became the first provisional governor of the State of Mississippi after the Civil War, and he was a close family relation.

---

[19] *Ada's Journal and Emma's Letters*, 119 (originally from *Vicksburg Herald* in Jan 1871).
[20] *A History of the Irish Settlers in North America* by Thomas D'Arcy McGee, found https://www.libraryireland.com/IrishSettlers/Sharkeys.php, accessed 28 Nov 2022.

Figure 12 – 1875 Map - Madison Parish Louisiana - Dep. of Transportation and Development, Plantations and Land Ownership,
Note W. B. Pittman, likely William Buckner Pittman, owner of both "Mountain" plantation and "Monocacy" as of 1875
Also, note that Mountain Plantation says "Omega 57" – Omega Plantation was well known in the mid-1800s in this area.

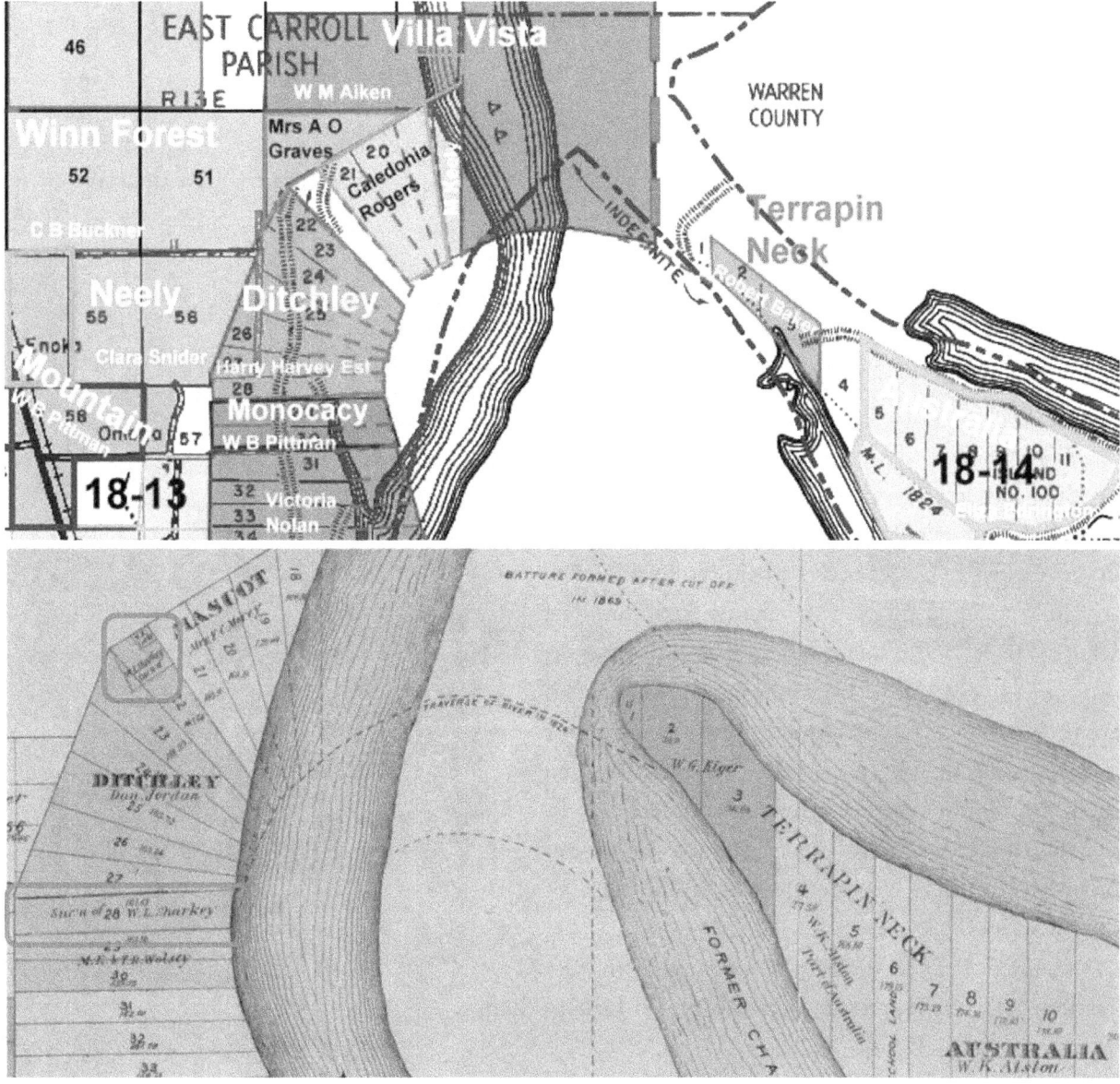

Figure 12 - 1891 Map courtesy of Library of Congress
Top square reads in part: "W. L. Sharkey Suc'n of" and bottom rectangle reads: "161.64 Suc'n of W. L. Sharkey"

Note: It is interesting that a plantation owned by William Sharkey, or William Lewis Sharkey, Jr. became known as "Monacacy," which is the name of a famous Civil War battle in which Sharkey's cousin William Raine Peck, served as senior colonel. "Peck often led the brigade as the senior colonel, and his role in the July 1864 Battle of Monocacy drew praise from his division commander, Maj. Gen. John B. Gordon. He was wounded in the right thigh by a shell fragment at the Third Battle of Winchester in September. He did not return to the field until December. Peck was promoted to brigadier general on February 18, 1865. He was paroled in Vicksburg on June 6 of that year. Following the Civil War, Peck returned to his Louisiana plantation and resumed active management of the business. Plagued by poor health from his military service, he died six years after the war near

Milliken's Bend, Louisiana, of congestive heart failure."[21] See the *Sawbones: Volume II* Appendix for a description of early plantation life and slavery in Madison Parish, LA.

Also to note: William Sharkey wrote a letter to President Andrew Johnson on behalf of his cousin Gen. William Raine Peck, as follows:

From William L. Sharkey

Executive Office, Jackson, Miss.
August 30th 1865.

His Excellency Andrew Johnson President &C
Sir

I take the liberty of introducing to you my friend & relation, Genl. W R Peck,[22] who is son of Judge [Jacob] Peck[23] of east Tennessee, who is probably an old acquaintance of yours. Genl. Peck desires very much to have an interview with you, and will himself explain his object. I will take the liberty of saying however that he is desirous of being a loyal citizen, and fully acquesces [sic] in the changed condition of affairs. He feels the solicitude in accomplishing his purpose on account of his Father and mother who are now old and destitute, and depend upon him for a support, as they have no other son who can aid them. Some time since I presented his case to Mr. Speed, but received no reply. I hope it may be in your power to aid him consistently with your sense of duty.

General Peck has shown me a letter from East Tennessee which represents a terrible State of things there.

Figure 13 - Young William Lewis Sharkey, photo of original by the author, original shared with author courtesy of Loosa Yokena Plantation, Vicksburg, Mississippi

Very respectfully Your Obt Servt
W. L. Sharkey
Provisional Govr of Miss[24]

---

[21] William Raine Peck, Plantation Owner and Civil War General, by Richard P. Sevier, https://sites.rootsweb.com/~lamadiso/bios/peckwr.htm, accessed 28 Nov 2022.

[22] William R. Peck (1818-1871), a planter in Louisiana since the early 1840s, rose from private to brigadier general in the Confederate army. He claimed to have known Johnson "well in my early youth when a student at the College of Dr Coffin near Grenville Tenn." Warner, *Gray*, Peck to Johnson, June 6, 1865, Amnesty Papers (M1003, Roll 29), La., William Raine Peck, RG94, NA.

[23] Jacob Peck (1779-1869), a lawyer and state senator, was a member of the Tennessee supreme court (1822-1834) and publisher of a volume of the court's decisions. *BDTA*, 1:577.

[24] During the succeeding weeks, General Peck tried at least twice to see the President regarding his pardon. Finally, on October 13, 1865, his pardon was issued. *Washington Morning Chronicle*, Sept. 28, Oct. 12, 1865; Amnesty Papers (M1003, Roll 29), La., William Raine Peck, RG94, NA. Author's question: Why couldn't Isham come to the aid of his parents?

Figure 14 – Vicksburg, Mississippi, downtown looking north, Mississippi River on the left, view from 10 South Rooftop Bar & Grill, Photo by the Author, 14 Jun 2023

Loosa Yokena Plantation

William Lewis Sharkey and wife Minerva lived at the Loosa Yokena Plantation, located south of Vicksburg. "Acquired by James Hyland as an English land grant in the latter part of the 1700s, Loosa Yokena, which means "Black Dirt," was named for the last Choctaw Indian chief in the area."[25] Isham and brother William may have spent some of their formative years on Loosa Yokena, learning first-hand about cotton planting and managing a plantation close to the Mississippi.

Figure 15 - Author Andy Peck with Dee Hyland, owner of Loosa Yokena Plantation, "secretary" of William Lewis Sharkey in the background, photo taken by Drew Peck, author's father, 15 Jun 2023. Dee is the mother of Jan Hyland Daigre, Warren County Circuit Clerk as of July 2023.

Figure 16 - Author Andy Peck, dad Drew Peck, son Justice (red shirt), son Hudson (middle), and Warren County Circuit Clerk Jan Hyland Daigre, photo taken 15 Jun 2023 at Warren County Courthouse. "Cousin" Jan is related to William Lewis Sharkey.

The following two pages show an "Agreement with Freedmen" document showing the arrangement made with former slaves to work.

---

[25] Terri Cowart Frazier, Loosa Yokena plantation has a deep, rich history and a legacy of loving owners, *The Vicksburg Post*, Vicksburg, Mississippi, 3 Apr 2020, http://tinyurl.com/LoosaYokenaHistory

AGREEMENT WITH FREEDMEN.

THIS AGREEMENT, Made and entered into this *1st* day of *February*
A. D. 186*5*, by and between *Wm. L. Hyland*
of the *County* of *Warren*, and State of *Mississippi*
of the first part, and the persons hereinafter named and undersigned, Freedmen of the same place, parties hereto of the second
part, WITNESSETH:

That for the purpose of cultivating the plantation known as the *Hyland Plantation*
Situation in the *County and State* aforesaid,
during the year commencing on the *1st* day of *February* A. D. 1865,
and terminating on the First day of January, A. D. 1866, the said parties do hereby mutually agree that the Regulations as
prescribed by General Orders No. 84, Headquarters Department Mississippi, March 23, 1865, hereto annexed, providing for the
employment and general welfare of Freedmen, and the local rules in pursuance thereof, all of which are hereto annexed, and are
hereby incorporated in and made a part of this agreement as fully as if here recited.

The said *Wm. L. Hyland*, for the considerations and on the conditions
and stipulations hereinafter mentioned, agrees to pay to the said laborers, the rates of monthly wages agreed upon and as
specified in the orders hereto annexed: one-half of such wages to be punctually paid upon the 1st days of May, August, and
November, 1865, and the remainder to be paid on or before the 31st day of January, 1866. Said
Wm. L. Hyland further agrees to furnish to the said laborers and those rightfully dependent
on them, free of charge, clothing and food of good quality and sufficient quantity, as prescribed by the orders hereto annexed;
good and sufficient quarters, a separate tenement for each family, fuel and medical attendance; to see that the premises thus
furnished are kept in a good sanitary condition; to allot from the lands of said plantation for garden purposes, to each family, the
amount of land specified in orders hereto annexed; such allotment to include a reasonable use of tools and animals; to exact only
ten hours work per day in summer and nine hours in winter, and no labor whatever on Sundays; and if any labor in excess of
the above per day is rendered, the same is to be paid as extra labor, upon such terms as may be agreed upon by the parties
hereto; to grant to such laborers one-half of each and every Saturday, to enable them to cultivate the portions of land allotted
to them, also, the fourth day of July; to co-operate in the establishment of any school for the education of the children of said
laborers; finally, the said *Wm. L. Hyland*, agrees to comply in all respects with the
rules and regulations above referred to and made part hereof.

AND IN CONSIDERATION of the faithful performance by the said *Wm. L. Hyland*, of all
the obligations assumed by *him*, and of the punctual payment by *him* of the wages agreed upon as aforesaid,
the said laborers do hereby severally, and each for himself, agree with the said *Wm. L. Hyland*,
heirs and assigns, to well and faithfully perform the labor herein stipulated for the term aforesaid, in strict conformity with the
conditions aforesaid; and they further agree to observe and comply with the rules and regulations above referred to.

AND IT IS FURTHERMORE AGREED: That in case the said *Wm. L. Hyland* shall fail, neglect
or refuse to fulfil any of the obligations assumed by *him*, or shall furnish said parties of the second part with bad or
insufficient food or clothing, or insufficient or unhealthy quarters, or shall be guilty of cruelty to them, he shall, besides the legal
recourse left to the particular party or parties aggrieved, render this contract liable to annulment, at the option of the Provost
Marshal of Freedmen.

And in case any laborer shall voluntarily absent himself from, or shall neglect or refuse to perform the labor herein
contracted for, and the fact shall be proved to the satisfaction of the proper officer, the one-half of the wages due to said party so
offending, retained in the hands of the said *Wm. L. Hyland*, as aforesaid, shall be forfeited,
one-half thereof to the said *Wm. L. Hyland*, and the other half to the United States, to aid
in supporting the helpless, and the party so offending may be discharged from said employment.

AND IT IS FURTHERMORE MUTUALLY AGREED by the said *Wm. L. Hyland* and the
following named laborers to-wit:

John Roe   Charles Burnham
and Bob Sharkey

that in lieu of the half wages to be paid to them at the end of the year, the said laborers shall be entitled to, and agree to accept,
the share of the nett profits of carrying on the plantation during the period aforesaid, respectively set opposite their names below.

AND IT IS FURTHERMORE AGREED, That any wages or share of profits due the said laborers under this agreement, shall
constitute a first lien upon all crops or parts of crops produced on said plantation or tract of land by their labor. And no

Figure 17 – Agreement With Freedmen document, Page 1 on previous page, Page 2 here, 1 Feb 1865 by William S. Hyland and John Roe, Charles Burnham, and Bob Sharkey, agreeing to pay them $10.00 per month.
Photos of original by author, originals shared courtesy of Loosa Yokena Plantation, photographed 15 Jun 2023.

Figure 18 – 2023 Google Earth Map showing approximate location of "The Fifty Acre Glass Tract" on the north side of the city, in blue, and Isham's Plantation on the southern border of the city, in green, and "Peck and Reading's Saw Mill", in brown, all locations based on 1849 City of Vicksburg Map which follows. Colors visible in hardcover version of Sawbones, or see Sawbones Resources webpage. www.crossmountainbooks.com/sawbones-resources

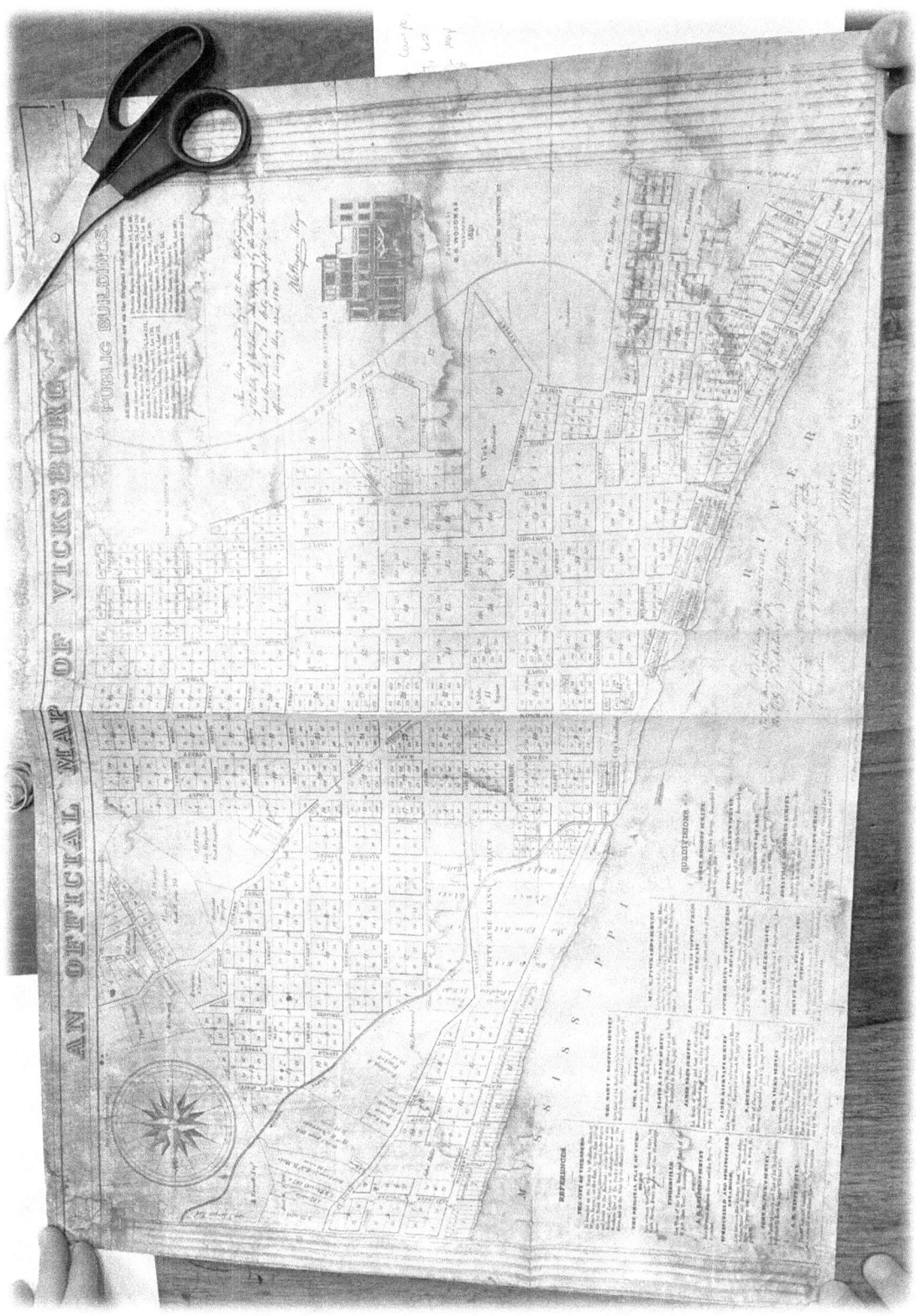

Figure 19 - Map by A. M. Winn, City Engineer of the City of Vicksburg, adopted as the official survey on 22 May 1848. Photographed by the author. Original courtesy of the Old Court House Museum, Vicksburg, Mississippi. Special thanks to Jordon Rushing, Assistant Director/Curator. Note location of Isham's plantation on right side of map.

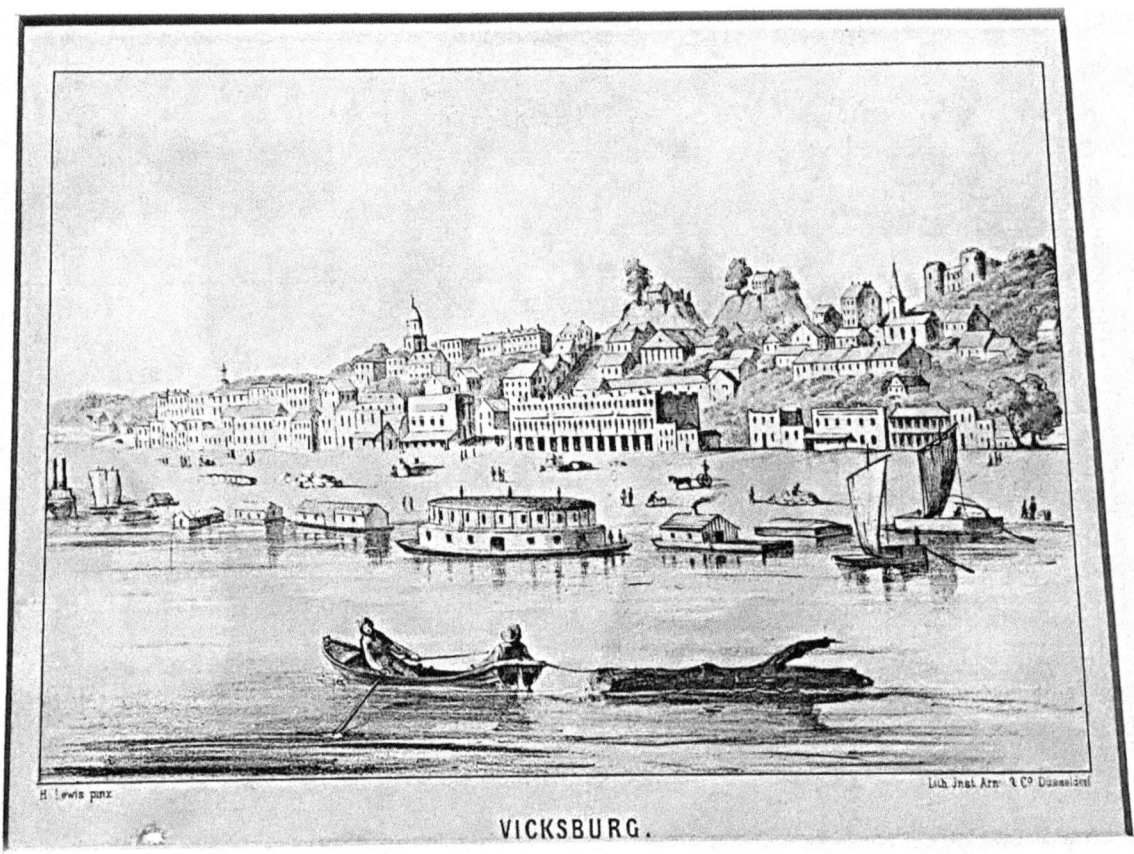

VICKSBURG.

Figure 20 - "Vicksburg" Sketched by Henry Lewis and Published in Dusseldorf, Germany, in 1854 in Das Illustrirte Mississippithal. Photo of original by author. Original courtesy of the Old Court House Museum in Vicksburg, Mississippi.

Plantation Owner and Planter

Isham married his second wife, Helen D. (Rapalje) Glass on 18 May 1837. This marriage will be covered more extensively in the next section on marriages. But it is relevant here because when Isham married Helen at the age of 26, he inherited her plantation, properties, and at least 37 slaves. Here are other "newsworthy" things that happened to Isham or on his plantations during his time living in or at least owning property in and around Vicksburg in Warren County. One important note, during Isham's time in Vicksburg, he is consistently listed as T. J. Peck, especially in newspapers. It seems that he may have gone by the name "Talbot" during his time in Vicksburg. And also, the script version of "I" and "T" appear very similar to "T" and "J".

From 1837 to 1840s, Isham and wife Helen were involved in court cases that went all the way to the Mississippi Supreme Court regarding Helen's former husband's land, see next chapter on marriages.

The 1840 Warren, MS Census lists Isham as owning 52 slaves.

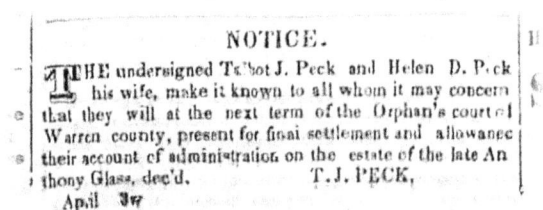

NOTICE.

THE undersigned Talbot J. Peck and Helen D. Peck his wife, make it known to all whom it may concern that they will at the next term of the Orphan's court of Warren county, present for final settlement and allowance their account of administration on the estate of the late Anthony Glass, dec'd.   T. J. PECK,
April 3w

Figure 21 - Notice regarding Orphan's Court, Vicksburg Tri-Weekly Sentinel, Vicksburg, MS, 29 May 1840, 3.

On 29 May 1840 Isham and wife Helen gave notice that they desired "final settlement and allowance their account of administration on the estate of the late Anthony Glass, dec'd" during the next "Orphan's court". [26]

In Sep 1840, Isham was appointed as a Whig delegate by the Tippecanoe club of Vicksburg to represent Warren County at the convention held in Jackson, Mississippi on 5 Oct 1840.[27]

In March 1841, Isham met with abolitionist Ezekiel Birdseye, giving him information about a Mr. Worthington who lived in Washington County, Mississippi, 100 miles above Vicksburg. In this exchange, Isham is helped Birdseye to assist a man named Gerrit Smith free a slave girl and her family, and reunite them with each other.[28]

On 30 Sep 1842, the *South-Western Farmer* published a note that reported on "More Brag Picking" from Isham's Plantation. It read:

> *More Brag Picking.*—We learn, from the Vicksburg Sentinel that six hands on the plantation of Dr. Peck, under the management of Mr. Porter, picked in one day 1921 pounds of cotton, as follows:

Ranney	365
Cud	335
Port	320
Jim	310
Bill	301
Martha	290
Total	1921

The average to each hand was 320 1/6 lbs.[29]

The issue of a "Commissioner's Sale" continued and multiple notices appeared in the papers in 1843. One dated 28 Mar 1843 read:

> By Virtue of a decree of the Hon. Probate court of Warren county, rendered at the December term, 18__ in the caes of T. J. Peck and Helen D., his wife, petitioners, against the legatees and devisees of Anthony Glass, deceased. The undersigned Commissioner therein appointed, will proceed to sell to the highest bidder,
>
> On the 24th day of April next, at the residence of the said T. J. Peck, near Vicksburg, a Credit of Nine Months, the following Negro slaves, Wash, Jim, Jack, Bill, Irwin, Lewis, Jess, Joe, Dan, A?, Sawney, Spence, Pont, Fay, Charles, Sal, Charlotte and her four children, Rany and her two children, Rody, M? and her two children, Nice and her three children, Frances?

---

[26] *Vicksburg Tri-Weekly Sentinel*, Vicksburg, MS, 29 May 1840, 3.

[27] *Vicksburg Daily Whig*, 19 Sep 1840, 2.

[28] Durwood Dunn, *An abolitionist in the Appalachian South: Ezekiel Birdseye on slavery, capitalism, and separate statehood in East Tennessee, 1841-1846*, The University of Tennessee Press, Knoxville, 142, 146.

[29] *South-Western Farmer*, Raymond, Mississippi, 30 Sep 1842, 5.

and her two children, Sarah and Ann. Also __ mules and one horse; also at the same time and place, a credit of twelve months, the following described real estate, lying and being in the city of Vicksburg, __ Part of lot No 60, in square no 10, front on 2__ Street 24 feet 9 inches, and running back 80 feet from_ on Walnut street, running back 73 feet 9 inches off the south end of said lot; also part of lot no 38, square no 7, fronting on 2d East street 36 feet 6 ½ inches running back 147 feet 6 inches, (said lot no 38, being subject to a lease of about 10 years;) also part of lot no __ in square no 37, fronting on Monroe street 73 feet 9 inches, and on China street 147 feet 6 inches; also part of no 61, in square no 9, commencing about 32 feet from North east corner of said lot on 2d East street, round thence west 91 feet and back 95 feet 4 inches; and also no 291, in square of no 61. Also the following described real estate lying and being in the county of Warren, Lot no 5 of section 34, T 16, range 3 east, containing _ acres; the undivided half of lot no 4, section 34, T _ range 3 east, containing about 82 acres; section two _ nine T sixteen, range three east, containing 642 73__ acres, less 133 56/100 granted to C. Steele and __ley Mathis, which will appear by reference to title par___ fractional section no 25, T 16, range three east, __ district of land offered for sale at Washington, Mississippi containing 53 acres; lot no 1 of fractional section __ T 16, range three east, containing 127 52/100 acres fractional section no 25, T 16 range three east, bounded __ east by the south west quarter of fractional section 2__ on the west by lands belonging to Anthony Glass, west half of the south west quarter of section no 5___ range 4 east, containing 76 9/100 acres, more or less, __ sectional no twenty-three, T sixteen, range there in the district of Washington, Mississippi, containing __ acres, and part of section no 22. T 16, range 3 east in __ land district West of Pearl River, lying and being near the city of Vicksburg, and bounded as follows: commencing at a post corner to Levi Mitchell, thence south ___ eight degrees, east twenty one chains and twenty ___ a post on the road leading to Vicksburg, and ___ Wm M Pinckard, thence with the meanders of said __ south nine degrees, west seven chains and seventy links to a post, thence south thirty deg. W 8 chains __ fifty links to a post, thence south three chains and __ links to a post, thence S 7 degrees, west 4 chains __ corner of A. Glass, thence south 80 degrees 30 m, __ chains and fifty links to a locust tree on the swamp, ___ to A. Glass, thence north 10 degrees 15 m., east __ chains and seventy three links to the beginning, (no ___adon being allowed in courses,) containing by estimate 53 ¾ acres and twenty perches. The said described realty belongs to the estate of Anthony Glass, deceased and will be sold, or so much thereof as will be sufficient as to the sum of twenty thousand five hundred and twenty ___ dollars and ten cents, with six per cent interest ___ from the 16th day of December 1842 until paid; being __ amount ordered to be made by said decree. The said ___ to be first sold. Bonds with approved security will be required of the purchasers, together with a lien on the property. Hours of sale from 12 to 4 o'clock, and to be continued from day to day until the whole sum aforesaid __ made, or until the whole of said property is disposed.

STEPHEN STAFFORD
Commissioner

march 9 w 6t prs fee 28[30]

One month later, a summary of the sale was posted in the *Whig*:

By virtue of a decree of the Hon. Probate court of Warren county, Mississippi, rendered at the December term, 1842, in the case of T. J. Peck and Helen his wife, petitioners against the legatees and divizees of Anthony Glass, dec'd, will be sold
on the 24h of April, 1843,
at the plantation of T. J. Peck, one mile from Vicksburg,

37 NEGROES
On a Credit of Nine months.
1078 ACRES OF LAND,
Comprising the plantation now occupied by Dr. T. J. Peck, and
Six Houses and Lots in Vicksburg,
On a Credit of Twelve months,
[Etc…][31]

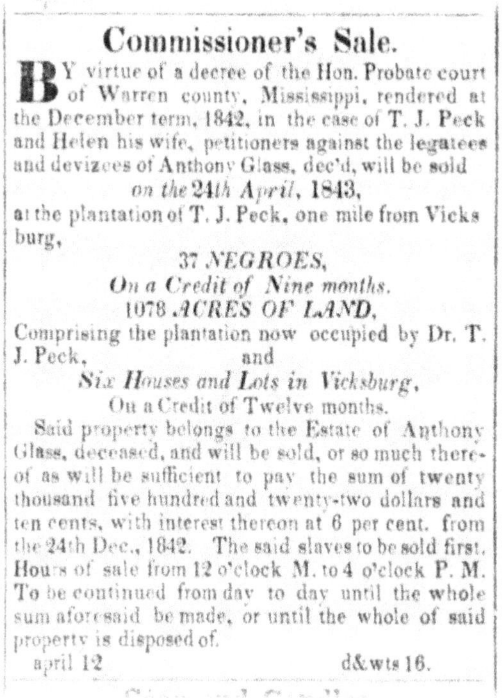

Commissioner's Sale.

BY virtue of a decree of the Hon. Probate court of Warren county, Mississippi, rendered at the December term, 1842, in the case of T. J. Peck and Helen his wife, petitioners against the legatees and devizees of Anthony Glass, dec'd, will be sold *on the 24th April, 1843,* at the plantation of T. J. Peck, one mile from Vicksburg,

37 NEGROES,
On a Credit of Nine months.
1078 *ACRES OF LAND,*
Comprising the plantation now occupied by Dr. T. J. Peck, and
Six Houses and Lots in Vicksburg,
On a Credit of Twelve months.

Said property belongs to the Estate of Anthony Glass, deceased, and will be sold, or so much thereof as will be sufficient to pay the sum of twenty thousand five hundred and twenty-two dollars and ten cents, with interest thereon at 6 per cent. from the 24th Dec., 1842. The said slaves to be sold first. Hours of sale from 12 o'clock M. to 4 o'clock P. M. To be continued from day to day until the whole sum aforesaid be made, or until the whole of said property is disposed of.
april 12 d&wts 16.

Figure 22 - Commissioner's Sale notice, lands of T. J. Peck and wife Helen, Vicksburg Daily Whig, 20 Apr 1843, 3.

Isham wrote the following note to the *Daily Whig* on 25 Jan 1844 about a new cotton gin he was very proud of:

For the Whig.
VICKSBURG, Jan. 25th, 1844.

MR. EDITOR :– I saw a notice some days since in your paper, that some person had written you a communication, speaking in high terms of Kelley's patent Gin. Well, I was not that man, neither do I know who wrote it; but I yesterday put in operation one of the only two Gins of Kelley's patent that was ever manufactured, and I think I have the best Gin in the world. Persons interested in such matters would do well to call and see this Gin in operation soon, as I have but little cotton, it will only run a few days.   TALBOT J. PECK.

The other Gin is in operation at Dr. J. B. Warren's, in this county.[32]

Just four months later, Isham's plantation was blooming with cotton, and it made the paper:

---

[30] Commissioner's Sale, *Sentinel and Expositor for the Country*, Vicksburg, MS, 14 and 28 Mar 1843, 4. "march 9 w 6t prs fee 28" is original to the article, possibly a notation for how many weeks this notice is supposed to run & that it is paid up
[31] Commissioner's Sale, *Vicksburg Daily Whig* (Vicksburg, MS), 20 Apr 1843, 3.
[32] *Vicksburg Whig*, Vicksburg, Mississippi, 29 Jan 1844, 2.

COTTON PLANTATION.   EINE BAUMWOLL-PFLANZUNG.

Figure 23 - Plate 70, A Cotton Plantation, Eine Baumwoll-Pflanzung, Das Illustrirte Mississippithal, or,
The Valley of the Mississippi Illustrated, artist Henry Lewis, 1854, courtesy of SIUE Digital Collections.

COTTON BLOOMS.– We neglected to mention in our last paper, that Mr. Porter, the manager on Dr. Peck's plantation, near this city, sent to our office, on the 21st inst., two full grown cotton blooms. Mr. P. states that there are many more in his field. These, however, were not the first of the season. We understand Maj. A. G. Creath had a bloom on his plantation on the Yazoo river, on the 9th inst.[33]

Just 3 months later, a Jackson newspaper shared that one of Isham's cotton bales was the first to arrive in New Orleans:

MISSISSIPPI PRODUCES THE EARLIEST COTTON.—The three first bales of the present cotton crop landed at New Orleans, were severally from the plantations of Mrs. Lucinda Davis[34], ex Gov. McNutt[35], and Dr. Peck, citizens of this state. The cotton arrived on

---

[33] *Vicksburg Whig*, Vicksburg, Mississippi, 27 May 1844, 2.
[34] Lucinda Farrar Davis (1797-1873), sister of Jefferson Davis, President, CSA
[35] Alexander G. McNutt, Twelfth Governor of Mississippi: 1838-1842. Interestingly, Gov. McNutt wrote articles for the *Spirit of the Times* just like Isham, https://www.mshistorynow.mdah.ms.gov/issue/alexander-g-mcnutt-twelfth-governor-of-mississippi-1838-1842.

NEW-ORLEANS (LOUISIANA)   ©SIUE|siue.edu/digitalcollections

Figure 24 - (Top) A Mississippi Landing, Library of Congress, at Vicksburg, Publisher Detroit Publishing Co, Circa 1900-1906, https://www.loc.gov/item/2016795012/ and (Bottom) New Orleans (Louisiana), by Henry Lewis, Das Illustrirte Mississippithal, or, The Valley of the Mississippi Illustrated, artist Henry Lewis, 1854, courtesy of SIUE Digital Collections.

the 22d ult. Last year the earliest cotton bale received in New Orleans was on the 17th August; two bales were then received. Madison county Misp., sent one and Opelousas, La. the other. Cotton has matured this year twenty-six days earlier than last.[36]

Just three months after Isham is celebrated for getting his cotton to New Orleans so quickly, his overseer, Patterson Porter, murdered a man named Mr. Watrous (also spelled Waters, Walter, and Waturs in various articles), at the bar of the Prentiss House. This Prentiss house most likely belonged to Seargent Smith Prentiss, a well-known figure in Vicksburg at the time.[37]

> It is our painful duty to record another, to the long list of murders, becoming so prevalent, from one end of the country to the other. On Friday morning last, James Patterson Porter, killed a Mr. Watrous, with a Bowie knife, at the bar of the Prentiss House. Watrous received three stabs, which terminated his existence instantaneously. The Coroner's Jury rendered a verdict of wiful [sic] murder against Porter. Porter will undergo a judicial investigation this day; the court it is presumed, for the sake of consistency, and in accordance with an established rule of some thirteen months standing, will admit him to bail.[38]

Another account shared a few additional details, and gave two different spellings for the victim's name.

> MURDER MOST FOUL.—On yesterday, about 12 o'clock, Patterson Porter, overseer for Dr. Peck, stabbed John S. Waters, a carpenter, at the Prentiss House. From the statements related to us, Mr. Porter commenced the attacked [sic] without any provocation whatever, by striking Mr. Walter with his whip, which he caught. Porter then drew a knife and stabbed him three times in the side, of which wounds he died in about ten minutes. Porter is in custody.[39]

This wasn't the only difficulty Isham faced in Vicksburg, he also lost a building in a fire in Feb 1846.

Destructive Fire.

On Saturday morning, about daylight, a fire broke out in a frame building next to the river, at the foot of Jackson street, belonging to Judge Bodley, and temporarily occupied by some slaves belonging to Mr. Vick, who were brought here to be shipped up the river to his plantation. They kindled a fire upon some earth that had been formerly placed there, and on which a stove had stood, and it is supposed it communicated to the floor. It then caught the two houses occupied by the Messrs. Dickerson, which were stored with hay and corn; from thence it communicated to the old building formerly occupied as the Whig Office. It then spread to the Commission Warehouse of Mr. James Gwin, entirely consuming that and 4 adjoining frames; then crossed Washington street and swept the buildings form the corner of Jackson to Main; and from thence up Main street to Walnut—Mr. Fraisse's brick building alone being saved. The north side of Main street, from Washington to Walnut, is a heap of

---

[36] *Southern Reformer*, Jackson, Mississippi, 3 Aug 1844, 3.

[37] Seargent S. Prentiss (1808-1850) Politician, http://mississippiencyclopedia.org/entries/seargeant-s-prentiss/

[38] *Vicksburg Weekly Sentinel*, Vicksburg, Mississippi, 20 Aug 1844, 2.

[39] *Vicksburg Whig*, Vicksburg, Mississippi, 19 Aug 1844, 2.

ruins, as well as the north side of Walnut street as far as the residence of Mrs. Shockney, which was consumed.

The wind was very high at the time, and one half the town would have been burned but for the recent rain—the roofs of the houses being very wet—blazing shingles and boards falling very thick over the whole of Springfield. A great deal of property has been destroyed, and many families in moderate circumstances have lost nearly their all.

The losers were Judge Bodly, 3 houses; Mr. Chinn, (of N.O.) 1; Mr. Armstrong 1; store of Messrs. Aikin & Gwinn, belonging to some one in Philadelphia; Hartwell Vick's heirs, several houses; Planter's Bank 1; U.S. Bank 1; S. C. Field 2; E. D. Downs 1; Rail Road Bank 1; J. A. Klein 1; H. Stidger 1; **Dr. Peck 1**; E. B. Lilly 1; A. H. Arthur 1; N. H. Vick 3; and Messrs. Dickinsons and others, their stock of stores.

Messrs. Field and Klein were the only parties whose property were insured, as far as we know.– *Vicksburg Whig.*[40]

In November of 1846, a well-dressed man was found hanging dead in Isham's field:

CORONER'S INQUEST. – The Coroner held an inquest yesterday on the body of a man found hanging form a limb of a cotton wood tree in Dr. Peck's field, about a mile from town. He was well dressed, apparently from 22 to 25 years of age, and appears to be a stranger, as he has not been recognized. Every article of his clothing is new and of fine quality. He had in his pockets two sovereigns and between $3 and $4 in silver, an open-end or tailor's thimble, a piece of cloth having several needles in it, and a new trunk key. From appearances he had first tied himself to a limb with his cravat, the limb being too low he had untied the cravat from his neck and left it hanging; he then took a silk pocket handkerchief and tied it to another limb by which he was suspended when found. It is supposed that the act was committed between the rains which fell on Saturday night and Sunday night last. There was no evidence perceivable of his having been an intemperate man while living, and no papers were found upon his person.

If any of our boarding-house keepers have missed a boarder, by informing the Coroner, (who has the key of his trunk,) some information may be gleaned as to his name and late residence.[41]

One month later, on Christmas day, Isham's plantation was up for rent. "FOR RENT. THE Plantation adjoining Vicksburg, occupied for several years by Dr. T. J. Peck. Possession given immediately. Enquire of C. STEELE."[42]

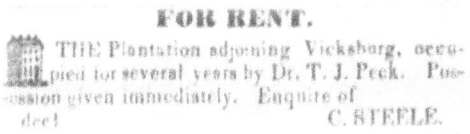

Figure 25 - Isham's Plantation for rent, 25 Dec 1846.

[40] Destructive Fire, *The Guard*, Holly Springs, Mississippi, 27 Feb 1846, 2, emphasis added.
[41] Coroner's Inquest, *Vicksburg Daily Whig*, Vicksburg, Mississippi, 6 Nov 1846, 2.
[42] For Rent, *Vicksburg Daily Whig*, Vicksburg, Mississippi, 25 Dec 1846, 3.

While owning his plantation or plantations in and around Vicksburg, Isham was also involved with issues of the church. While it is possible that the "Mr. I. T. Peck" referred to here was not Isham, this author believes that it was. Future articles mention how he spent much of his time resolving church disputes during his life, maybe slavery was one of them.

METHODIST CONFERENCE, June 4th.
DECLARATION FROM SOUTHERN MEMBERS.

MR. LONGSTREET presented the following document, signed by fifty-two delegates from the Southern Conferences: –

The delegates from the Conferences in the slave-holding states take leave to declare to the General Conference of the Methodist Episcopal Church, that the continued agitation on the subject, of slavery and abolition in a portion of the Church, the frequent action of the General Conference on the subject, and especially the extra judicial proceedings in the case of Bishop Andrew on Saturday last, in their virtual suspension of him from his office, must produce a state of things in the South which renders a continuance of the jurisdiction of this Conference over those Conferences inconsistent with the success of the ministry in the slave-holding states.

Mr. McFerrin moved the following resolution:

Resolved, That the committee appointed to take into consideration the communication of the delegates from the Southern Conferences be instructed, provided they cannot, in their judgment, devise a plan for an amicable adjustment of the difficulties now existing in this Church on the subject of slavery, to devise, if possible, a constitutional plan for a mutual and friendly division of the Church.

Mr. I. T. PECK opposed. He could not consent to such a resolution without discussing it, and there was not now time for that. It was against his judgement to allow the Conference to be pressed into a division by brethren who wishes to erect themselves into a separate Church.

Mr. MCFERRIN said it was not worth while for brethren to take the stand the brother had just taken. There were now but two things that could be done – either they must agree upon an amicable adjustment of the question of slavery, or there must be a division of the Church. Why then not do it pleasantly, and not talk in the strain that brother **Peck** had adopted?

The paper and resolution were referred to a Committee of nine.[43]

In short, with limited time to discuss the full implications of it, Mr. McFerrin wanted the church to vote on a split over the issue of slavery, and Isham opposed the measure, saying that there must be discussion of such a far impacting decision. Isham was then praised for his tone by the writer of the article.

---

[43] *Republican Banner*, Editor Donald Macleod, Volume XXXI., Later called *The Tennessean*, Nashville, TN, 17 Jun 1844, 1, emphasis added.

In January 1842, a bill appeared in the *Vicksburg Daily Whig* about incorporating the city of Vicksburg. Setting out what land the city of Vicksburg will include, it said (*emphasis added*):

SEC. I. – *Be it enacted by the Legislature of the State of Mississippi*, That the limits and boundaries of the City of Vicksburg shall be as follows, to wit: Beginning at the mouth of Glass's Bayou, where an extension of the Eastern line of First North Street would strike the same, thence South with the said line to the Vicksburg and Jackson Rail Road; thence in a Westerly direction with the Northern line of said road, to the Western line of Cherry street, **thence South with the same to a point where an extension of the Northern boundary line of the property known as the plantation of Talbot J. Peck**, would strike the same; thence with the said line to the Mississippi river, thence up the same, with its meanders, to the place of beginning; and including within said limits as far as the State Boundary on the Mississippi River extends, and the jurisdiction of the City, so far as boats trading with said city are concerned, shall extend upon the said river for one mile above and one mile below these limits, and the said city shall be laid off into seven Wards, the limits and boundaries of which shall be designated by the board of Aldermen.

Figure 26 – Section of Map by A. M. Winn, City Engineer of the City of Vicksburg, adopted as the official survey on 22 May 1848. Photographed by the author. Original courtesy of the Old Court House Museum, Vicksburg, Mississippi. See full map for context. Bottom left reads, "Peck & Reading's Saw Mill". To the right of it, "Dr. Peck's Plantation". Photo enhanced for clarity.

Isham's plantation was located just to the south of Vicksburg. Technically, Isham's plantation provided the border of the city limits of Vicksburg. See images of the 1848 map in this volume. First a closeup of Isham's plantation, and then the full map. Under the references section of this official city map, it reads:

The City of Vicksburg

Is bounded on the North by Watkins, Glass, or Winn's Bayou, on the East, by the East side of the 1st North Street, extended North to the Bayou and South to the Railroad, on the South by the Railroad, Eastern line of Washington Street and Northern line of **Dr. Peck's** Plantation to the River, and on the West by the Mississippi River.[44]

One of Isham's letters indicated that he owned the Water Works and Banking Company building on Jackson Street which housed Dr. James Hagan's *Sentinel and Expositor For the Country* newspaper in the rear of the building.[45]

An 1883 article indicated that J. W. Vick sold land to Isham on an unknown date.[46]

Isham's brother William Raine Peck was listed as one of the registered voters in the Vicksburg Mayoral and City Council election in March 1843.[47]

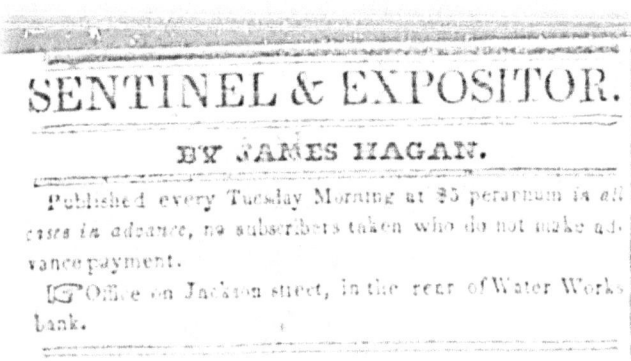

Figure 27 - Sentinel & Expositor by James Hagan, note the location of the newspaper, "in the rear of Water Works bank", 12 Apr 1842, 1.

Though we do not know what happened to his 2nd wife, Helen Rapalje, we know that Isham married Emma Henderson in 1848, and continued to be active in planting cotton. He then focused more on the East Carroll and Madison Parishes of Louisiana. In 1852, Isham's remedy for beating the boll weevil, made its way to the newspapers by way of his dad, Judge Jacob Peck.

From the Alabama Planter.

Remedy for Boll Worm in Cotton.

Messrs. Editors. – I notice, your paper and others, accounts of the destructive ravages of the boll worm on cotton. A remedy is of course desirable and important. Is the following new to you? Destroy the stalks of last year's crop, and the present year the crop will be free from the worm. The philosophy of it is, that the worm deposits an egg in the stalk which remains there during the winter and produces a new worm next season.

---

[44] Official City of Vicksburg Map published by O. O. Woodman, Vicksburg, 1849, emphasis added.
[45] See Sawbones article from 8 Jul 1877 in this volume
[46] *Vicksburg Evening Post*, Vicksburg, Mississippi, 5 Jul 1883, 4.
[47] *Sentinel and Expositor for the Country*, Vicksburg, Mississippi, 14 Mar 1843, 3.

This information was communicated to me a few days ago, in convention, by Judge Peck, an intelligent old gentleman of our part of the state. He has a son, **Mr. Isham Peck**, a planter of Milliken's Bend, Louisiana, who, he told me, had professed to have discovered the above remedy. His crop having suffered from the worm, he was led to investigate the matter with a view to find a preventative. On examination, he found a small hole in the old stalk, and on breaking it open saw the egg left there by the old worm. He concluded to burn the stalks, and was not troubled, by the worm any more. The thing looks reasonable.

I asked Judge Peck if his son had given general circulation to the supposed discovery through the newspapers. He replied, he had not. He had only mentioned it in conversation. It is for this reason I communicate the intelligence to you. If, in your estimation, it is worth any. thing to southern planters, I am persuaded you will let them have it.

JOSEPH H. MARTIN

KNOXVILLE, Tenn., Sept. 1853.[48]

Isham's brother William had a plantation called Mountain, also at Milliken's Bend, and this was the state of things there in 1867:

TERRIBLE MORTALITY.– We learned on yesterday that the cholera, some weeks ago, broke out among the negroes on Buckhorn plantation, in Louisiana, near Milliken's Bend. The overseer, the only white person on the place, becoming alarmed, went off. Dr. Dancey was sent for and on arriving, found fifteen dead and unburied. Those who had not been taken with the disease paid no attention to either the dead of the dying, positively refusing to assist in burying the dead. The Doctor went to Gen. Peck's plantation, a few miles off, for the purpose of procuring help. The negroes there at first refused to go, but after being stimulated highly with whisky, finally consented. In the meantime twenty more had died—and in a day or two forty-eight, making in all eighty-three.—This dreadful mortality is supposed to have been occasioned by the eating of fish which were caught in large quantities in some lakes in the neighborhood, which had been nearly dry, the water remaining being very muddy, stagnant and offensive. There were about one hundred negroes on the place.

Vicksburg Herald, 18*th*.[49]

To learn more about Madison Parish in the mid-1800s, see the *Sawbones: Volume II* Appendix for EARLY PLANTATION LIFE IN MADISON PARISH, LA.

Cotton was king during this era of our American story, and Isham was in the middle of it. The evil of slavery is a terrible stain on our American conscience, and a disappointing reality in the lives the Pecks who lived in that era.

---

[48] Remedy for Boll Worm in Cotton, *The Yazoo Democrat*, Yazoo City, Mississippi, 22 Dec 1852, 4, emphasis added. Fun note, the parents of the author of *Sawbones* were both raised in Enterprise, Alabama, where there is a monument to the boll weevil.
[49] Terrible Mortality. *The Weekly Democrat*, Natchez, Mississippi, 2 Dec 1867, 4.

The National Museum of African American History has an excellent online exhibit detailing the rise of slavery and how it is interwoven with cotton in America.[50]

The following photos attempt to depict some of the realities of slavery during this time.

SALE OF ESTATES, PICTURES AND SLAVES IN THE ROTUNDA, NEW ORLEANS

Figure 29 - Sale of Estates, Pictures and Slaves in the Rotunda, New Orleans, 1842; Courtesy of The Historic New Orleans Collection, 1974.25.23.4

Figure 28 - (Left) A Slave-Pen at New Orleans - Before the Auction. (Right) Slavery Sale, Courtesy of the Historic New Orleans Collection.

---

[50] Slavery & the Making of a New Nation, www.searchablemuseum.com/slavery-and-the-making-of-a-new-nation

Cotton plantations were prevalent throughout the South, but especially along the Mississippi.

Figure 30 - Hauling the Whole Week's Picking, 1842, by William Henry Brown. This collage, depicting a family of slaves, was part of a series created to decorate the rooms of the masters' children on the Nitta Yuma plantation in Vicksburg, Mississippi. Brown specialized in the art of silhouette, which involved using scissors to cut portraits of people from black paper. Watercolor on paper. Courtesy of The Historic New Orleans Collection.

Figure 31 - (Left) Launey & Goebel. Picking cotton, Savannah, Ga., early Negro life. [between 1867 and 1890] Photograph. Library of Congress. (Below) Weighing Cotton. Thomas County, GA, 1895. National Museum of African American History.

Figure 32 – Top & Bottom, Cotton picking and cotton scale as featured at the Vicksburg Civil War Museum, owned and operated by Charles Pendleton. Visit the Museum at 1123 Washington St / Vicksburg, MS 39183. Learn more at www.vicksburgcivilwarmuseum.org

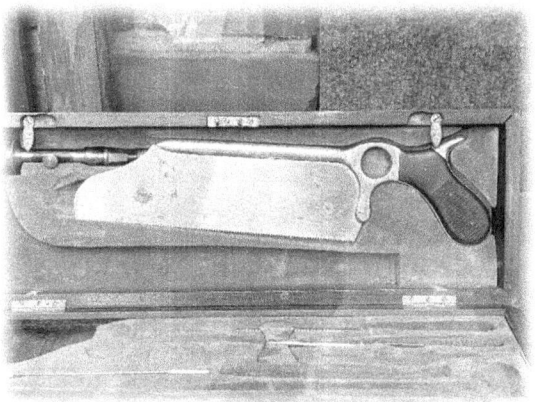

Figure 33 - Right column of photos from Old Courthouse Museum of Vicksburg. (Top) Conf. General Pemberton informs his troops he is going to surrender to General Grant. (Middle) Confederate Battle Flag. (Bottom) Old Courthouse Museum, learn more at https://oldcourthouse.org

Figure 34 - Left column of photos from Vicksburg Civil War Museum. Top two photos by the author, slave cabin, civil war surgeon "Sawbones" saw, bottom photo is actors playing Gen. Grant and Pemberton with museum owner Charles Pendleton. www.vicksburgcivilwarmuseum.org

Figure 35 –
CMB LIVE
(Left)
Vicksburg
Videos, (Right)
Vicksburg
History,
Waterfront,
and Murals

MARRIAGES

First Wife – Cordelia M. Talbot

Isham's first marriage was to his cousin "Cordelia M. Talbot". One article shared, "Cordelia M. Talbot was not yet a teenager when her mother died. Although the records are scant and sometimes contradictory, we believe that she married Isham T. Peck, perhaps a cousin, and that they lived together for a short period of time. Apparently, there were no children from this marriage and the marriage dissolved. The few available records how that Cordelia suffered from mental illnesses and was institutionalized a good part of her life. Isham Talbot [Cordelia's father] provided for her care quite generously in his will and refers to her as "my unfortunate daughter, Cordelia M. Peck." She died in 1860 and was buried at the Frankfort Cemetery."[51] Interestingly, Cordelia's dad was Isham Talbot, Jr. (wife Margaret Garrard) who was a lawyer, politician, and U. S. Senator from Kentucky. Isham Talbot, Jr.'s dad was Isham Talbot, Sr. (who was the son of Matthew Talbot and Jane Clayton). Isham Talbot, Jr. had Cordelia Talbot on 8 Aug 1808. This would make her 3 years older than Isham Peck. Perhaps they had somewhat of an arranged marriage (between cousins), but then Isham had military duty and other things that occupied him. They never had any children and perhaps divorced when she went away for one of her stays in the mental institution. One of Senator Talbot's daughters was indeed named Cordelia.

Cordelia married a man who shared the same name as her father and grandfather…her dad being Isham Talbot, Jr. and then her husband being named Isham Talbot Peck![52] The records for the Kentucky State Senate show that [Senator] Isham Talbot, Jr. presented a petition "praying a divorce" for his daughter from Isham T. Peck on 4 Feb 1835.[53] On 11 Feb 1835 Mr. Wingate, from the committee of religion, reported a bill for the benefit of Cordelia M. Peck;" and on 27 Feb 1835 they passed "An act for the benefit of Cordelia M. Peck." On 18 Feb 1835 it was announced that the Governor of Kentucky had signed the bill in favor of the "act for the benefit of Cordelia M. Peck." Additionally, a MyHeritage site lists Cordelia as remarrying an Erasmus B. Talbot in 1833 in Kentucky.[54]

By analyzing the life timeline provided in this book, it is evident that there was a connection between Isham's traveling with the military, and the dissolution to his marriage with Cordelia. He married her on 19 Nov 1832 when he was 21 years old, and less than a year later (22 Sep 1833) he applied for his passport to Mexico (application signed by her dad, Senator Isham Talbot). He departed for Mexico on an unknown date, and returned home on 30 Jan 1834 (at age 23). Four days later, Cordelia's dad petitioned the Kentucky Senate to grant his daughter a divorce from Isham. They had

---

[51] http://freepages.rootsweb.com/~fww64/genealogy/isham_talbot_senator.htm

[52] The Invincible, A Magazine of History chronicles some of these marriages and histories - https://play.google.com/books/reader?id=NmNbAAAAMAAJ&pg=GBS.PA3

[53] Journal of the Senate of the Commonwealth of Kentucky: Begun and held in the town of Frankfort, on Wednesday the 31st of December, in the Year of our Lord 1834, and of the Commonwealth the forty-third. Frankfort, by Albert G. Hodges, Printer for the State, 1834. P223, p255, p390, p394

[54] https://www.myheritage.com/names/cordelia_talbot

been married for 1 year, 2 months, 2 weeks, and 2 days (442 days). Why did they marry? Why did they divorce? This remains a mystery.

Isham then moved to Mississippi and married a wealthy widow.

Second Wife – Helen D. (Rapalje) Glass

Figure 37 – See 5 Dec 1837 - Vicksburg Weekly Sentinel (Vicksburg, MS) - Probate Court Notice for Warren County, MS

On 18 May 1837, Isham married Helen D. (Rapalje) Glass, widow of Anthony Glass. He was 26 years old. As referenced above by Ezekiel Birdseye, Helen was a slave-owning plantation widow. An 1840 Mississippi Supreme Court case sheds light on where they lived. Anthony Glass, Helen's previous husband, owned 50 acres in Vicksburg, Mississippi, located next to Glass's Bayou, close to what is now the Vicksburg National Military Park. After Anthony's death, there arose a dispute about his land holdings, and by my reading, the court allowed Isham and Helen to sell the land, then distribute the proceeds to various heirs. See map that follows.

Isham appeared in a 5 Dec 1837 *Vicksburg Sentinel* article filing for the disputed land (Scan QR Code to left for newspaper clipping). And a *Vicksburg Daily Whig* clipping dated 4 Jan 1840 mentioned the same situation. One genealogy website mentions Helen Glass as his wife, but no other information is provided about her (dates of birth, death, etc...).[55] You can read about the Mississippi Supreme Court Case on the Sawbones Resources website (Scan QR code to right). As a historical note of interest, Isham's cousin, Judge William Lewis Sharkey (1797 – 1873), was on the bench during the case, but he recused himself from the decision. This was likely

Figure 36 - See 1840 Mississippi Supreme Court Case involving Isham and wife Helen Glass

due to their close family connection. Judge Sharkey was Isham's 2nd cousin, 1x removed. It is not known what happened to Helen (Rapalje) Glass, whether she died or they divorced. But Isham did eventually name his second daughter Helen. One theory is that Helen died, and Isham remembered her fondly.

Helen's maiden name was Rapalje. According to Kelli Breland, Glass family researcher at Mississippi College in Clinton, Mississippi, Helen D. Rapalje was the daughter of Isaac Rapalje. The Rapaljes were a wealthy and very prominent family from New York. According to research available, Helen was daughter to Isaac Rapalje, sister to George Rapalje, Jr., and niece of Jacques Rapalje. Isaac and Jacques Rapalje were the sons of Gerrit Rapalje and Helena De Neys. As more is discovered about the Rapalje's, updates will be posted to the Sawbones Resources Page: https://www.crossmountainbooks.com/sawbones-resources.[56]

---

[55] https://www.geni.com/people/Dr-Isham-Peck/6000000047582310884
[56] More info about the Rapaljes in Warren County can be found in *Becoming Southern: The Evolution of a Way of Life, Warren County and Vicksburg, Mississippi, 1770-1860* by Christopher Morris, especially pages 37-39.

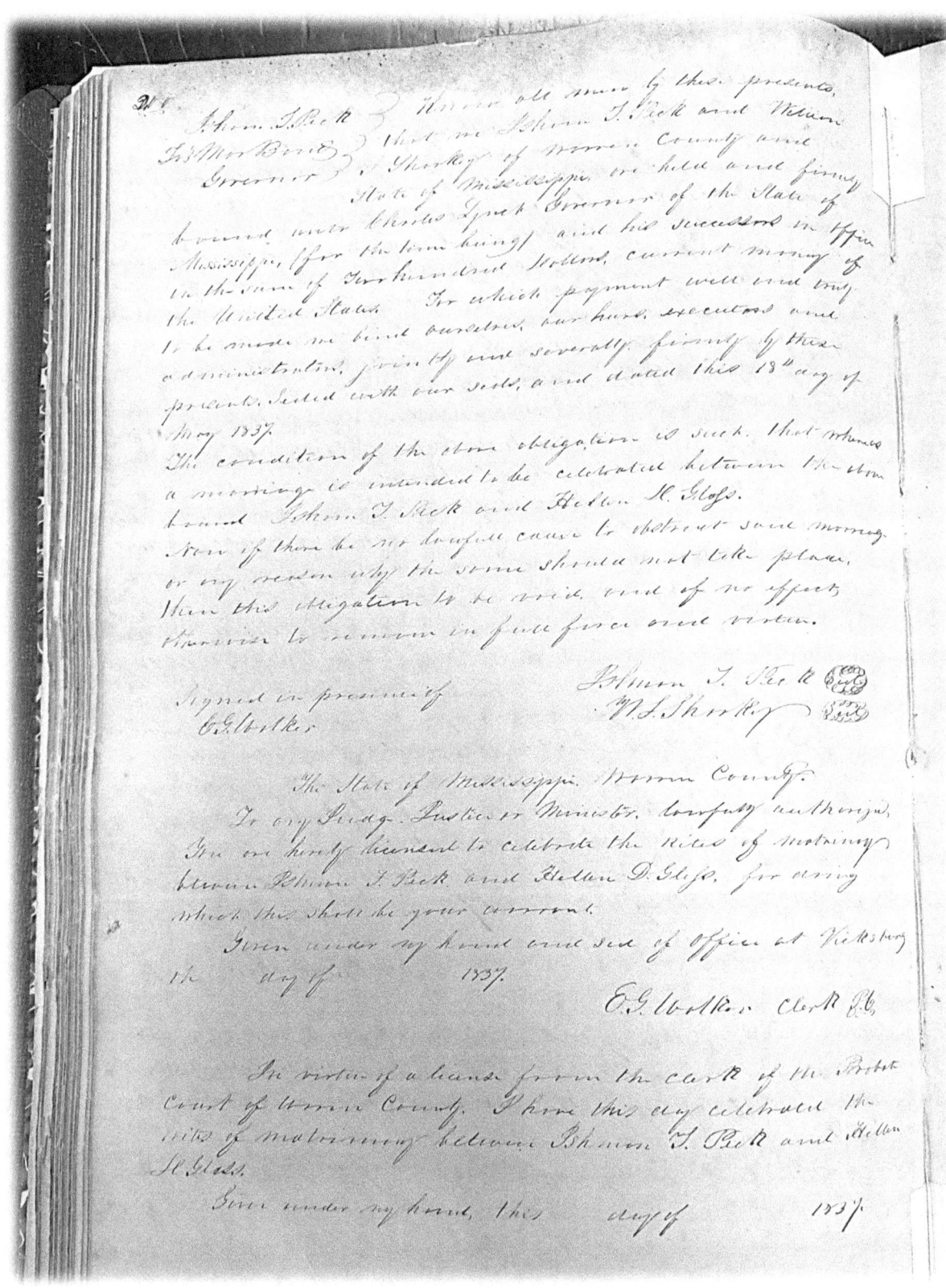

Figure 38 - Original marriage record for Isham T. Peck and Helen D. Glass, dated 18 May 1837, photographed by the author 15 Jun 2023, Vicksburg County Courthouse, County Clerk Office,
Warren County White Marriage Records, Aug. 1834-July 1840, Book E, 200.
Photo sharpened 35% and brightness increased 5% for clarity. See following page for transcription.

Marriage Record Transcription – Isham T. Peck and Helen D. Glass
[Page] 200

Isham T. Peck } Know all men by these presents,
 To: Mr. Bond } that one Isham T. Peck and William
     Governor } L. Sharkey of Warren County and State of Mississippi, one held and firmly bound unto Charles Lynch Governor of the State of Mississippi, (for the time being) and his successors in office in the sum of two hundred dollars, current money of the United States. For which payment well and truly to be made me bind ourselves, our kind, executors and administration, jointly and severally, firmly by these presents, sealed with our seals, and dated this 18th day of May 1837.

The condition of the above obligation is such that whereas a marriage is intended to be celebrated between the above bound Isham T. Peck and Helen D. Glass.

Now if there by no lawful cause to obstruct such said marriage or any reason why the same should not take place, then this obligation to be void and of no effect, otherwise to remain in full force and virtue.

Signed in presence of   Isham T. Peck {Seal}
E. G. Walker   W. L. Sharkey {Seal}

The State of Mississippi. Warren County.
To any Judge, Justice or Minister, lawfully authorized, You are hereby licensed to celebrate the rites of matrimony between Isham T. Peck and Helen D. Glass, for using? which this shall be your warrant.

Given under my hand and seal of office at Vicksburg the   day of   1837.
                             E. G. Walker. Clerk {Symbol}

In virtue of a license from the clerk of the probate court of Warren County. I have this day celebrated the rites of matrimony between Isham T. Peck and Hellen [sic] D. Glass.

Given under my hand, this   day of   1837.

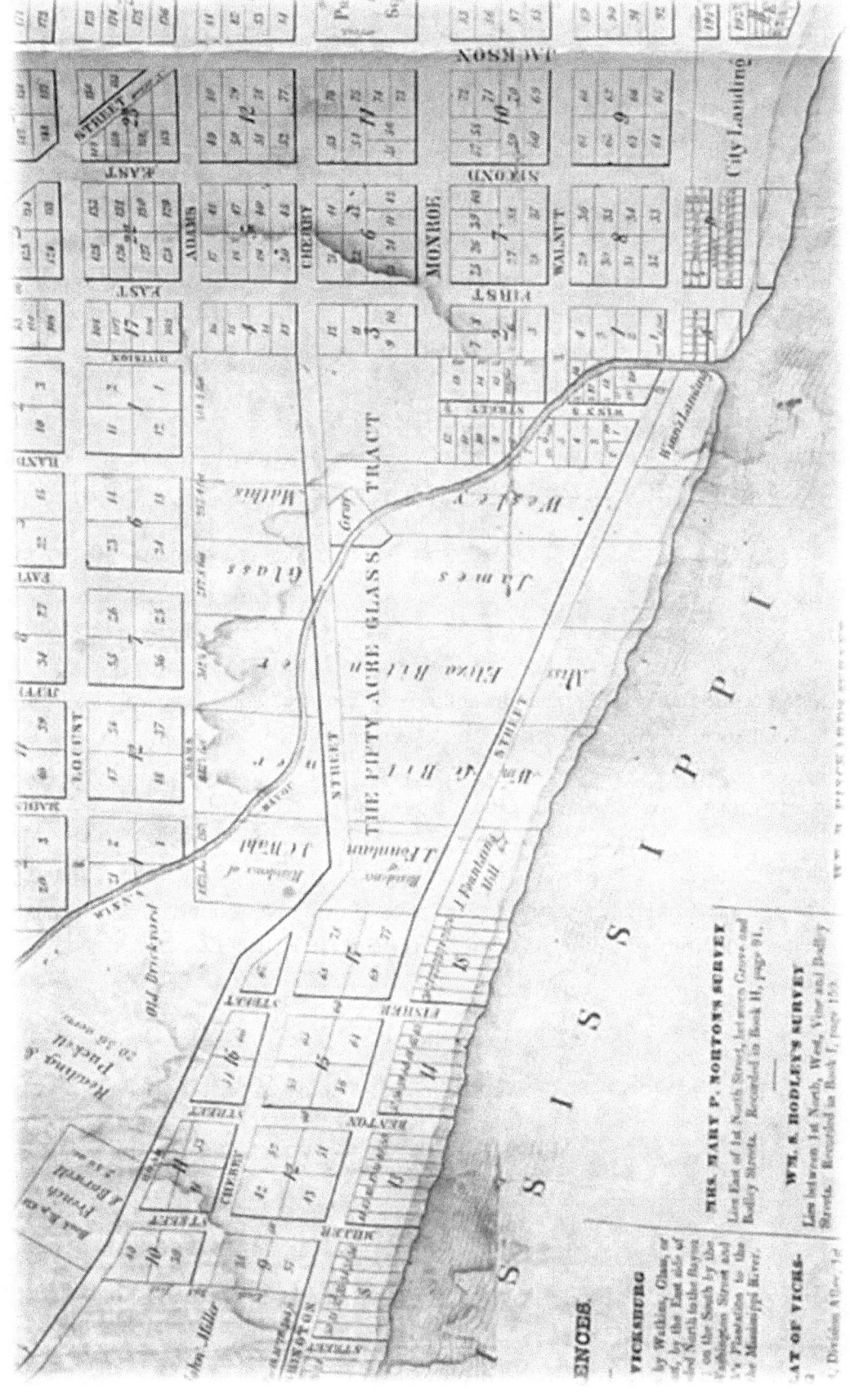

Figure 39 – 1849 Vicksburg Map showing close-up of "The Fifty Acre Glass Tract," divided by inheritance, published by O. O. Goodman. Map drawn by A. M. Winn, City Engineer, and adopted by the Mayor and City Council as the official survey on 22 May 1848. Photo by author. Original courtesy of the Old Courthouse Museum of Vicksburg.

Third Wife – Emma Elizabeth Henderson

Figure 40 - Emma Henderson Peck - Photo in Peck Family Collection - Digitized by Author at home of Arnette Peck King 2017, Colorized using MyHeritage.com

On 12 Oct 1848, Isham married his third wife, Emma Elizabeth Henderson, in East Carroll Parish, Louisiana. Isham was 37 and Emma was approximately 15 years old at the time of their marriage. Emma was from East Carroll Parish which is about 56 miles by highway, and 30 miles north on the Mississippi from Vicksburg, MS. For a good description of Emma, with details about her family and land holdings in Louisiana, please see the About the Author section of *Ada's Journal and Emma's Letters*, Cross Mountain Books, 2021.

She is listed on the 1850 Census from the Western District of Carroll Parish as being 19 years old and being born in Mississippi (estimated DOB 1831). She is listed on the 1870 Jefferson County, TN Census as being 37 years old (est. DOB 1833). The 1880 Census from Big Creek in Cocke County, TN lists her as 44 years old (est. DOB 1836). So from these dates we can narrow down that she was born sometime between 1831 and 1836. One more stray date appears in her death notice posted in the *Knoxville Journal and Tribune* on 17 Sep 1899 on page 5, saying she was "aged about seventy-five years." This date would mean she was born in 1824 (which is clearly in error). At the oldest she was 17 when they got married, and at the youngest she was 12. Their first daughter, Ada, was born 25 Jul 1853 in Mossy Creek at their farm called Oakland. She would have been anywhere from 17 to 22 when Ada was born. For consistency, we will use 1833 as the date of her birth, even though we do not have it "in stone" anywhere.

The 1850 Census lists her dad as William Henderson, born 1800 in Tennessee, and her mom, "Mrs. William" [Louise] as born 1812 in Missouri. They married in Warren County, Mississippi on 13 Dec 1827. From *Ada's Journal* we know that William had a twin brother, but the author has not been able to locate additional conclusive information about William's origins or family. He was born around 1800 and died Sep 1867.[57] William was one of the largest slaveholders in Louisiana and owned what was known as Henderson Plantation. By 1860, he owned 143 slaves and had 36 slave dwellings on his plantation.[58] From *Ada's Journal and Emma's Letters*, we can glean snippets about William's personality,

---

[57] Kate Stone, *Brokenburn*, 3rd edition. (Baton Rouge: Louisiana State University Press, 1995), 373.
[58] Joseph Menn, *The Large Slaveholders of Louisiana-1860*. (1860)

but not much more. He and his wife Louise travelled by steamboat, railroad, and stagecoach to visit their daughter Emma at Oakland and later their home in Wolf Creek, TN.[59] He was a brave man, as he pulled a crazed buck off of Isham in April 1855, and Emma credited him with saving her husband's life. In the summer/fall of 1862, William and his wife Louise stayed at their plantation, knowing that the Union Army was advancing on Vicksburg at the time, just 40 miles below their property.[60] According to Louise, in Jan 1856, William was "as fat and jolly as ever, our climate agrees so well with him." He had a sense of humor, as Louise quoted him as saying "hard times does not keep the ladies from shopping" after he couldn't even enter some of the stores in New Orleans because of the crowds of women in Nov 1857.[61] Louise reveals another nugget about her husband in January 1861, that he didn't like to write letters.[62] Emma must have thought highly of her father, and wanted to honor him, because she and Isham named their first son, William Henderson Peck, after her father.

Much could be said and written about Emma's mom Louise, as she was an excellent writer, who used pithy phrases, and cared deeply for her family. Pages 73-86 in *Ada's Journal and Emma's Letters* contains seven lengthy letters written by Louise. Please review these letters for a full picture. Additionally, her obituary is found on pages 113-114 in *Ada's Journal*. To quote the obituary, "Among her relatives and friends Mrs. Henderson was affectionately known as 'Gam,' and her cheerful and considerate manner gained for her friends, in all her household, who regarded her as an 'optimist.' Her ready humor and bright intellect, which, constantly, drew on a large store house of knowledge, made her always a most agreeable companion." She was born 4 Mar 1813 in St. Genevieve, Missouri and died 13 Feb 1897.

Truthfully, Emma deserves her own biography. Born in Mississippi, raised in Louisiana down the road from another famous writer, Kate Stone (see *Brokenburn*), she is educated, cultured, and intelligent. Her penmanship was excellent, and she also played the piano. The author was entrusted with Emma's Songbook, and hopes to publish it in due time. It contains approx. 40 songs (piano sheet music) published around the 1830s/1840s and includes songs by Jenny Lind, the Star Spangled Banner, music published by Charles Horton in New Orleans, and Osbourn's Music Saloon in Philadelphia.

Emma kept a journal from the perspective of her first-born child and daughter Ada from 1853-1855. The final entry was made on Ada's second birthday, 25 Jul 1855. This journal was published by Cross Mountain Books in 2021 and is called *Ada's Journal and Emma's Letters: The Civil War Era Journal and Letters of Emma Peck*. The second half of this book contains

Figure 41 - Front cover of Emma's Songbook, text reads "Elizabeth E. Henderson", photo by Author

[59] Emma Peck, *Ada's Journal and Emma's Letters: The Civil War Era Journal of Emma Peck*, 1st. (Scott AFB, IL: Cross Mountain Books, 2021), 37).
[60] Ibid, 65.
[61] Ibid, 76.
[62] Ibid, 81-82.

approx. 40 letters from Emma written to her best friend Emma Allen in Wolf Creek from 1854-1894. These letters shed incredible light on what it was like to be a wife, mom, and daughter before, during, and after the Civil War. Other letters from Isham, Louise Henderson, and others are included as well.

Emma gave birth to nine children. Her last child, Robert Lee Peck, was born 29 Apr 1874, when Emma was about 41 years old (and Isham 63). After Isham died in 1887, Emma lived with her son Paul in Lake City, Florida. Additionally, in her old age, she lived with her mom, Louise Henderson, who everyone called "Gam," and her son's mother-in-law, Mrs. King. Emma died 16 Sep 1899. Additional biographical details can be found in the "About the Author" section of *Ada's Journal and Emma's Letters*. Emma was faithful to Isham, and endured the struggles of life, war, and burying five children with him. As he wrote his letters to the editor of the *Morristown Gazette*, she wrote her letters to her friend Emma Allen. Because she wrote, we can learn much about her life and times as well.

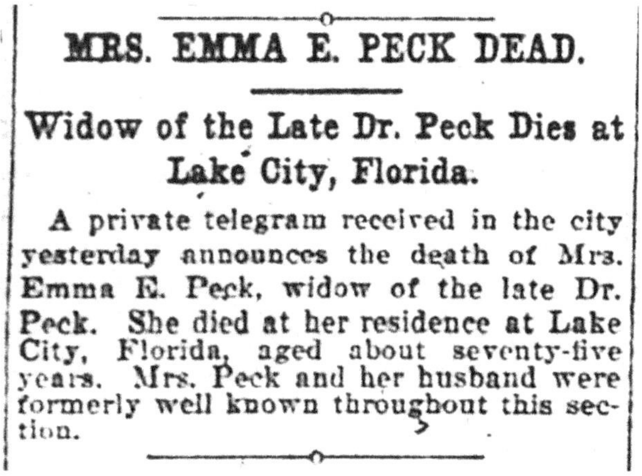

MRS. EMMA E. PECK DEAD.

Widow of the Late Dr. Peck Dies at Lake City, Florida.

A private telegram received in the city yesterday announces the death of Mrs. Emma E. Peck, widow of the late Dr. Peck. She died at her residence at Lake City, Florida, aged about seventy-five years. Mrs. Peck and her husband were formerly well known throughout this section.

Figure 42 - 17 Sep 1899, *The Journal and Tribune* (Knoxville, TN), 5.

Figure 44 - Emma (Henderson) Peck, photograph by Knoffs in Knoxville, circa 1880, Courtesy of Peck Family Collection

Figure 43 - 28 Mar 1893, Emma Peck (middle) with who is likely her daughter-in-laws Fannie Gibbens Peck and Ella R. King Peck, Photograph was taken by S. P. Burgert in Jacksonville, FL, more info here: https://tampapix.com/burgert3.htm, Courtesy of Peck Family Collection

MILITARY SERVICE

PERSONAL.

E. G. Budd, the Murfreesboro correspondent of the *American*, arrived in the city last night.

Miss Ida and Addie Fletcher, of Cincinnati, are on a visit to Mr. Jacob Bloomstein and family.

Mr. Paul Nicholson, of Fryer's Grand Opera Troupe, left last night for Louisville.

Dr. Talbot Peck, of Wolf Creek, Cocke county, Tennessee, arrived in the city yesterday from his Louisiana plantation, en route to his home in the mountains, and is quartered at the Maxwell. In his younger days the doctor was a Surgeon in the United States Army, and was stationed at Des Moines and Chicago when they were but small villages on the frontier. He has been a great traveler, in this country and abroad, and is remarkably familiar with the personal history of the Southern men who have been most prominent in public life during the past forty years. Keeping thoroughly posted as to what is going on in the outer world, by taking a large number of newspapers, he lives quietly and contentedly in the midst of his thirty thousand acres of East Tennessee possessions, embraced in which is a mountain of specular iron that for extent and richness has no rival save the famous Iron Mountain of Missouri.

Figure 45 - *The American*, now *"The Tennessean"* (Nashville, TN), 25 Dec 1877, Pg 4

According to one article (left), during Isham's "younger days," he was a surgeon in the US Army and was stationed at Des Moines and Chicago, when they were small villages on the frontier.[63] The article goes on to say "He has been a great traveler, in this country and abroad, and is remarkably familiar with the personal history of the Southern men who have been most prominent in public life during the past forty years. Keeping thoroughly posted as to what is going on in the outer world, by taking a large number of newspapers, he lives quietly and contentedly in the midst of his thirty thousand acres of East Tennessee possessions, embraced in which is a mountain of specular iron that for extent and richness has no rival save the famous Iron Mountain of Missouri." This article was written when he was 66 years old, and just 10 years before his death. Based on a little period research, the author estimates that he served in the Army off and on between 1831 and 1850. This would make him 20-39 years old during his service, allowing him time to receive his medical training, and allowing him to serve at least a full 5 year of enlistment (even though he would have been an officer).

U.S. Military Milestones in the 1830s-1840s.[64]

- 1830 May 28 – Indian Removal Act of 1830, signed into law by President Andrew Jackson
- 1831 Spring – American emigrants settled on Indian lands, Sac and Fox Indians under Chief Black Hawk burned settlers houses in Western Illinois
- 1832 Aug 2 – Col. Henry Atkinson, Jefferson Barracks Commander, takes 500 regulars and 500 volunteers to defeat the Indians at confluence of the Bad Axe River and the Mississippi (Isham was there – see 6 May 1874

Figure 46 - From "The Regular Army Before the Civil War 1845-1860 by Clayton R. Newell, pg 16 (Originally "The American Soldier, 1847, by H. Charles McBarron (U.S. Army Art Collection)

---

[63] *The Tennessean*, Nashville, Tennessee, Tue, Dec 25, 1877, 4.

[64] Richard Stewart, *American Military History Volume 1: The United States Army and the Forging of a Nation, 1775-1917*, Center of Military History, Washington, D.C., Chapter 7, 166-172.

Sawbones article about Rock Island, IL and the cholera epidemic)

- 1832 – Treaty with the Seminoles at the direction of Secretary Cass, the U.S. Indian commissioner in Florida, ratified in 1834. Deadline for removal of Indians from Florida to Arkansas set at 1 Jan 1836.
- 1835 – Seminoles resisted and by Dec 1835, there were 9 companies of artillery and 2 of infantry, 536 officers and men under the command of Bvt. Brig. Gen. Duncan L. Clinch.
- 1835-1842 – Second Seminole War
- 1820s-1830s – Army pioneered expeditions from Ft. Leavenworth seeking to make treaties with the Great Plains Indians to protect trading caravans
- 1825-1830 – "Between 1825 and 1830, approximately 15,000 immigrants with several thousand African American slaves poured into Texas. In March of 1836 they proclaimed their independence from Mexico."
- 1835 Oct 2 – Texans fired the first shot at the Mexican Army, leading to the start of the Texas Revolution[65]
- 1835 Oct 28 – Texan Army laid siege to San Antonio, there was a clash at Mission Concepcion, Texans were victorious over Mexican Army troops led by General Martin Perfecto de Cos.
- 1835 Nov 26 – Texan Army defeated the Mexican Army in the Grass Fight
- 1836 Feb 23 – Mar 6 – Siege of the Alamo – Santa Ana's Mexican troops defeated the Texans including native Tennessean Davy Crockett
- 1836 Apr 21 – Maj. Gen. Sam Houston (Tennessee State Governor 1827-1829) defeated Santa Ana at San Jacinto
- 1836 Jul-Dec – General Gaines occupied Nacogdoches across the Sabine River
- 1842-1843 – 2d Lt John C. Fremont led expeditions to explore and map the Platte River country for the benefit of emigrants moving over the Oregon Trail
- 1845 – Col Stephen Kearny marched 5 companies of the 1st Dragoons over the Oregon Trail to protect emigrants
  - 1845 Mar 1 – Congress jointly resolved to admit Texas into the Union under President Polk
  - 1846 Apr 25 – 2 Feb 1848 – Mexican-American War

Fort Des Moines (Iowa) and Fort Dearborn (Chicago)

The first Fort Des Moines was "established 19 May 1834 as Camp Des Moines by Lt. Colonel Stephen Watts Kearny, 1st U.S. Dragoons to control and protect the Sac and Fox Indians. Abandoned 1 Jun 1837 and the buildings were sold to private owners. The fort site became the town of Montrose [*Iowa*]."[66] This is located just across the river from Nauvoo, Illinois, the site which became so famous as the location of early Mormon settlers when they fled from Missouri in late 1839. The second Fort Des Moines was "established 20 May 1843 at the

Figure 47 - Article about "Old Fort Des Moines", also available here: https://pubs.lib.uiowa.edu/annals-of-iowa/article/13503/galley/121954/view/

---

[65] The Alamo, www.thealamo.org/remember/battle-and-revolution

[66] A great retelling of the history of Fort Des Moines can be found here: Polk, H. H., (1962) "Old Fort Des Moines", *The Annals of Iowa* 36(6), p.425-436. doi: https://doi.org/10.17077/0003-4827.7643, accessed 22 Jan 2022

junction of the Des Moines River and the Racoon River by Captain James Allen and elements of the 1st U.S. Dragoons.[67] [68] The post protected the Sac and Fox Indians before they were removed to Missouri. The Sac and Fox Indian Agency moved to Missouri in 1846 and the post was abandoned 12 March 1846."[69] "*The Opening of the Des Moines Valley to Settlement*" shares extensive information about Fort Des Moines and its operations.[70] The only U.S. Army Fort in operation in Chicago during this period was Fort Dearborn. The Fort was constructed in 1805, rebuilt in 1816, and decommissioned by 1837.[71] If Isham served at Fort Dearborn until it decommissioned in 1837, he may have served somewhere else between 1837 and 1843, when the second Fort Des Moines opened.

Note the fact that both the first and second Fort Des Moines had dragoons as a significant part of their troops. Later, during the Civil War, Isham used his resources to equip "The Peck Light Dragoons" formed under prominent Mossy Creek entrepreneur Benjamin Branner. It is quite possible that Isham saw the usefulness of light dragoons during his pre-Civil War service, and this inspired him to invest in a similar military unit when the War Between the States started.

Figure 48 - Birthplace of Des Moines. Fort Des Moines No. 2 (1843-1846) Wood Cabin. Photo by Megan Bannister, and found here: https://olioiniowa.files.wordpress.com/2015/01/imgp1724.jpg, accessed 21 Jan 2022.

It is very difficult to find accounts of medical operations at either Fort Dearborn in Chicago or Fort Des Moines. But here is one from the approximate time when Isham would have been at Fort Dearborn. "As far as posts in the West were concerned, transportation presented a greater problem than purchasing. Ships came to grief from time to time and floods could delay the delivery of much-needed goods. Some forts appear to have been particularly unfortunate. In March 1845, for example, a packet ship loaded with supplies for Forts Snelling and Crawford, as well as for Forts Leavenworth, Atkinson, **Des Moines**, and Scott, was wrecked, and only three months later, when another ship, bound for New Orleans, met misfortune on the coast of Florida, the mishap deprived Fort Crawford of sixteen iron bedsteads and Fort Snelling of another twelve."[72]

Another account from the same book includes this account of a cholera outbreak in 1832. "On board the Sheldon Thompson, cholera did not appear until after a stop at Fort Gratiot, where some

---

[67] http://www.fortwiki.com/James_Allen

[68] http://www.fortwiki.com/1st_U.S._Dragoons

[69] http://www.fortwiki.com/Fort_Des_Moines_(2)

[70] Description of Fort Des Moines in "The Opening of the Des Moines Valley to Settlement", *Iowa Journal of History & Politics*, Vol. 14 No. 4 (Oct. 1916), 520 ff.

[71] https://chicagology.com/fortdearborn/

[72] Mary C. Gillett, *The Army Medical Department, 1818-1865*, 83. http://tinyurl.com/ArmyMedicalDept1818-1865, emphasis added.

of her passengers were put ashore because of serious overcrowding on board. On 8 July She stopped at Fort Mackinac and left off four more who were sick. She then proceeded to **Fort Dearborn, at Chicago**, where three passengers died, their illness not immediately recognized as cholera. The day after the ship left Fort Mackinac, more passengers fell ill, and the diagnosis of cholera became unavoidable. By the time the ship reached **Chicago** on 10 July, seventy-seven cases of cholera had been identified. **Fort Dearborn** was quickly converted into a hospital and its garrison ordered to pitch camp several miles away. While his men were being cared for by two assistant surgeons, General Scott warned all comers away from the fort in order to prevent the spread of the disease to troops actually engaged in fighting. At the fort, however, 200 men had been taken into the hospital in the space of a week, and 58 died."[73]

Mexican-American War

The introduction to *Gateway South: The Campaign for Monterrey* gives a thorough, yet succinct summary of the Mexican War.

Figure 49 – Fort Dearborn - U. S. Marine Hospital. Big Locust Tree. Storehouse, Magazine. Block-house. Soldier's Barracks. Officer's Quarters. Light-house. Stables, Artillery. Commandant's Quarters. Light-keeper's House. Ferry Slip.

"The Mexican War (1846-1848) was the U.S. Army's first experience waging extended conflict in foreign land. This brief war is often overlooked by casual students of history since it occurred so close to the American Civil War and is overshadowed by the latter's sheer size and scope. Yet, the Mexican War was instrumental in shaping the geographical boundaries of the United States. At the conclusion of this conflict, the U.S. had added some one million square miles of territory, including what today are the states of Texas, Arizona, New Mexico, and California, as well as portions of Colorado, Wyoming, Utah, and Nevada. This newly acquired land also became a battleground between advocates for the expansion of slavery and those who fought to prevent its spread. These sectional and political differences ripped the fabric of the union of states and eventually contributed to the start of the American Civil War, just thirteen years later. In addition, the Mexican War was a proving ground for a generation of U.S. Army leaders who as junior officers in Mexico learned the trade of war and later applied those lessons to the Civil War.

The Mexican War lasted some twenty-six months from its first engagement through the withdrawal of American troops. Fighting took place over thousands of miles, from northern Mexico to Mexico City, and across New Mexico and California. During the conflict, the U.S. Army won a series of decisive conventional battles, all of which highlighted the value of U.S.

---

[73] Ibid, 51, emphasis added.

> Military Academy graduates who time and again paved the way for American victories. The Mexican War still has much to teach us about projecting force, conducting operations in hostile territory with a small force that is dwarfed by the local population, urban combat, the difficulties of occupation, and the courage and perseverance of individual soldiers."[74]

The War With Mexico: The Taylor and Kearny Campaigns by the U.S. Army Medical Department / Office of Medical History, gives a look back at surgeons during the Mexican War.[75] Another section of this history details the ranking of surgeons in the Army, "Section 2 of the act of Congress 'To increase and regulate the pay of the surgeons and assistant surgeons of the army,' approved June 30, 1834, provides that surgeons 'shall be entitled to receive the pay and emoluments of a major, assistant surgeons who shall have served five years the pay and emoluments of a captain, and those who shall have served less than five years the pay and emoluments of a first lieutenant.'"[76] If Isham was a primary surgeon, rather than an assistant, then he would have had the equivalent rank of a Major.

Later in life, we know from newspaper articles that Isham spent considerable time with Major Henry Heiss and Green Allen. Maj Heiss was a part of Captain Payne's Company, First Battalion Tennessee Cavalry (Lieut. Col. F.N. McNairy), 1861.[77]

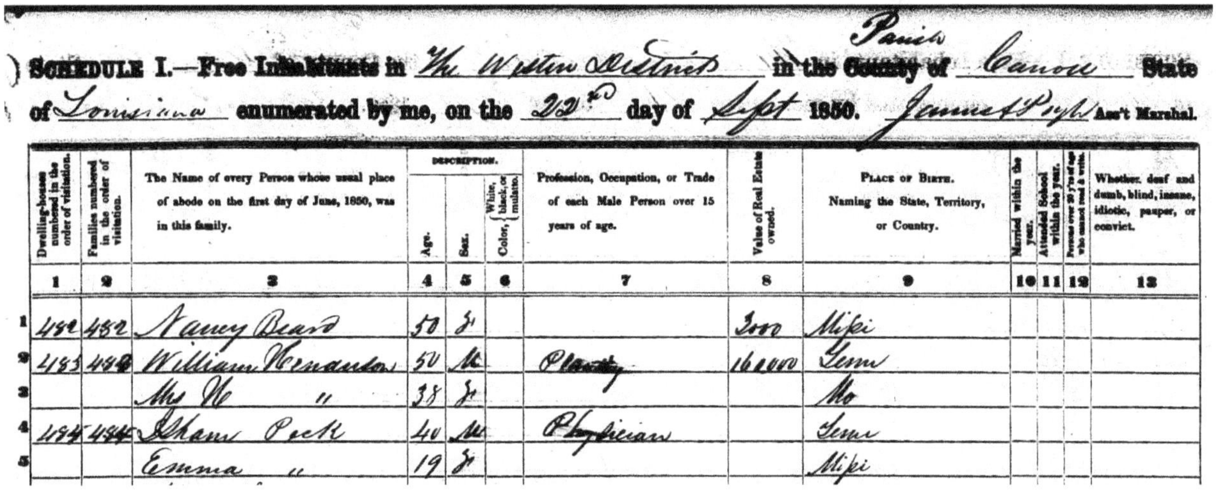
SCHEDULE I.—Free Inhabitants in The Western District in the Parish of Carroll State of Louisiana enumerated by me, on the 22nd day of Sept 1850. James ... Ass't Marshal.

	Dwelling-houses numbered in the order of visitation.	Families numbered in the order of visitation.	The Name of every Person whose usual place of abode on the first day of June, 1850, was in this family.	Age.	Sex.	Color, (White, black, or mulatto.)	Profession, Occupation, or Trade of each Male Person over 15 years of age.	Value of Real Estate owned.	Place of Birth. Naming the State, Territory, or Country.	Married within the year.	Attended School within the year.	Persons over 20 y'rs of age who cannot read & write.	Whether deaf and dumb, blind, insane, idiotic, pauper, or convict.
	1	2	3	4	5	6	7	8	9	10	11	12	13
1	482	482	Nancy Beard	50	F			3000	Missi				
2	483	483	William Henderson	50	M		Planter	160000	Tenn				
3			Mrs H "	38	F				Mo				
4	484	484	Isham Peck	40	M		Physician		Tenn				
5			Emma "	19	F				Missi				

Figure 50 - 1850 Western District - Carroll Parish, Louisiana Census.
Dwelling 483 – William Henderson (Age 50) Planter with 160000 acres, born in Tennessee, Wife "Mrs. H." (Age 38), born in Missouri. Dwelling 484 – Isham Peck (Age 40), Physician, born in Tennessee, Emma Peck (Age 19), born in Mississippi
William Henderson and Louise (Donohue) were Emma's parents, living on their sprawling "Henderson Plantation"
*Note that Isham's father-in-law is 10 years older than him, and mother-in-law is 2 years younger than him.

---

[74] The Occupation of Mexico, May 1846-July 1848, https://history.army.mil/brochures/Occupation/Occupation.htm
[75] The Army Medical Department, 1818-1865, The War With Mexico: The Taylor and Kearny Campaigns, https://achh.army.mil/history/book-civil-gillett2-amedd-1818-1865-chpt5, accessed 4 Dec 2022.
[76] https://achh.army.mil/history/book-civil-gillett2-amedd-1818-1865-chpt2, accessed 4 Dec 2022.
[77] HISTORY Of DAVIDSON COUNTY, TENNESSEE, WITH ILLUSTRATIONS AND BIOGRAPHICAL SKETCHES of its PROMINENT MEN AND PIONEERS BY PROF. W. W. CLAYTON Philadelphia: J. W. Lewis & Co. 1880. Press of J. B. LIPPINCOTT Manuscript scanned and digitized in 2009 by: Ginger L. Christmas-Beattie, 189, http://www.tngenweb.org/records/davidson/history/clayton/1-192_PT_1.pdf, accessed 19 Mar 2020.

Mexico Trip – Passport and Ship Record

We have two time-stamped documents that give us anchors for Isham's travel. The first is his passport application, and the second is a ship manifest of his return from Mexico. Here is their transcription.

Passport Application[78]
Received Sept. 28 1833

Frankfort. KY. Sep. 22d: 1833

Dear Sir

In behalf of a dear relative of mine Doctor Isham T. Peck, a son of Judge Peck of Tennasee [sic]. I have to ask the favor I have made out for Him: a Passport. Which shall authorize him to travel through the Territory of Mexico. Which He is desirous of exploring [.] His person may be thus descended in stature about 6 feet 3 inches in length [.] Complexion and Hair: Blue Eyes. and Nose slightly Aquiline [.] If you will have the goodness to have this Document Passport Bgthe[?] proper officer in your Department and enclosed to Doctor Peck of Louisiana in this State. as early as economical. *Unintelligible Marking*

[Page 2] your will confer appeal from on news with peal? Newport? [*or* your passport].

Isham Talbot

[Outside of Letter/Envelope]

Isham T. Peck

Passport Tent

Sept 28th 1833

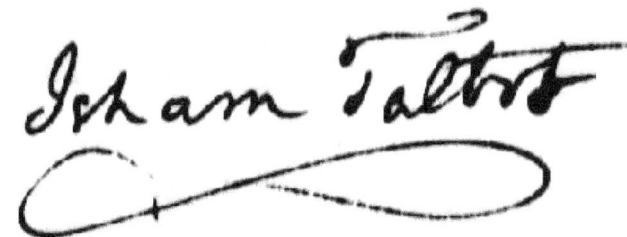

The Honorable

Louis Mc.Lane

Secretary of State

Washington

DC.

Figure 51 – Signature of Senator Isham Talbot from 1833 passport application

Secretary of State Louis McClane
Louis McClane served as the Secretary of State from 29 May 1833 – 30 Jun 1834 under President Andrew Jackson. A well written history detailing the various offices he held can be found at Wikipedia: https://en.wikipedia.org/wiki/Louis_McLane. The more significant name here is the one found at the end of the application. Isham Talbot, of Frankfort, Kentucky, requested Isham's passport. And he calls Isham his "dear relative".

---

[78] National Archives and Records Administration (NARA); Washington D.C.; NARA Series Passport Applications, 1795-1905; Roll #: 2; Volume #002 – 13 May 1833 - 31 Dec 1834

Senator Isham Talbot, Jr.

Senator Isham Talbot, Jr. calls himself our Isham's "dear relative", and was his half great uncle, soon to be father-in-law, and an accomplished statesman. Here is his biography from an 1897 account.[79]

ISHAM TALBOT, United States senator and lawyer, was born in Bedford county, Virginia, in 1773. In his youth his father emigrated to Mercer county, Kentucky, where with few advantages and without the aid of teachers he acquired an extensive knowledge of languages, ancient and modern. He was a student of law under Colonel George Nicholas, and commenced the practice at Versailles, moving soon afterward to Frankfort, where he took a prominent place at the bar. He was elected to the state senate in 1812 and to the United States senate in 1815, as the successor of Jesse Bledsoe, continuing in office by re-election until 1825. He died at his residence "Melrose," near Frankfort, September 21, 1837.

Figure 52 - Senator Isham Talbot, Jr. (1773-25 Sep 1837). Oil painting by Matthew Harris Jouett (1788-1827). Public Domain.

Mr. Talbott was an accomplished lawyer and eloquent speaker. His rapidity of utterance was extraordinary. He once argued a case before the supreme court of the United States and spoke for four hours; his address was marked by impassioned eloquence, his words flowed like a torrent and his velocity of speech was a topic of conversation with the judges after adjournment. Judge Washington wittily observed, "A person of moderate wishes could hardly desire to live longer than the time it would take to repeat deliberately that four-hour speech of Mr. Talbot's." In his long career in the United States senate, as shown by the reports of the debates of that body, his course was one of conservative patriotism and his voice in eloquent language was raised in behalf of all those measures leading to the advancement of national prosperity. As a lawyer in practice at the bar his contemporaries were Henry Clay, Joseph H. Daviess, George M. Bibb, Jesse Bledsoe, and John Rowan. Mr. Talbot was esteemed one of the brightest of that galaxy of noted men.

It is noteworthy that the next official correspondence we have from Senator Talbot concerning Isham is when he is petitioning the court to grant his daughter a divorce from him. (See earlier section regarding Isham's first marriage to Cordelia Talbot).

---

[79] *Lawyers and Lawmakers of Kentucky*, by H. Levin, editor, 1897. Published by Lewis Publishing Company, Chicago. Reprinted by Southern Historical Press., Franklin County, 117.

Ship Passenger List

The Ship manifest of the Schooner Express dated 30 Jan 1834 lists the following passengers returning from Mexico into the port of New Orleans. [80]

W. P. Harris, 37, Merchant
W. G. Griffin, 35, Merchant
G. H. Allen, 27, Merchant
I. Vellers, 37, Merchant
J. Bower, 29, Farmer
R. Wilson, 41, Merchant
C. Churchill, 25, Merchant
P. D. Dicky, 30, Farmer
I. T. Peck, 23, Physician
Clarke, 24, Merchant
P. Pepprey, 31, Mariner
H. Charm, 23, Farmer
F. Benningmane, 33, Mechanic
A. Weatherbay, 22, Mechanic
Fords, 40, Physician

Figure 53 – Schooner (pictured here) is very similar to the Schooner Express that Isham traveled upon back from Mexico. Painting circa 1850, "Schooner Madawaska Maid, by Elisha Taylor Baker. The Maid was built on the west bank of the Kennebec River at Phippsburg, just south of Bath, Maine. Launched in 1832 at the yard of William Reed she was a 130-ton coaster, 78 feet long with a 23-foot beam and drawing just over 8 feet of water (weight-length-draft). The American merchant ensign flies from her gaff-peak." https://commons.wikimedia.org/wiki/File:Schooner_Madawaska_Maid,_by_Elisha_Taylor_Baker_13172_600.jpg, accessed 21 Jan 2022.

The Schooner Express was most likely a military ship, built in Dorchester County, MD in 1826. It weighed 119 19/95 tons; was 78 ft. 9 in. x 22 ft. 8 in. wide x 7 ft. 8 in. It had one deck, two masts, square stern, and a billethead. At the time Isham sailed on it, it was registered as No. 31, 10 Apr 1832. According to some records, the owner was Jean Juste Nartigue of New Orleans, and its master was John Giraudel.[81] Alternately though, the actual passenger document lists the master for this trip as "Thompson."

[80] Ancestry.com. *New Orleans, Passenger List Quarterly Abstracts, 1820-1875* [database on-line]. Provo, UT, USA: Ancestry.com Operations, Inc., 2011. Original data: Quarterly Abstracts of Passenger Lists of Vessels Arriving at New Orleans, Louisiana, 1820–1875. M272, 17 rolls. Records of the U.S. Customs Service, Record Group 36. National Archives and Records Administration, Washington, D.C., emphasis added.
[81] Ship Registers and Enrollments of New Orleans, LA, Prepared by The Survey of Federal Archives in Louisiana, Service Division, Work Projects Administration, Vol III, 1831-1840, 78.

PECK FAMILY AND THE CIVIL WAR

The Civil War revealed the political and ideological differences between members of the Peck family. Some members of the family were Unionists, Isham funded a Confederate unit, and multiple family members fought for the Confederate States of America. Isham's Uncle Moses Looney Peck had one son who fought for the Union and one who fought for the Confederacy, see their info below.

Though the author does not know exactly where Isham's dad stood on the issue, it is clear that Judge Jacob fought for slaves' rights during his lifetime. Two decades before the Civil War, in 1841, he advocated alongside Ezekiel Birdseye to form the new State of Frankland, which was proposed to be a state free of slavery. The effort did not materialize, but showed Judge Jacob's sentiments.[82]

Isham's Uncle, Moses Looney Peck, who was recognized as the leader and pioneer of Mossy Creek Methodism, was outspoken in his support for the Union. He was one of 13 delegates from Jefferson County, who joined 500 others, to meet in Knoxville on 30 May 1861. "They adopted several resolutions in favor of the Union." After adjourning until a vote on 8 Jun 1861, the delegation head, James P. Swann (attorney from Dandridge), wrote the following to the Knoxville *WHIG*,

> 1 Jun – If our brethren of the South commit national sin, let them account for themselves…if Tennesseans violate the laws of the land, let them be punished.[83]

> 8 Jun - We urge, we implore every man to go to the polls on the 8th of June and vote it down. Vote on your ticket No Separation, No Representation. Our beloved Washington called upon us to beware of sectional differences and yet you hear it from every mouth, you are compelled to do for the North or south, using all their efforts in urging on this sectional difficulties to destroy us. This is bad spirit.[84]

Union Tennessee Volunteer

- Madison Henry Peck (Dec 1832 – 12 Apr 1907) – Enlisted 15 Feb 1862, discharged 1 Apr 1863, served as First Lieutenant in Union Army with 3rd Tennessee Cavalry, Company K. Suffered from bronchitis and scurvy as a result of his service. Son of Moses Looney Peck (1793-1888) and his wife Susan Lyon Mynatt (1792-1873). Isham's first cousin.

On the side favoring secession and the Confederate States of America, there were a number of Peck family members. On 25 Jun 1861, two weeks and three days after Tennessee seceded from the Union (8 Jun 1861), Isham funded the "The Peck Light Dragoons" which were organized at Mossy Creek under Benjamin M. Branner.[85] See the following section for more information on the Dragoons.

---

[82] *Broken Hearts – Broken Lives, Jefferson County, Tennessee, 1860-1868, Civilian Life In the Civil War*, East Tennessee Historical Society, Restore Our County, 1986, 5.

[83] Knoxville *Whig*, 1 Jun 1861.

[84] Ibid, 8 Jun 1861.

[85] *Broken Hearts – Broken Lives*, 12.

Confederate Family Members

Isham's Brothers:

- Lt. Adam Clayton Peck (12 Mar 1814 – 5 Jun 1864) – 6' 9", blue eyes, sandy hair, 1 Sergeant to 1 Lieutenant - 2d Co. D. Walker's Battalion, Thomas' Legion, North Carolina Troops. A Methodist preacher who fought and died in the Battle of Piedmont. Enlisted 30 Sep 1862 at Strawberry Plains, TN. Commissioned on 9 May 1863. See 6 Sep 1876 "An Open Note to Sawbones" for more info on Adam.

- Brig. Gen. William Raine Peck (31 Jan 1818 – 22 Jan 1871) – "The forty-five-year-old native of Jefferson County, Tennessee, had moved to Louisiana in the early 1840s. He purchased land near the hamlet of Milliken's Bend in Madison Parish, on the opposite side of the Mississippi River from Vicksburg, fifteen miles to the southeast. His farm prospered and Peck acquired other land, piecing together a profitable cotton planting business. He subsequently built a large mansion known as "The Mountain." A fiery secessionist and states right advocate, Peck was a signatory to Louisiana's Ordinance of Secession in January 1861. With war looming, "Big Peck," despite his wealth and political prominence, enlisted as a mere private in the Milliken's Bend Guards. He rose steadily through the ranks to finish the war as a brigadier general."[86] He led the 9th Louisiana in the battles of Wilderness, Spotsylvania, Cold Harbor, and then the Overland Campaign. He was the final commander of the famed "Louisiana Tigers."

Figure 54 – Brig. Gen. William Raine Peck, CSA, imaged by Heritage Auctions, HA.com, Sharpened by Ancestry

- Private John Henry "Jack" L. Peck (11 Aug 1826 – 1892) – 6' 7", blue eyes, dark hair, Private in Company D, 1 Regiment Thomas' Legion, North Carolina Troops. Enlisted 24 Aug 1863 at Strawberry Plains. Multiple hospital stays throughout war including Abingdon, VA in Oct 1863, Bristol, TN on Dec 1863 - Apr 1864, Emory Hospital in Washington County, VA on 29 Oct 1864, took Oath of Allegiance at Chattanooga, TN on 24 May 1865. Sometimes listed as John Henry Peck, Jr.[87]

Isham's Uncle:

- Private Adam Peck, Jr. – (14 May 1791 – 5 Apr 1866) – Enlisted in the 11th Battalion, Georgia State Guards, Company B (CSA) at the age of 72, Adam was the son of Adam Peck, Sr.

---

[86] Scott L. Mingus, *The Louisiana Tigers in the Gettysburg campaign*, June-July 1863, 2009, 11-12, quoting Warner, *Generals in Gray*, 231.

[87] It is unknown why he is listed as a "Jr." occasionally. He did not share the name of his dad. If one investigates and discovers the cause of this, please inform the author at info@crossmountainbooks.com

Isham's First Cousins:

- Jacob Young Peck (1822 – Dec 1863) – Enlisted 20 Sep 1863 in Georgia, 66th Infantry, Company H (CSA), died before 31 Dec 1863 from disease, took sick at Missionary Ridge, TN with pneumonia fever, then transferred to Medical College Hospital in Atlanta, GA.[88] Jacob was the son of Adam Peck, Jr. (1791-1866) and Eliza Gayle (1792-1874).

- 1st Lt. Lafayette Peck (22 Jun 1828 – 25 Mar 1864) – Son of Isham's Uncle Moses Looney Peck. After graduating West Point and becoming an officer in the U.S. Army, Lafayette resigned his commission on 23 Aug 1861 and pledged to support the CSA starting on 1 Sep 1861. A letter of recommendation was sent from John R. Branner, President of the E. Tenn. and VA Railroad Company, to General G. A. Henry in Lexington, VA, saying that Lafayette was his "neighbor and friend." He took rank on 16 Mar 1861, was confirmed on 28 Jan 1862, and accepted into service on 20 Sep 1862. Lafayette was assigned as the Commander, Camp of Instruction, Confederate States Artillery, in Knoxville, TN, on 1 Oct 1862. He was nominated for a promotion to "Major of Conscripts, at Rogersville, TN" (by numerous high-ranking individuals), and recommended to stay in place as Commander of Instruction, but the CSA Senate denied the promotion. On 8 Oct 1863 he was authorized to recruit for the 1st Regiment Tennessee Heavy Artillery. He died on 25 Mar 1864 at Tuscumbia, AL.

LAFAYETTE PECK, TENNESSEE
Instructor; died of disease
in Alabama, 1864; Lieutenant.

Figure 56 - Courtesy of Ancestry.com, Colorized by Ancestry

Figure 55 - West Point Class Ring of Lafayette Peck, Image Courtesy of Max "Ed" Stiner, Jr., Descendent of Moses Looney Peck

- Note: Lafayette Peck's West Point Class Ring is owned by Ed Stiner, Register of Deeds for Jefferson County, TN. He sent a photo of the ring to the West Point Archivist and she verified that it matched the style of rings from the time period. Many thanks to Ed for sharing his photo!

POSSIBLE CIVIL WAR SERVICE

This author has only found one mention in print saying that Isham was a Civil War Surgeon, but cannot attest to its veracity. It says: "Dr. Peck was a surgeon during the Civil War and also owned land in Louisiana."[89] He was a physician and a surgeon, but whether he used his skills to directly support the war efforts is yet to be verified.

---

[88] Roster of Confederate Soldiers of Georgia 1861-1865
[89] Finding Aid for *Wolf Creek Papers*, UT Knoxville, Betsey B. Creekmore Special Collections and University Archives

CIVIL WAR: THE PECK LIGHT DRAGOONS

After the Civil War broke out, Isham donated $1,000 to his friend Benjamin Branner to outfit the first confederate fighting unit formed in Mossy Creek, The Peck Light Dragoons. The Salt and Light History told by the Jefferson City Methodist Church, tells part of this story, "In 1861, in the fervor of this feeling, Ben Branner formed the first Confederate fighting unit in the county at Mossy Creek, calling it "The Peck Light Dragoons." A newspaper from the period said this, "Dr. Peck, of Jefferson county, with a generosity characteristic of the man, has presented to the Peck Light Dragoons one thousand dollars to aid in their equipment."[90] There was a history of "light dragoons" in the

Figure 57 – U.S. Army Cavalry / Dragoon exhibit. National Infantry Museum and Soldier Center, Columbus, GA. Photo by author, 28 Nov 2021.

area; a petition from 1799 asked for the establishment of a militia unit known as the Volunteer Light Dragoons.[91] According to the National Infantry and Soldier Museum in Columbus, GA exhibit on dragoons, "the first cavalry organizations to serve in the United States Army were dragoons. Typically, dragoons were mounted infantry that used horses for transport but fought on foot; American dragoons, however, were trained as light cavalry, which meant troops stayed mounted and acted as scouts for the main army. Early dragoons were trained to use sabers and charge directly at the enemy. However, because of terrain and practicality, most dragoons served as scouts or messengers. It would not be until the Mexican-American War that an enemy would experience the full impact of an American Cavalry charge."

A research paper about the Botetourt (Virginia) Dragoons in the Civil War sheds light on dragoons during the Civil War.[92] Isham's grandpa, Adam Peck, Sr., was from Botetourt, so this description relates in multiple ways.

> Overall, the Dragoons formed a rather elite group. Unlike the infantry, cavalrymen provided their own horses and equipment. Each man had to sign a bond promising to return or pay for his revolver and sabre, valued at sixty-six dollars. Obviously, the average man could not afford such expensive cavalry accouterments, not to mention a good horse. As a consequence, many of these men came from relatively wealthy slaveholding families, especially

---

[90] *The Athens Post* (Athens, TN), 5 Jul 1861, 1.
[91] *Tennessee Petitions*, 1799, Petition Number 35, Session 2.
[92] *The Botetourt Dragoons in War and Peace*: An Honors Thesis Submitted to the History Faculty in Candidacy for the Bachelor of Arts Degree in History Department of History by Michael G. Henkle Richmond, VA, May 2000, 4-5.

those who became officers. However, money or slaveholding alone fail to explain the motivations of these men and their ability to rise through the ranks. Education also played a major role in promotion. Most officers attended colleges, such as Washington College, the College of William and Mary, the University of Virginia, Virginia Military Institute, and the University of Pennsylvania. A VMI degree seemed an especially valuable asset given the Breckinridges' success. [. . .] Despite the expense, numerous middle class or even poor men also joined the Dragoons.

How did such men afford to equip themselves? Unfortunately, the record fails to reveal the answer, but it seems likely that the more propertied Dragoons helped to cover the cost of the horses, sabres, pistols, and so forth for these men. Lucy Breckinridge, a Botetourt resident and the sister of the Breckinridge Dragoons, lent credence to this when she noted that Beverly Whittle, a Dragoon, sent his younger brother, Stafford, to borrow a horse from the Breckinridge estate. If the relatively wealthy Whittles supplied their son through the Breckinridges' generosity, it seems likely that others did also. In addition, it became common for the men to equip themselves from captured Union horses and goods.

The Peck Light Dragoons were a part of the 4th (Branner's) Tennessee Cavalry Battalion, also called the 1st, and 2nd. "The East Tennessee Cavalry Battalion was organized 29 Aug 1861; mustered into Confederate service 4 Oct 1861; reorganized 24 May 1862, and consolidated with the 5th Battalion to form 2nd (Ashby's) Cavalry Regiment. Field officers were Lt. Col. Benjamin M. Branner and Major John N. Bridgman. . . . Benjamin M. Branner, A. C. Plumlee, F. M. Jackson, formed company E. The Peck Light Dragoons were organized at Mossy Creek, Jefferson County, now Jefferson City, on 25 Jun 1861, and included men from Jefferson and Knox Counties. It was accepted into confederate service on 4 Oct 1861 at Cumberland Ford, Kentucky. It became Company "I", 2nd Regiment."[93]

Figure 58 - CSA Lt Col Benjamin Manasseh Branner, Age 31, younger brother of John Roper Branner, and commander of the 4th Tennessee Cavalry, 1861 and 1862. Enhanced. Courtesy of Randy Huber, Ancestry.com

The account of one its soldiers shares even more history of the unit.

William W. Lloyd was born in Grainger, County, Tenn., December 20, 1835; and died near Sipe Springs, Tex., May 28, 1909, in his seventy-fourth year. Comrade Lloyd was one of the first men to enter the Confederate service from his native county and the first man of his company to reenlist for the war. He was mustered into service at Mossy Creek (now Jefferson City), Tenn., with the "Peck Light Dragoons" May 26, 1861. This company became Company

---

[93] *Battle Of Barboursville Kentucky*, by Ray Adkins, 2005, p24.

E of the 3d (Branner's) Battalion Tennessee Cavalry, and later Company I, 2d Regiment Tennessee Cavalry, Col. H. M. Ashby. Comrade Lloyd was elected and served as its first corporal from its organization until the surrender under Gen. J. E. Johnston, April 28, 1865, and was well known in the regiment as "The Corporal," on account of his long service in that position. He was frequently offered promotion; but his ambition was to be "the ranking corporal of the Confederate army," and it is probable that he was. No man in his company rendered more continuous or faithful service than Corporal Lloyd, and he escaped with only one wound, as now remembered by the writer.[94]

Figure 59 - U.S. Army Cavalry / Dragoon exhibit. National Infantry Museum and Soldier Center, Columbus, GA. Photo by author, 28 Nov 2021. Pictured items include: horses, uniforms, pistols, sabers and scabbards, hall carbines, helmets, and bugles.

The article mentioning Isham's donation says that money was to "aid in their equipment." This equipment would have likely included items like uniforms, pistols, sabers and scabbards, hall carbines, helmets, and bugles.

---

[94] *Confederate Veteran*: Published Monthly in the Interest of Confederate Veterans and Kindred Topics. United States: n.p., 1909, 358.

Another account shares the following about the Dragoons, "Last evening, about dusk, Capt. Plumlee's company, the Peck Light Dragoons, from Cumberland Gap, escorted twenty-three prisoners through town to quarters at Camp Cummings. They are said to be a Union company from Hancock county, under command of one Capt. Jarvis, who were arrested by a party of Virginians, while attempting to make their way through the mountains into Kentucky. We learn they had a drum and flag, several guns, and a quantity of pistols. Considerable sympathy was expressed on our streets for these deluded men, and there was no lack of indignation expressed against their leaders here and elsewhere, who first deluded and then deserted them – who, having shrewdly 'knocked under,' in the 'nick of time,' are now walking the streets with unblushing effrontery, while their deluded, but probably honest victims, are marched as prisoners through the town, to be tried for that vilest of crimes known to the criminal calendar – treason.–*Knoxville Register, 11th.* "[95]

Figure 60 – Flag of the Peck Light Dragoons, 4th Tennessee Cavalry Battalion (Branner) (Private Collection). The unit designation, "Peck Light Dragoons of East Tenese," is centered on the flag; the slogan "Our Native Land" is centered on the reverse side. Additional details and history of flag available in *Civil War Flags of Tennessee* by Stephen D. Cox, 2020, UT Press, 418-419. Photo of flag also available at the Jefferson County Courthouse, Dandridge, TN.

---

[95] 14 Sep 1861, *Daily Nashville Patriot*, 2.

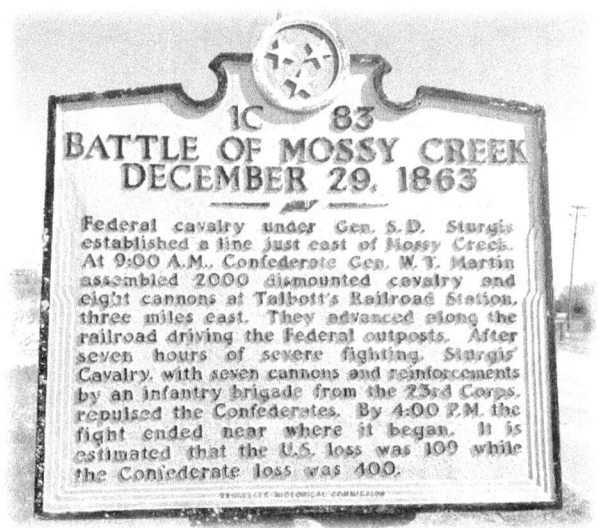

Figure 61 - Battle of Mossy Creek Historical Marker, Jefferson City, Tennessee. Inscription reads, "1C 83, Battle of Mossy Creek, December 29, 1863, Federal cavalry under Gen. S. D. Sturgis established a line just east of Mossy Creek. At 9:00 A.M., Confederate Gen. W. T. Martin assembled 2000 dismounted cavalry and eight cannons at Talbott's Railroad Station, three miles east. They advanced along the railroad driving the Federal outposts. After seven hours of severe fighting, Sturgis' Cavalry, with seven cannons and reinforcements by an infantry brigade from the 23rd Corps, repulsed the Confederates. By 4:00 P.M. the fight ended near where it began. It is estimated that the U.S. loss was 109 while the Confederate loss was 400. (Tennessee Historical Commission)"
Image courtesy of David Aldrich, March 2023

The Battle of Mossy Creek was fought in December 1863 around Mossy Creek (modern-day Jefferson City, Tennessee). Colonel Foster, Union Army, actually setup his headquarters at Isham's home, and the Union Calvary with General Elliott setup his headquarters at Isham's dad Judge Jacob Peck's house.

HEADQUARTERS CALVARY CORPS
December 27, 1863—1.30 p. m.
General ELLIOTT,
Judge Peck's:
GENERAL: Yours of 12.45 received. If you think best to attempt turning the right of the enemy, Colonel Foster will be near enough to support you. His headquarters are at **Dr. Peck's**. On account, however, of the large force of cavalry at Mansfield's Gap, it was my intention to have Foster Occupy such a position in your rear as to act in that direction more directly. I will not hamper you, however, if you deem it best to try their right and Colonel Foster will give what support you may call for, so far as his small division may be able.

Yours,

S.D. [Sturgis]
Brigadier-General.[96]

HEADQUARTERS FIRST DIVISION CAVALRY
Peck's House, *December 25, 1863.*

I have just come from our lines; our pickets are within 200 yards of the enemy. They informed the citizens, while falling back, that they would have re-enforcements by daylight and whip us out. I have ordered Colonel LaGrange to hold his position and act on the defensive unless otherwise ordered. I suppose probably they will attack in the morning. They sent in a flag of truce while I was down at headquarters for the bodies of 2 of their officers killed to-day. Our position is good, and I will await

[96] War of the Rebellion: Serial 056 Page 0510 Chapter XLIII. KY., SW. VA., Tennessee, MISS., N.ALA., AND N.GA., https://ehistory.osu.edu/books/official-records/056/0510, emphasis added, accessed 28 Nov 2022.

your orders in the morning. The ammunition in two regiments is a little short. I would like to have Campbell's brigade up in the morning if you can spare it.

Very respectfully, your obedient servant,

EDWARD McCOOK
Colonel, Commanding

Lieut. W. L. SHAW
Acting Assistant Adjutant-General.[97]

Figure 62 – Edward M. McCook, circa 1864, Library of Congress, Public Domain, "At the start of the Civil War, Moody worked as a spy for the federal government, gathering information to help the military. He then enlisted as a cavalry lieutenant in the regular army before becoming a captain in the Second Indiana Cavalry. McCook's skills led to a series of promotions, and he reached the rank of brevet major general by the end of the war. While in the Union army, McCook became friendly with General Ulysses S. Grant. This friendship later helped McCook secure appointments as minister to the Hawaiian Islands and governor of Colorado Territory." https://coloradoencyclopedia.org/article /edward-m-mccook

HEADQUARTERS,
***Dr. Peck's**, December 26, 1863—11 a. m.*

General ELLIOTT: I have just received a message from one of Colonel McCook's staff to the effect that a considerable body of the enemy's cavalry has got around your left flank, and was moving up toward Mossy Creek. I presume you will be able to check them without Colonel Garrard. Please look out for their flank moves, and rather fall back slowly than risk being turned, as from information I have I will fall back anyway rather than advance, unless I received orders from Foster to the contrary. There is no doubt but Longstreet's infantry is near Morristown, I think.

S[amuel]. D. STURGIS,
Brigadier-General.

HEADQUARTERS CAVALRY CORPS,
***Dr. Peck's**, December 26, 1863—1 p. m.*

General ELLIOTT:

GENERAL: Yours of 12.40 is received. I feel easier now that you have covered the roads from Dyer's Ferry and from Chucky Bend by Colonel McCook's command. You will perceive by dispatches I sent you from Flat Gap that the enemy has not advanced in that direction, so that it will not be necessary for you to fall back any father at present as a simple precaution. Please give me some particulars of the firing. The last few

Figure 63 - Washington Lafayette Elliott (March 31, 1825 – June 29, 1888) was a brigadier general in the Union Army during the American Civil War. He led a division of IV Corps at the Battle of Nashville in 1864. In 1866, he was awarded the honorary grade of brevet major general, U.S. Army. Wikipedia

---

[97] War of the Rebellion: Serial 054 Page 0634 KY., SW. VA., Tennessee, MISS., N. ALA., AND N. GA. Chapter XLIII., https://ehistory.osu.edu/books/official-records/054/0634, emphasis added, accessed 28 Nov 2022.

guns (some ten minutes since) appeared to be farther round on your right than the first firing. Please keep my hasty notes.

Yours,

S[amuel]. D. STURGIS,
Brigadier-General, Commanding.[98]

HEADQUARTERS CAVALRY CORPS,
***Dr. Peck's**, December 26, 1863—2 p. m.*
General ELLIOTT: I am perfectly convinced of the existence of a large infantry force at Morristown and of the desire of the enemy to entire us in that direction. as it would not, therefore, be prudent for us to advance (especially while their cavalry is at Dandridge), and as there are no special reasons for our remaining in the positions our troops now occupy, you will please fall carefully back when you can to this side Mossy Creek keeping a good show of force to the front and picketing all roads leading out to the front and flanks of your new position.

I am, general, very respectfully,

S. D. STURGIS,
Brigadier-General, Commanding Cavalry.

Figure 64 - Samuel D. Sturgis, U. S. Army, circa 1864, Brady-Handy photograph collection, Library of Congress, Prints and Photographs Division. Public Domain
"Samuel Davis Sturgis (June 11, 1822 – September 28, 1889) was a senior officer of the United States Army. A veteran of the Mexican War, Civil War, and Indian Wars, he attained the rank of brevet major general." Wikipedia

No. 6.
Report of Oscar H. La Grange, First Wisconsin Cavalry, commanding Second Brigade.

HDQRS. SECOND BRIGADE, FIRST CAVALRY DIVISION,
DEPARTMENT OF THE CUMBERLAND,
Talbott's House, near Mossy Creek, East Tennessee, December 27, 1863.
CAPTAIN: I have the honor to report that, at 8 a.m. on the 24th instant, two small brigades of the enemy, under General Armstrong, advanced on the position occupied by this brigade near **Dr. Peck's house, 2 1/2 miles west of Mossy Creek Station**. Our picket on the Morristown road was re-enforced, and an important position on the right occupied. About half of our force was gradually drawn into the engagement. The enemy was driven back 3 1/2 miles, leaving several dead, including 1 lieutenant, on the field. We camped for the night at Mossy Creek Station. Our loss was 2 killed and

---

[98] War of the Rebellion: Serial 056 Page 0505 Chapter XLIII. CORRESPONDENCE, ETC.-UNION., https://ehistory.osu.edu/books/official-records/056/0505, emphasis added, accessed 28 Nov 2022.

Figure 65 - Oscar Hugh La Grange (April 3, 1837 – January 5, 1915) was an American lawyer and abolitionist activist. He served as a Union Army officer in the American Civil War, and received an honorary brevet to brigadier general. Wikipedia

9 wounded. Had we been permitted to assume the offensive, it is though the enemy might have been severely punished.

Captain Hackleman, and Lieutenants Stover and Thomas, Second Indiana, deserve special mention for the gallant manner in which they held an important position, with only two companies, against a greatly superior force.

On the 26th, drove back the enemy's pickets and made a demonstration to the front, but did not advance. On returning to camp, the Fourth Indiana found its ground occupied by the enemy, and, after a brisk skirmish, compelled him to retire, leaving 5 dead and 2 wounded on the field. Our loss during the day was only 2 slightly wounded.

On the 27th, advanced, by order, to the ground occupied on the previous day, and drove the enemy 3 miles on the right of the Morristown road, our advance occupying his camp and capturing arms, cooking utensils, &c. Darkness put an end to the engagement. We had 2 men killed by a shell, and 4 others slightly wounded. Enemy's loss unknown.

On the 28th, Major Torrey, First Wisconsin Cavalry, made a movement on the enemy's left flank, and after a brisk skirmish occupied Talbott's Station, capturing 5 of the enemy with horses, arms, and equipments, without loss.*

Very respectfully,

O. H. LA GRANGE,
Colonel, Commanding.[99]

From the introduction to *Ada's Journal and Emma's Letters*:

"In a book called *Bent Twigs in Jefferson County*, Jean Patterson Bible mentions Dr. Isham Peck's home and the "vault" where Ada lay on page 58. It says, "At about twelve noon the Yankee battery moved down the road and went into position in the front yard of doctor's home Dr. Isham Peck - Mr. Neil Manley now lives where this house once stood) *[as of the year 2023 it is the Summit Medical Group-Tn Valley]*. During a lull in the firing of cannoneers [,] had a chance to look the house over. One Yankee said, 'this old English doctor is very nicely situated here. He has everything a sportsman could ask for, guns, fishing gear, etc., which we "borrow" from him. He must be of a rather eccentric nature as he has his family vault not twenty feet from the front door.' Actually, this was the grave of Dr. Peck's daughter, Ada, who died at the age of five on a

[99] War of the Rebellion: Serial 054 Page 0639 Chapter XLIII. OPERATIONS NEAR MOSSY CREEK, Tennessee, ETC. https://ehistory.osu.edu/books/official-records/054/0639, emphasis added, accessed 28 Nov 2022. Notice the location given, *"Talbott's House, near Mossy Creek,"* it seems Isham was known by Talbot(t) in Mossy Creek and Vicksburg.

trip south. Her body was returned and buried in a vault in the year in 1859. Later her remains were removed to Westview Cemetery where her tombstone can still be seen."[100]

David Needs, Mossy Creek/Jefferson City Historian, shared with the author that the Elizabeth Chapel, originally constructed by Isham's grandpa Adam Peck, Sr., was used as a hospital for the Union wounded during and after the Battle of Mossy Creek. A number of soldiers were even buried close by in the Westview Cemetery (though later disinterred and removed to the Knoxville National Cemetery). A concise summary of the Battle can be found in the Tennessee Encyclopedia online.[101]

In July 2017, the author interviewed David Needs on the banks of Mossy Creek on the campus of Carson-Newman University. **Experience Cross Mountain Books (CMB) LIVE: Scan the QR code below for the full interview.** Topics include the Battle of Mossy Creek, Isham's home used as Headquarters, the founders of Mossy Creek, grist mills, the quarry, the zinc mine, the original Mossy Creek Baptist Church, and more.

Figure 66 - Author Andy Peck with Jefferson City Historian David Needs (right), 12 July 2017 Banks of Mossy Creek, Carson-Newman campus

Figure 67 - **CMB LIVE**: Battle of Mossy Creek Interview with historian David Needs https://www.youtube.com/watch?v=eg7n411Gxz4

---

[100] Emma Peck, Andy Peck, *Ada's Journal and Emma's Letters: The Civil War Era Journal and Letters of Emma Peck*, Cross Mountain Books, 2021, xix-xx.

[101] Battle of Mossy Creek by Spurgeon King, https://tennesseeencyclopedia.net/entries/battle-of-mossy-creek/

GOLD RUSH LETTER FROM WILEY TO MARTHA

During the California Gold Rush of 1848-1855 (most likely), Isham's brother Wiley wrote a letter to their sister Martha. It is included here because of its description of Isham, Emma, and Emma's mom Louise. But it also has other fun historical tidbits!

Milliken's Bend L^a
Feb 18th

Dear Sister

When I came down from Mr Henderson's, on the day before yesterday, William handed me a letter from you. I was gratified I assure you.

I had a much more pleasant trip down than I expected — My money held out so well that I travelled on a fine boat, and actually had five whole dollars left when I landed at the bend.

I am going to California — Shall start in a few days. William furnishes me with an outfit. I expect to join the company from Halton. Write to me immediately, and direct to St Louis. You shall hear from me again before I leave "the white settlements;" and instruct you how to direct letters to California so that there will be a probability of my receiving them. Are there any persons going from Jefferson? If so, who are they?

William & brother are very well. Isham is quite fat, and by far the noblest looking man I ever saw. I was at Mr Henderson's several days, — Brother's wife is very amiable, and her mother is one of the pleasantest

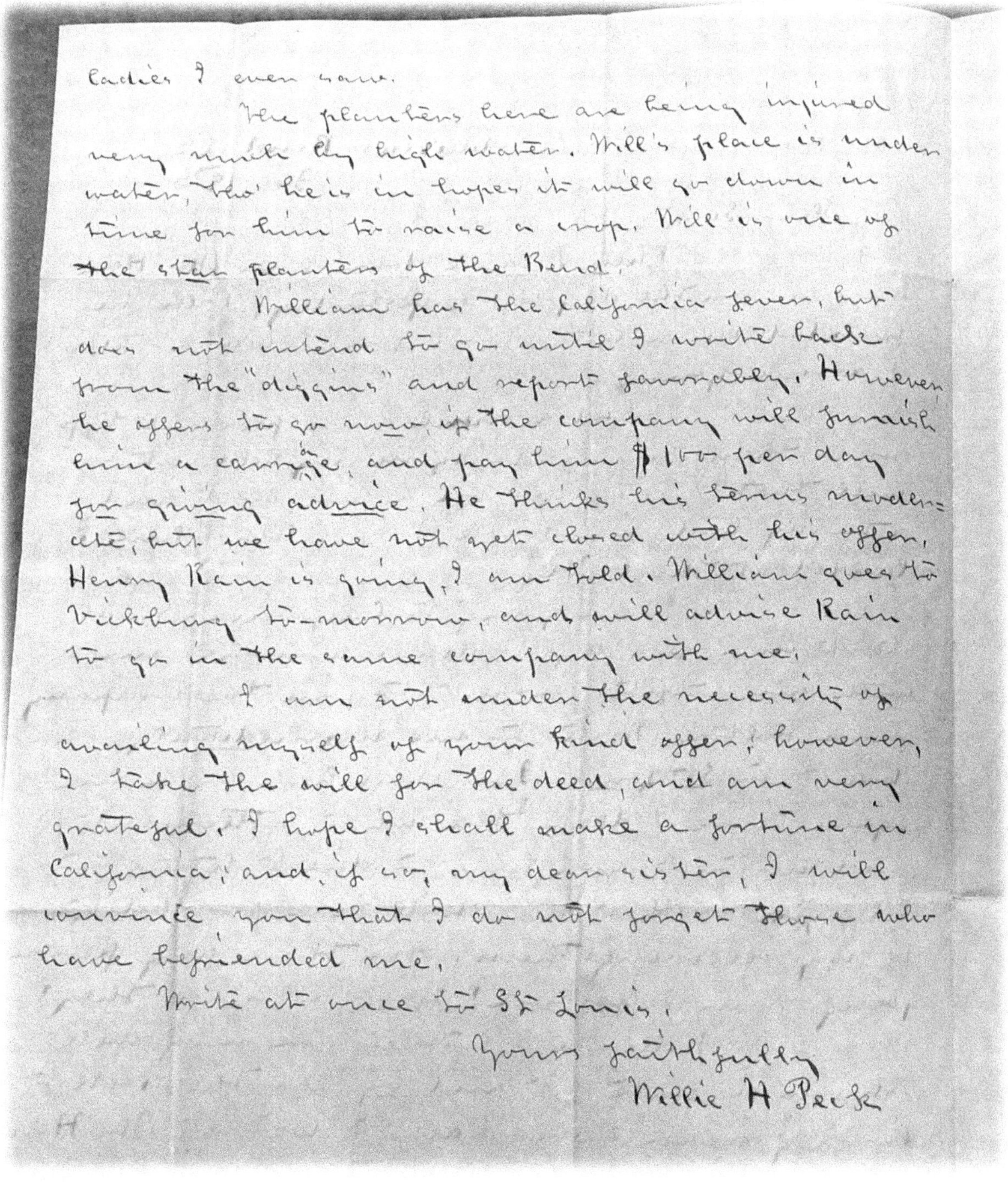

Figure 68 - Gold Rush Letter from Wiley to Martha Peck, written from St. Louis to Martha in New Market, Tennessee, Courtesy of the Calvin M. McClung Historical Collection, Knox County Public Library, Tennessee, Peck Family Letters, Box C505-08

Transcription:

Envelope: From Memphis [Postmarked] MEMPHIS FEB 25

Miss Martha A. F. Peck
New Market
Jefferson County
Tennessee

Milliken's Bend Lᵃ
Feb 19ᵗʰ

Dear Sister

When I came down from Mr. Henderson's, on the day before yesterday, William handed me a letter from you. I was gratified I assure you.

I had a much more pleasant trip down that I expected _ My money held out so well that I travelled on a fine boat, and actually had five whole dollars left when I landed at the bend.

I am going to California _ Shall start in a few days. William furnishes me with an outfit. I expect to join the company from Jackson. Write to me immediately, and direct to St Louis. You shall hear from me again before I leave "the white settlement:" and instruct you how to direct letters to California so that there will be a probability of my receiving them. Are there any persons going from Jefferson? If so, who are they?

William & brother are very well, Isham is quite fat, and by jov the noblest looking man I ever saw. I was at Mr. Henderson's several days, _ Brother's wife [Emma] is very amiable, and her mother is one of the pleasantest [end of page 1] ladies I ever saw.

The planters here are being injured very much by high water. Will's place is under water, tho' he is in hopes it will go down in time for him to raise a crop. Will is one of the star planters of the Bend.

William has the California fever, but does not intend to go until I write back from the "digging" and report favorably. However [,] he offers to go now, if the company will furnish him a carriage, and pay him $100 per day for giving advice. He thinks his terms moderate, but we have not yet closed with his offer, Henry Rain is going, I am told. William goes to Vicksburg to_morrow, and will advise Rain to go in the same company with me.

I am not under the necessity of availing myself of your kind offer, however, I take the will for the deed, and am very grateful. I hope I shall make a future in California, and if so, my dear sister, I will convince you that I do not forget those who have befriended me,

Write at once to St. Louis,

Yours faithfully,
Willie H Peck

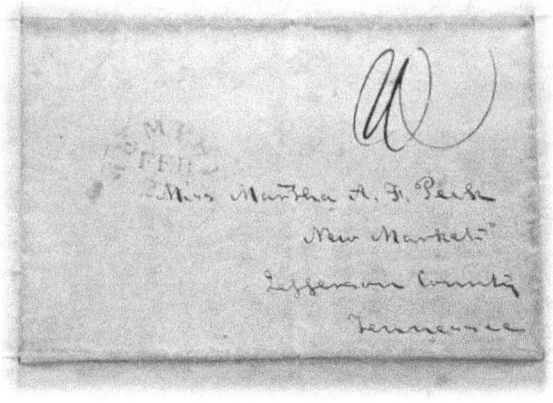

POST CIVIL WAR TO END OF LIFE

The following Life and Times Timeline will give the reader most facts known about Isham's life, cradle to grave and beyond. To summarize, he was 55 years old when the Civil War ended on 5 Apr 1866. Five of his children had been born, but four were still to come, including Louis in 1865. His youngest son Robert Lee Peck was not born until 1874, when Isham was 63 years old. Though he was the oldest son of his parents, he outlived all but one of his 8 siblings, Jack, who lived until 1892. In the latter half of his life, after the Civil War, he lost 6 of 8 siblings, and 4 of his 9 children. He had seen cholera claim the lives of dozens of soldiers at Rock Island in 1832 and 1835, then his daughter Ada in 1859, then former slaves across the plantations around Henderson Plantation in Louisiana. As a physician, this must have been incredibly difficult to witness, and possibly generated a feeling of helplessness to the power of such a terrible illness.

After his father, Judge Jacob, died at the age of 89 in 1869, Isham spent a significant portion of his time fighting in courts over the land that was left to him and his relatives. It is unknown what state their "Oakland" / Mossy Creek farm home was left after the Union Army used it as their Headquarters during the Battle of Mossy Creek. Regardless, Isham and Emma retired to their Glen Ada home in Wolf Creek, Tennessee during the 1870s. We know that their son Charley traveled to Europe and South America, and they may have travelled as well. But they were still raising small children. Robert Lee was only 13 when Isham died in 1887. Isham spent his time smoking his meerschaum pipe, reading papers from around the world, hiking and fishing, tending to church matters, and writing letters to the editor of *The Morristown Gazette*. His son Charley started the Mossy Creek *Independent* newspaper in 1876, and Ashby started his paper *The Mountain Boomer* in 1877. Their son Edward, the author's second great grandfather, graduated from Vanderbilt Medical School at the age of 20 in 1879. The same year, Charley wrote his epic southern novel, *Mary Anderson and Peacock the Mineralogist: The Bad Luck of a Young Southern Girl*. The serial novel was published to a newspaper, clipped out and pasted into Charley's form book. Discovered again in 2021, this author transcribed the novel, added 89 illustrations, maps, and charts, and published it as *Charley's Novel* (2022), Cross Mountain Books. There are dozens of references to Peck family members in the book, and Mary's father, Mr. Anderson, is at least partially based on Isham's life.

Referring to Mr. Anderson, but clearly hearkening to Isham's life, *Charley's Novel* says in Chapter 1, "[Father] had been a great traveler and a great hunter in his younger days and had lived in Louisiana, and would often amuse us with stories of his deer and boar hunts long before the war, when he was a large slave owner, and the way the war set them free which broke him up and compelled him to leave with the little he had left to him. He came to this healthy place where he could live cheaper and better, and educate his children—so you see we were not rich, not what you call wealthy, but we always had plenty to go on and a nice comfortable home. [. . .] What the house lacked in beauty was made up by nature's surrounding beauties, hills and plains. Nearly all rough places were covered with vines and flowers. And best of all we were contented and cheerful."[102]

This opening to the novel describes life in Wolf Creek, Tennessee for the Peck family. Interestingly, a few months after writing his novel, Charley deeded his land to brother Ed, and then depart for Brazil for a pleasure trip. The editors from *The Morristown Gazette* visited Isham at his Wolf Creek Property in May 1882, and their article (relayed in *Sawbones: Volume II*) paints a picture of Isham with his pipe, surrounded by his papers.

He had written articles for Bill Porter's *Spirit of the Times* as a younger man, but when he discovered a plot by the newspaper men of North Carolina to invent "volcanoes in the Smokies," he couldn't help but take up the pen again. On 25 Mar 1874, at the age of 63, he wrote his first article for the *Gazette* under the pen name Sawbones, and exposed the "volcano" for the farce that it was. His article(s) gained national attention, and started getting circulated by papers around the country. Soon, and continuing for years after, people from around Tennessee and the country would write responses to Sawbones, and he would sometimes write them back. These articles, replies, and responses, provide the bulk of knowledge about Isham and his life and times.

Isham was friends with notable people around Wolf Creek and Jefferson County, TN, and he and Emma were close with the Rumbough family of Hot Springs, NC. Daughter Helen became close with one of the Rumbough daughters and they went off to Salem Female Academy together in Winston-Salem, NC. Tragically, Helen got sick and died during her first semester at the school. Isham planted a huge white cross on the mountain across from Glen Ada in the summer of 1887. On 27 Nov 1887, Ashby committed suicide by taking laudanum down in Florida. The news was wired to Wolf Creek, and as soon as Isham heard that another of his sons had killed himself, and his 5th child had died, his heart stopped. He died on the spot. They conducted a double funeral for him and Ashby in Mossy Creek.[103]

His wife Emma fought for his land as he had, in the courts, while also fighting for reparations from the government for her family's plantation in Louisiana. In the end, it seems that taxes, large companies, and decades long court battles were too much to keep the land together and in the family. Emma moved to Florida and lived with her sons, her mom Louise aka "Gam", and her son's mother-in-law, Mrs. King. She died nearly 12 years after Isham died.

Son Dr. Edward Jerome Peck, who had lived in Atlanta, and also in Newport, TN, lived in the Wolf Creek area until the early 1890s when he moved to New Bern, NC with his wife Cora and children. After Cora divorced him in 1900, he moved back to Wolf Creek, and began practicing in Wolf Creek and Hot Springs, NC. He kept the Glen Ada land and home, but turned his focus to the Mountain Park Hotel and served as a Railway Surgeon. When he died in 1927, the people of Hot Springs, NC and the Rumbough family erected a monument to him "IN MEMORY OF OUR BELOVED DOCTOR." His story and the stories of his siblings are shared in the book, *He Loved the*

---

[102] Charles Talbot Peck, *Charley's Novel: Mary Anderson and Peacock the Mineralogist, the Bad Luck of a Young Southern Girl*, 2022, Cross Mountain Books, 1-2.

[103] The author has visited the Westview Cemetery (Jefferson City, TN) where many Peck family members are buried and searched for the grave of Isham and Ashby, with no success. If you are able to locate these gravestones, in the Westview Cemetery or elsewhere, please share the photos and location with the author at info@crossmountainbooks.com.

Folks: Dr. Edward Jerome Peck of Hot Springs, North Carolina, by the same author and published by Cross Mountain Books.

7 DEC 1887 SAWBONES IS BURIED IN MOSSY CREEK ALONGSIDE SON ASHBY[104]

Dr. Wm. [Isham Talbot] Peck of Wolf Creek, Cocke county, well known throughout East Tennessee, died at his residence on the 28th ult. He was formerly one of our best correspondents. Hundreds of our readers will remember his contributions to THE GAZETTE published under the nom-de-plume of "Saw Bones" his reports and theories about the Bald Mountain (N. C.) phenomena were particularly interesting and copied by the press throughout the country. The doctor's son, A. H. Peck died on the same day at Jacksonville Fla from an overdose of morphine, taken accidentally, we are informed, for neuralgia. The remains of both father and son were taken to Mossy Creek and there buried at the same time. The singularly afflicted family have our sincerest sympathy.

Dr. Wm. Peck, of Wolf Creek, Cocke county, well known throughout East Tennessee, died at his residence on the 28th ult. He was formerly one of our best correspondents. Hundreds of our readers will remember his contributions to THE GAZETTE, published under the nom-de-plume of "Saw Bones"; his reports and theories about the Bald Mountain (N. C.) phenomena were particularly interesting and copied by the press throughout the country. The doctor's son, A. H. Peck, died on the same day, at Jacksonville, Fla., from an overdose of morphine, taken accidentally, we are informed, for neuralgia. The remains of both father and son were taken to Mossy Creek and there buried at the same time. The singularly afflicted family have our sincerest sympathy.

The author has visited the Mossy Creek cemetery (Westview Cemetery, Jefferson City, TN) where Isham's family members are buried, including children Ada and Charley, brother William, and sibling Juliet, but did not find the grave stone for Isham or for Ashby. If the reader locates these gravestones, in the Westview Cemetery or elsewhere, please inform the author and share photos.[105] Photos of Peck Family gravestones can be found in the *Sawbones: Volume II* Appendix.

---

104 Editors, [Sawbones is Buried In Mossy Creek Alongside Son Ashby], *The Morristown Gazette*, 7 Dec 1887, 3.
105 Please write to the author at info@crossmountainbooks.com. Thank you!

LIFE AND TIMES TIMELINE

1811 Feb 23 (Age 0) – Birth in Mossy Creek, TN

1811 (Age 0) – Dad Judge Jacob, Uncle Adam Peck, Jr., and Uncle Benjamin pose for their silhouettes to be cut on the streets of New Orleans (see photo to right)

1811/1812 Winter (Age 1) – New Madrid tremors rocked the Midwest[106]

1812 (Age 1) – Sister Eliza Jane Talbot Peck born in Mossy Creek, TN

1812 (Age 1) – Cousin Louisa Ann Peck (dau. of Uncle Patrick Peck, then adopted by Uncle Adam Peck, Jr.) born in Feliciana Parish, LA

1812 Apr 18 (Age 1) – Uncle Adam Peck, Jr. writes to the Secretary of War thanking him for appointing him an "Ensign of Infantry" in the Virginia Infantry (24th Regiment) and is sent to fight at the Canadian border at Fort George and Fort Niagara

1813 Mar 4 (Age 2) – Future mother-in-law Louise (Donohue) Henderson is born in St. Genevieve, Missouri (date from obituary, see *Ada's Journal* Pg 113)

1813 Dec 19 (Age 2) – Uncle Adam Peck, Jr. captured at Fort Niagara and marched 590 miles to Quebec, Canada until paroled on 4 May 1814 (4 months 15 days)

1814 Mar 12 (Age 3) – Brother Adam Clayton Peck born at Oakland, TN

Figure 69 - Inscription below print reads: "Men pictured were three brothers, left to right, Adam Peck, Benjamin Peck, and Jacob Peck. Silhouettes were made in New Orleans, LA., circa 1811, by the artist, who did not know the Pecks but stopped them on the street, being struck by their height and personal appearance and requested permission to 'cut' their silhouettes. The three brothers were sons of Adam and Elizabeth Sharkey Peck, who were the first settlers of Mossy Creek, now Jefferson City. On an old tombstone in Jefferson City may be found the following inscription: 'Sacred to the memory of Adam and Elizabeth Peck, pioneers from Virginia to the West in 1788.'" Image courtesy of Hank Peck, Knoxville.

1814 Dec 3 (Age 3) – Uncle Patrick Peck dies during the Battle of New Orleans (War of 1812) from dysentery, surrounded by his brothers (Isham's Uncles) Moses and Adam Peck, Jr.

1814 Dec 3 (Age 3) – First cousin William Lewis Sharkey fights in Battle of New Orleans (age 17)

1816 Mar 31 (Age 5) – Sister Juliet N. Peck born in Mossy Creek, TN

1816 Jul 30 (Age 5) – Uncle Adam Peck, Jr. marries Elizabeth "Eliza" Gayle (widow of Isham's Uncle Patrick)[107]

1817 Feb 13 (Age 5) – Grandpa ADAM PECK, SR. dies

1818 (Age 7) – Uncle James Hawkins Peck practices law in St. Louis (Missouri Territory) until 1822

1818 Jan 31 (Age 6) – Brother William Raine Peck born in Mossy Creek, TN

1818 Oct 15 (Age 7) – Uncle Henry Hopkins Peck marries Aunt Elizabeth "Eley" Cox

---

[106] https://www.usgs.gov/natural-hazards/earthquake-hazards/science/summary-1811-1812-new-madrid-earthquakes-sequence?qt-science_center_objects=0#qt-science_center_objects, accessed 20 Apr 2020

[107] Read extended account of Adam Peck Jr.'s life, Patrick's military service, and more in *Adam the Younger, 1791-1866 in the War of 1812: The Second American Revolution* by Susan Moore Teller, 2016

1818 Dec (Age 7) – Cousin John Gayle Peck (son of Uncle Adam) born in Mossy Creek, TN

1819 (Age 8) – Cousin Mary Jane Peck (dau. of Uncle Henry H. Peck) born

1819 Aug 26 (Age 8) – Sister Martha Ann Featherstone Peck born in Mossy Creek, TN

1820 (Age 9) – Cousin Virginia Peck (dau. of Uncle Adam) born in Mossy Creek, TN

1820 Jun 25 (Age 9) – Cousin Wiley Blount Peck (son of Moses Looney Peck) born

1821 (Age 10) – Dad Judge Jacob becomes a Tennessee State Senator

1821 Aug 4 (Age 10) – Davy Crockett runs successfully for a seat in the Tennessee General Assembly, representing Lawrence and Hickman counties. He rapidly becomes known for his strong anecdotal oratory skills.

1821 (Age 10) – Date Estimated: Isham and his brother William R. Peck move to Vicksburg, MS and "spend their boyhood" there. No exact dates are known for this period of their lives.[108]

1821 (Age 10) – Cousin Elizabeth Sophia Peck (dau. of Uncle Henry) born in TN

1821 Nov 11 (Age 10) – Cousin William Mynatt Peck (son of Moses L. Peck) born

1822 (Age 11) – Cousin Jacob Young Peck (son of Uncle Adam) born in Mossy Creek, TN

1822 (Age 11) – Dad Judge Jacob Peck becomes a Tennessee Supreme Court Justice

1822 Jan 10 (Age 10) – Brother Wiley Hawkins Peck born in Mossy Creek, TN

1822 Mar 26 (Age 11) – Uncle James Hawkins Peck nominated to be Judge for the U.S. District Court for the District of Missouri. His nomination was confirmed by the Senate on 5 Apr 1822.

1823 Sep 15 (Age 12) – Cousin Joseph Hawkins Peck (son of Uncle Moses Peck) is born

1824 Dec 21 (Age 13) – Cousin Martha Jane (dau. of Uncle Adam) born in Mossy Creek, TN

1825 (Age 14) – Sister Cordelia Sophia Peck was born and died the same day

1825 Feb 6 (Age 14) – Cousin Lydia Ann Peck (dau. of Uncle Moses Peck) born

1826 (Age 15) – Brother John Henry "Jack" Peck born

1826 Aug 7 (Age 15) – Cousin Harriet Pocahantes Peck (dau. of Uncle Moses Peck) born

1826 Aug/Sep (Age 15) – Isham begins attending Greeneville College in Greeneville, TN

1827 Jan 14 (Age 15) – Cousin Mary Catherine Peck (dau. of Uncle Adam) born in Mossy Creek

1827 Dec 13 (Age 16) – Future father and mother-in-law William Henderson and Louise Donohue get married in Warren, MS

1828 Jun 22 (Age 17) – Cousin Lafayette Peck (son of Uncle Moses) is born

1828 (Age 18) – First cousin William Lewis Sharkey serves in Mississippi Legislature until 1829

1830 Apr 24 (Age 19) – Uncle and Judge, James Hawkins Peck impeached on the charge of abuse of the contempt power by the U.S. House of Representatives

1830 Jun 30 (Age 19) – Cousin James Henry Peck (son of Uncle Adam) born in Mossy Creek

1830 Sep 25 (Age 19) – Cousin Nancy Ludy Peck (dau. of Uncle Moses) is born

1831 Jan 31 (Age 19) – Uncle James Hawkins Peck acquitted by 1 vote and continues to serve on the United States District Court for the District of Missouri until 1836 when he dies.

1831 Jun 11 (Age 20) – Grandma Elizabeth Sharkey Peck dies at age 74 (Born 16 Feb 1757)

---

[108] Obituary for General William Raine Peck in *Ada's Journal & Emma's Letters*, 2021, p 119.

1832 (Age 21) – First cousin William L. Sharkey serves as Chief Justice of Mississippi Supreme Court from 1832-1851

1832 (Age 21) – Grandpa ISHAM TALBOT, SR. (Mom's dad) dies in KY at age of 94

1832 Aug 6 (Age 21) – Isham's sister Eliza "Jane" Peck marries Madison Henry McEffee

1832 Oct 6 (Age 21) – Isham witnesses cholera at Rock Island, Illinois after the Black Hawk War

1832 Nov 19 (Age 21) – Isham marries 1st wife, Cordelia M. Talbot, in Franklin Co, KY

1832 Dec 12 (Age 21) – Cousin Madison Henry McEfee Peck born (son of Uncle Moses)

1833 Sep 22 (Age 22) – Isham's U.S. Passport is issued. Application says he is "desirous of exploring the Territory of Mexico." Also that he is 6'3" tall, light complexion, blue eyes, and slightly aquiline nose.[109] Request says to send to "Doctor Peck at Louisiana."

1833 (Age 22) – 3rd Wife EMMA ELIZABETH HENDERSON born in Mississippi

1833 Oct 11 (Age 22) – Brother-in-law Madison McEffee (Sister Jane's husband) dies

1833 Jul 22 (Age 22) – Niece Juliet "Ellen" McEffee born to sister Jane and brother-in-law Madison Henry McEffee

1834 Apr 26 (Age 23) – Aunt Elizabeth Cox Peck (wife of Uncle Henry Hopkins Peck) dies at age 35 in Mossy Creek, TN

1834 May 29 (Age 23) – Greene County, January Session advertises that Isham T. and Adam Peck (could be Uncle Adam Peck, Jr. or brother Adam Clayton Peck) have 5,000 acres "lying on the waters of Paint Creek" that they did not pay taxes on in 1833 and now owe double.

1834 Jan 30 (Age 23) – Returns to Port of New Orleans on the Schooner Express from Mexico – listed as a 23-year-old physician

1834 Feb 4 (Age 23) – His father-in-law Isham Talbot petitions the Kentucky Senate to grant his daughter, Cordelia M. Talbot, a divorce from Isham. They had been married for just over 2 years.

1835 (Age 24) – His dad retired as a TN Supreme Court Justice

1835 May 18 (Age 24) – After losing the 1835 congressional election, Davy Crockett decides to leave politics and travel to Texas. He later fights in the Texas War of Independence.

1835 Jun 29 (Age 24) – Cousin Virginia (dau. of Uncle Adam) marries Thomas Poteet in Dahlonegah, Lumpkin Co, GA at the age of 15 (living in Cherokee County, NC in 1850)

1835 Aug 17 (Age 24) – Isham witnesses the cholera epidemic at Rock Island, Illinois while serving as a physician with the Army, there were 68 cases through 17 Aug.[110]

1835 Sep 18 (Age 24) – His dad is granted a U.S. patent for the harvesting and collecting of grain and grass seeds, signed by President Andrew Jackson

1836-1839 (Age 24-27) – Brother Adam C. Peck is a volunteer for Talbott's Company, 2nd Tennessee Mounted Infantry during the Cherokee War

1836 Jan 23 (Age 24) – Cousin John Peck (son of Uncle Moses) is born

---

[109] "An **aquiline nose** (also called a **Roman nose** or **hook nose**) is a human nose with a prominent bridge, giving it the appearance of being curved or slightly bent. The word aquiline comes from the Latin word aquilinus ("eagle-like"), an allusion to the curved beak of an eagle." From https://en.wikipedia.org/wiki/Aquiline_nose, accessed 20 Apr 2020
[110] Army and Navy Chronicle, 29 Sep 1835

1836 Mar 6 (Age 25) – Davy Crockett is killed fighting in the final Battle of the Alamo. Crockett was 49 years old.

1836 Apr 29 (Age 25) – Uncle James Peck dies in St. Charles, Missouri from pneumonia

1836 Dec 10 (Age 25) – Dad Judge Jacob Peck applies to TN Governor Newton Cannon for job of surveying the Charleston and Cincinnati Railroad route through Tennessee

1836 Dec 24 (Age 25) – George Branner (father of John Roper Branner) writes a letter of recommendation to Gov. Cannon for Judge Jacob to get the job of surveying the Charleston, Cincinnati, and Louisville Railroad

1837 (Age 26) – Panic of 1837 hit America. Huge financial crisis that started a major recession which lasted until the mid-1840s.[111]

1837 May 18 (Age 26) – Isham marries Helen D. (Rapalje) Glass in Vicksburg, MS

1838 Oct 8 (Age 27) – Isham's brother Adam C. Peck writes a letter to Chief John Ross (head of the Cherokee Nation) declining the position of Assistant to "Mr. Putnam", supervising the Cherokee Removal in one of the "emigrating parties."

1838 Dec 28 (Age 27) – Isham's cousin Horace Prentice, Jr. is born in Lake Providence, LA[112]

1839 Jul 30 (Age 28) – Grandpa ISHAM M. TALBOT (Sophia's dad) dies at the age of 79

1840 (Age 29) – Living in Warren, Mississippi according to U.S. Census

1844 Jun 17 (Age 33) – Possible reference to him attending a 4 Jun 1844 Methodist Conference and opposing a resolution for a "friendly and mutual division" of the Methodist Church over the issue of slavery.[113]

1844 Aug 19 (Age 33) – Isham's plantation overseer, Patterson Porter, whips and then stabs John S. Waters, a carpenter, at the "Prentiss House" – Porter is arrested.[114]

1846 (Age 35) – Cousin William Richbourg Peck (son of Uncle Patrick, then adopted by Uncle Adam) dies in Harrisburg, Poinsett Co., Arkansas

1846 Oct 8 (Age 35) – Cousin Mary Catherine Peck (dau. of Uncle Adam) marries John Abercrombie, Jr. in Dahlonegah, Lumpkin Co, GA)

1848 Oct 12 (Age 37) – Marries Emma Elizabeth Henderson (3rd wife) in East Carroll Parish, Louisiana

1849 Dec 2 (Age 38) – Cousin Joseph Hawkins Peck (son of Uncle Moses) dies at age 26

1850 (Age 39) – Cousin Virginia Peck (dau. of Uncle Adam) commits suicide by slitting her throat in the Peck Chapel in Mossy Creek, TN because she "was such an unhappy wife."

1850 (Age 39) – Listed as Physician on U.S. Census

1851 (Age 40) – First cousin William L. Sharkey serves as the U.S. Consul in Havana, Cuba until 1854

1853 Jul 25 (Age 42) – First daughter Ada is born in Mossy Creek, TN at 2am

1853 Sep 9 (Age 42) – Family traveled to Knoxville by stagecoach, steamboat from Knoxville to Decatur, railroad to Tuscumbia, AL, 4 days in stagecoach to Lagrange, TN, railroad to Memphis,

[111] https://en.wikipedia.org/wiki/Panic_of_1837, accessed 20 Apr 2020
[112] https://www.findagrave.com/memorial/53256470, accessed 3 May 2020
[113] *The Tennessean* (Nashville, TN) 17 Jun 1844, 1.
[114] *Vicksburg Whig* (Vicksburg, MS) 19 Aug 1844, 2.

stayed one week in Memphis (yellow fever was bad at this time), then took Steamboat James Robb to Henderson Landing in East Carroll Parish, LA ("home")

1854 Mar (Age 43) – Family is at Henderson Plantation and Isham's brother Bill gave Ada 3 bales of fine cotton and they bought rocking chairs for Judge Jacob and Sophia Peck back in Tennessee

1854 May 3 (Age 43) – Family leaves LA for Tennessee, travels on Steamboat R.J. Mara, stayed one night at Smithland, LA, then took another boat to Nashville (after stopping in Memphis), then a train to Loudon, TN, and stagecoach to Knoxville. Scarlet fever was very bad along their route and they couldn't stop.

1854 May 25 (Age 43) – Ada rides around in the carriage that Isham and his brother "Jack" built for her. Chairs arrive from Louisiana for Judge Jacob and Sophia Peck. Took ~2 months to come.

1854 May 26 (Age 43) – They watched the Solar Eclipse together (photos linked in Ada's Journal)

1854 Jun 13 (Age 43) – Family (including Ada's "Aunt Pattie" and "Mary") visits Judge Jacob Peck in Carrol County, VA where he owns part of a copper mine

1854 Jun 23 (Age 43) – Judge Jacob connects with them, and they go "visiting" around Jonesborough, TN (not far from Greeneville, TN)

1854 Jun 25 (Age 43) – Isham's family stays at Capt Roper's and they enjoy it

1854 Jul 1 (Age 43) – Family stays in Kingsport, TN where Isham's sister Eliza "Jane" lives

1854 Jul 13 (Age 43) – Family arrives back at Oakland (Mossy Creek, TN) after their 1-month trip. Eliza Jane's daughter, Juliet "Ellen" McEffee, comes back with them. She is almost 1 year old.

1854 Jul 22 (Age 43) – Family has a fish fry "at a pretty shady place on the Holston River"

1854 Jul 25 (Age 43) – They celebrate Ada's 1-year birthday with a picnic dinner under a "fine old Oak" and they drink Blackberry Cordial. Isham puts up a swing for Ada, Judge Jacob has a swing has well and they swing together.

1854 Aug 1 (Age 43) – Isham and family, including his brother "Big Peck," depart "Oakland" to visit Warm Springs, NC

1854 Aug 1/2 (Age 43) – They stay overnight at Major Franklin's (Fairfax Inn in White Pine, TN) to rest en route

1854 Aug 3 (Age 43) – Isham and family stay at "Mrs. Allen's." Ada gets in Wolf Creek for the first time.

1854 Aug 8 (Age 43) – Family travels to Warm Springs, they see the "Chimnies" and Paint Rock. They see the Patton Hotel in Warm Springs and it looks beautiful. They stay at the hotel about 9 days and Isham and Emma enjoy live music each day and music and dancing each night.

1854 Aug 17 (Age 43) – Family returns to the Allen's and plan to stay "until cool weather"

1854 Aug 21 (Age 43) – Isham and Emma pick out "Glen Ada" in Wolf Creek where they plan to build their "Mountain Home"

1854 Sep 6 (Age 43) – Family departs Wolf Creek for Oakland. Brother "Jack" (possibly John Henry Peck) travels with them. Sister Eliza "Jane" and Sister Juliet come visit them at Oakland. Ada spends time with Isham's nephew Harry Rhoton

1854 Oct 6 (Age 43) – Family leaves Oakland for Henderson Plantation in LA with Isham's sister Martha "Pattie", Isham's niece Ellen McEffee (sister Jane's daughter), and brother Jack (John Henry)

1854 Oct 21 (Age 43) – Isham and family arrive at Henderson Plantation after taking the Steamboat Bulletin down the Mississippi

1854 Nov 8 (Age 43) – Big Peck hosts Isham and family for a "grand dinner" in honor of their return to Louisiana at his "Mountain" plantation

1854 Dec 29 (Age 43) – Nephew Henry Clay Rhoton (Juliet's son) dies at age 1 yr 7 mo.

1855 Jan 16 (Age 43) – Isham's nephew Harry Rhoton dies from scarlet fever

1855 Mar 25 (Age 44) – Isham and family watch the Steamboat Bulletin burn on the Mississippi River, Emma's gun was on board

1855 Apr 2 (Age 44) – Isham is attacked by a buck on the Henderson Plantation; he is saved by his father-in-law, William Henderson, and his brother "Uncle Willie," as Ada calls him

1855 Apr 29 (Age 44) – Isham travels to New Orleans to receive care for his broken arm

1855 May 6 (Age 44) – Isham returns to East Carroll Parish with news his arm is broken and will "never be straight or strong again"

1855 May 31 (Age 44) – Family tries to board Steamboat Eclipse but it does not stop for them

1855 June 3 (Age 44) – Brother Willie travels to Vicksburg and gets the Steamboat Niagara to stop for Isham and family the next day. It stops and they board for their trip back to TN.

1855 June 10 (Age 44) – Isham and family arrive in Nashville, TN

1855 Jun 10 (Age 44) – Isham and family leave Nashville in railroad "cars" and reach Knoxville, TN 6pm the next day, Jun 11th

1855 June 12 (Age 44) – Isham and family arrive home at "Oakland" in Mossy Creek, TN

1855 June 19 (Age 44) – Isham travels to Mrs. Allen's in Wolf Creek, TN and is "very sick"

1855 June 25 (Age 44) – Isham returns home and is "most dead he was so sick." His brother-in-law Dr. Rhoton, "Uncle Doctor" doctors him, giving him medicine, and vaccinates daughter Ada. Isham recovers fairly quickly and the family leaves to go stay with the Allens at the Wolf Creek Inn.

1855 July 25 (Age 44) – Family celebrates Ada's 2nd birthday. Father-in-law William Henderson and "Jane" come up from Louisiana on 15 July and everyone is staying in Wolf Creek. Family has been there one month at this point.

1855 Nov 30 (Age 44) – First son William "Willie" Henderson Peck is born in Louisiana

1857 Nov 16 (Age 46) – Son Charles "Charlie / Charley" Talbot Peck is born in Louisiana

1857 Aug 2 (Age 46) – Cousin Harriet Pocahontas Peck (dau. of Uncle Moses) dies at age 30

1858 Mar 18 (Age 47) – Uncle Henry Hopkins Peck dies at the age of 58

1858 Aug 7 (Age 47) – Niece Juliet "Ellen" McEffee (married to George M. Backman) dies at the age of 24 years old

1858 Oct 31 (Age 47) – 1st cousin 1x removed Adam Sharkey Peck (son of Cousin James Henry Peck) is born in Dahlonegah, Lumpkin Co., GA

1859 Mar 27 (Age 48) – First child Ada dies at 8 o'clock in the morning after taking ill from cholera on 26 Mar 1859 at the age of 5[115]

---

[115] *Ada's Journal and Emma's Letters*, 22 Apr 1859 letter from Emma Peck to Emma Allen, p 51-52

1859 Apr 13 (Age 48) – Isham's wife Emma's cousin Horace Prentice, Jr. (son of Horace and Minerva Prentice) dies from typhoid fever[116]

1859 Oct 12 (Age 48) – Cousin Elizabeth Sharkey Peck (dau. of Uncle Patrick, then adopted by Uncle Adam) dies in Jefferson County, TN at the age of 49

1859 Oct 14 (Age 48) – Son EDWARD JEROME PECK is born in Tennessee

1859 Dec 4 (Age 48) – Emma Peck writes to Emma Allen and says "Doc [Isham] does not do much else but settle church difficulties" and that it will take him until fall 1860 to be ready to handle some of the "cases" he is taking depositions for.

1860 (Age 48) – Isham is listed as living in Jefferson County, TN according to U.S. Census

1860 Jan (Age 48) – Isham's brother Col. Wiley Hawkins Peck, member elect of the LA State Legislature from Madison Parish, shoots and stabs Charles N. Harris of Carroll Parish to death in the St. Charles Hotel in New Orleans

1860 Jan-Feb (Age 48) – Isham travels to New Orleans to support his brother Wiley while he stands trial for murder. Wiley is acquitted and it is ruled self-defense. Isham returns to Oakland on 8 Feb 1860.

1860 Jun 25 (Age 49) – Isham writes to friend Wash Allen informing him that "Mr. Shepherd Brown of New Orleans" would occupy his Wolf Creek mountain home (Glen Ada) during summer of 1860

1861 Jan (Age 49) – Brother William Raine Peck becomes a signatory due to the Louisiana Ordinance of Secession

1861 Apr 12 (Age 50) – Civil War officially begins when Confederate troops fire on Fort Sumter in Charleston Harbor

1861 Jun 25 (Age 50) – Isham donates $1,000 to the "Peck Light Dragoons" of Jefferson County "to aid in their equipment"

1861 Aug (Age 50) – "Peck Light Dragoons" organized under Capt Benjamin M. Branner – Part of 4th Battalion, TN Cavalry (CSA), merged into 2nd (Ashby's) TN Cavalry Regiment May 1862

1861 Jul 7 (Age 50) – Brother William R. Peck enlists as a private in the 9th Louisiana Infantry

1862 (Age 51) – Son Ashby Henderson Peck is born in Tennessee (named after Gen. Turner Ashby, CSA)

1863 Feb (Age 51/52) – Detachment of Gen. Grant's Army stationed at Millken's Bend takes $30,000 in bushels of corn, 60 head of cattle, and 120 cords of wood from the Henderson Plantation in LA.

1863 Mar 29 (Age 52) – Brother and CSA soldier Adam C. Peck writes to their mom Sophia from Strawberry Plains, TN expressing concern at hearing of Juliet's condition. He says that he has been preaching regularly at the Methodist Church.

1863 May 18 – Jul 4 (52) – Siege of Vicksburg takes place – ends in Union victory after 47 days[117]

1863 Jun 7 (Age 52) – Battle of Milliken's Bend takes place just south of Henderson Plantation

1863 Jul 14 (Age 52) – Cousin Lafayette Peck (son of Uncle Moses), Wet Point graduate, dies in Tuscaloosa, AL as a Confederate soldier

---

[116] Ibid, 1 Jul 1859 Letter from Emma Peck to Emma Allen, p 52-53 and https://www.findagrave.com/memorial/53256470, accessed 3 May 2020
[117] https://www.battlefields.org/learn/civil-war/battles/vicksburg, accessed 29 Nov 2022

1863 Aug 1 (Age 52) – Uncle Adam Peck, Jr. enlists as a Private in the 11th Battalion, Georgia State Guards at the age of 72 for a period of 6 months

1863 Oct 8 (Age 52) – Brother William R. Peck is promoted to Colonel of the 9th Louisiana to succeed Leroy A. Stafford

1863 Dec 11 (Age 52) – Emma's Uncle Horace Prentice dies from pneumonia and Kate Stone's mom visits Isham's Aunt Minerva in her distress[118]

1863 Dec 13 (Age 52) – Emma's Uncle Horace Prentice is buried. Kate Stone stays with Minerva for the rest of the day and her mom stays with her the entire night.[119]

1863 Dec 24 (Age 52) – Brig. Gen. S. D. Sturgis records that Colonel Foster's (Union) Headquarters are at Dr. [Isham] Peck's house in Mossy Creek, TN

1863 Dec 24 (Age 52) – Col. Oscar H. La Grange records (on 27 Dec) that on this day two small Confederate brigades under Gen Armstrong advanced on the Union position close to Isham's house (2.5 miles west of Mossy Creek Station); the Union army drove the CSA troops back 3.5 miles and then camped for the night at Mossy Creek Station.

1863 Dec 25 (Age 52) – Col Edward M. McCook writes from Isham's home listing it as "Headquarters First Division Cavalry"

1863 Dec 31 (Age 52) – Cousin Jacob Young Peck (son of Uncle Adam) dies as a Confederate soldier in Atlanta as it was under siege

1864 Jan 9 (Age 52) – Future daughter-in-law Cora Brownrig Ward is born on the Ward Plantation in Greene County, North Carolina (she later marries son Dr. Edward Jerome Peck) in 1885

1864 May 25 – Cousin Mary Catherine Peck (dau. of Uncle Adam) dies from cholera in Lake Co, FL

1864 Jun 5 (Age 53) – Brother Adam Clayton Peck dies in New Hope, VA in the Civil War Battle of Piedmont[120] [121]

1864 May/Jun (Age 53) – Brother "Big Peck" leads the 9th Louisiana in the battles of Wilderness, Spotsylvania, and Cold Harbor, followed by the Overland Campaign

1864 July (Age 53) – Brother Big Peck leads his brigade as Senior Colonel and draws praise from his division commander, Maj. Gen. John B. Gordon for his role in the Battle of Monocacy

1864 Sep 19 (Age 53) – Brother Big Peck is wounded in his right thigh by a shell fragment in the Third Battle of Winchester.[122]

1864 Sep 15 (Age 53) – Sister Juliet (Rhoton) dies and is buried in Mossy Creek, TN

1865 Feb 18 (Age 53) – Brother Big Peck is promoted to Brigadier General

1865 May 15 (Age 54) – Son Louis Sharkey Peck is born in Tennessee

1865 Apr 9 (Age 54) – Gen. Robert E. Lee surrenders his Army of Northern Virginia to Union Gen. Ulysses S. Grant

---

[118] From *Brokenburn: The Journal of Kate Stone 1861-1868*, Edited by John Q. Anderson, p264 says, "Mamma and Mrs. Carson have gone out to see Mrs. Prentice. Her husband died last night leaving her a childless widow alone in a strange land. He had been ill for a week with pneumonia, and both Johnny and Jimmy have been sitting up with him."

[119] Ibid, p266

[120] See 1876 *Morristown Gazette* article addressed to Sawbones where "Whitehead" says, "There are not many of us left. Adam fills a gallant soldier's grave, in the Valley of Virginia, where he fell in the battle of Piedmont,"

[121] https://en.wikipedia.org/wiki/Battle_of_Piedmont, accessed 21 Apr 2020

[122] https://en.wikipedia.org/wiki/Third_Battle_of_Winchester, accessed 21 Apr 2020

1865 Apr 15 (Age 54) – President Abraham Lincoln is assassinated

1865 Jun (Age 54) – First cousin William Lewis Sharkey appointed as the provisional governor of Mississippi by President Andrew Johnson following the Civil War. He serves until Dec 1865.

1865 Jun (Age 54) – Brother Big Peck is paroled in Vicksburg

1866 Jan (Age 54) – Brother Wiley Hawkins Peck dies at the age of 43. He has a sudden "hemorrhage of the lungs" while visiting Big Peck at his "Mountain" Plantation[123]

1866 Apr 5 (Age 55) – Uncle Adam Peck, Jr. dies in Dahlonegah, GA at the age of 75

1866 Aug 20 (Age 55) – President Andrew Johnson announces end of the Civil War

1866 Sep 17 (Age 55) – Mother-in-law Louise Henderson is "sick"[124]

1867 Sep 22 (Age 56) – Isham's Father-in-law William Henderson dies, and Kate Stone along with Mr. Rhotan stay for 7-10 days with Minerva and Louise[125]

1867 Nov 24 (Age 56) – Isham is in Louisiana working on the plantation, Emma is at Oakland, she expects Isham "home" before 1 Jan 1867. Many of the "negroes" die of cholera on Isham's Louisiana Plantation. 83 died on a nearby plantation close to Milliken's Bend. Things are terrible in Louisiana; people are selling their plantations for 50 cents/acre. One man moves to Honduras. Another tries to sell for $1/acre but no one will buy it.[126]

1868 (Age 57) – Sister Eliza "Jane" Talbot McEfee Lynn dies at the age of 56 and is buried in Kingsport, TN (Boatyard Methodist Episcopal Church Cemetery)

1868 May 15 (Age 58) – Uncle Dr. John Moil Talbot (mom's brother) dies in Louisville, KY (87 y.o.)[127]

1869 Mar 23 (Age 58) – Son Paul Eve Peck is born in Tennessee

1869 Jun 10 (Age 58) – Dad Judge Jacob Franklin Clayton Peck dies at the age of 89

1869 Nov 3 (Age 58) – Isham and family ask that his dad's extensive land holdings and mining interests be sold and revenue distributed accordingly to surviving family members. This becomes TN Supreme Court Case (originating in Jefferson County) called "Peck v. Rhoton" and references 30 different land holdings containing tens of thousands of acres.

1870 (Age 59) – Living in Mossy Creek, Jefferson County, TN according to U. S. Census

1871 Jan 22 (Age 59) – Brother, General William Raine "Big Peck" dies at the age of 52 at his "Mountain" plantation in Madison Parish, Louisiana

1871 Jun 4 (Age 60) – Mom Sophia Westerner Talbot Peck dies at the age of 83 in Talbot, TN

1871 Feb 27 (Age 60) – First son Willie commits suicide by laudanum at age 15

1871 Nov 21 (Age 60) – Youngest daughter Helen is born at Glen Ada in Wolf Creek

1872 (Age 61) – Son Charley begins attending Reagan High School for Boys in Morristown, TN

---

[123] *Ada's Journal and Emma's Letters*, 65-66, Letter from Emma Peck to Emma Allen dated 1 April 1866 from Oakland (Tennessee)

[124] Ibid, 67, 17 Sep 1866 Letter from Emma Peck to Emma Allen written from Oakland (TN)

[125] *Brokenburn*, 373, "Mr. Rhotan and I became quite chummy when I went to stay a week or ten days with Mrs. Henderson after Mr. Henderson's death. We thought her so desolate and alone until her sister, Mrs. Prentice, came to stay with her—two lonely, elderly widows."

[126] 24 Nov 1867 Letter from Emma Peck to Emma Allen written from Oakland (TN), See *Ada's Journal & Emma's Letters*

[127] https://www.findagrave.com/memorial/109667776/john-moil-talbot, accessed 29 Nov 2022

1873 Mar 30 (Age 62) – First cousin William L. Sharkey dies in Washington, D.C. and is buried in Greenwood Cemetery, Jackson, Mississippi. Sharkey County, Mississippi is named in his honor

1874 Apr 29 (Age 63) – Youngest son Robert Lee Peck is born at Glen Ada in Wolf Creek

1874 Jul 23 (Age 63) – Aunt Elizabeth "Eliza" Gayle Peck (wife of Uncle Adam) dies in Russell Spring, Russell, Kentucky

1874 Sep (Age 63) – Son Charley enrolls in and attends one year at Washington and Lee University

1876 May (Age 65) – Son Charley starts a weekly newspaper called the Mossy Creek *Independent*

1877 May 19 (Age 66) – Son Ashby starts his newspaper called *The Mountain Boomer* in Wolf Creek

1877 Nov 28 (Age 66) – Isham "visits his plantations in Louisiana"

1877 Dec 24 (Age 66) – Isham returns home from visiting Louisiana, headed to his home in Wolf Creek, and stays "at the Maxwell" in Nashville, TN. He is listed as having 30,000 acres of East Tennessee possessions.[128]

1878 Apr 24 (Age 67) – Isham endorses James Swaggerty, Esq. of Newport for TN Governor

1878 Sep (Age 67) – Son Charley returns from England with family member George W. Peck

1878 Oct 23 (Age 67) – Isham spends a day in Morristown, TN and is listed as having neuralgia in the face. He cannot visit his friend Maj Heiss in Nashville due to the spread of yellow fever throughout Louisiana

1878 Nov 20 (Age 67) – His friend Maj Harry Heiss and State Fishing Commissioner Col Akers visit him and fish on the French Broad River

1879 Feb 27 (Age 68) – His son DR. EDWARD J. PECK graduates Vanderbilt Univ. Medical School in Nashville, TN at the age of 20 years old

1879 Mar 31 (Age 68) – Isham travels on the J. M. White boat so his son Ed can get better treatment. Ed was in "feeble health."[129]

1879 Apr (Age 68) – Son Charley writes his epic southern novel during his idle hours. Published now as *Charley's Novel: Mary Anderson and Peacock the Mineralogist, the Bad Luck of a Young Southern Girl* (Cross Mountain Books, 2021). Numerous references to Isham and other family throughout.

1879 Apr 23 (Age 68) – Isham travels to Vicksburg, MS to care for his son DR. ED PECK who had a serious health attack (at the age of 20). Isham returns with Ed, "the invalid," and takes the train for his home. Isham is listed as being in "robust health" and Ed "as well as could be expected."

1879 Sep (Age 68) – Charley deeds his portion of the Wolf Creek land over to his brother EDWARD.

1879 Dec 3 (Age 68) – Isham takes the train west from Morristown (unknown destination)

1880 Feb (Age 69) – Son Charley travels to Brazil and returns by way of California

1880 Nov 2 (Age 69) – James Garfield is elected President of the United States

1882 Feb 18 (Age 70) – Son Charley is "stricken with an apoplectic fit" and found prostrate in a street in Cincinnati. Officials telegraph for his brother DR. ED PECK to come from Atlanta to help him.

1882 Feb 22 (Age 70) – Son Charley dies in Cincinnati just hours after Ed arrives.

1882 Feb 25 (Age 71) – Isham and family bury Charley at Westview Cemetery in Mossy Creek

---

[128] *The Tennessean* (Nashville, TN) 25 Dec 1877, 4.
[129] *Vicksburg Herald*, Vicksburg, MS, 1 Apr 1879, 3.

1882 May 3 (Age 71) – Editors from the *The Morristown Gazette* visit Isham at his Wolf Creek property and find him smoking his meerschaum and reading his newspapers. He shows them around the property.

1882 Aug 10 (Age 71) – Sister Martha Ann Featherstone dies in Mossy Creek, TN

1884 Feb 14 (Age 72) – Isham, daughter Helen, and son Ed stay at Battle House (Hotel) in Knoxville, TN[130]

1884 Dec 19 (Age 73) – Isham travels to Vicksburg on the Will S. Hays boat[131]

1885 Aug 22 (Age 74) – Son DR. EDWARD JEROME PECK marries CORA BROWNRIG WARD in Cocke County, TN

1885 Nov 24 (Age 74) – Isham files lawsuit in Cocke County Chancery Court against Elza Houston, William Houston, Jr. (Elza's son), Samuel Mooneyham, and Rhoton Keys for 5,000 acres of land

1886 (Age 75) – Son Louis Sharkey Peck moves to Tallahassee, FL

1886 Aug (Age 75) – Cousin Lydia (dau. of Uncle Moses) dies at age 60

1887 May 27 (Age 76) – Youngest daughter Helen dies after two-week illness at Salem Female College

1887 Summer (Age 76) – Isham erects a cross monument in Helen's honor on the top of "Cross Mountain" on the heights of his Wolf Creek, TN property where she used to read books

1887 Nov 27 (Age 76) – Son Ashby commits suicide at the age of 25 in FL by taking laudanum

1887 Nov 28 (Age 76) – Isham falls dead after receiving the news that Ashby had killed himself

Timeline Continued After Isham's Death

1888 Sep 12 – Paul Eve Peck is appointed Depot Agent at the Newport, TN Railroad Office

1888 Nov 7 – Louis Sharkey Peck marries Frances "Fannie" Perkins Gibbens in Leon, FL

1891 Jan 7 – Paul Eve Peck marries Ella R. King in Columbia, FL

1891 Nov 4 – Paul's son (Isham's Grandson) Richard King Peck is born in Lake City, FL

1897 Feb 13 – Mother-in-law LOUISE DONOHUE HENDERSON dies

1899 Sep 16 – Wife Emma Elizabeth (Henderson) Peck dies in Lake City, FL

1901 Jan 9 - Robert Lee Peck marries Isabella Elizabeth "May" Purden in Orange, FL

1901 May 3 – Massive fire strikes Jacksonville, FL – leaves more than 10,000 people homeless

1901 Nov 3 – Louis writes letter to friend Harry Heiss Allen informing him that he's been working in the Dispatcher's Office in Jacksonville, FL for 3 weeks

1902 Sep 19 – Fannie (Louis's wife) and her mom visit Mr. & Mrs. John Currier in Knoxville, TN and Louis is trainmaster of the Seaboard Air Line (a railroad) in Florida[132]

1914 Oct 26 – Paul's daughter (Isham's granddaughter) Elizabeth "Betty" Peck is born in Jacksonville

1916 Dec 29 – Paul's daughter (Isham's granddaughter) Violet "Irene" Peck is born in FL

---

[130] *The Daily Chronicle*, Knoxville, TN, 14 Feb 1884, 1.
[131] Vicksburg *Herald* Pg 4, 20 Dec 1884
[132] *The Journal and Tribune*, Knoxville, TN, 19 Sep 1902, 6.

PEN NAME "SAWBONES"

Isham wrote under the pen name Sawbones and the following articles give us an incredible window into his life and times. Before we begin looking at each article, it behooves us to pause and examine this name "Sawbones." Why did Isham choose it for himself? The truth is that it is a nickname for doctors, especially surgeons…and has fallen into disuse for the most part. We know that Isham was a doctor, sometimes listed as a physician on the census. In the 1850 Louisiana Census, just 2 years after his marriage to Emma, he is listed as "Physician." He was listed as a "farm laborer" in the 1870 Census, but a "Dr of Medicine" on the 1880 Census at age 69 years old.

In a well-written article on the subject of limb surgery, Doctor Robert G. Slawson, MD, FACR writes extensively on the practice of amputation before, during, and after the Civil War.[133] He says, "Necessary amputations had been done for some time. During the Napoleonic wars, amputation was practiced even though effective anesthesia was not available. It was the fastest way to treat the largest number of wounded in a very short window of time. They had found that forty-eight hours after the injury was the magic time. After that, the probability of dying from infection was very high. During the Crimean War in the mid-1850s, it had been demonstrated again that primary amputation was the best way to save the most lives.[4] They also found that amputations done days later were seldom as effective in preventing death.[3,5] Because of this fact, early amputation became the recommended treatment in the Civil War. Resistance to this was frequent among surgeons at the beginning of their service and many conservative approaches were tried. Most of these ended fatally. Many surgeons who initially opposed amputation came to see the benefits of this procedure in survival.[6]

Figure 70 - Amputation scene, Fortress Monroe. Courtesy of the Library of Congress.

---

[133] The Story of the Pile of Limbs, originally published in 2017 in the Surgeon's Call, Vol 22, No. 1, http://www.civilwarmed.org/surgeons-call/limbs/

Because of the devastating effects of amputation on the lives of most of the survivors, the public objected to this treatment. The term "invalid" actually meant that the person was an incomplete person and not a valid person. Certainly, it was difficult for a laborer or a farmer to function well afterwards, especially if the limb was an arm. A huge public outcry arose. Many both in and out of the army complained that surgeons were too quick to amputate. In the early part of the war, some unnecessary amputations may have been done by inexperienced surgeons or by some who simply wanted the experience of learning to do amputations. The army responded to this and developed criteria for amputation to limit the procedure to those in whom it was medically necessary. **Military surgeons came to be called "sawbones," a nickname that is still applied to surgeons, although most people don't realize the origin of the term."**[134]

Figure 71 - General Daniel Sickles (center) with General Joseph B. Carr (left) and General Charles K. Graham (right), visiting the location on Gettysburg Battlefield where Sickles was injured. Photograph circa 1886. Courtesy of the Library of Congress.

There is a certain irony in Isham choosing "Sawbones" as his pen name. As a surgeon in pre-Civil War America, he may have been required to perform numerous amputations…depending on how much combat he saw. In medical practice, limbs were severed due to pain and the risk of infection setting in after an injury. Not to stretch the metaphor too far, but Isham had at least five children whose lives were **cut** short by suicide or illness while he was alive. The ones who committed suicide must have had such acute psychological pain that they did not feel they could continue in this world. Similar to amputees, Isham and Emma lived on with the memory of their lost children, but not their presence. After losing 2 children within a 6-month span during his 77th year, and upon hearing the news that his son Ashby had committed suicide by laudanum, Isham literally fell dead. His pain was too much too bear, and his old heart could not bear it. He and Ashby were buried the same day. More of Ashby's story is shared in *He Loved the Folks: Dr. Edward Jerome Peck of Hot Springs, NC.*

---

[134] Ibid, emphasis added.

SAWBONES ARTICLES BY ISHAM, IN CHRONOLOGICAL ORDER

At Wolf Creek, just west of Paint Rock, a large cross shines white from a mountain peak. It is a landmark that instantly attracts attention. The conductor of the train said it had been standing there for thirty years, but he did not know who erected it, or why it was placed there. A man who, had boarded the train at Paint Rock, said he thought it marked the dividing line between North Carolina and Tennessee. We set about to learn the history of this cross and eventually uncovered a sweet little story of fatherly devotion. The cross was erected on this mountain peak nearly forty years ago, by the late Dr. Edward Peck, as a memorial to his daughter. The young woman died suddenly while attending school in Asheville. The spot where the cross is placed was her favorate retreat for reading and study. It overlooks the French Broad valley and commands a view of a great range of mountains. Dr. Peck was well known to newspaper readers in the western part of the State. He was a man of much literary attainment and contributed to the papers under the name of "Sawbones." He died eight years ago. His name, however, still lives. A son, Dr. Edward Peck, practices his profession in Hot Springs.

Figure 72 - *The Evening Chronicle*, Charlotte, North Carolina, 30 Sep 1911, 4.

As the author began family research efforts in the months leading up to a 2017 Peck family reunion at Fort Rucker, Alabama, celebrating (early) his Grandma Bea Dot (Smallwood) Peck's 90th birthday, he began combing through all the articles available on newspapers.com, searching for any mention of the Peck family. One article mentioned Wolf Creek, Dr. Edward Peck, and even the fact that his dad was a doctor as well. The article got three things wrong…one, it calls Isham "Dr. Edward Peck," but it is most certainly referring to Isham. It mentions the Memorial Cross that he erected on the top of what is now referred to as "Cross Mountain" (because of the cross he erected there), and shares that he put it there in memory of Helen who had died at the Salem Female Academy, a private boarding school in Salem, North Carolina (not Asheville as the article says, that's the second mistake). But the key line that stood out was this one, "He was a man of much literary attainment and contributed to the papers under the name of "Sawbones." The article gets a third detail wrong; it says that Isham died "8 years ago," when in reality he died in 1887 (which was approx. 34 years before the article was written). Ed was still living at the time the article was written.

Transcription: "At Wolf Creek, just west of Paint Rock, a large cross shines white from a mountain peak. It is a landmark that instantly attracts attention. The conductor of the train said it had been standing there for thirty years, but he did not know who erected it, or why it was placed there. A man who, had boarded the train at Paint Rock, said he thought it marked the dividing line between North Carolina and Tennessee. We set about to learn the history of this cross and eventually uncovered a sweet little story of fatherly devotion. The cross was erected on this mountain peak nearly forty years ago, by the late Dr. Edward [*actually Isham*] Peck, as a memorial to his daughter. The young woman died suddenly while attending school in Asheville [*actually Salem, NC*]. The spot where the cross is placed was her favorite retreat for reading and study. It overlooks the French Broad valley and commands a view of a great range of mountains. Dr. Peck was well known to newspaper readers in the western part of the State. He was a man of much literary attainment and contributed to the papers under the name of "Sawbones." He died eight years ago. His name, however, still lives. A son, Dr. Edward Peck, practices his profession in Hot Springs."

Once this 112-year-old hidden gem was found, the fact that Dr. Isham Talbot Peck was a prolific writer who wrote under the pen name "Sawbones," it opened up a world of writing by Isham that is quite exciting. After extensive research, the author has found 41 articles written by, addressed to, or about "Sawbones." These articles are primarily found in *The Morristown Gazette*, based in Morristown, TN (about 17 miles away from Isham's Mossy Creek, TN home). But at least one article was picked up by the Nashville *Union and American*, based in Nashville, TN. The articles were written between 25 Mar 1874 and 13 Oct 1886 (a span of approx. 12 years). Before moving on, one more piece of corroborating evidence is found in *The Morristown Gazette* on 3 Dec 1879 on page 2, where it says, "Dr. Peck, the inimitable "Sawbones," of Wolf Creek, came over on the Buncombe and took a western bound train Saturday night." With Isham's authorship cemented, let us turn to the actual articles.

Dr. Peck, the inimitable "Sawbones," of Wolf Creek, came over on the Buncombe and took a western bound train Saturday night.

Figure 73 - Cross Mountain across from Glen Ada, Wolf Creek, Tennessee. The cross Isham planted stood on this mountain from 1887 until the mid-late 20th century. Photo by the author, 29 Oct 2020.

BALD MOUNTAIN.—[Drawn by A. Wordsworth Thompson.]

Figure 74 – "Bald Mountain. – [Drawn by A. Wordsworth Thompson.]". Digital surrogates [Rutherford County:
Landscapes: Rumbling Bald Mountain, 11-18 April 1874, Harper's Weekly, 313] of originals in image box 037, folder 1313,
North Carolina County Photographic Collection, no. P0001, North Carolina Collection Photographic Archives,
The Wilson Library, University of North Carolina at Chapel Hill. Public Domain. Photo enhanced.

25 MAR 1874 "Sawbones" Elucidates the Mystery![135]

STARTLING VOLCANIC FACTS. THE CUSSEDNESS OF NEWSPAPER HUMANITY.

Near the Volcanic Regions, March 19. 'H—U afloat in the Mountains!'— 'Old Bald-y" Preparing to Eruct (sic)! —Volcano? —Smoke! —Fire!!—The Earth Quaking! —Things Tottling!'
To the Editor of the Morristown Gazette:

I heard all this, and I could not stand it. I had never seen a volcano, so I mounted my horse and put out for "old Bald." The news got worse the farther I went. As I approached the mountain I met the natives a getting'-men, women, children and dogs. They begged me to turn back, and sung, 'Turn, sinner, turn,' and I think some of them prayed for me. It beat old Mrs. Ward's saloon at Greeneville. To get out of the fuss I pushed on. I struck a leading spur of old Bald, and rode up, up as far as I could ride. Then I dismounted, hitched my horse and walked on. Where the spur joined the main mountain my way was obstructed by perpendicular rocks. I could see smoke from the top, but I could not hear the rumbling. I climbed up and around the mountain to avoid the rocks. After proceeding for some time, I began to hear the rumbling. It appeared to be below me, and farther around the mountain. I got on a high point, from which there was a commanding view below. The rumbling from this point was terrible and unaccountable. Just here I saw a sight that astonished me more than if the earth had yawned at my feet. I saw a wagon, with four mules, driven furiously around the side of the mountain. It had on it an old fashioned wagon-bed, and from the noise, there was a few loose rocks in it. How the thing held together, bouncing about over the rocks, is unaccountable. It went a few hundred yards, and turned round. It stopped about ten minutes as if to rest the mules, then, here it came again. The road (if it could be called a road,) was about four hundred yards long. It would turn and rest the mules at each end. I saw it make several trips. Then I took a drink from my flask, and scrambled down to this Devil's Turnpike. I placed myself by the side of the road, to wait for the wagon. In a few minutes here it came. The driver did not see me until he was within fifty steps of me. He appeared astonished, stood up in his stirrups, (he was riding one of the mules,) and tried to bluff me by yelling out: 'Get out of the way, you d – d fool!' As soon as he spoke I knew him. It was George Sikes. He used to live over in Buncombe when Madison was part of Buncombe. I picked up a couple of rocks and placed myself in the middle of the road. Then he stopped and I went for him. Said I, 'George, if you don't want to be lifted from that mule with one of these dornicks[136], talk fast.' 'Talk what?' said he. 'Volcano!' said I. 'Now look here, Sawbones.' (he always called me Sawbones,) 'you know that I am a poor man. I am paid by the editors to do this.' 'But how about the smoke and fire?' He said one of his boys was on top and with sticks and wet leaves he kept up a smoke. At night they built a fire. 'How about the blow out?' Here George laughed outright. He said the natives were very skittish when they heard the rumbling, but when 'the blow out' came, they incontinently toddled! He had buried a keg of powder about eight feet deep, inserted a tin tube in the keg, tramped in the dirt, lit a slow match and then she blew out! 'They say they hear this rumbling at Old Fort?' 'O, yes! They hear it there! They will hear it in New York soon, the news is spreading mighty fast! Sawbones, for

---

[135] Dr. Isham Peck, "Sawbones" Elucidates the Mystery, *The Morristown Gazette* (Morristown, TN) Wed, 25 Mar, 1874, 2.
[136] Dornick = "a small stone small enough to throw," https://www.merriam-webster.com/dictionary/dornick

God sake give me all the tobacco you have about you – go home to your family and keep your mouth shut.'

I did go home to my family. The old quilt saw me coming and ran to meet me. The first word was 'volcano!' I told her the volcano was all right, but that the cussedness of human nature was breaking my heart, and that if she didn't get in the house and make me a strong cup of coffee, there would be a volcano right there. She went – not being a strong-minded crusader, she consequently does what I ask her to do.

If you are in the 'volcano' business you can suppress this. I do not want to injure any man's business; and this volcano-earthquake news is mighty exciting reading. SAWBONES."

On 27 March 1874, just 2 days after this story was published in *The Morristown Gazette*, The Nashville *Union and American* picked up the story and published it as well. The only difference is that they added the words "BALD MOUNTAIN" at the top of the story.[137] It seems clear to me from reading these articles, that this was likely Isham's first time writing to the newspaper under the name "Sawbones." He explains the nickname in the article, "'Now look here, Sawbones.' (he always called me Sawbones,)." Isham doesn't explain his nickname in any other article he writes. The fact that the newspapers (must not have been the *Gazette*) were paying old George Sikes to make a ruckus and blow things up at the top of Bald Mountain so that people thought there was a volcano or an earthquake…just to make a profit and sell papers, was enough to get Isham to speak up about the hubbub. The deception that the newspaper editors drummed up, had its intended effect. People travelled from all over the country to "investigate" the rumblings and possible volcano in the Smoky Mountains. To this day, there is a resort, on Lake Lure, called "Rumbling Bald" that tells the story of how Bald Mountain rumbled back in 1874. This author has traveled there twice with family, once with just his father, and again with father, uncles, and cousins, when they played a "Peck Golf Week" at the resort. There are two beautiful golf courses at the Rumbling Bald Resort, "Rumbling Bald" and "Apple Valley."

The author contacted Rumbling Bald Resort Management and attached the articles written by Isham and others about these events. He went on a boat tour of Lake Lure, and after the boat guide told the "official" story about Rumbling Bald and its history, he asked her if he could share another story about Rumbling Bald and she agreed. He then told the story of Sawbones and him coming upon George Sikes on the mountain. She had never heard of it.

The possibility of a volcano in the Smokies was big news throughout North Carolina, Tennessee, and across the country. Listen to these accounts and stories from the *The People's Press* (Winston-Salem, North Carolina) published just one day after Isham's article was published…

---

[137] Sawbones' volcano account was also carried in *The Herald and Mail* (Columbia, TN) 10 Apr 1874, *The Home Journal* (Winchester, TN) 9 Apr 1874, and The Milan Exchange (2 Apr 1874).

26 Mar 1874 IS BALD MOUNTAIN A VOLCANO? GREAT RELIGIOUS EXCITEMENT

The North Carolina Volcano – in Prospect.

In relation to the phenomenon that is now terrifying the people in the neighborhood of Bald Mountain, candor forces me to admit that I do not believe their fears are altogether groundless.

I was on the mountain on the night of the 1st inst. The noise seemed to be under the ground in a small valley between what is called the Round and the Stone mountains, though I could not exactly determine the locality. Sometimes the shocks are very heavy, accompanied by sounds similar to the detonations of artillery, and the earth is shaken for miles around. A very perceptible movement is seen among the trees when vibrations take place, and the houses are sufficiently jarred to arouse children from their nightly slumber, when they manifest their fright by cries and screams.

The sound is more distinctly heard in the valley than any other place. The people who live in the vicinity are very much alarmed, and many of them are preparing to emigrate. A protracted meeting is in the immediate neighborhood, and upwards of forty persons have professed religion and joined the Baptist church – the only denomination in this section. Prayer-meetings prevail, in which all take an active part, from the worst sinners to the best and purest Christians. I attended one of these meetings, and feel safe in saying that it was the first religious assembly I ever witnessed where every one was so deeply interested in the salvation of the soul. If this noise is followed by no destructive eruption, it will be a good thing for these people in a religious point of view. These subterranean sounds are not constant, but are heard more of less distinctly every day. – *Asheville Pioneer*

Since the above, we have additional sketches embracing the following:

"Since the middle of February last there has been considerable excitement in the section of the mountain.

The prayer meetings were commenced at the house of a Mr. Camp, and have since become general all through this region."

The following from the Asheville *Expositor* will give some idea of the excitement:

On March 3, J. M. Lumly, {formerly of this place,} a Methodist minister, in charge of Broad River missions, was importuned to attend and preach, and promptly complied with the request. From an eye-witness the scenes are described as most strange and extraordinary. The people came flocking in crowds of fifteen and twenty, including men, women and children, all presenting the most terrible state of fear, despair and penitence. On the day Mr. Lumly preached the house was literally packed, the preacher barely having room to stand. So great was the rush to hear that many rushed up the side of the walls and crowded on the joists above. Only a portion of the upper story having a floor, and many not being able to enter the house, crowded their heads in the door and all around the house manifesting the most intense interest.

When the call was made for mourners the people rushed from all parts of the house and from the outside, with almost frantic yells, and fell upon the floor and upon each other, all praying and supplicating in the most heartfelt and agonizing manner ever witnessed on earth. These exercises continued incessantly for sixteen days and nights, with but little intermission.

The New York *Herald* correspondent writes under date of March 21ˢᵗ, as follows:

Last night there was a succession of terrific shocks on the sides of Bald Mountain, accompanied by a sharp thunder storm. Simultaneously with the thunder, quick and loud reports could be heard from the mountain sides. I stopped at the house of an old farmer, who welcomed me and said that he would like to have a hundred in the house, as the mountain had scared him nearly out of his life. During the night, when the rumbling was at its height he got up, and assembling his family around him, held a family prayer meeting. The whole neighborhood was aroused in like manner. The shaking of the earth was quite perceptible, and it was almost impossible to sleep. As yet no one has been able to give any definite account of the source of the convulsion.

I started up the mountain this morning at seven o'clock, and had ridden over three-quarters of a mile when a sudden shock occurred, which so terrified my horse that he became unmanageable. He ran me against a tree, and unhorsing me, left me on the ground so much bruised in the left side and leg that I was unable to remount. I have a guide who will go up with me if I am able, when I shall be able to send full and definite information.

After sixteen days of prayer meeting, during which time the people left their cattle and crops to take care of themselves, they seem now awaiting some terrible calamity, and in many instances their anxiety is really distressing. Nearly 200 converts to religion are reported.

Bald Mountain is situated between Crooked Creek in McDowell county, and Stone Mountain, Rutherford county, and since 1812 there has been no symptoms similar to those now experienced. In that year (1812) the shocks were as severe, so says one of the oldest inhabitants.

VOLCANIC HUMORS. – A part of an article in the New York *Graphic* on the Bald Mountain pertubations [sic] is as follows:

Nothing could be more unfair than to require a new volcano to equal at the very start, volcanoes that have been in constant use for centuries. Only give the North Carolinians time to thoroughly comprehend the thing and they will doubtless produce as good an article of volcano as can be found in any of the effete monarchies of Europe.

Persons whose motives are plainly of the most unpatriotic and envious character scoff at the North Carolina volcano, and insist that science has shown that all volcanoes are situated on the sea coast, and are due to salt water leaking through the bottom of the sea, and coming in contact with boxes of potassium and jars of acids stored away in the heart of the neighboring mountains. But it is open to the North Carolinians to reply that in the centre of Thibet, at a distance of more than 1,000 miles from the sea, are two extraordinarily lively volcanoes. Now, if the degraded Thibetians can produce volcanoes without water, surely the free and enlightened citizens of North Carolina can do as much. There does not seem to be any sufficient answer to this argument, and fairminded men will have to admit there is no scientific impossibility involved in setting up a volcano in the west of North Carolina and making it, if not a pecuniary, at all events a spectacular success. As to the rumor that the so-called volcano is the creation of the diseased mind of an illicit distiller who had consumed his own stock rather too recklessly, it is not deserving of contradiction. Every cultivated North Carolinian knows that whisky may produce monkeys and snakes, but that by no possible process of revolution can it produce volcanoes.

Even were we to admit the truth of the scientific theory that no volcano can exist at a distance from the sea, we should only be postponing the possibility of a volcano in the North Carolina mountains. The sea is gradually eating into our Atlantic coast, and in course of time will break at the foot of the Alleghanies. Then all the scientific conditions for the production of volcanoes will be at hand. The sea will leak into the sub-cellars of the mountains and begin its chemical labors, and as soon as a sufficient amount of steam and gas shall be generated by this process the lid, so to speak, of the Alleghanies will fly off, and we shall have volcanoes of unlimited horse-power, and in quantities amply sufficient to suit every demand of our great and populous country. [End of 26 Mar 1874 article]

BALD MOUNTAIN, NORTH CAROLINA. THE SCENE OF THE EARTHQUAKE PHENOMENA AND THREATENED VOLCANO.—SKETCHED BY THOMAS C. MORTON.—SEE PAGE 90.

Figure 75 – "Bald Mountain, North Carolina, The Scene of the Earthquake Phenomena and Threatened Volcano. – Sketched by Thomas C. Morton. – See Page 90.". Digital surrogates [Rutherford County: Landscapes: Rumbling Bald Mountain, 11-18 April 1874, Harper's Weekly, 89] of originals in image box 037, folder 1313, North Carolina County Photographic Collection, no. P0001, North Carolina Collection Photographic Archives, The Wilson Library, University of North Carolina at Chapel Hill.

A few days later, *The Morristown Gazette* publishes the next entry in the Rumbling Bald Saga…

1 APR 1874 The Volcano (Update)[138]

"THE VOLCANO. —We have nothing new concerning the volcanic symptoms published about Bald Mountain. Mr. Russell, of Newport, informed us on Saturday that he had read a letter, written by a reliable gentleman residing in close proximity to the embryo crater, to a relative in Newport, in which the writer spoke of the tremorousness of the earth to the extent of jarring the cubbardware in his house, of a continual rumbling noise in the mountain and smoke constantly arising from its summit. The writer stated that the people of the locality were alarmed and making preparations to leave. But all of this has already been published. and until some better proof of its volcanic nature is exhibited the theory of our friend 'Sawbones' should allay undue excitement."

THE VOLCANO. —We have nothing new concerning the volcanic symptoms published about Bald mountain. Mr. Russell, of Newport, informed us on Saturday that he had read a letter, written by a reliable gentleman residing in close proximity to the embryo crater, to a relative in Newport, in which the writer spoke of the tremorousness of the earth to the extent of jarring the cubbard ware in his house, of a continual rumbling noise in the mountain and smoke constantly arising from its summit. The writer stated that the people of the locality were alarmed and making preparations to leave. But all of this has already been published. and until some better proof of its volcanic nature is exhibited the theory of our friend "Sawbones" should allay undue excitement.

People in the area were legitimately scared and leaving the area for fear of their lives. The newspaper editors' desire to print a good selling story came at the peril of people's feelings of safety and security.

The next day, *The Milan Exchange* covers the story on page 2 of their paper. Milan is 358 miles from Morristown, a 5.5-hour drive by car on nice roads. In that day, it would have been a multiple day journey by stage coach, train, or otherwise, depending on what was available for travel between the two cities.

After a few more days, Sawbones couldn't hold his tongue anymore and decided to go on record again regarding the eruptions…

Figure 76 – Settler's Cabin on the Side of Bald Mountain.-[Drawn by A. Wordsworth Thompson.], Digital surrogates [Rutherford County: Landscapes: Rumbling Bald Mountain, 11-18 April 1874, Harper's Weekly, 313] of originals in image box 037, folder 1313, North Carolina County Photographic Collection, no. P0001, North Carolina Collection Photographic Archives, The Wilson Library, University of North Carolina at Chapel Hill. Public Domain.

SETTLER'S CABIN ON THE SIDE OF BALD MOUNTAIN.-[DRAWN BY A. WORDSWORTH THOMPSON.]

---

138 1 Apr 1874 Article by Editors, *The Morristown Gazette*, 3.

8 APR 1874 Bald Mountain. DISPATCH FROM SAWBONES.[139]

OUR REPORTS IN A HOT PLACE—GEORGE GETS A NEW TEAM AND MORE POWDER—AWFUL TIME JUST AHEAD—LATEST ITEMS OF INTEREST.

To the Editor of the Morristown Gazette:

RIGHT IN THE VOLCANO, April 4.

And mighty hot for your Reporter! It requires a man of nerve to go through with it!

A note just received from George. He has received a fresh team of mules, and a wagon load of powder!

It will be awful from this time out!

Old Major Bender (the illicit distiller who came down from the mountain and was converted,) is in exstacies (sic) since the Revenue officers were scared off!

He supplies George with whisky, and his stills are working to their full capacity!

The nigger[140] preacher and his white assistant retreated, with their flock, to what they considered a safe distance; but after the publication of Prof. Kennedy's startling theory, they took a fresh start, and some of them are as far as Wolfe Creek Depot, Tenn.!

They say that a branch of the Gulf Stream passes under the mountain, and the noise is caused by the rocks 'a drappin' in'!

They think this earth a very unsafe place, anyhow, and want to go to Heaven!

A Narrow Gauge road to that place would do a big business now!

If the lava stream should turn in your direction I will give you timely notice, so that you may be saved!

In the meantime, reflect upon your latter end!

SAWBONES.

About a month later, there are literally people who have travelled from New York to see the phenomenon of the Smoky Mountain volcano! Isham cannot help but to send in another entry…

---

[139] Dr. Isham Peck, Bald Mountain. DISPATCH FROM SAWBONES, *The Morristown Gazette*, 8 Apr 1874, 2.

[140] Personal note from author: "I despise this word, and am saddened that my 3rd great-grandfather used it in any context, but it is included here for historical accuracy."

6 MAY 1874 FROM THE MOUNTAINS – LETTER FROM SAWBONES[141]

LETTER FROM SAWBONES.

GEOLOGICAL SPECIMEN—THE REAL MT. SINAI—WILLING TO DO HIS PART—PROUD OF MOSES—LEFT A GOOD POLITICAL RECORD—WOLF CREEK'S BLUFF—FROZEN FOG—ROCK ISLAND—THE LONG, LONG AGO—CAN'T GIVE UP THE MOUNTAINS—TESTIMONY OF A PREACHER—DEADHEAD PASSES—DODGING WASH ALLEN—LATEST FROM GEORGE—THE SELL ACKNOWLEDGED.

IN THE MOUNTAINS, April 29.

To the Editor of the Morristown Gazette:

I sent you a specimen of geology, merely that you may see it.

Dr. Beik, an Englishman, finding it necessary to his peace of mind that he should find the real Mount Sinai, went with a party to the delectable region known as the Peninsula of Sinai, and they found the Simon-pure-no-mistake Mount: as evidence, they found bones on the side of the Mountain, (where sacrifices had been offered,) and an old clay pipe, on which were Hebrew characters, which being interpreted by the learned Rabbi, Manassa, is – Moses!

There is such a thing as over proving a case!

If any responsible man will believe the pipe part, I will undertake to believe the bones!

I yield to no man in respect to Fore-father Moses!

We see few such men now! His manner of crossing seas, and fetching water from the living rock has seldom been equaled and never excelled!

His head was also very level on the hog question!

But here is what they certainly found. The geology of the mountain is identical with the rock I sent you, color and all. It is feldspar, and nothing but diamond will cut it!

The specimen I send is part of a boulder taken from Wolf Creek. It comes from what we call the Bluff. Wolf Creek comes out of the bluff, and the mountain there rises to four thousand three hundred feet!

I go there sometimes. Everything is magnificent – just as it came from the Great Creator's hands; and the modest descendants of a hairy animal, with pointed ears, have not attempted any improvement there yet. An old hunter told me to go there when the *fog freezes!* He says it hangs from tree to tree!

The Milan Cathedral has been five hundred years building, and not finished yet, with its hundreds of spires pointing the way to heaven. It is but a poor imitation of what we see here!

Figure 77 – Painting of Milan Cathedral / Duomo, "Ansicht des Mailänder Doms. Aquarell/Gouache auf Papier", Circa post 1803, Public Domain, photo enhanced.

---

[141] Dr. Isham Peck, Letter From Sawbones, *The Morristown Gazette*, 6 May 1874, 1.

Figure 78 - Rock Island in the pre-arsenal years, following the Black Hawk War of 1832 with a view of the U.S. Army post Fort Armstrong, circa 1839, by Octave Blair, early Captain with the Corps of Engineers. The painting, which depicts what currently serves as the Rock Island Arsenal, was painted from the Illinois side of the Quad Cities, showing the hills and trees of Davenport in the background. Public Domain.

I read recently in a newspaper of a fellow who went to Heaven. When he told that he was from Rock Island[142], they advised him to go right back!

Now, I happen to know all about Rock Island. It is a pretty place – as beautiful as any place can be without mountains! In the long, long ago, I used to have fine sport catching bass and pike round that Island, and grouse shooting on both sides of the river, where large towns stand now; but I saw cholera doing awful work there in '32 and again in '35! And then they have nothing but limestone water!

Faugh!

People don't leave here to go anywhere, except one man. He hitched his two little oxen to his cart and went to Platte county, Missouri.[143] He made the trip there and back just as quick as it could be made with oxen. When he returned I asked him why he left that fine land and came back to the smoky mountains? He said he did not get a drop of water fit to drink from the time he left till he returned!

A preacher was sent in here once to preach the Word! That chosen

Figure 79 - 1877, Edwards Brothers of Missouri, A drawing of the Platte County Court House in Platte City, Missouri, included in an 1877 plat book of Platte County, Missouri. Public Domain.

vessel did not stay but a few days! He returned to the valley, and when asked if he would again visit the mountains, he said – 'No; the Almighty has nothing against them people!'

I regret you refuse free-passes! Otherwise you could come here in hot weather and go to the Bluff where there are ice cool springs everywhere.

I never held but one free-pass! That was in Wash Allen's canoe across the French Broad. I paddled the canoe myself, and if Wash finds it out, he'll make me pay for it yet!

I told you George would make it lively for them! I saw two victims here Tuesday! They had come all the way from New York to see Old Bald blow out! On the same day when the New York papers

---

142 Isham is likely referring to Rock Island, IL, but if in this reference he is speaking of Rock Island, TN, please see a photo and video from Rock Island, TN, https://tnstateparks.com/parks/rock-island.
143 The author spent from 1994-1999 in Platte County, MO and attended Park Hill High School in that place.

said the earth shook for one hundred miles, *they were on the mountain!* All quiet on old Bald that day! They acknowledge the sell!   SAWBONES.

This letter from Sawbones covers a number of topics, evidenced by its long title. Along with his article, Isham sends a "specimen of geology" that was taken from "The Bluff" at Wolf Creek. The rock he sent was feldspar, and it reminded him of an expedition by one Dr. Beik, an Englishman who claimed to find the real Mount Sinai. See Exodus and Deuteronomy 5 for the Biblical account of the events concerning Moses and the people of Israel.

Feldspar - "Feldspar is the most abundantly found rock forming mineral on Earth. It constitutes about 60% percent of Earth's surface. Feldspar is the foundation of the Earth's surface and even the oceans. It is used to provide strength, as a fluxing agent, reduce production costs and bring in gloss and shine in a finished product. Several popular *gemstones* are Feldspar minerals. These include moonstone, sunstone, labradorite, amazonite and spectrolite."[144]

Figure 80 - Labradorite is a type of Feldspar mineral that exhibits an iridescent play-of-color. Image from Feldspartech.com

Pecks and Geology / Mineralogy - Isham, and his dad, Judge Jacob Peck, were heavy into mineralogy. His dad was a well-known amateur geologist, and one of the mountains in Wolf Creek was even called "Peck's Iron Mountain." See Appendix VII of *Charley's Novel: Mary Anderson and Peacock the Mineralogist*, 2021, for more information and articles about the Pecks and Geology. One article copied there, from 1 Oct 1881, references "Wolf Creek Granite" and the fact that one "Professor Bradley" named Wolf Creek Granite "unakite" because it was not found anywhere else in the world." Also, at least 3 articles between 1878 and 1883 reference gold on Wolf Creek. See Sawbones Resources online for the articles.[145]

Figure 81 - Overlooking the French Broad River at Weaver's Bend, Photo courtesy of C. Bowman, themonkeysmask.weebly.com

Creation – Isham reports that he enjoyed going to the Bluff at Wolf Creek, and admiring God's creation. This is similar to the report of his daughter Helen, who enjoyed going up to possibly the same bluff, and enjoyed reading her books while looking out over the French Broad River and the mountains around her.

---

[144] FeldsparTech Solutions, *What is Feldspar?*, 8 Oct 2020, https://www.feldspartech.com/post/what-is-feldspar
[145] https://www.crossmountainbooks.com/sawbones-resources

Milan Cathedral – Isham says that the Milan Cathedral, also known as The Duomo of Milan, cannot compare to God's creation. This assuredly speaks to one of the reasons that Isham decided to make his final abode Wolf Creek. But his comments were not only referring to Wolf Creek, for he soon moves on to speaking of the beauty of Rock Island, Illinois.

Rock Island, Tennessee – When this author first read Isham's comments about Rock Island, he thought it surely referred to Rock Island, Tennessee. Rock Island State Park sits at the confluence of two rivers and along the old stagecoach road, and is truly a sight to behold. So great was this author's confidence that Rock Island, Tennessee was the place, that he took his family there, despite his wife's weary calls for "another time" at the end of a long road trip. After further research and review, it was discovered that Isham was in fact referring to Rock Island, Illinois, and to his military work there during/after The Black Hawk War of 1832 and later in 1835, when cholera was killing the troops and Native Americans alike. See the *Sawbones: Volume II* Appendix for a brief history of Rock Island State Park. **CMB LIVE: Journey to Rock Island, Tennessee and its beautiful waterfalls with the author and his family.**

Figure 82 - **CMB LIVE**: Journey to Rock Island, Tennessee, https://youtu.be/5K5Q WwgOmAI

Rock Island, Illinois – In 1832 and 1835, the years Isham says he witnessed cholera at Rock Island, there was a U.S. Army Fort called Fort Armstrong sitting where the modern-day Rock Island Arsenal stands. From Wikipedia: The **Rock Island Arsenal** comprises 946 acres (383 ha), located on **Arsenal Island**, originally known as **Rock Island**, on the Mississippi River between the cities of Davenport, Iowa, and Rock Island, Illinois. It lies within the state of Illinois. Rock Island was previously used as the summer camp site for Sauk Native Americans, and the dispute over tribal ownership led to the Black Hawk War of 1832, after the primary leader of the Sauk, Black Hawk. It is now home of First Army headquarters, and the US Army's Center of Excellence for Additive Manufacturing.[3] The island was originally established as a government site in 1816, with the building of Fort Armstrong. It is now the largest government-owned weapons manufacturing arsenal in the United States.[4] It has manufactured military equipment and ordnance since the 1880s."[146]

Clues to the fact that Rock Island, Tennessee was the proper Rock Island include the cholera epidemic, which is noted in numerous newspaper articles and histories of the Black Hawk War, and to Isham's phrase "as beautiful as any place can be without mountains!" Rock Island, Tennessee is quite mountainous. Additionally, this small add on phrase from Isham "but I saw cholera doing awful work there in '32 and again in '35!" gives a huge insight into Isham's whereabouts and activities during the thirties.

Black Hawk War – The Black Hawk War occurred in 1832, and based on Isham words, he was there.

---

[146] Rock Island Arsenal, https://en.wikipedia.org/wiki/Rock_Island_Arsenal, accessed 31 Dec 2022.

Here is a description of the events from Wikipedia: "On June 15, 1832, President Andrew Jackson, displeased with Atkinson's handling of the war, appointed General Winfield Scott to take command.[128] Scott gathered about 950 troops from eastern army posts just as a cholera pandemic had spread to eastern North America.[129] As Scott's troops traveled by steamboat from Buffalo, New York, across the Great Lakes towards Chicago, his men started getting sick from cholera, with many of them dying. At each place the vessels landed, the sick were deposited and soldiers deserted. By the time the last steamboat landed in Chicago, Scott had only about 350 effective soldiers left.[130] On July 29,

Figure 83 - Map of Black Hawk War (1832), Encyclopædia Britannica, Inc.

Scott began a hurried journey west, ahead of his troops, eager to take command of what was certain to be the war's final campaign, but he would be too late to see any combat.[131]"

Dr. Neil Gale, Ph.D. adds the following concerning cholera and General Winfield Scott. "General Winfield Scott - In 1832, President Andrew Jackson ordered Winfield Scott to Illinois to take command of the Black Hawk War conflict. General Winfield Scott led 1,000 troops, to Fort Armstrong, to assist the U.S. Army garrison and militia volunteers stationed there. While General Scott's army was en route, along the Great Lakes, his troops had contracted Asiatic cholera, before they left the state of New York; it killed most of his 1,000 soldiers. Only 220 U.S. Army regulars, from the original force, made the final march, from Fort Dearborn, in Chicago to Rock Island, Illinois. Winfield Scott and his troops likely carried the highly contagious disease with them; soon after their arrival at Rock Island, a local, cholera epidemic broke out, among the whites and Indians, around the area of Fort Armstrong. Cholera microbes were spread, through sewery-type, contaminated water,

Figure 84 - Fort Armstrong, circa 1835, https://drloihjournal.blogspot.com

which mixed with clean drinking water, brought on by poor sanitation practices, of the day. Within eight days, 189 people died and were buried on the island. By the time Scott arrived in Illinois, the conflict had come to a close with the army's victory at the Battle of Bad Axe. Also known as the Bad Axe Massacre it was a battle between Sauk (Sac) and Meskwaki (Fox) Indians and

Figure 85 - Model of Fort Armstrong, Illinois, circa 1835, https://drloihjournal.blogspot.com

United States Army regulars and militia that occurred on August 1st and 2nd of 1832. This final battle of the Black Hawk War took place near present-day Victory, Wisconsin."[147]

Isham "saw cholera doing awful work there in [18]32 and [18]35!" Maybe he was one of the "Army Regulars" who came down from Fort Dearborn with General Scott. We know, from other articles, that he was stationed at Fort Dearborn around this same period.

An article dated 6 Oct 1832 mentions cholera at Rock Island, "FROM THE WEST.—We have been favored with the following extract of a letter from Bellevillve [sic], near St. Louis, in the State of Illinois. It is without date, but its contents show that it is later than any intelligence which has been before received. 'A part of the troops at Rock Island deserted and came down on Friday, in a Mackinaw boat. Two died of cholera on their way down, and several have taken it at Jefferson Barracks, below St. Louis. The boat sunk at the Barracks on her arrival, but all would not do—the awful scourge is near us. It will be in St. Louis in a day or two, and great must be the loss of lives, for there is a great amount of dissipation. The Cholera has been bad at Rock Island. General Scott's troops brought it to our state.'"[148]

Notably, three future presidents took part in the actions surrounding the Black Hawk War, Abraham Lincoln, Col. Zachary Taylor, and Jefferson Davis (CSA). Also, to note, Andrew Jackson was president during the Black Hawk War, and he is the only one Isham claimed to have met and spent time with. Jackson served from 1829 to 1837. Click on the QR code to the right, and then choose "Black Hawk War Phases" for more info about the future presidents' involvement in the war.

Figure 86 – Black Hawk War by James E. Lewis, Jr., Kalamazoo College, https://digital.lib.niu.ed u/illinois/lincoln/topics /blackhawk/intro

Cholera at Rock Island in 1835 - Though it is tempting to share more here about the Black Hawk War, please see QR codes and other sources for lengthy coverage of this frontier conflict. Isham's passing remark mentioned 1832 **and** 1835, and focused on the beauty of the area, and the great hunting and fishing he was able to enjoy. Sadly, 24 years later, Isham would watch helplessly as his daughter Ada died of the same disease. This must have brought back terrible memories for him. See the following article describing the recurrence of cholera in 1835.

---

[147] Neil Gale, Ph.D., The History of Fort Dixon located on the Rock River in the Dixon's Ferry, settlement of Illinois. (1830 -1843), 11 Sep 2018, https://drloihjournal.blogspot.com/2018/09/history-of-fort-dixon-located-along-the-banks-of-the-rock-river-in-the-settlement-of-dixons-ferry-illinois.html.

[148] *Burlington Weekly Free Press*, Burlington, Vermont, 6 Oct 1832, 3.

"The St. Louis Herald of the 14ᵗʰ ult. States, on the authority of a gentleman just from Council Bluffs, that the Cholera was making its ravages among the Pawnee and Otto Indian tribes. A number had died, and many were sick. It was rumored also that the Cholera was prevalent among the Omahaws.

The Cholera has re-appeared at Fort Armstrong, on Rock Island, near the mouth of the Rock river. Up to the 17ᵗʰ of August there had been 67 cases in all—several of them mild, but a majority of them were severe; five deaths had occurred, three of which were new recruits, and two old soldiers."[149]

Figure 87 - Daly, Walter J. "The black cholera comes to the central valley of America in the 19th century - 1832, 1849, and later." *Transactions of the American Clinical and Climatological Association* vol. 119 (2008): 143-52; discussion 152-3.

And also this article about the same topic:

"The Cholera has again broken out among the recruits at Fort Armstrong, on Rock Island, near the mouth of the Rock river. At the latest account there had been 68 cases in all, and five deaths. 'The commanding officer deemed it prudent to evacuate the post temporarily; the greater part of the troops were therefore marched several miles west of the Mississippi and encamped.'"[150]

A 29 Sep 1835 article adds, "The quarters had been stripped of bunks and other fixtures, well whitewashed, and strict police established in the fort, inside and out, and it was hoped the troops might return with safety in two or three weeks. The introduction of the cholera at this time is attributed to the arrival of a detachment of recruits about the middle of July, as not a single case of any kind of disease had occurred prior to their arrival.—Army and Navy Chronicle."[151]

Figure 88 - George Catlin, Rock Island, U.S. Garrison, 1835-1836, oil on canvas, Smithsonian American Art Museum, Gift of Mrs. Joseph Harrison, Jr., 1985.66.328. Cropped by author.

---

149 *Vermont Chronicle*, Bellows Falls, Vermont, 8 Oct 1835, 3.
150 *South Branch Intelligencer*, Romney, West Virginia, 3 Oct 1835, 2.
151 *The Pittsburg Gazette*, Pittsburg, Pennsylvania, 29 Sep 1835, 2.

Isham the Sportsman – Despite the difficulty of watching dozens of soldiers die from cholera around Rock Island, Isham focuses on the hunting and fishing he was able to do there, and the beauty of the place. He caught bass and pike around the Island, and shot grouse on "both sides of the river." As of 2022, Rock Island High School has a Bass Fishing club, so it's still a popular sport in the area.

Figure 90 - Fly-Fishing for Black Bass, National Museum of American History, Publisher Bradlee Whidden, Lithographer Forbes Lithograph Manufacturing Company, Artist Sherman Foote Denton, Harry T. Peters "America on Stone" Lithography Collection, DL.60.2731, date 1890. Painting brightened for this publication by the author. Public Domain.

Isham also read and contributed to *The Spirit of the Times*, a popular sporting newspaper started in 1831.

Figure 89 - Pike, Lake St. John (Ouananiche Fishing), Watercolour over graphite, 1897, Winslow Homer (American, 1836–1910), Courtesy of Harvard Art Museums

Figure 91 – Above: Ruffed Grouse, sometimes called "the king of game birds" because they are swift fliers and make for challenging prey.

Left: Grouse Shooting in Nova Scotia, 1855, from the Illustrated London News, Public Domain.

Life at Fort Armstrong - The following request for commissary items was placed 1 July 1835, with delivery needed to pass through St. Louis by 15 Apr 1836 for Fort Armstrong.

Commissary Request by

	Office of Commissary General of Subsistence At Fort Armstrong, Mississippi River
120	barrels of pork
250	barrels of fresh superfine flour
250	bushels of new white filed beans
1760	pounds of good hard soap
800	pounds of good hard tallow candles
40	bushels of good clean dry salt
450	gallons of good cider vinegar

Similar orders, with different quantities, based on troop populations, were needed for: New Orleans, Baton Rouge, Fort Jessup (25 miles by land from Natchitotches), Fort Towson (mouth of the Chiemichi), Fort Coffee (10 miles above Fort Smith, Arkansas), Fort Gibson (mouth of the Verdigris 140 miles above Fort Coffee, Arkansas), Jefferson Barracks (10 miles below St. Louis), Fort Leavenworth (mouth of Little Platte), Fort Crawford (Prairie du Chien, Mississippi River), Fort Snelling (Saint Peters), Fort Winnebago (on the Fox river, at the portage of the Fox and Ouisconsin rivers), Fort Gratiot, Fort Howard (Green Bay), Fort Brady, Sault de Ste. Marie, Fort Mackinaw, Fort Dearborn (Chicago), Hancock Barracks (Houlton, Maine), Fort Sullivan (Eastport, Maine), Fort Preble (Portland, Maine), Fort Constitution (Portsmouth, NH), Fort Trumball (New London), Fort Walcott (Newport, RI), Governor's Island (New York Harbor), Fort McHenry (Baltimore), Fort Severne (Annapolis), Fort Washington, Fort Monroe (Old Point Crowfort), Fort Johnson (Smithville, NC), Fort Moultrie (Charleston, SC), Oglethorpe Barracks (Savannah, GA), Arsenal (four miles from Augusta, GA), Fort Marion (St. Augustine, FL).

This list gives a fairly comprehensive list of American military posts as they stood in 1835. Additional instructions given to the potential bidders include: "The hogs of which the pork is packed, to be fattened on corn, and each hog to weigh not less than 200 pounds; and, except where the quantity is otherwise designated, will consist of one hog to each barrel, excluding the feet, legs, ear and snout. Side pieces may be substituted for the hams.—The pork is to be carefully packed with Turks' Island Salt, and in pieces not exceeding ten pounds each. The pork to be contained in seasoned heart of white oak or white ash barrels, full hooped.—The Vinegar in iron bound casks; the beans in water-tight barrels; and the soap and candles in strong boxes, of convenient size for transportation. Salt will only be received by measurement of thirty-two quarts to the bushel. The candles to have cotton wicks."[152]

On the same day that Isham's letter was published, the editor of The *Morristown Gazette* writes an article ABOUT Sawbones and his writings…

---

[152] Office of Commissary General of Subsistence, Kentucky Gazette, Lexington, Kentucky, 18 Jul 1835, 2.

6 MAY 1874 SAWBONES. [OLD VICKSBURG RESIDENT'S SULPHUROUS WORDS COVERED AROUND THE COUNTRY].[153]

Another of the inimitable epistles of our correspondent 'Sawbones,' written for our private delectation, graces our first page to-day. The geological specimen accompanying it has been placed in our collection of minerals, though we confess a lack of appreciation for fragments of such crystalline masses of granite, gneiss, porphyry or other volcanic dornicks, compared to the originality and wit of our esteemed friend. His letter of a few weeks since 'About the Volcano; or the Cussedness of Newspaper Humanity,' has had an unprecedented publicity in the newspapers throughout the United States, it was copied by the Nashville, St. Louis, Cincinnati and New York Co-Operative Unions into all their editions, and the more respectable and sturdy home-made journals have nearly all given it a prominent place in their columns, The Vicksburg *Herald*, now before us, introduces it with this editorial preface: The volcano in North Carolina having had a pretty extensive run in the newspapers and on the telegraph lines, an old and esteemed friend of ours, a former resident of this city, well known to all of our old citizens, and now residing in the vicinity of Bald Mountain, North Carolina, has investigated "old Baldy," and the result of his researches have been furnished to the MORRISTOWN, (Tenn.) GAZETTE. The writer is an educated gentleman, who belongs to the profession indicated by his signature, and his amusing account of his ascent of 'old Baldy' will be read with great interest by all the readers of the HERALD. It opens a sulphurous smell, but as his subject is a volcano, 'Sawbones' may be pardoned the use of sulphurous words."

Despite George's pleadings for him to keep quiet, Isham wrote his article, and it was covered from Nashville to St. Louis to Cincinnati to New York!

Rumbling Bald - Listen now to the history given by "Rumbling Bald: Resort on Lake Lure" on their website: "Rumbling Bald Resort takes its name from the beautiful ridges and cliffs of Rumbling Bald Mountain that surround the resort and provide some of the most dramatic scenery in Western North Carolina. Yet the mountain was not always known by its current name. On the evening of February 9, 1874, a local preacher prayed at one such revival for God to move the hearts of sinners by "making the mountain to shake and tremble beneath their feet." The next day, Old Bald began to rumble. For the local people the earthquake-like sounds and trembling created a time of terror. Many sincerely believed that the world was about to end, and local farmers turned out their livestock into the woods, convinced that they would not be around to care for them anymore. Scientists later theorized that the tremors and sounds were caused by rocks falling into the extensive cave system that underlies the mountain. The rumbling continued intermittently for six months, and then the mountain became silent again, and except for very occasional rumbles, has remained so ever since. Folks rounded up their animals again and life went on as before, but the mountain has been known as

---

[153] Editors, "Sawbones," [Old Vicksburg Resident's Sulphurous Words Covered Around the Country] title added by Andy Peck, *The Morristown Gazette*, 6 May 1874, 3.

Shaking Bald, Quaking Bald, and finally Rumbling Bald ever since. For those with a historical bent, the USGS has collected some newspaper clippings about the 1874 rumblings that are worth a read."[154]

The link given in Rumbling Bald's history page takes you to a page called "U.S. Volcanic Eruptions: "Non-Volcano Eruptions" Newspaper Clippings which lists the following regarding our subject.

"March 18, 1874 ... (March 17)

Bald Mountain, North Carolina

Denver Daily Times, Colorado "**THE VOLCANO.** Raleigh, N.C., March 17. -- Passengers from the west, on this morning's train, confirm the reports of the rumbling noises on the surface, and the general upheaving of Bald mountain. The people living on and near the mountain are moving, and a heavy volcanic eruption is expected. Reporters left this afternoon for the mountain to view the scene and to ascertain the extent of the eruption.

New York, March 18. -- A special from Salisbury, N.C., says one report from a scientific source is that the internal noises heard in Bald mountain, resemble those heard in Mount Etna, preparatory to a volcanic eruption. It is heard throughout the county and from a distance of sixteen miles, extending into the adjoining counties. These sounds are not only heard, but a trembling and reverberation of the earth is perceptibly felt. No signs of fire or lava have been discovered.

AMERICAN VOLCANO.

New York, March 17. -- Raleigh, N.C. dispatches say that Bald Mountain, in the Western part of the State, is in a state of volcanic eruption; that houses and cottages on the side, and at the base have been thrown down. The inhabitants in the locality are terror stricken, and are seeking safety in flight. A thin vapor sinks from the top of the mountain, and a low rumbling sound is constantly heard.[155]

---

[154] https://www.rumblingbald.com/blog/3-facts-you-might-not-know-about-rumbling-bald/, accessed on 22 Mar 2020
[155] Colorado's Historic Newspaper Collection Website, 2007.

VOLCANIC DISTURBANCE IN NORTH CAROLINA.

KNOXVILLE, Tenn., March 17.—We have no positive information of the volcanic disturbance reported from Raleigh. It is reported from Ashville as being between that place and Old Fort, and not at the Bald Mountains. The rumbling sounds have been heard and tremors felt frequently during the last two or three weeks for some distance in that vicinity.

THE REPORTS CONFIRMED.

RALEIGH, N. C., March 17.—Passengers from the west on this morning's train confirm the reports of the rumbling noises and the general upheaving of the Bald Mountain in Western Carolina. People living on and near the mountain are moving out, and a volcanic eruption is momentarily expected.

"March 18, 1874 ... (March 17) Bald Mountain, North Carolina

The New York Times, New York

VOLCANIC DISTURBANCE IN NORTH CAROLINA.

KNOXVILLE, Tenn., March 17. – We have no positive information of the volcanic disturbance reported from Raleigh. It is reported from Ashville as being between that place and Old Fort, and not at the Bald Mountains. The rumbling sounds have been heard and tremors felt frequently during the last two or three weeks for some distance in that vicinity.

THE REPORTS CONFIRMED.

RALEIGH, N.C., March 17. – Passengers from the west on this morning's train confirm the reports of the rumbling noises and the general upheaving of the Bald Mountain in Western Carolina. People living on and near the mountain are moving out, and a volcanic eruption is momentarily expected."[156]

For geographical context, see the following snip from Google Maps of the distance from Wolf Creek (where Isham spent much of his time, owned a home, etc…) and where the Bald Mountains of North Carolina are located.[157]

[156] *New York Times* Archives, 2008

[157] Google Maps, https://tinyurl.com/mrxw4rna

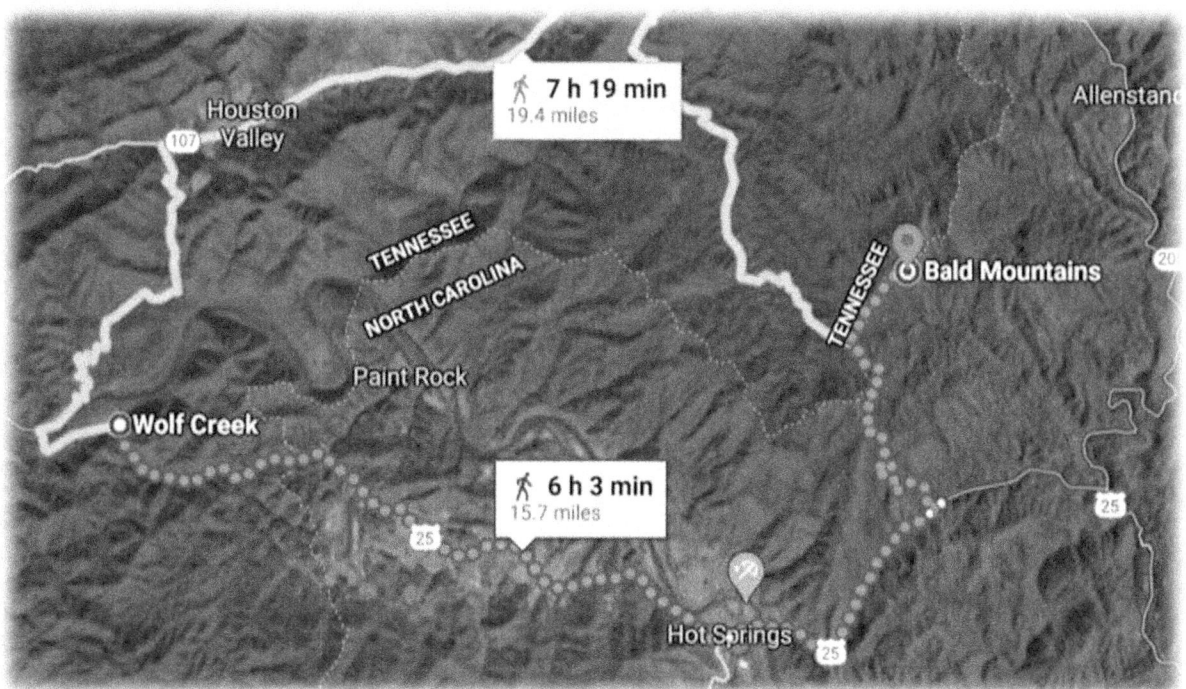

In Google's estimation, one could complete the 15.7-mile hike on foot in about 6 hours, if they take the route through Hot Springs. But Isham was on horseback until he reached the actual mountain, so it wouldn't have taken him nearly as long. Probably a couple hours to get there for him. This makes sense and certainly seems doable for him. Interestingly though, "Rumbling Bald" above the resort on Lake Lure, is much farther away. For comparison's sake, Google Maps estimates the hike to be 77.8 miles and that it would take a person 26 hours on foot.[158] It seems there were multiple mountains where newspaper men and locals claimed to hear "rumblings." All that being said, according to Isham, no mountain in the area had any "natural" rumblings to begin with. The newspaper editors of the day had a field day with the possibility of a volcano in the Smokies, but it was all a sham.

Interestingly, a modern-day newspaper equivalent, the www.visitmysmokies.com blog, published an entire article called "Active Volcano Discovered Under the Great Smoky Mountains" in 2016. It is well-written, and even has a graphic of the blast radius that would affect Gatlinburg and Pigeon Forge…but alas, it was an April Fool's joke, published on April 1st.[159]

Here are some more articles regarding Bald Mountain and Sawbones…

---

[158] https://tinyurl.com/3bxujtjf
[159] "Active Volcano Discovered Under the Great Smoky Mountains", Visit My Smokies.com, 1 Apr 2016,
https://www.visitmysmokies.com/blog/smoky-mountains/active-volcano-discovered-under-great-smoky-mountains/

27 May 1874 "FOR THE MOUNTAINS."[160]

—Prof. Bradley of E[ast]. T[ennessee]. University with his geology class passed through town Saturday on their way to Bald Mountain. We commend them to the kind consideration of our correspondent 'Sawbones,' with the belief that their visit to the mountains will be exceedingly pleasant if they are so fortunate as to meet with that genial gentleman."

FOR THE MOUNTAINS. — Prof. Bradley of E. T. University with his geology class passed through town Saturday on their way to Bald Mountain. We commend them to the kind consideration of our correspondent "Sawbones," with the belief that their visit to the mountains will be exceedingly pleasant if they are so fortunate as to meet with that genial gentleman.

 Professor Frank Howe Bradley (20 Sep 1838 – 27 Mar 1879) graduated Yale College in 1863. He became the Professor of Mineralogy and Geology at East Tennessee University in Knoxville in Sep 1869. He resigned to undertake the development of a gold mine in Northern Georgia in 1875. He died in his gold mine when a bank fell near Nacoochee, Georgia.[161]

Figure 92 - East Tennessee University, Knoxville, 1874. Renamed University of Tennessee in 1869. *Scribner's Monthly*, 1874, 27.

COLLEGE — KNOXVILLE.

---

160 Editor, "For the Mountains," *The Morristown Gazette*, 27 May 1874, 3.
161 Frank Howe Bradley, https://en.wikipedia.org/wiki/Frank_Howe_Bradley, accessed 27 Mar 2023

3 JUN 1874 FROM THE MOUNTAINS. LETTER FROM "SAWBONES."[162] HE IS 'IN AT THE DEATH'—WELCOMES RETURNING MOUNTAINERS—VISITING SCIENTISTS—GEORGE IS FORTUNATELY OUT—WASH ALLEN'S MOUNTAIN HOUSE—THE BANGERS AND THE GRANGERS.

IN THE MOUNTAINS, May 30, 1874. MR. HELMS:- The farce is ended! The lights are out, the curtain down - the wirery spasms have ceased! George has turned out his mules - the old wagon is at the blacksmith shop, and Old Bald has settled down for a long nap! When the inhabitants of Pompeii, who were so fortunate as to escape from the dry rain that subcindered that city, returned to seek their marble palaces they did not find them!

The inhabitants of Old Bald have returned to find their log palaces intact except the smashing of widow Nandy's mud chimney! The natives who *got* religion when destruction was impending, have all backslid, and are worse than they had been! George thinks they are trying to make up for lost time!

George is here - dressed in a suit of store clothes and is using the longest and most unintelligible words I ever heard! He learned them from the scientists who visited the volcano! He has turned scientist himself! He thought of adopting the Farmer's Friend or the Vegetable Bitters business, but he says the Science business is the thing!

He will lecture this summer on the cause of earthquakes, volcanos, origin of man, and such like.

He rejects the Garden of Eden theory and substitutes one of his own, which is both novel and startling! He will lecture in your town and then you will know how it is yourself.

He has adopted the Glazical theory! – has found scratches at the foot of Bald! (His son tells me that all the scratches there were made by widow Nandy's children!)

I saw the Geologists en route for the volcano! They were in uniform, except the Chief, who was distinguished by a remarkably shaped hat! It is known as the Bald mountain hat, and is in shape like the Bald mountain!

The Chief had also a metal box at his side I did not examine it, but I think it is the instrument invented by the late Lieut. Derby, U. S. N. The box contains clock works, with a dial on top. A metal rod about two feet long passes down inside the pants, and is strapped to the leg. The action of the leg when walking operates the machine, and by looking at the dial you can tell how far you have travelled. Derby called it a goometer.

George met them, and is uneasy!

Being in uniform - one of them having a gun – and that strange hat, may induce old Belcher, (the distiller.) to mistake them for Revenue officers! Then there will be trouble?

Besides, rattle snakes are bad this spring!

I look forward with great interest for their report! Old Bald has been playing tricks on the Scientists! There are so many of these that they will surround the mountain and catch her at it! I am glad George is out! Col. Wash, has been after me about that old canoe! (It is the same 'Old Canoe' we read about - in fact, it is suspicioned that Wash wrote that poetry!)

---

[162] Dr. Isham Peck, "From The Mountains: Letter from Sawbones," *The Morristown Gazette*, 3 Jun 1874, 3.

He has repainted and refurnished his hotel, and it is the most pleasant summer retreat in the mountain! I regret the Colonel is unhappy in his domestic relations - in this: that he has no wife of his own!

But he makes out first rate considering!

I see by the papers that the Bible-bangers (the Richmond *Dispatch* during the war, called them 'Hen-Huzzies[163]!') are down on the Grangers!

The Grangers might conclude to winter fewer of that kind of stock hereafter!

These bangers are at the bottom of a heap of devilment hidden behind women's petticoats!

SAWBONES."

The 5 June 1874 Nashville *Union and American* covers the 3 June 1874 article from the *Gazette*, but reduces its size and ends the story after this line, "There are so many of these that they will surround the mountain and catch her at it!" The end of the article references George, Col. Wash, talks about "Bible-bangers" and the Grangers. This may have been too personal and too local for them to want to publish…plus the language of "Bible-bangers" would probably have been incendiary to their readership.

Sawbones Turns to Other Topics

The next article doesn't appear until July 29, 1874 and begins to take on topics unrelated to Bald Mountain.

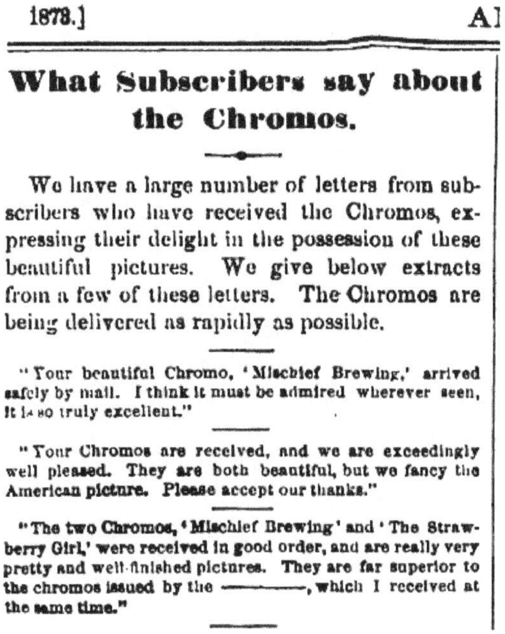

1873.]   A]

What Subscribers say about the Chromos.

We have a large number of letters from subscribers who have received the Chromos, expressing their delight in the possession of these beautiful pictures. We give below extracts from a few of these letters. The Chromos are being delivered as rapidly as possible.

"Your beautiful Chromo, 'Mischief Brewing,' arrived safely by mail. I think it must be admired wherever seen. It is so truly excellent."

"Your Chromos are received, and we are exceedingly well pleased. They are both beautiful, but we fancy the American picture. Please accept our thanks."

"The two Chromos, 'Mischief Brewing' and 'The Strawberry Girl,' were received in good order, and are really very pretty and well-finished pictures. They are far superior to the chromos issued by the ————, which I received at the same time."

Figure 93 - Chromo Ad - *The Agriculturist*, 1873, 239

---

[163] Hen-Huzzy/Hen-Hussy: a) A man who performs tasks that traditionally belong to a woman., b) a man who meddles with women's affairs. Reference: wiktionary.org and finedictionary.com

"CHROMOS AND CREATURES.

AN UNSOPHISTICATED MOUNTAINEER SENDS US A SPECIMEN CHROMO WITH A PUNGENT CRITICISM ON NEW YORK CHROMOS AND CREATURES.

To the Editor of the Morristown Gazette:

I sent to New York sometime ago for a picture paper for the children, and they sent me the thing accompanying this note for what they call the 'premium chromo!' Look at the — thing dispassionately! Did you ever see such a specimen of art before? Is there some one in your office who can efface the wings and substitute a gun or pistol? And the old woman would look much more comfortable with a pipe in her mouth! The face and attitude of the angel is exactly that of Nancy Sykes, as we see her in Oliver Twist!

Figure 94 – 1873, "Love or Duty" chromolithograph of a painter and a nun; published in Paris by Hangard-Mangué. His painting of a family is symbolic of what he offers her should she break her vows. Painter Gabriele Castagnola (1828-1883). Public Domain

The papers are filled with the Tilton-Beecher nastiness! The police should take the case and if he and the lamb are guilty, give them six months in the workhouse! Some time since Beecher said the South had been robbed enough; but his congregation went for him, and he immediately apologized, said he did not mean it that he only sloshed over!

The doings of these old clerical bucks make mighty interesting family reading! Tilton, it appears, did not consider the lamb damaged, as he continued to live with her! It reminds me of an incident of years ago, when the Mahomedans pitched into the Druses and Christians, at Mount Lebanon and Damascus, wiping out about forty thousand. A Yankee missionary wrote that the heathens had ravished his wife and sisters and ruined the *running gear of a good clock!* He laid great stress on the clock! SAWBONES."

---

[164] Dr. Isham Peck, "Chromos and Creatures," *The Morristown Gazette*, 29 Jul 1874, 1.

"Premium Chromo" is a reference to a premium chromolithograph…which is a picture produced by chromolithography.[165]

Figure 96 - Henry Ward Beecher, circa 1878

Figure 95 - Elizabeth Richards Tilton, circa 1870

"Love or Duty", on the previous page, is a chromolithograph of a painter and a nun; published in Paris by Hangard-Mangué.[166] His painting of a family is symbolic of what he offers her should she break her vows. It was painted by Gabriele Castagnola in 1873, just one year before Isham wrote his article on "Chromos and Creatures."[167]

Henry Ward Beecher was the brother of Harriet Beecher Stowe, author of Uncle Tom's Cabin, and also a very famous Congregationalist preacher. Wikipedia has an excellent article on him…explaining that he was a supporter of the abolition of slavery, he emphasized God's love in his preaching, and coverage for his 1875 adultery trial was extensive.[168] The photo of him here was taken around 1878, the year he was appointed chaplain of the New York National Guard's 13th Regiment.[169] Other photos of him available online show him appearing younger with softer features. Elizabeth Richards Tilton was an American suffragist, a founder of the Brooklyn Women's Club, and a poetry editor of *The Revolution*, the newspaper of the National Woman Suffrage Association.[170]

Instead of trying to summarize this complicated case of Beecher and Tilton, I defer to the summary description found on Amazon for the book *The Most Famous Man in America: The Biography of Henry Ward Beecher."* It reads,

"No one predicted success for Henry Ward Beecher at his birth in 1813. The blithe, boisterous son of the last great Puritan minister, he seemed destined to be overshadowed by his brilliant siblings—especially his sister, Harriet Beecher Stowe, who penned the century's bestselling book *Uncle Tom's Cabin.* But when pushed into the ministry, the charismatic Beecher found international fame by shedding his father's Old Testament–style fire-and-brimstone theology and instead preaching a New Testament–based gospel of unconditional love and

---

165 https://en.wikipedia.org/wiki/Chromolithography
166 https://en.wikipedia.org/wiki/Chromolithography#/media/File:Love_or_dutyb.jpg
167 https://en.wikipedia.org/wiki/Gabriele_Castagnola
168 https://en.wikipedia.org/wiki/Henry_Ward_Beecher#%22The_Beecher-Tilton_Scandal_Case%22_(1875)
169 https://en.wikipedia.org/wiki/New_York_Army_National_Guard
170 https://en.wikipedia.org/wiki/Elizabeth_Richards_Tilton

Figure 97 – Testimony in the great Beecher-Tilton scandal case illustrated / des. & drawn by James E. Cook 46 Desplaines St.; Commercial Lith. Co. 180 Clark St., circa 1875, LOC, http://hdl.loc.gov/loc.pnp/cph.3c21959

healing, becoming one of the founding fathers of modern American Christianity. By the 1850s, his spectacular sermons at Plymouth Church in Brooklyn Heights had made him New York's number one tourist attraction, so wildly popular that the ferries from Manhattan to Brooklyn were dubbed "Beecher Boats."

Beecher inserted himself into nearly every important drama of the era—among them the antislavery and women's suffrage movements, the rise of the entertainment industry and tabloid press, and controversies ranging from Darwinian evolution to presidential politics. He was notorious for his irreverent humor and melodramatic gestures, such as auctioning slaves to freedom in his pulpit and shipping rifles—nicknamed "Beecher's Bibles"—to the antislavery resistance fighters in Kansas. Thinkers such as Emerson, Thoreau, Whitman, and Twain befriended—and sometimes parodied—him.

And then it all fell apart. In 1872 Beecher was accused by feminist firebrand Victoria Woodhull of adultery with one of his most pious parishioners. Suddenly the "Gospel of Love" seemed to rationalize a life of lust. The cuckolded husband brought charges of "criminal conversation" in a salacious trial that became the most widely covered event of the century, garnering more newspaper headlines than the entire Civil War. Beecher survived, but his reputation and his causes—from women's rights to progressive evangelicalism—suffered devastating setbacks that echo to this day.

Featuring the page-turning suspense of a novel and dramatic new historical evidence, Debby Applegate has written the definitive biography of this captivating, mercurial, and sometimes infuriating figure. In our own time, when religion and politics are again colliding and adultery in high places still commands headlines, Beecher's story sheds new light on the culture and conflicts of contemporary America."[171]

Isham was tired of hearing about this sordid affair and decided to write about it!

There is a nearly a four month lull in the articles from Sawbones, and then we find a note about another newspaper, *The Daily Graphic*, wanting to hire Sawbones to write for their paper as well, but how the editor of the Gazette "persuades" him to just pay for the privilege of copying their Sawbones articles.[172]

---

[171] https://www.amazon.com/Most-Famous-Man-America-Biography/dp/0385513976
[172] https://en.wikipedia.org/wiki/The_Daily_Graphic, accessed 22 Mar 2020

"Col. Lee Crandall, one of the most whole-souled, genial gentlemen, and the best off-had stump speaker belonging to the State of Alabama, now connected with the New York *Daily Graphic*, was a passenger on Sunday's eastern train, bound for the *Graphic* office. He halted long enough to tell us he had secured 'Sawbones' as a regular contributor to his paper; but when we threatened to bust up Wash. Allen with damage suits if the thing wasn't stopped, he came to more satisfactory conclusions, and pays handsomely to copy from the GAZETTE."

This historical note about Col. Lee Crandall shows the people that Isham associated with, and those who sought him out. Here is info about Col. Crandall after his death at 94 years of age in 1926. **Col. Lee Crandal** - "NOTE: Col Crandall's records contain a newspaper clipping from a Washington, D. C. newspaper, including his picture, dated Monday, September 13, 1926. And reads as follows:

COL. LEE CRANDALL DIES AT AGE 94

CONFEDERATE VETERAN AND OLDEST FEDERAL
EMPLOYEE WAS ILL ONLY TWO DAYS

Col. Lee Crandall, aged 94, a soldier of the Confederacy who later served his reunited States as loyally as he had served the cause of the South in the Civil War, died yesterday morning at his home, 1822 Calvert street. He was the oldest Federal Government employee.

Death came as a result of a severe cold recently contracted. Which kept him away from his Federal duties last Friday and Saturday, the only two days of absence on account of sickness in his more than 12 years of service as deputy collector of internal revenue. In those 12 years Col. Crandall took only 5 days of annual leave, whereas he was

---

[173] Editors, "New York Daily Graphic Tries to Hire Sawbones", title by Andy Peck, *The Morristown Gazette*, 11 Nov 1874, 3.

entitled to 30 days each year. He was located in the offices at 1423 Pennsylvania Ave.

A man of unusual vigor for his age, the sturdy veteran time after time had proven himself superior in strength to men of much younger years. On the occasion of the funeral of President Harding, Col. Crandall, through the sweltering heat of that sad day, toiled the full length of the funeral march up Pennsylvania Ave from the White House to the Capitol, wearing the warm woolen gray uniform of a confederate colonel. He kept on, trudging up the hill at the Capitol, where many veterans of the World War had dropped out of line, overcome by the heat. He was always at his office early and was known among his associates for his tireless activity.

Loyal to Modern Youth

Full of enthusiasm and faith in the younger generation, was known for his energetic gestures while conversing. He would slap his hand down on a table or pound his knee with great gusto while relating an incident and never complained of ill health.

His death cuts short hopes he had cherished for years of celebrating his one hundredth birthday and the two hundredth George Washington anniversary now in prospect.

It was Col Crandall's pride that he served as confidential staff officer to Gen. "Stonewall" Jackson and during Jackson's campaign in the Valley of Virginia was the only aide permitted to enter the general's tent, day or night on special business.

His love for the Confederacy and his pride in the wounds and imprisonment he suffered as a soldier of the South were matched by his devotion to his reunited country of today and his respect for the modern youth and life.

"The girl of today," according to Lee Crandall, in an interview on his recent last birthday, "despite her short skirts, her cigarette case, her lipstick and her penchant for the Charleston, is just as good morally and mentally as the more demure young lady of the days of the long dress and the minuet."

"No sir," he insisted at that time, "I don't believe in all this talk about the world getting worse. I've lived a long time and watched a lot of generations grow up, and I will stick to my contention that times are improving right along."

THE DAILY GRAPHIC

Temperate in his diet, Col. Crandall for years had abstained from meat, was fond of soups and milk, and religiously drank every morning before breakfast a pint of warm water.

Born in New York

Born in 1832 at South Berlin, N.Y., Col. Crandall went South and entered the Confederate army as captain of Company I of the 8th Louisiana Infantry. He took part in the first battle of Bull Run. He was with Gen. Jackson through the Valley of Virginia, and at Cross Keys was wounded in the wrist. He was promoted to major by Gen.

Jackson and later the Confederate secretary of war ordered him to report to Gen. Price at Little Rock. He was made colonel of the 47th 'Arkansas' Cavalry, organized there, which was in the raids through Kansas. At Mine Creek, Col. Crandall, with five other field officers, was captured by the Union forces and sent to Johnson's Island, Ohio, where he remained a prisoner until the close of the war.

Afterward Col. Crandall lived in Louisiana for a while and was a delegate from that State to the post-war commercial convention in 1868 at Memphis. He later lived in Louisiana, Alabama and Philadelphia where he represented the old New York Daily Graphic, and later came to Washington, where he founded the National View. This paper he edited until 1895, championing the causes of the American Bimetallic League, of which he one time was secretary.

He went to Arizona and took part in politics, but returned to Washington. In 1914 he was appointed deputy collector of internal revenue.

Funeral services will be held at the home tomorrow afternoon at 1 o'clock, in charge of Robert E. Lee Camp, Confederate Veterans, before the body is taken to Arlington Cemetery for interment."[174]

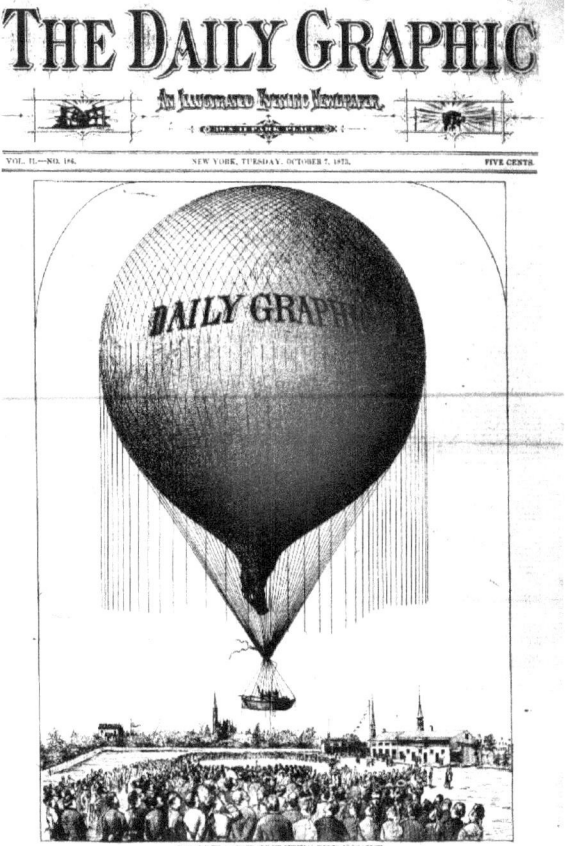

Figure 98 - Front page of the Daily Graphic (New York), 7 October, 1873, showing the ascent of Washington Donaldson's unsuccessful attempt sponsored by the newspaper to cross the Atlantic. Public Domain. https://en.wikipedia.org/wiki/The_Daily_Graphic#/media/File:Daily_Graphic_7_October_1873.png

One week after the publication of the article regarding Col. Crandall, Sawbones writes again!

[174] 47TH (CRANDALL'S) ARKANSAS CAVALRY REGIMENT, http://www.couchgenweb.com/civilwar/47thf&s.html, originally from National Archives, accessed on 22 Mar 2020

18 NOV 1874 LETTER FROM "SAWBONES." – [WOLF CREEK INN, GEORGE PRENTICE, AND VICKSBURG EDITORS!][175]

A MOMENTOUS DAY—OLD BALD COMES TO TIME—WASH. ALLEN STANDS A SIEGE—GEORGE D. PRENTICE, &c., &c.

MR. HELMS : —The 3d was the greatest day since the day of the upsetting of them tables in the Temple!

The scoundrels will now take to their dens, and the scum will go to the bottom!

Did you hear me yelling?

It is but forty miles. You might have heard me but I suppose you were hard at it yourself!

We had no gun, but we got up steam on old Bald, and she is doing her best! The victory was so great and so unexpected that we were not prepared as we were last summer!

We had an army of preachers here on their way to the mountains. Each had a large carpet-bag stuffed full. I supposed they were filled with the glad tidings of salvation, until one fell from the stage and burst open and filled the road with fried chicken and ball biscuit!

The first thing on leaving the train was to eat everything in the bags! They then made a rush for the hotel!

And such pushing and crowding!

The landlady says she has seen soldiers and hog-drivers eat, but they are insignificant in interest to a crowd like this! (Judge Longstreet tells us of a sand-lapper, at a crowded hotel, who kept yelling, 'more cowcumbers!' 'more cowcumbers!' until the landlord took him by the coat collar and 'dragged him on the outside!" One of the chosen vessels kept yelling 'more coffee!' at this place until the landlady was making arrangements to have him 'drapped out!' when he subsided!

Wash. has rules for his hotel, from which he never deviates! He speaks it out so that all can hear!

Preachers pay for dinner 25 cents, but gentleman ante to the tune of 50 cents!

My opinion as regards Wash's chance for salvation is the same as that expressed by Father Fatsides in Dalgetty's case!

I have not heard much from up the country, except that the corn is frost bitten and the hogs are dying of cholera. It is thought the disease was introduced there.

I see you are in partnership with the *Courier-Journal*. I was a subscriber for that paper up to two years ago, when them fellers said the Democratic party was dead. Then I quit!

I was one of many who gave Geo. D. Prentice a public dinner at a Louisville hotel, on his first appearance at Louisville. The acquaintance continued as long as he lived.

As a fighter, he was not a success! I witnessed his fight with George Trotter. His fight with (free) Tom Moore, at Harrodsburg, was no better!

The Vicksburgh editors were the boys for a fight! I could write all day, giving my experience there. But enough.

Sawbones."

---

[175] Dr. Isham Peck, "Letter from Sawbones," [WOLF CREEK INN, GEORGE PRENTICE, AND VICKSBURG EDITORS!] title addition by Andy Peck, *The Morristown Gazette*, 18 Nov 1874, 2.

Mr. Helms refers to John E. Helms, editor and publisher of *The Morristown Gazette*. A personal profile for Mr. Helms follows from *Tennessee: The Volunteer State, 1769-1923, Vol 4* by John Trotwood Moore, Austin Powers Foster.

Figure 99 - Col. John Edward Helms (1827-1906), Courtesy of Joe Moore, Hamblen County Historian

John Helms, Morristown Gazette Editor

"JOHN E. HELMS. John E. Helms, editor and publisher, and who recently retired as postmaster of Morristown, was born in Knoxville on the 2d of August, 1857. His forefathers were of English stock, his ancestors having come to this country and settled in Frederick county, Virginia. His forebear, Rev. John Helms, was born in Winchester, Virginia, about 1740. He was a pioneer Methodist minister and is said to have been the first west of the Alleghany mountains. He settled in Fincastle, Virginia, and died in Botetourt county in 1821. The subject of this sketch was the son of John Edward and Margaret Lones Helms. His father was one of the most prominent men of his day. A native of Fincastle, Virginia, born in 1827, he came to Tennessee as a mere boy and located in Claiborne county. Later he removed to Knoxville, where he learned the printer's trade under E. G. Eastman, in the Knoxville Standard office. Completing his apprenticeship, he engaged in the newspaper business, publishing the Knoxville Plebian and other papers in that city before the Civil war. In 1873 he came to Morristown. purchasing The Morristown Gazette, in the conduct of which he was active until a short time before his demise. He was principal clerk of the Tennessee state senate in 1874 and 1876; was secretary of the first railroad commission in this state; was a member of the Tennessee Historical Society and president of the Tennessee Press Association. Mr. Helms was postmaster of Knoxville one term prior to the Civil war. He was a veteran of the Mexican war. One of his brothers, Rev. William S. Helms, served as a chaplain in the Confederate army. Mr. Helms was prominent in fraternal circles and had the distinction of being the first man to be initiated into the Independent Order of Odd Fellows in East Tennessee. In Knoxville was celebrated the marriage of Mr. and Mrs. Helms. Mrs. Helms was born and reared in Knox county, a member of one of the pioneer families of this section of the state. To the union of Mr. and Mrs. Helms eight children were born, four sons and four daughters, two sons and four daughters living, John E. being the fourth in order of birth.

The private schools of Knoxville afforded John E. Helms his early education. When he was sixteen years of age he entered the printing business in association with his

Figure 100 - Margaret Lawson (Lones) Helms (1828-1878), Photo courtesy of Joe Moore, Hamblen County Historian, and the Hamblen County TN History Facebook Group

father, becoming joint publisher with him of The Morristown Gazette. He purchased his father's interest in the paper and conducted it on his own account until he was appointed by President Wilson postmaster of Morristown in 1914, which position he filled for eight years and four months. The paper is now being published by John E. Helms, Jr. It was consolidated with the Evening Mail of Morristown and is now being issued as a daily under the name of The Daily Gazette and Mail. It is Morristown's only daily newspaper and it contains extensive advertising. Its circulation is large and steadily increasing, extending throughout Hamblen and the adjoining counties. John E. Helms, Jr., represents the third generation of the family in newspaper circles. In politics, Mr. Helms is a democrat. He served as a member of the state democratic committee in 1910-11-12 and was chairman for six years of the democratic congressional committee of the second district. He was alderman of Morristown for three terms, frequently acting as mayor pro tem.

On the 11th of June, 1890, was celebrated the marriage of Mr. Helms and Miss Mary Whiteside, who was born in Chattanooga, Tennessee, November 15, 1866. She is a daughter of Foster and Miranda Whiteside, highly esteemed residents of Morris town. To their union three children have been born: Margaret is the wife of J. H. Richardson of Hawkins county, and they are now living in Greeneville, South Carolina. Harris W. is engaged in the Insurance business in Morristown. John E., Jr., is publisher of The Gazette and Mail. He married Constance O'Keefe of Greeneville, who is associated with him in the publication of the paper. Harris served in the army of the World war, and John in the navy.

The religious faith of Mr. Helms is that of the Methodist Episcopal church, South, and for a number of years he was active as a member of the board of stewards of that church. Retiring as postmaster, due to a change in the national administration, Mr. Helms has resumed his newspaper vocation and is assisting his son in the editorial work of The Daily Gazette and Mail."[176]

Figure 101 – Home of Col. John E. Helms, built 1868, photo taken by Joe Moore circa Feb 2022. Courtesy of Joe Moore, Hamblen County Historian. Address: 400 E 2nd N St/ Morristown, TN 37814

[176] *Tennessee: The Volunteer State, 1769-1923, Illustrated, Volume IV,* Chicago, Nashville, The S. J. Clarke Publishing Co., 1923, 925-926, http://tinyurl.com/JohnHelms, accessed 22 Mar 2020.

Please see the *Sawbones: Volume II* APPENDIX IV: HISTORY OF THE MORRISTOWN GAZETTE for additional information about John Helms and *The Morristown Gazette*.

There are numerous family connections to this Helms' family history. Isham's grandpa, Adam Peck, Sr. was born in Fincastle, Botetourt County, Virginia, the same place where John Helms' father lived before moving to Tennessee. In addition, Helms' grandfather was a pioneer of Methodism, and Isham's uncle Moses Looney Peck was active in the Methodist ministry as well. Isham's grandfather Adam founded the first Methodist church (Elizabeth Chapel) in the area (Mossy Creek) and installed his slave Uncle John Peck as its pastor. Isham must have felt like he had a kindred spirit in John Helms, and this may have been an additional reason he felt comfortable to send in his articles to the paper.

Figure 102 - "Old Stage Coach Inn and Drovers' Stand, The Allen Inn, Wolf Creek, Cocke County, Tennessee", Clifton Johnson, Highways and Byways

The next person mentioned is Isham's good friend George Washington "Wash" Allen. The home that Isham and Emma built in Wolf Creek, was very close to the Allens. In addition, Emma Peck and Emma Allen were the best of friends, and so extended time is warranted establishing the connection between "the Pecks and the Allens (in the words of Ms. Betty Walker)."

Glen Ada, where they located their home, may have been situated on a Tennessee land grant dated 7 Jun 1830 in Isham's name. Multiple land grants were executed on that date for Isham, his brother Adam, and other family members, connected to lands owned by Judge Jacob Peck.

The following article by Iris Wagner speaks about The Wolf Creek Inn and history of the area.

Old Stage Coach Inn and Drovers' Stand

The Allen Inn, Wolf Creek, Cocke County, Tennessee

by Iris Teta Eubank Wagner

3rd great-granddaughter of Margaret Hoss Wolf [177]

"Published genealogical records are uncertain as to the man's name who built the original small cabin in Cocke County, Tennessee, where Wolf Creek flows into the French Broad River. I have not found specific documents to prove my theory, yet accumulated circumstantial evidence shows my third great grandparents to be William Wolf and his wife, Margaret Hoss Wolf, and that they built the small cabin in the late 1790's. Their small log cabin was later covered with siding and it is shown attached to the larger structure, the Allen Inn, in the photo above, taken in the late 1800's. Fanny Hoss Wolf was a daughter of Margaret Wolf and, by my theory - William Wolf. Fanny was born September 5, 1811, wife of James Allen, born September 16, 1806, son of "John, the Bricklayer" Allen, known as Jack Allen. James and Fanny were married January 15, 1827. They lived at Cosby, Tennessee, near Jack Allen. [...]

Reubin Allen family built the Drovers' Stand & Inn

In the photo above, the long extension to the right of the smaller cabin structure was known as the Allen Inn and Drovers' Stand, built in the 1820's. Descendants through the Reubin Allen family were owners and proprietors of the inn until the inn itself was destroyed by fire in 1975.

The inn was built in the decade of the 1820's during which the road through the French Broad River Valley to North Carolina was completed. The road connected Knoxville, Tennessee, with Asheville, North Carolina. The new road brought heavy drover traffic through the valley, and the road was also the main stage coach route for travelers between Knoxville and Asheville, and farther south. The new road completed in 1828 connected to the Buncombe Turnpike at Asheville.

With the completion of the Buncombe Turnpike, the drover traffic increased year by year. George Washington "Wash" Allen, son of Reubin and Mary, managed the inn with his mother after the death of Reubin, who died in 1825.

---

[177] Iris Teta Eubank Wagner, *Old Stage Coach Inn and Drovers' Stand,*
https://www.ancestraljourneys.website/allen_inn_wolf_creek_story.htm, accessed 4 Dec 2022.

From his visit to the Allen Inn in the late 1800's, travel author Clifton Johnson wrote in his book *Highways & Byways*, "In those old days the thoroughfare . . . was enlivened with constant traffic, and the dwellers along the way could rarely look out on it and not see some passing team or horseback rider."

Figure 103 - Home of John "Jack" Allen, Cocke County, TN

George Washington "Wash" Allen operated the Drovers' Stand and Stage Coach Inn at Wolf Creek

The Allen Inn was an inviting overnight stay for weary travelers at the end of the day. The Allen family provided comfortable rooms at the inn and good corral and feeding for them.[178] Among my grandmother Fanny's archived papers, I found a list of stands (below) that were located along the old drovers' road from Wolf Creek "Wash" Allen Inn to John Collett's in Anderson, South Carolina. My grandmother and Charlie B. Mims of Newport were correspondents, and he provided my grandmother with this list of stands and inns.

After decades of growing prosperity, in the later years of the 19th into the early 20th century, the Allen Inn evolved into an hospitable, peaceful place to which artists, writers, and tourists came to stay for a few days, a week, or live for a summer. There were fewer stock drives - stock was being shipped by rail car to markets in the south. When the Civil War began, railroad construction through the valley to North Carolina halted at Wolf Creek until the end of the war. When construction was resumed it took another few years for completion to Asheville. Stage coach travel was discontinued after the railroad was completed into North Carolina about 1883.

(below) This photo of the Allen Inn is from the late 19th or early 20th century at a time after the railroad was completed through the French Broad Valley from Knoxville to Asheville. The Inn was host to well-known artists and writers and dignitaries known nationally as well as regionally.

---

[178] Learn more about the Buncombe Turnpike at Anchor, a North Carolina History Online Resource, *The Buncombe Turnpike*, https://www.ncpedia.org/anchor/buncombe-turnpike, accessed 5 Sep 2023.

This photo was published with an article written by Betty Walker, widow of Ward Walker, great-great grandson of Reubin Allen and wife Mary Jones. The article by Mrs. Walker was published in October, 2003 in *The Newport Plain Talk*, the county newspaper. In the same

Figure 105 - Wolf Creek Inn, published in the *Newport Plain Talk* in Oct 2003

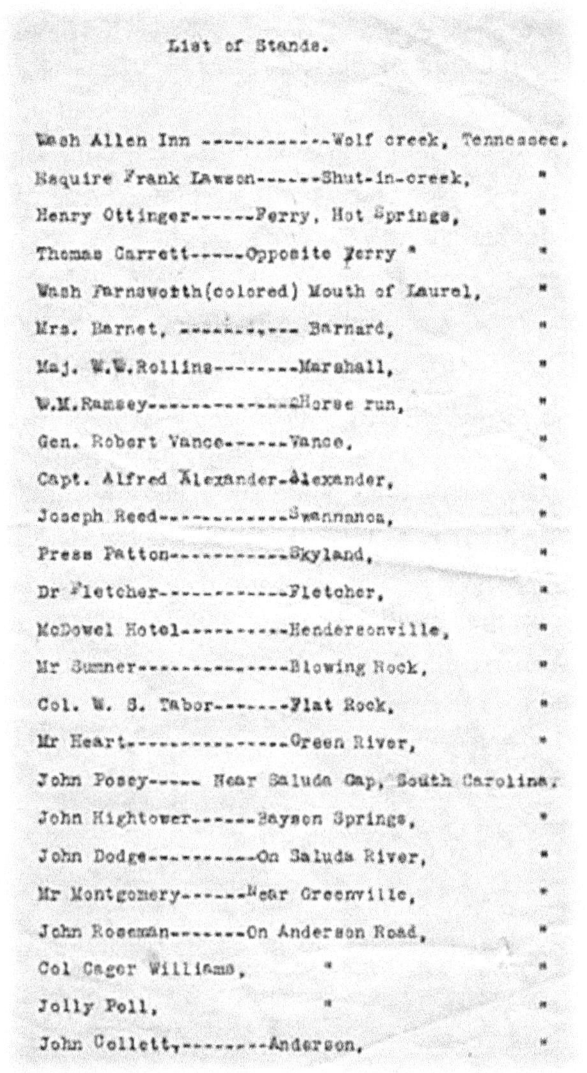

issue, Mrs. Walker wrote a quite thorough history of the railroad coming to Newport and Wolf Creek.

Back when the passenger train stopped at Wolf Creek Station, just a few hundred feet from the French Broad River, travelers disembarking there followed a short path to the waiting hospitality at the inn. My mother remembered a visit to the inn in the summer of 1927. She held memories of a beautiful, historic place shaded by tall evergreen spruce and hemlock, and the soft rushing of Wolf Creek – she was lulled to sleep in the feather bed, in her front room above the creek.

The descendants of Reubin and Mary Jones Allen developed this place through the 19th and into the 20th century. They designed and developed and cared for the ornamental gardens - and boxwoods and rose bushes, flowers and herbs. English ivy covered the grounds. […]

The Allens establish their inn at Wolf Creek in the early 1820's

Not knowing facts about the circumstances of Reubin Allen's family when they came to live at Wolf Creek in the early 1820's, I would think that they saw an economic opportunity in establishing a tavern and inn along the drovers'

List of Stands.

Wash Allen Inn -------------Wolf creek, Tennessee.
Esquire Frank Lawson--------Shut-in-creek,   "
Henry Ottinger------Ferry, Hot Springs,   "
Thomas Garrett------Opposite Ferry *   "
Wash Farnsworth(colored) Mouth of Laurel,   "
Mrs. Barnet, ------------- Barnard,   "
Maj. W.W.Rollins--------Marshall,   "
W.M.Ramsey---------------Horse run,   "
Gen. Robert Vance------Vance,   "
Capt. Alfred Alexander-Alexander,   "
Joseph Reed------------Swannanoa,   "
Press Patton-----------Skyland,   "
Dr Fletcher------------Fletcher,   "
McDowel Hotel----------Hendersonville,   "
Mr Sumner--------------Blowing Rock,   "
Col. W. S. Tabor-------Flat Rock,   "
Mr Heart---------------Green River,   "
John Posey----- Near Saluda Gap, South Carolina.
John Hightower------Bayson Springs,   "
John Dodge----------On Saluda River,   "
Mr Montgomery-------Near Greenville,   "
John Roseman--------On Anderson Road,   "
Col Cager Williams,   "   "
Jolly Poll,   "   "
John Collett,--------Anderson,

Figure 104 - List of Drovers' stands from the "Wash Allen Inn" in Wolf Creek to John Collett's Stand in Anderson, SC Image courtesy of the Fanny Swagerty Eubank archive

road through the French Broad valley that would connect to the Buncombe Turnpike, already under construction north of Asheville just across the mountain in western North Carolina that would lead to roads south of Asheville into South Carolina. They likely bought the place from Margaret Wolf. The county courthouse fire in Newport in late 19th century destroyed records that would have told us.

There is no known specific document to reveal the name of Margaret's husband. We don't know for sure what happened to him. However, on the 1820 Buncombe County, North Carolina census, there is entered a man named William Wolf, born between 1775-1794, a young female 16-26, and 3 young children under 10 years of age."

The following is the article that Ms. Betty Walker wrote about the Allen Inn, eventually known as the Wolf Creek Stagecoach Inn. It appeared in January 1986 issue (Volume 25, No. 3, Pages 66-67) issue of *The Boxwood Bulletin*. Reprinted here with permission from the author.

WOLF CREEK-AN OLD STAGECOACH INN SURROUNDED BY BOXWOODS

By Betty M. Walker

Reuben Allen came from Rockingham County, Virginia in the mid 1700s to a section of Tennessee now known as Cocke County. Reuben liked this mountain country. He built a log house, 90 by 40 feet, with four chimneys, a great porch, and a 'dog trot' Mr. Allen went back to Virginia in 1805 and married Mary (Polly) Jones, a relative of Admiral Nelson. In the same year he brought his bride home to the Smokies of Tennessee.

Figure 106 - The Allen House – Wolf Creek Stagecoach Inn – in the 1890s.

A few years before Allen's arrival in Tennessee a Frenchman from Canada, named Wolfe, built a small cabin beside a bubbling creek in the area. The creek bordering the front of Wolfe's property, which later became Reuben Allen's property, was soon known as Wolf Creek. This creek emptied into the mighty French Broad River about one-fourth of a mile from the Allen home.

Over the next twenty years ten children were born to Mary and Reuben Allen. Emma Allen, one of the young daughters, was a natural artist. She designed the boxwood garden on the east side of the two-story house. Emma used the Mount Vernon Gardens for her model. She combined the common box for the borders with the dwarf box for the geometric designs. Emma used the common box on each side of the paths leading to the spring house, the barn, the school house and the cabins which housed guests when the 13-room house was filled. A single path led toward the railroad and the French Broad River and to the cemetery where today one

Figure 107 - A picture taken in the Wolf Creek gardens around 1890.

finds the graves of Reuben Allen, his wife, several of Reuben's children and David Ward Allen, Reuben's nephew who became owner of the Allen home in the late 1800s. David's wife, Maggie, and their five children are also buried among the many boxwoods in the family cemetery.

After the boxwoods were well established, with many fragrant blooming flowers planted in the centers of the designs, a sister of Emma Allen died in Arkansas. The funeral cortege of the deceased sister was traveling slowly to Wolf Creek. While traveling through the swamp area of Arkansas, Cynthia Cowan broke several branches of bald cypress to be used as funeral greenery. Seeing a small cypress seedling, she pulled it up. Upon arriving at Wolf Creek, Cynthia planted the cypress seedling in a circle of boxwood in the formal garden. Today, that bald cypress is the largest cypress in East Tennessee. It has given years of good mulch and much protection to the many boxwoods at Wolf Creek.

In 1867 when the East Tennessee, Virginia, and Georgia Railroad made its appearance, Wolf Creek was the terminal. The train stopped at Wolf Creek and passengers were taken by stagecoach to Hot Springs and Asheville, North Carolina. Many notable personages spent the night at Wolf Creek, including several United States presidents. By this time the old home had taken the name of The Allen Inn. Later it became known as the Wolf Creek Stagecoach Inn.

When Woodrow Wilson was a young professor at Princeton University, he visited Wolf Creek. During the visit he spoke of being a "school teacher." One of the four little girls of the David Allen household rose to the occasion and said "Well, if you are a teacher maybe you'd like to see the Allen Academy." Nell Allen, that little girl, took Mr. Wilson along the boxwood path to the little school where she and her sisters and a brother did their lessons with a governess. Nell Allen became Mrs. W. M. Walker in August of 1924. After a brief period of living in Statesville, North Carolina, she, her husband, and two small sons came back to Wolf Creek where she kept the gardens and the old house in excellent condition until her death in 1953.

The first post office in this area was at Wolf Creek. A telegraph office also was located at the Inn. Wolf Creek became a summer resort for artists and vacationers. The formal boxwood gardens were a popular place for weddings of family members and friends. The stately old home burned in May 1975 but the chimneys and the many boxwoods are reminders of the varied activities that have taken place for over two centuries. In June of 1978 James Ward Walker, Nell Allen Walker's son, and his family returned to Wolf Creek and began the enlightening experience of rebuilding.

A June wedding reception recently held for a sixth-generation descendant of Reuben Allen in the garden that Emma Allen designed in the mid 1800s was an appropriate way of paying tribute to a great beginning in East Tennessee. Each generation has added to the boxwood collection at Wolf Creek, and as Tennessee prepares for 'Homecoming 86' Wolf Creek seems to have a head start.

More could be said of this friendship, and letters between the Emma's (Peck and Allen) are rich with personal history and events. Please see the book *Ada's Journal and Emma's Letters: The Civil War Era Journal and Letters of Emma Peck*, 2021, by Cross Mountain Books, for the full collection of letters exchanged between Isham's wife Emma Peck and Emma Allen of the Wolf Creek Allen Inn.

Augustus Longstreet (Judge) - Judge Longstreet refers to Augustus Baldwin Longstreet, an attorney, minister, educator, and humorist who became well known for his primary literary work called *Georgia Scenes, Characters, Incidents, Etc. in the First Half Century of the Republic* in September 1835. It received a hearty endorsement from poet Edgar Allen Poe and became quite popular.[179] [180]

The mention of "Father Fatsides in Dalgetty's Case" comes from a book *The Legend of Montrose*, contained

Figure 109 - Augustus Baldwin Longstreet, Photo available from Wikipedia

[179] https://en.wikipedia.org/wiki/Augustus_Baldwin_Longstreet, accessed on 22 Mar 2020
[180] https://www.georgiaencyclopedia.org/articles/arts-culture/augustus-baldwin-longstreet-1790-1870, accessed on 22 Mar 2020

Figure 110 - A Legend of Montrose illustration. From 1872 edition published by James R. Osgood and Company, Boston, Public Domain, Wikipedia

within a series of books called *Tales of My Landlord* by Walter Scott, published in 1817.[181] [182] The transcription here comes from Project Gutenberg.[183] From Chapter 2.

The Legend of Montrose

"And may I ask," said Lord Menteith, "why you, Captain, being, as I suppose, in the situation you describe, retired from the Spanish service also?"

"You are to consider, my lord, that your Spaniard," replied Captain Dalgetty, "is a person altogether unparalleled in his own conceit, where-through he maketh not fit account of such foreign cavaliers of valour as are pleased to take service with him. And a galling thing it is to every honourable soldado, to be put aside, and postponed, and obliged to yield preference to every puffing signor, who, were it the question which should first mount a breach at push of pike, might be apt to yield willing place to a Scottish cavalier. Moreover, sir, I was pricked in conscience respecting a matter of religion."

"I should not have thought, Captain Dalgetty," said the young nobleman, "that an old soldier, who had changed service so often, would have been too scrupulous on that head."

"No more I am, my lord," said the Captain, "since I hold it to be the duty of the chaplain of the regiment to settle those matters for me, and every other brave cavalier, inasmuch as he does nothing else that I know of for his pay and allowances. But this was a particular case, my lord, a CASUS IMPROVISUS, as I may say, in whilk I had no chaplain of my own persuasion to act as my adviser. I found, in short, that although my being a Protestant might be winked at, in respect that I was a man of action, and had more experience than all the Dons in our TERTIA put together, yet, when in garrison, it was expected I should go to mass with the regiment. Now, my lord, as a true Scottish man, and educated at the Mareschal-College of Aberdeen, I was bound to uphold the mass to be an act of blinded papistry and utter idolatry, whilk I was altogether unwilling to homologate by my presence. True it is, that I consulted on the point with a worthy countryman of my own, one Father Fatsides, of the Scottish Convent in Wurtzburg—"

181 https://en.wikipedia.org/wiki/A_Legend_of_Montrose, accessed on 22 Mar 2020
182 https://en.wikipedia.org/wiki/Tales_of_My_Landlord, accessed on 22 Mar 2020
183 http://www.gutenberg.org/files/1461/1461-h/1461-h.htm, accessed on 22 Mar 2020

"And I hope," observed Lord Menteith, "you obtained a clear opinion from this same ghostly father?"

"As clear as it could be," replied Captain Dalgetty, "considering we had drunk six flasks of Rhenish, and about two mutchkins of Kirchen-wasser. Father Fatsides informed me, that, as nearly as he could judge for a heretic like myself, it signified not much whether I went to mass or not, seeing my eternal perdition was signed and sealed at any rate, in respect of my impenitent and obdurate perseverance in my damnable heresy. Being discouraged by this response, I applied to a Dutch pastor of the reformed church, who told me, he thought I might lawfully go to mass, in respect that the prophet permitted Naaman, a mighty man of valour, and an honourable cavalier of Syria, to follow his master into the house of Rimmon, a false god, or idol, to whom he had vowed service, and to bow down when the king was leaning upon his hand. But neither was this answer satisfactory to me, both because there was an unco difference between an anointed King of Syria and our Spanish colonel, whom I could have blown away like the peeling of an ingan, and chiefly because I could not find the thing was required of me by any of the articles of war; neither was I proffered any consideration, either in perquisite or pay, for the wrong I might thereby do to my conscience."

"So you again changed your service?" said Lord Menteith.

"In troth did I, my lord; and after trying for a short while two or three other powers, I even took on for a time with their High Mightinesses the States of Holland."

The author's interpretation of this old story basically amounts to Isham taking a friendly stab at his buddy Wash Allen, saying that he has no chance at salvation.

He briefly mentions hog cholera and frost bit corn, and for our purposes here, know that hog cholera is also called swine fever. It is a disease transmitted from infected pigs by a number of carrier agents, including vehicles which pigs are conveyed from place to place, dealers who journey from farm to farm, and farm attendants. More info can be found on the Encyclopedia Britannica website, where this information was obtained.[184]

The next mention is of a Geo. D. Prentice, who is George Dennison Prentice, one of the co-editors of the *Courier-Journal,* who died in 1870. The Louisville *Courier-*

Figure 111 - Louisville Journal GEORGE PRENTICE Sue Mundy ~ Antique 1877 Art Print Engraving

---

[184] https://www.britannica.com/science/hog-cholera, accessed 22 Mar 2020

Journal still exists, and its website gives this part of its early history.[185]

The Marse Watterson Years

The first edition of the Courier Journal on Sunday, Nov. 8, 1868, was only four pages, but it was packed with news. The print was tiny, and there were no photographs or illustrations.

One of the stories that first day told how 37 people had died in the previous week, six from consumption, as tuberculosis was then called, four from measles, three from pneumonia, two each from apoplexy, typhoid fever and "softening of the brain." The death toll includes 11 children under 3 years old.

From the beginning, the paper set its sights high.

Formed through the merger of the Louisville Daily Journal, which had opposed slavery, and the Louisville Morning Courier, which supported the Confederacy, it boasted in a note to readers that the new paper immediately "assumed a circulation, influence and value enjoyed by no paper out of New York." It was an unlikely alliance. The two papers had fought one another so bitterly that 11 years earlier, their editors fought a duel. They both survived.

Figure 112 – Photo from Courier Journal), original caption reads, "Mr. Watterson's editorial staff in 1868, when the three daily newspapers of Louisville were united into the "Courier-Journal." Mr. George D. Prentice and Mr. Watterson are in the center.

Now one of them, an ailing George Prentice, who would die in 1870, recruited Watterson, who was only 28, to edit the paper. Prentice had run the Journal, notoriously editorializing against Catholics and immigrants, whom he derided as "pestilent foreign swarms," brewing hatred and hysteria that culminated in the "Bloody Riot" of 1855 in which 22 people in Louisville were killed as they tried to vote.

---

[185] https://www.courier-journal.com/story/news/2018/11/08/courier-journal-150-anniversary-justice-fairness/1200347002/, accessed on 22 Mar 2020

A sign of the times, the George Prentice Statue which sat in Louisville in that spot for 104 years was removed on Dec 11, 2018. Prentice's own *Courier Journal* covered the story, "A controversial statue of an anti-immigrant and anti-Catholic figure was removed Tuesday from the grounds of the downtown Louisville library.

Workers used a crane to pull the statue of George Dennison Prentice, the founder and editor of the Louisville Journal in the mid-1800s, from its spot behind the Louisville Free Public Library, 301 York St.

Prentice was known for writing anti-immigration and anti-Catholic editorials. He was seen as an instrumental figure in the 1855 Bloody Monday riots, where more than 20 people were killed after Irish and German immigrants were attacked by members of the American Know-Nothing Party.

Background: Statue of anti-Catholic outside Louisville library to be removed[186]

The Prentice statue, as well as the John B. Castleman statue in Cherokee Triangle, was vandalized with orange paint in February 2018.

The statue will be placed in a city storage facility on Lexington Road. What will happen to the Prentice statue has not been determined. The city said in a statement that Cave Hill Cemetery, where Prentice is buried, declined to take the statue.

The Prentice statue originally sat in front of the Courier Journal building but was moved to a spot in front of the Louisville Public Library in 1914."[187]

A balancing article written on 28 Aug 2019 by James M. Prichard, a Louisville historian, shed new light on George Prentice. Prichard said that Prentice became a scapegoat when in reality there were numerous people to blame, and not Prentice primarily. He shared that Prentice had a 40-year career and he is also remembered as the man

Figure 113 - State of George D. Prentice in Louisville, KY with orange paint from vandalism, 2018.

who helped "save Kentucky for the Union."[188] He argued in his article that the Prentice statue should have been moved back to the *Courier Journal*, its original location, rather than into storage.

---

[186] https://www.courier-journal.com/story/news/local/2018/12/10/mayor-fischer-louisville-prentice-statue-removed-week/2263641002/, accessed on 22 Mar 2020

[187] https://www.courier-journal.com/story/news/2018/12/11/controversial-louisville-statue-george-prentice-removed-downtown-library/2274285002/, accessed on 22 Mar 2020

[188] https://www.leoweekly.com/2019/08/giving-devil-due-george-d-prentice-statue-not-moved/

Farther down in Isham's letter, he writes, "As a fighter, he was not a success! I witnessed his fight with George Trotter." There are various accounts of this "fight." One from Putnam's monthly, Vol 3, published in 1908 says,

"'George Trotter of the *Louisville Gazette* fired at him on Market Street, Mr. Prentice, knife in hand, threw him to the ground.' Prentice was a storm centre and a hard hitter."[189]

Another account is found in *Harper's Magazine*, Vol 50. It offers a different sequence of events, and includes some of the words thrown back and forth between Prentice and Trotter. It is rather lengthy, but gives some context and the fight, and alludes to duels in that day:

"He was not in the least considerate of the feelings or sensibilities of those persons he had reason to dislike. His opponents did not forbear him, nor did he forbear them. He gave as good as he received, usually a little better. His mode of treating what is named in the South the private quarrels of gentlemen maybe judged by this (his [Prentice's]) account of an affray in Lexington (July,1835) among several members of his craft:

"Mr. Trotter, without provocation, attempted to shoot Mr. Clark in the street: the parties exchanged shots twice without effect. Mr. O'Hara, a friend of Mr. Trotter, made an attack upon Mr. Bryant, the associate of Mr. Clark; Mr. Bryant gave Mr. O'Hara an effectual cudgeling, and then laid his cane over the head and shoulders of Mr. Trotter till the latter cried for quarter. There the matter ended, Mr. Clark retiring to reload his pistols, Mr. Bryant to procure a new cane, and Messrs. Trotter and O'Hara to get their heads mended.

"Trotter (George James), then the editor of the Kentucky Gazette, retorted in his columns upon Prentice in a virulent article, closing with something like these words: "The infamy of George D. Prentice is notorious. He is shunned by all honorable men. The mark of Cain is on his brow."

"Prentice's sole rejoinder in the Journal was: "Mr. George James Trotter says that the mark of Cain is on our brow. We don't know about that; but we do know that the mark of cane is on his back."

"Of course this made Trotter a theme for laughter, and, burning with rage, he went to Louisville with the deliberate intent to shoot Prentice on sight. Discovering the chief of the Journal on his way to the office, he pulled his pistol without-notification, and fired upon Prentice, only a few feet distant, wounding him on the breast. Prentice, quick as thought, leaped at Trotter, caught him in his arms, took away his weapon, threw him powerless to the ground, and drew a bowie-knife.

"Meanwhile a crowd that had gathered cried out, "Kill the scoundrel! Kill him on the spot!

"Prentice simply said," I can not take the life of a disarmed and helpless man;" and releasing his hold, put up his knife, and walked away amidst enthusiastic cheers evoked by his magnanimity.

---

[189] Putnam's Monthly: A Magazine of Literature, Art, and Life, Vol 3, published 1908 by G. P. Putnam's Sons The Knickerbocker Press, New Rochelle, New York, Copyright 1907, 1908 by Putnam's Monthly Company, 396-398, available free here: https://tinyurl.com/4xnubuym

There always were one or two, sometimes three, newspapers in Louisville opposed to the Journal. Hardly any of them had long life or assured success, and the result was that they hated Prentice with a feminine intensity. The rival editors were unremittingly at war, generally with their pens, sometimes with their pistols.

William E. Hughes, of the Democrat, now gathered to the shades, having wasted all the ink he could afford in a bitter controversy, waited upon his antagonist, and sent up his card.

"Tell Mr. Hughes," said Prentice, "that I will meet him in front of the office as soon as I load my pistols."

"In two minutes he was in the street: the journalists exchanged four shots without effect. The police, by some unaccountable accident, interfered, and hostilities were at an end — until the next time."[190]

Two pages later in Harper's Monthly, even more light is shed on Isham's article, perhaps explaining why Isham withdrew his subscription:

"The rebellion aroused all that was patriotic and noble in the old Whig war-horse [Prentice]. The first gun fired on Sumter rendered him a more ardent and unflinching Unionist than ever. Subscribers withdrew in large numbers. Many of his life-long friends were on the other side; his interests all seemed to point in the same direction. He was entreated, warned, threatened. His two sons, his only children, entered the Southern army. Nevertheless, Prentice's fidelity to the republic could not be shaken, and he fought a heroic fight. To his editorial exertions more than to any other one cause was attributed the non-secession of Kentucky. Though better perhaps for the contest that she should have gone out, his credit for trying to keep her in should be none the less.

When the news of the first battle of Manassas reached Louisville, the excitement was at white heat. The Stars and Stripes had long been floating over the Journal office, and at that particular time a carpenter was on the roof of the building to repair the flag-staff. This gave rise to the rumor that somebody was up there to pull down the flag. The editor, his eyes flashing fire, thundered out, "Go up at once, and throw the scoundrel into the street. If it isn't done in five minutes, by Jove I'll do it myself!" The order was quickly obeyed, so far as to insure the rapid descent of the guileless mechanic, and his ignominious propulsion down several flights of stairs.

His treatment of angry Confederates is shown by the following correspondence:

"UNIVERSITY OF VIRGINIA, MAY 17, 1861 "GEORGE D. PRENTICE,—Stop my paper. I can't afford to read Abbolition (sic) journals in these times. The atmosphere of Old Virginia will not admit of such filthy sheets as yours has grown to be."   "GEORGE LAKE."

---

[190] Melville, H., Alden, H. Mills. *Harper's new monthly magazine.* New York: Harper & Bros, 1875, 198. Available for free here: https://tinyurl.com/harpers1875

"LOUISVILLE, May 24, 1861. "GEORGE LAKE —I think it a great pity that a young man should go to a university to graduate a traitor and a blackguard, and so ignorant as to spell 'Abolition' with two *b*'s.   GEORGE D. PRENTICE."

The close of the war saw Prentice broken in health and spirits. The terrible struggle had buoyed him up, had touched his mind with the ancient fire. His life work was done, and he knew it. Soon after, the Journal, effectually an extinction, was consolidated with the Courier, and he retained with it a merely nominal connection. His wife, too, died; and he had already lost a son in battle. His dearest friends had slipped away; he had survived his generation; Louisville, Kentucky, the South, had, in more than one sense, undergone a revolution. There was little left to fear, and, worse still, nothing left to hope. Bending beneath the tempests of many years, rent by the force of a thousand contests, it is not strange he walked to the grave with trembling limbs but undaunted soul, murmuring at the last," I am glad to go!"[191]

Thomas Patrick Moore - Before summarizing, please note another historical figure mentioned by Isham, "(free) Tom Moore[192]." Thomas Patrick Moore (1797-1853) was a Representative from Kentucky. He was appointed Lieutenant Colonel of the Third United States Dragoons in the war with Mexico and served from March 3, 1847, to July 31, 1848.[193] In *George Keats of Kentucky: A Life* by Lawrence M. Crutcher, the author describes the interaction (duel between Prentice and Moore) this way,

"Probably the most colorful of the society's trustees, however, was Prentice himself, the *Louisville Journal's* Whig editor and a close friend of the Keats family. Prentice's paper sparred editorially and libelously throughout the 1830s with Shadrack Penn's *Louisville Public Advertiser* in one of the great American newspaper wars. One of Prentice's milder retorts to a Penn editorial was this: 'We prefer that they should accept our hand open and ungloved, but if they would rather have it in the shape of a FIST it is still at their service.'[59] A subsequent sketch of Prentice stated, 'Next to being a good writer, it was also useful to be a good shot.'[60] Prentice was both. In 1838, the year the Historical Society opened in Louisville, it was reported: 'Mr. Prentice, of the Journal, fought another pistol battle August 14th – this time with Major Thomas P. Moore, at the Harrodsburg Springs, both parties coming out of the conflict without physical injury.'[61]"[194]

Isham brings up his comments because he had learned that *The Morristown Gazette* was in partnership with the *Courier-Journal*. George Prentice had died 4 years before Isham wrote his letter,

---

[191] Ibid, Pg 200
[192] https://en.wikipedia.org/wiki/Thomas_Patrick_Moore, accessed 22 Mar 2020
[193] https://bioguideretro.congress.gov/Home/MemberDetails?memIndex=M000921, accessed 22 Mar 2020
[194] George Keats of Kentucky: A Life, https://tinyurl.com/4ffsdasb, accessed 22 Mar 2020
Quotes within *George Keats of Kentucky include*
      [59] – Alice Ford, *John James Audubon* (University of Oklahoma Press, 1964), 104-5.
      [60] – John Goff, "The last Leaf," Register of the Kentucky Historical Society 59 (1961): 331-42. And
      [61] – U.S. Genealogy Net, 2001.

but he was still bitter that the *Journal* had sided with the Union. His comments give us a window into the newspaper feuds and duels of the 1800s, but also his personal political stances. It can be inferred that Isham was a Democrat, and we know from other sources that he supported the Confederacy during the Civil War. He mentions that the "Vicksburgh editors were the boys for a fight!" We know from multiple sources that Isham's second wife was from Vicksburg, MS which sits in Warren County. According to the 1840 Federal Census in Warren, MS, Isham and his wife owned 52 slaves at that time. Here is a transcription of that record:

1840 United States Federal Census Warren, Miss. – I. T. Peck

Free White Persons - Males - 20 thru 29:	3
Free White Persons - Males - 30 thru 39:	1
Free White Persons - Females - 30 thru 39:	1

Slaves - Males - Under 10:	12	Slaves - Females - Under 10:	5
Slaves - Males - 10 thru 23:	7	Slaves - Females - 10 thru 23:	5
Slaves - Males - 24 thru 35:	9	Slaves - Females - 24 thru 35:	4
Slaves - Males - 36 thru 54:	5	Slaves - Females - 36 thru 54:	5

Persons Employed in Agriculture	28
Free White Persons - 20 thru 49	5
Total Free White Persons	5
Total Slaves	52
Total All Persons - Free White, Free Colored, Slaves	57

Isham married Helen (Rapalje) Glass 3 years prior to this 1840 census, and when he married her, he inherited her land and slaves (at least for a time). His friends, brother, numerous family members fought for the Confederacy, and he contributed to the war effort monetarily. His contribution and other events surrounding the Civil War are covered earlier in this volume. The key point, in the author's view, is that as Isham's focus becomes less and less about the fake Bald Mountain volcano in his writing. He now increasingly allows his feelings, political views, friendships, reading, and experiences show in his Sawbones articles. The window into his life is getting larger and larger.

After nearly a year of newspaper silence, Isham writes again. It had been so long, that the article is called, " 'SAWBONES' REDIVIVUS." Redivivus is an old word that means to come back to life, or to be reborn.[195] SAWBONES HAS COME BACK TO LIFE, or more satirically, "SAWBONES IS REBORN!"

---

[195] https://www.merriam-webster.com/dictionary/redivivus, accessed 23 Mar 2020

1 SEP 1875 "SAWBONES" REDIVIVUS[196]

THE STRIDES OF TRUE INWARDNESS—UNAUTHORIZED TICKET SELLERS—A SPECIMEN PASS—CAPT. TAYLOR AND HIS INEXORABLE RULE—COL. WASH AND HIS PROSPECTS.

To the Editor at the Morristown Gazette:

We bad just begun to recover from the Beecher stench, when I find his 'true inwardness' is breaking out all over the country!

No wonder Beecher's salary has been raised to one hundred thousand dollars, and that his church has had an accession of one hundred members of whom eighty are females! There is but one safe remedy for this true inwardness—that is buckshot!

One dose is sufficient—if properly administered it stops the spread of the disease!

These self styled men of God profess to be 'drummers for the Kingdom!'

Drummers are not always reliable—better do business directly with the principal!

And besides they charge a heavy percent!

Salvation is without money and without price, and I cannot understand by what authority they sell tickets on that line!

When Christ delivered the keys to Peter, at Bandis, be gave him no such authority!

After the killing of some of the fanatic mob who were burning, robbing and murdering recently at San Miguel, passes like this were found in their pockets: 'Peter, open to the bearer the gates of Heaven, who has died for religion.' Signed by the Priest.

If these fellows had come by this route that pass would not have been worth shucks on the Cincinnati, Cumberland Gap and Charleston road!

There never was a pass written by human hands that would pass a man over that road!

I have seen it tried!

Capt. Taylor's rule is—pay or walk!

There's no dodging that arrangement!

Do you recollect the fellow who went to heaven from Chicago, a few years since? When he arrived there, Peter asked him where he was from. 'Chicago,' he said. Peter told him it would not do—that there was no such place as Chicago. The Chicago man asked if there was a map of the United States handy, and when one was placed before him he pointed out Chicago. 'Sure enough, here it is,' said Peter, 'but you are the first man who ever came here from Chicago!'

You inquired recently about Colonel Wash!

I have been waiting hoping I could say something good of him but it is no use waiting!

He does at times appear to lie deeply concerned about the future state—of the money market, and he did promise me that he would join the Young Men's Christian Association!

But that was before the Beecher business!

When I mention it now, he uses such language as I don't care to hear in hot weather!

He did think of the holy-bonds-of-matrimony business, and went so far with it as to buy a cradle!

---

[196] Dr. Isham Peck, "Sawbones Redivivus", *The Morristown Gazette*, 1 Sep 1875, 3.

But this 'true inwardness' has been too many for him!

He says he begins to understand things now that at one time were mysteries to him!

SAWBONES."

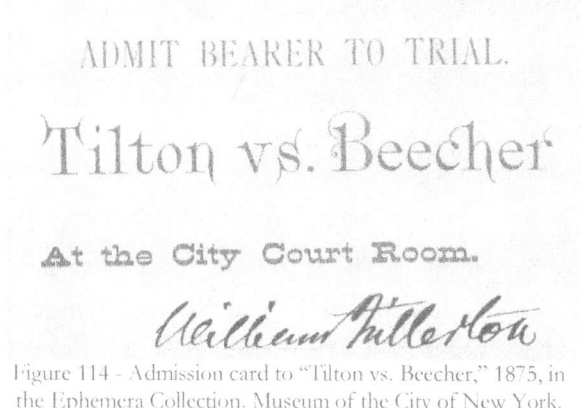

Beecher's "True Inwardness" Letter Trial

Here are actual court proceedings from Beecher's "True Inwardness Letter" Court Trial:

"MR. BEACH CONTINUES HIS ARGUMENT.

Mr. Beach—On the 8th day of March, 1871 --the letter which I last read of Mr. Beecher bearing date Feb. 7, 1871—Mrs. Tilton writes this communication to Mr. Beecher:

WEDNESDAY.

'DEAR FRIEND: Does your heart bound towards all as it used.'

The words "towards all," italicized, seeming to indicate an intention under that general phrase to make a personal application to herself.

'So does mine! I am myself again. I did not dare to tell you until I was sure; but the bird has sung in my heart these four weeks, and he has covenanted with me never again to leave. "Spring has come." Because I thought it would gladden you to know this and not to trouble or embarrass you in any way I now write. Of course I should like to share with you my joy, but can wait for the Beyond!

When dear Frank says I may once again go to old Plymouth I will thank the dear Father.' Following that Mr. Beecher writes this letter to her:

'The blessing of God rest upon you. Every spark of life and warmth in your own house will be a star and a sun in my dwelling. Your note broke like Spring upon Winter, and gave me an inward rebound to life. No one can ever know, none but God, through what a dreary wilderness I have wandered. There was Mt. Sinai, there was the barren sand, and there was the alternation of hope and despair that marked the pilgrimage of old. If only it might lead to the

Promised Land—or, like Moses, shall I die on the border? Your hope and courage are like medicine. Should God inspire you to restore and rebuild at home, and while doing it to cheer and sustain outside of it another who sorely needs help in heart and spirit, it will prove a life so noble as few are able to live, and in another world the emancipated soul may utter thanks.'

"THE "TRUE INWARDNESS" LETTER.

It is a little surprising, it seems to me, that Mr. Beecher should find occasion under these circumstances to resort to Mrs. Tilton to be cheered and sustained, professing that he sorely needed help in heart and spirit. And why? If Mr. Beecher was so entirely free from any sentiment toward this lady that was not justified by their relation, and his character and position, if he was so entirely cheerful and comfortable and innocent in all his conscience with reference to associations with this lady, why is it that he should need from her cheer and comfort! It was a cheer and comfort to be rendered to him in addition to the rebuilding and reinstatement of her own home and position. It was a personal appeal to this lady to pour upon him her sympathies and affections, to cheer and console him in the desolation of his life outside of her association. No other construction can be given to it.

If it would be a comfort to you [the "you" italicized], now and then, to send me a letter of true inwardness ["inwardness" italicized]—the outcome of your inner life—it would be safe, for I am now at home here with my sister; and it is permitted to you ["permitted to you" italicized], and will be an exceeding refreshment to me, for your heart experiences are often like bread from heaven to the hungry. God has enriched your moral nature. May not others partake?

"If it would be a comfort to you to send me a letter of true inwardness, it would be safe." If this phrase referred only to that permissible and proper communication which should pass between an afflicted and Spirit broken woman and her considerate and careful pastor, of course no exception could be taken to it. But why was it necessary to give assurance to Mrs. Tilton that such a communication would be safe? What hazard was there about communion of that sort? Why was it that the pastor and parishioner should feel that there was a hazard or peril in the permissible intercourse? Why should Mrs. Tilton need the encouragement or the assurance that it would be safe for her to pour out her true inwardness upon Henry Ward Beecher, who appeared, not as the Christian comforter, as the solacer in affliction, but as the beggar at her heart, to be cheered and comforted by her; not rendering pastoral service, not solacing her with prayer and with precept, but bending his head in affliction at her side, and praying the consolation of her countenance. "All this will be safe, Mrs. Tilton. permitted to you, for I am now at home with my sister." What does that mean, gentlemen? It is written by Henry Ward Beecher to this lady, all communication with whom he but a few days before pronounced as un wise and improper. Why does he tell her that she may communicate her inward thoughts to him because he is alone with his sister, his wife absent! Some significance must be given to this language. It must be construed in connection with the other circumstances in this case. It must be made rational with reference to the proven intercourse between these parties. idea, it presented some request to the mind of Mrs. Tilton, and was it an idea or request which would be likely to soothe and quiet the disturbance of her own heart, as Mr. Beecher describes it, or the uneasiness which existed in her own home, as he represents it? Was it a letter to be addressed under these circumstances by a pastor professing the condition of things Mr. Beecher states upon this stand!" [197]

So, basically the Beecher-Tilton Affair remains in the news, and as things are happening in the courtroom in Brooklyn, NY . . . items are continually flowing through the press. In June of 1875 "the truth inwardness letter" from Henry Ward Beecher to Mrs. Tilton comes to light. The letter had been written on 7 Feb 1871, but had just now made its way into the courtroom, and into the papers afterwards. Isham and his friend Wash Allen are fed up with the publicity of the whole "affair." He is venting his frustration to the *Gazette*. The ticket to the trial and Harper's Weekly drawing from the previous page are from the Museum of the City of New York Blog: *New York Stories.* [198]

The *MCNY Blog* summarizes the trial well,

> "The Beecher-Tilton Affair was alleged to have taken place during the 1860s, when, due to conflict in the relationship and Theodore's extended absences related to his work, Elizabeth sought the companionship of Beecher. In 1870, Elizabeth confessed to her husband that she had engaged in an adulterous relationship with Beecher. The confession was soon well-known among certain influential members of Plymouth Church, and eventually reached the ears of Woodhull, who then made the confession public. Beecher and Theodore badgered Elizabeth to retract her confession, then retract the retraction, respectively. By 1873, Theodore Tilton was no longer editor of the *Independent,* and in fact the journal came down hard against Tilton and in support of Beecher. Tilton was also excommunicated from the Plymouth Church congregation.
>
> Despite much published evidence of the affair, Plymouth Church exonerated Beecher, leading Theodore Tilton to bring suit against him in 1874 for "criminal intimacy" with his wife.
>
> The trial was opened in January of 1875, and captivated the nation. The significance of the trial was not lost on Beecher, as evidenced in the letter below, which states "But this poor note may have an <u>extrinsic</u> interest as being written at the climax of this remarkable trial."
>
> At the close of the trial in July of 1875, the jury deliberated for six days, but could not reach a verdict. Following the trial, Plymouth Church exonerated Beecher once again. Theodore Tilton moved to Paris following the trial, where he lived out the remainder

---

[197] Theodore Tilton Vs. Henry Ward Beecher, Action for Crim. Con. Tried in the City Court of Brooklyn, Chief Justice Joseph Neilson, Presiding. Verbatim Report by the Official Stenographer, 981-982. Court Proceedings from Tuesday, 22 Jun 1875 as indicated on Pg 977. Published in New York: McDivitt, Campbell, and Co., Law Publishers, 1875. Digitized by Google. https://tinyurl.com/TiltonBeecherTrial, accessed on 23 Mar 2020

[198] Museum of the City of New York, *The Beecher-Titlon Affair*, https://blog.mcny.org/2012/10/23/the-beecher-tilton-affair/, accessed on 23 Mar 2020

of his life. Elizabeth Tilton remained a member of the Plymouth congregation until she, yet again, re-confessed to having an affair with Beecher in 1878. At that point, she was also excommunicated from Plymouth Church. Beecher remained a popular figure, though he never received quite the level of adulation he was accustomed to before the trial."[199]

To Isham's next point about Beecher's salary being increased to one hundred thousand dollars . . . it is true! After the verdict came back undecided, Beecher's church increased his salary so that he could pay his legal bills. Debby Applegate's biography addresses this very issue, "AFTER SIX MONTHS of testimony, eight days of debate, and fifty-two ballots, worn down by exhaustion and ill health, the jury finally gave up. Neither the Tiltons nor Henry were in the courtroom when the jury filled in, but Eunice was at her usual spot, waiting impassively, joined by her oldest son, Edward Beecher; Susan and Tasker Howard; and a retinue of attorneys.

'Have you a verdict?' asked the clerk.

'No we have not, I regret to say. We cannot,' replied the foreman. 'We ask to be discharged.' The judge agreed.[78]

Eunice's face did not even flicker with emotion. The attorneys looked stunned. The reporters leaped to chase down the jurymen as they gathered up their things to leave. Quickly the final tally was revealed: 9 to 3 in favor of Beecher. By the next day the papers had full analysis of the deliberations, broken down by each juror's occupation, religion, family life, social status, and personality. In the end, though, they simply could not agree on who was telling the truth. 'The mass of reading material helped rather than hindered the breach,' reported the *World*, with 'every man finding only support for his own opinion among its many pages.'[79]

'It can hardly be said that this is a victory for anybody,' concluded E. L. Godkin, 'but this is something very like a defeat for Mr. Beecher.' Even those who believed him innocent had seen too much of Beecher's weaknesses and poor judgment. The London *Daily Telegraph* echoed the opinion of many, maintaining that the minister had 'acted with an imbecility that would have disgraced an uneducated girl.'[80]

The next day, the Beecher house on Columbia Heights was jammed with well-wishers. Henry looked as if he'd returned to youth, and Eunice was treated like a hero, especially by the women. 'She accepted this as common sense and a matter of course, calling for no more exaltation than anything right and true,' the *Eagle* noted. The next evening Plymouth Church was overflowing with well-wishers, gathered to hear Beecher deliver a tender plea for forgiveness. 'Don't believe that all men are bad because you have seen some of their weaknesses, or even their sins. Of all the saints I know, stone

---

[199] Ibid, accessed 23 Mar 2020

throwing saints are the most unworthy,' he concluded.[81] In response the church trustees voted to increase Beecher's salary for the year to one hundred thousand dollars so he could pay his legal bills."[200]

If you'd like to read a rosy colored picture of Beecher, with no mention of the "affair," check out the "Beecher" page on Plymouth Church's website, which includes good info and nice photos. The following excerpt is from the website:

Henry Ward Beecher

Henry Ward Beecher was born in 1813 in Litchfield, Connecticut, the eighth of eleven children of the Rev. Lyman Beecher, minister of the established Congregational church there, and his first wife, Roxana Foote, who died when Henry was three. He grew up in a crowded parsonage with his father, who became one of the most prominent clergymen of that era, his stepmother, siblings and half siblings, and assorted relatives and servants. He was especially close to his sister Harriet, two years his senior, who later married Calvin Stowe and wrote Uncle Tom's Cabin. This friendship with Harriet continued throughout their lives, and she was still listed on the membership rolls of Plymouth Church when she died in 1896.

Henry, bashful and mumbling as a child, began his oratorical training at Mt. Pleasant Institution, a boarding school in Amherst, Massachusetts.

He graduated from Amherst College in 1834 and in 1837 from Lane Theological Seminary outside of Cincinnati, Ohio, which his father then headed. After serving Presbyterian churches in Lawrenceburg, Indiana, and in Indianapolis, he and his wife, the former Eunice Bullard, and their three surviving children moved to Brooklyn in the fall of 1847 where Beecher undertook with relish the creation of a new Congregational church.

---

[200] *The Most Famous Man in America: The Biography of Henry Ward Beecher*, by Debby Applegate, Pgs 451-452, quotes within are as follows:
    [78] – *Eagle*, 2 July 1875.
    [79] – *New York World*, July 3, 1875.
    [80] – *Nation*, 8 July 1875; Shaplen, *Free Love*, 258.
    [81] – *Eagle*, 3 June 1875; *New York Times*, 3 July 1875.

The most famous of these former slaves was a young girl named Pinky, auctioned during a regular Sunday worship service at Plymouth on February 5, 1860. A collection taken up that day raised $900 to buy Pinky from her owner. A gold ring was also placed in the collection plate, and Beecher presented it to the girl to commemorate her day of liberation. Pinky returned to Plymouth in 1927 at the time of the church's 80th anniversary to give the ring back to the Church with her thanks. Today, Pinky's ring and a copy of the bill of sale can still be viewed at Plymouth.

Despite these highly publicized activities, Beecher was viewed as a moderate compared to other abolitionists, and that perception greatly contributed to his influence. He never expected that a war would be required to free the slaves in the South, but when it came, the impact of his steadfast antislavery stance on public opinion helped the North endure horrific bloodshed.

From his earliest sermon in Brooklyn, Beecher made it plain that one cornerstone of his ministry at Plymouth would be his opposition to slavery, and it was that position, plus his powerful preaching, which quickly built Plymouth Church into the most prominent Protestant church of that era. His preaching was characterized by "originality, logic, pathos, and humor," in the words of a contemporary, and stalwartly and eloquently he preached and wrote that slavery was a sin. He also spoke out against U.S. arrogance toward Mexico, and against mistreatment of the Indians, but it was his antislavery preaching which made him famous. He sent rifles to the Kansas territory, he obtained the chains with which John Brown had been bound, trampling them in the pulpit, and he also held mock "auctions" at which the congregation purchased the freedom of real slaves.

In the early days of the Civil War, Beecher pressed President Lincoln to issue a proclamation of emancipation. He went on a speaking tour in England to explain the North's war aims and to undermine support for the South among the English, whose economy had been hurt by the embargo against Southern cotton. Just as the war was drawing to a close, Beecher was the main speaker when the Stars and Stripes were again raised at Fort Sumter, South Carolina, site of the war's first battle.

Although remembered today for his social activism, in his own time Beecher was always, foremost, a minister of the Christian gospel. He was one of the leaders in the movement known as Romantic Christianity, preaching not the harsh judgment of God, as had his ancestors, but rather the loving presence of God. He also espoused the concept of the freedom of the individual with a social conscience, a cornerstone of Congregational belief. After the war, Beecher championed such causes as women's suffrage, temperance, and evolution, and he spoke out against anti-Semitism.

Beecher suffered a stroke in March of 1887 and died quietly in his sleep two days later. Brooklyn, still an independent city, declared a day of mourning. The state legislature recessed, and telegrams of condolence were sent by national figures, including President Cleveland. His funeral procession to Plymouth Church--led by a Black commander of the William Lloyd Garrison Post in Massachusetts and a Virginia Confederate general and former slaveholder, marching arm in arm - paid tribute to what Beecher helped accomplish.

Henry Ward Beecher was laid to rest in Brooklyn's Green-Wood Cemetery on March 11, 1887, survived by his wife Eunice, and four of the nine children born to them: Harriet, Henry, William and Herbert."[201]

Isham mentions "Bandis." This is most likely a reference to Banias, modern-day Caesarea-Philippi.[202] The Biblical reference is plain, Christ giving the "keys of the kingdom" to Peter in Philippi: Matthew 16:13-20 (NASB) "[13] Now when Jesus came into the district of **Caesarea Philippi**, He was asking His disciples, "Who do people say that the Son of Man is?" [14] And they said, "Some *say* John the Baptist; and others, Elijah; but still others, Jeremiah, or one of the prophets." [15] He *said to them, "But who do you say that I am?" [16] Simon Peter answered, "You are the Christ, the Son of the living God." [17] And Jesus said to him, "Blessed are you, Simon Barjona, because flesh and blood did not reveal *this* to you, but My Father who is in heaven. [18] I also say to you that you are Peter, and upon this rock I will build My church; and the gates of Hades will not overpower it. [19] **I will give you the keys of the kingdom of heaven; and whatever you bind on earth shall have been bound in heaven, and whatever you loose on earth shall have been loosed in heaven."** [20] Then He warned the disciples that they should tell no one that He was the Christ."[203]

He then mentions the "burning, robbing, and murdering recently at San Miguel." The following article, dated 7 Oct 1875 tells the story…[204]

Rockhampton Bulletin (Qld. : 1871 - 1878), Thursday 7 October 1875, page 3

---

[201] http://www.plymouthchurch.org/beecher, accessed on 23 Mar 2020
[202] Caesarea Philippi (Banias), https://dannythedigger.com/banias/, accessed 7 Sep 2023
[203] https://www.biblegateway.com/passage/?search=Matthew+16%3A13-20&version=NASB, emphasis added.
[204] https://trove.nla.gov.au/newspaper/rendition/nla.news-article51781974.txt, accessed 23 Mar 2020

The Massacre at San Miguel.

(From the Panama Herald and Star.)

On the 20th June an outbreak of the populace took place at San Miguel, a town of forty thousand inhabitants, forty two miles distant from the Port of La Union, and the second city in San Salvador. There has been considerable discontent at San Miguel for some time past, owing to some regulations requiring dealers to use a new market which had been built. On the 20th (Sunday) a priest named Palacios preached a violent sermon, which was forbidden to be published, and that evening the mob rose, attacked the Commandancia, where they met with little or no resistance, murdered the general in command (Epinoza), liberated the prisoners, and set fire to both the Cabildo and Commandancia, which, with eight other of the principal houses in the town, were burnt and entirely destroyed. Eight other houses were pillaged of all their contents, except one, where a few things were left. It is estimated that 1,000,000 dollars worth of property has been destroyed, and grave commercial failures are dreaded inconsequence. The house of Senor Quiroz, one of the richest, citizens, was entered during the day by masked persons, who loaded 40,000 dollars on mules and took it away quietly into the country. After the row the Government soldiers were found to be with their colours.

In another communication from a Spanish, correspondent at La Union, under the same date, we have additional details connected with the outrages that have occurred in San Miguel, and which are as follows: The Very Rev. Bishop of Salvador it seems ordered the curates of the parish churches to read, on three consecutive feast days, a pastoral which his lordship had issued in which, amid many expressions of humility and charity he encouraged the faithful to rebel against the civil Government. The supreme authority, considering this an offence against the laws, decreed that the publication of the pastoral should be opposed by its department agents, requiring them to warn the parish priests for the first and second time, and defining what the punishment should be if they disobeyed the third warning.

Figure 116 - Cathedral San Miguel - https://www.britannica.com/place/San-Miguel-El-Salvador#/media/1/521514/14052

Don Jose Manuel Palacios, the curate of San Miguel, fearing that the Governor would carry the order referred to into effect on the day assigned (the 24th), had made preparations to frustrate it by the most diabolical of plans. The said curate got together a band of the worst characters in the population, and offered them spiritual blessings for the next world, and the pleasure of pillaging the rich storehouses of the merchants of San Miguel beside, if they would attack the Cabildo and set free the 200 prisoners there, who were his friends. This was done, after killing the sentinel on guard. They then burnt up the archives of the municipality, and rushed in a crowd to attack the barracks which are defended by the Governor and General in command, Don Felipe Espinoza, and his second in command, Juan Castro. The soldiers under their command fired their muskets at the rioters, charged with powder only. On General Espinoza finding, as soon as it was daylight, that his soldiers were favouring the intentions of the mob and obeying the dictates of the priest, he tried to persuade them to return to their duty, but without the least effect. General Espinoza was killed, his body cut in pieces and thrown at each other with a sort of satanic glee. General Castro had his skull cloven, and his body thrown over a wall, where it was found by his mother still living. After taking him home he lived three days longer. The best houses in the place were set fire to by the aid of kerosene. The people of the town of San Miguel, as can readily be imagined, were in the greatest consternation at seeing their city the prey to fire and deluged with blood. They had to endure this agony from the 26th at 11 p.m. until the same hour on the 23rd, when the forces of Honduras made their appearance under the brave Captain of the Porte of Ampala, Colonel Domingo Vasquez, by whose assistance the place was taken out of the hands of the mob.

The communication, which we translate, further states that a priest called Santiago Palacios has been put in irons, along with some hundred others of his followers, and that President Gonzalez had arrived at San Miguel with troops, and no one doubted but that he would see justice done and the law respected.

A letter from San Miguel to the Star and Herald of Panama, received to-day, says of the massacre:-- 'After the barracks had been taken nothing was heard but the savage yells of the assailants, dispersing in all directions, breaking open the door and windows of houses of merchants and others, robbing, pillaging, and assassinating in their fiendish occupations, and applying the torch to the houses and whatever else their whims chose. Amidst this the cry of 'Death to foreigners. Death to heretics!' was constantly heard. The town remained for three days at the mercy of the assailants. During that time all classes of crimes were committed, and even those who took refuge in the church were threatened with assassination by the mob. The losses in property will not fall short of one million of dollars. The President of the Republic has done all that he could to bring the offenders to punishment, but so numerous are they that they cannot be dealt with. The foreigners in the place have addressed their respective Governments for the purpose of making the Government responsible for the massacre.'

President [Santiago] Gonzalez [Portillo], of Salvador, had about fifty of those engaged in the recent fanatical outbreak shot in squads, at the towns between San Miguel and the capital, causing the padres who occasioned the riots to witness the executions. Many of these victims confessed they were set on by the padres by telling them they might rob the rich, provided they gave part to the Church. Great sorrow and indignation is expressed throughout Central America at the events in San Miguel in which respectable clergymen join.

The following is taken from a letter by an American resident in Costa Rica:--In July a number of Jesuits entered the Republic of Costa Rica from Guatemala, whence they were expelled. When they arrived within ten miles of the capital they were ordered to stop. Congress met the same day, and 200 masons, went in a body to the Congress hall and petitioned for the Jesuits' removal, as mischievous members of society. The president, who is a mason, and several members prominent in debate and influence made able speeches on the subject. Congress finally voted them 15,000 dollars for their immediate wants, and ordered them to leave the country."[205]

A more succinct version is found in *Romanism As It Is* by Rev. Samuel W. Barnum:[206]

Section 10. Central America. March 15, 1873, Senor Rufino Barrios, then lieut. gen. of the army, and provisional head of the government of Guatemala, since (May, 1874) elected president, signed a decree establishing liberty of worship throughout the republic of Guatemala. Previously the R. C. was the established and only worship.

June 20, 1875, at San Miguel the 2d city of the republic of San Salvador, a R[oman].C[atholic]. Priest, Jose Manuel Palacios, preached a violent sermon against the government and the rich. Thereupon a mob liberated the convicts, massacred the garrison with its officers and many honorable citizens, pillaged and fired the city, which was saved from destruction by the arrival of troops from a distance. The R. C. bishop of San Salvador and his clergy had been for some time hostile to the government because it organized public schools on the German plan, taxed R. C. church-property, &c.; and he had issued a pastoral letter which the government suppressed as seditious. After the outbreak the bishop and several of the clergy were banished for instigating it; 50 or more of the rioters were executed; and vigorous measures were taken by the president (Marshal St. Jago Gonzalez) to re-establish and preserve order. The governments of San Salvador, Guatemala, and Honduras exclude from their respective states the religious orders of the R. C. Church."

Isham felt that Beecher was fleecing his Plymouth Church congregation in New York, and he's making a comparison of the terrible abuses of the Catholic priests in San Miguel, El Salvador . . . ordering ruffians to commit crimes in the name of religion (and giving them a heavenly pass to do so), to Beecher.[207] He then turns his anger towards the priests who wrote the "passes." He says that their pass won't get the criminals into heaven any better than a hand written "ticket" would get someone a legitimate ride on the "Cincinnati, Cumberland Gap, or Charleston road." By the "road" Isham means the Railroad. Gustavus W. Dyer says the following in his *A School History of Tennessee*, "The Cincinnati, Cumberland Gap and Charleston Railroad is the Tennessee link in a line of roads from Cincinnati to

[205] https://trove.nla.gov.au/newspaper/page/5016517, accessed on 23 Mar 2020

[206] *Romanism as it is: An Exposition of the Roman Catholic System for the Use of the American People ... : and an Appendix of Matters from 1871 to 1876*, Connecticut Publishing Company, 1882, Pg 748.

[207] https://www.britannica.com/place/San-Miguel-El-Salvador, accessed 23 Mar 2020

Charleston, which is designed to enter the state on the north at Cumberland Gap, and passing out of it into North Carolina by way of French Broad River, at Point Rock."[208]

By "Capt Taylor," Isham is likely referring to Capt. Henry Harrison Taylor from Knoxville. "Capt Taylor enlisted in the Confederate army as a private for the first year, then became first-lieutenant, and finally captain of company H, Fifth Tennessee Confederate cavalry, commanded by Col. George W. McKenzie. He was captured October 11, 1863, on the retreat from the fight at Blue Springs, Tennessee, between the Confederate forces, commanded by Gen. John S. ("Cerro Gordo") Williams, of Kentucky, and the Federal army under Gen. Burnside. At the time of his capture he was on detached duty as inspector-general of Gen. A.E. Jackson's brigade [. . .] Capt Taylor was sent to Johnson's Island, Ohio, November 15, 1863, where he was detained a prisoner till June 12, 1865, when he was released, the war having terminated. [. . .]

Capt. Taylor's great-grandfather, Isaac Taylor, came to Tennessee from Virginia, and settled in Carter county among the pioneers of that country. His grandfather, Gen. Nathaniel Taylor, came to Tennessee from Rock-bridge county, Virginia, just after his marriage with Miss Mary Patton. [. . .]

Alfred W. Taylor, father of Capt. Taylor, was born on the Watauga river, Carter county, Tennessee, on a property that has been owned by the family for ninety years. [. . .] He was one of the original projectors of the East Tennessee and Virginia railroad, and was a director in that railroad company at the time of his decease."[209]

Since it was Capt Taylor's father, "Alfred W. Taylor" who was the director of the East Tennessee and Virginia railroad, either Isham got the two men confused, or Capt Taylor helped direct the railroad after his father passed away in 1856.

The end of the article focuses on Isham's friend Wash Allen. It seems that he was in bad health and people had been inquiring of him. Isham makes a joke that Wash is more concerned with the money market than he is his soul. He says that Wash promised to "join the Young Men's Christian Association!" It should be noted that in its origins and certainly at the time of Sawbones' letter, the YMCA was a solidly Christian organization. D. L. Moody was heavily involved in the YMCA in Chicago. A quick internet search revealed an article in *The Tennessean* from 16 Mar 1875 Page 1 giving announcement that "quite a number of the young men of Nashville and Edgefield met at 3 o'clock Sunday afternoon in the First Baptist Church, for the purpose of organizing a Young Men's Christian Association."[210] It goes on to list each persons' name who enrolled in the newly formed YMCA. Another history of the YMCA provided by StateUniversity.com lists the following information. After

---

[208] A School History of Tennessee – Gustavus W. Dyer, Copyright 1919, published by the National Book Company, Chattanooga, Tenn. Pg 136, available online for free at:
https://play.google.com/books/reader?id=33IAAAAAYAAJ&hl=en&pg=GBS.PA136

[209] *Sketches of Prominent Tennesseans* by William S. Speer, Pg 462, portions available at: https://tinyurl.com/2p9h6h5k
[210] https://www.newspapers.com/clip/28454977/ymca-1875/, accessed 23 Mar 2020

it was founded in 1844 in London by George Williams, the first American YMCA was established in 1851 in Boston.

> "By 1860 there were more than 200 YMCAs with more than 25,000 members in the United States. Most early YMCAs were open only to men, although a few accepted women members, often unofficially. Some YMCAs were established to serve particular ethnic or immigrant groups. The first YMCA for African Americans was established in Washington, D.C., in 1853 by Anthony Bowen, a freed slave. Beginning in 1875, YMCAs were founded in San Francisco, California, to serve the city's large Chinese population. Thomas Wakeman, a Dakota Sioux, started the first YMCA for Native Americans in 1879 in Flandreau, South Dakota.
>
> Early YMCA leaders were concerned with addressing the difficulties and temptations facing young men arriving in the cities, far from the stabilizing influence of home and family, during the American Civil War and the Industrial Revolution. In the United States revival meetings were the outstanding programs offered, and the associations sent out the first street workers to preach on street corners and around the wharves. They also sent out "gospel wagons" to distribute Christian tracts and Bibles and give sermons in city neighborhoods."[211]

As to Isham's talk about "the holy-bonds-of-matrimony business" and Wash buying a cradle, more in depth family research into the Allen family is needed to figure out details as to Wash's official marital status, whether he had children, etc. Suffice to say that Wash and Isham were both fed up by the clergical abuses of the day, Beecher and Fr. Palacios included. It would seem, though, that Isham at least considered himself a Christian, and probably that Wash did not.

Old Flint Article

The next article that appears in the *Gazette* referencing Sawbones is not from Isham, but by an acquaintance of his named "Flint." Flint writes an article decrying the Newport (TN) of 1875 and saying that you couldn't pay him to go there. Nevertheless, he spent time with Isham and Wash, and he thought the newspaper would want to hear about it. He uses racist terminology in the article, and for that, the author apologizes.

---

[211] https://education.stateuniversity.com/pages/2574/Youth-Organizations-YOUNG-MEN-S-CHRISTIAN-ASSOCIATION.html, accessed 23 Mar 2020

15 NOV 1875 "OLD FLINT: [NEWPORT AND HOW HE FOUND SAWBONES]"[212]

"OLD FLINT:

ON HIS CIRCUIT—HOW HE GOT TO NEW PORT AND HOW HE SCRATCHED A WAY—HOW HE FOUND SAWBONES AND THE LAST EXPRESSION OF THE YOUTHFUL ADONIS.

ON THE WING, Nov. 15, 1875.

Dear Gazette: —In the course of a recent business trip up the country, and 'out on the Buncombe,' it became necessary for me to go to Newport—I don't mean the neat, thrifty and pleasurable little Clifton, on the bank of the beautiful Pigeon, the very sight of which is enlivening to a wayfarer—but New Port, old New Port, a place situated about one and a half miles east of and across the river from Clifton. Once, and not many years ago. intelligence, education, refinement, wealth, big hearted hospitality and hog and hominy were associated with the very name of New Port; but now it is for the most part covered with filth, niggers and jailer dogs! My visit was quick, short and decisive, and I left hurriedly for Parrottsville—scratching as I went! I defy any one to pass through old New Port, and make a turn in the old court house, without scratching his way out! Duty, stern duty, might induce me to make another visit to old New Port in the day time, but if there was a bare possibility of night overtaking me there or thereabouts, I wouldn't go if the people of Cocke and Sevier would make me a warrantee deed to Wilson Dugan's old domain! I can but admire the bull dog tenacity with which one of her citizens held on and refused to give up his habitation to the bats and owls, but finally the blood of Pocahontas began to bile afresh in his veins, and off to the white settlement he moved and still lives to dispense justice to thousands.

Figure 118 – Photo of Wilson Duggan, Jr. (Son of Wilson Duggan) (Courtesy of Linda Arnold on FindAGrave.com)

On this trip I met with your correspondent, Sawbones, who had a full drum corps with him, under the leadership of G. Wash. Allen, who is very fond of drums and drummers generally, provided they do not (as they did on this occasion), keep up such a racket as to disturb a conversation between him and a pretty lass of 'sweet 18 or 20.' It was several hours after we got to Wolf Creek, before Wash recovered his usual equilibrium, and the last words we heard him say, as he was about to retire to his virtuous couch was, "dam them drums."

FLINT."

Because this is not an article written by Sawbones, but simply mentions him, less time will be spent explaining the various references. But a few notes are helpful for understanding. "Wilson Dugan" was a well-known character from Sevier County. Wilson L. Duggan (23 Sep 1803 – 14 Feb 1875) was heavily involved in the politics of the region. A findagrave.com entry by Linda Arnold says the following regarding Duggan. "Col. Wilson Duggan, was a lawyer in Sevier County. He was licensed

---

[212] Old Flint, [Newport and How He Found Sawbones], *The Morristown Gazette*, 17 Nov 1875, 2.

to practice law in December 1829 and practiced until his death in the 1870s. Wilson served as a representative to the Tennessee legislature in 1843-53 and 1865-67. Besides his extensive law practice, Col. Duggan owned a good farm and was a teacher in 1826-27. He was the son of Robert Duggan, and Margaret Dunn. Their children were: Reason Simeon, Lemuel, Pryor, Lisa, Jason, Margaret C. William H.H., Elizabeth, state Sen. Wilson L., and Robert Campbell."[213] Notably though, and in keeping with the racist language of Flint's article, he probably mentions Duggan because in 1866 Duggan was caught "in the embraces of a negro woman." He was thrown into jail and the papers had a field day with the news.[214] Today, white and black couples are commonplace, but this was not the case until the repeal of anti-miscegenation laws between 1948 and 1967. Wikipedia has fairly comprehensive coverage of the subject.[215]

Transcription of Duggan Article:

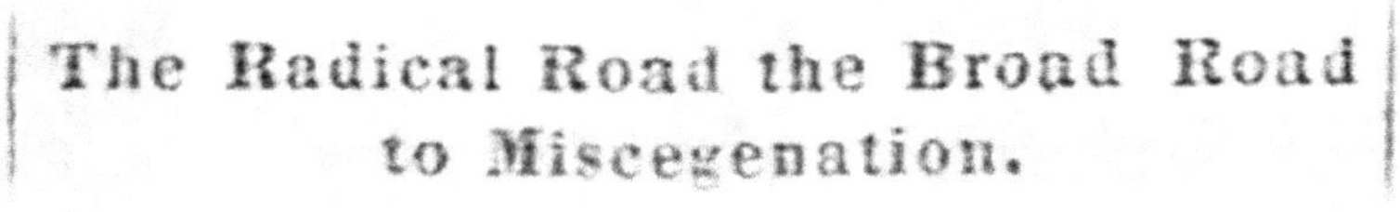

The Radical Road the Broad Road to Miscegenation.

Figure 120 - *The Nashville Daily Union* 4 Mar 1866, 1

The Radical Road the Broad Road to Miscegenation.

From the Union and American of the 3d.

An "honorable" gentleman, a representative from one or two of the counties of East Tennessee, by the name of Duggan, who is distinguished as a simon pure radical, was found by policeman Bergin and Edwards, in the centre of "Black Hall," (we refer to the map of the 9th Ward for the exact locality)—in the embraces of a negro woman, about the middle of the night of Thursday. Upon being taken thence to police headquarters, he pleaded drunkenness, said that he did not know whether his bedfellow was black or white, male or female. The Recorder took the testimony of the sable nymph, who stated that Duggan came to her house duly sober and offered her a princely compensation for her poor lodgings, herself included, which she could not resist—and the bargain was struck with the above result. Duggan submitted the case, and was let off with a fine amounting to two or three days of his *per diem*. We trust this is the very last one of *"Duggan's bills,"* either as a legislator or as an amateur Lothario[216], and law breaker, in this city. Duggan is about sixty years old, and should now go home, ask pardon of his constituents, and prepare himself for a better life."[217]

See Fig 133 on page 163 for "The Miscegenation Ball," a contemporary political caricature.

[213] https://www.findagrave.com/memorial/47124356/wilson-l_-duggan, accessed on 24 Mar 2020
[214] https://www.newspapers.com/clip/7371557/wilson-duggan/, accessed on 24 Mar 2020
[215] https://en.wikipedia.org/wiki/Anti-miscegenation_laws_in_the_United_States, accessed 24 Mar 2020
[216] "Lothario is a male given name that came to suggest an unscrupulous seducer of women, based upon a character in The Fair Penitent, a 1703 tragedy by Nicholas Rowe." https://en.wikipedia.org/wiki/Lothario
[217] *The Nashville Daily Union*, 4 Mar 1866, 1, quoting *The Union and American* from 3 Mar 1866.

31	492	492	Mary Allen	73	a				5500	17625			31
35			G. M. Allen	45	m		farmer	5500	16000				35
36			Emma	30	f								36
37			Martha Johnston	17									37
38			Mark Harris	26	m			1					38
39	493	493	Green Allen	61	a				2000	5500			39

Figure 121 – 1860 US Federal Census, Cocke County, TN - Mary Allen was 73; G. W. Allen, Mary and Reuben's son was 45; daughter Emma Allen, 30; son Green Allen, 61. Image from Ancestry.com.

The final paragraph of Flint's article addresses his time with Isham and Wash. Apparently Isham had a "drum corps" with him that was being led by Wash. Though in this instance Wash is annoyed by the drummers because he is trying to have a conversation with a young lady 18 or 20 years old, and the drummers are interrupting their conversation. According to the 1860 U.S. Federal Census, Wash was 45 at the time of the census. During this occasion, Wash was 60 years old.[218] All that to say, Wash seems to be an old bachelor and his main business is running the "Wash Allen Inn" as it is sometimes called.

As an additional source for info about Wash Allen, *A History of Transportation in Western North Carolina: Trails, Roads, Rails, and Air* is a treasure trove of information, photos, and other information. In that book, author Terry Ruscin says "Allen's Old Stand" was owned by George Washington "Wash" Allen who lived from 1812-1876 in Wolf Creek, Cocke County.[219] Describing the Buncombe Turnpike where Wash's hotel was located, Ruscin says:

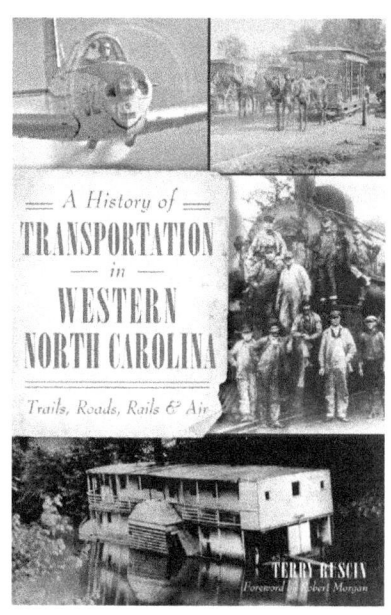

"A more famous early road was the Buncombe Turnpike across the mountains from Tennessee into South Carolina. This pike served as a road for drovers driving cattle, hogs, horses, sheep and even turkeys across the mountains to markets in South Carolina. Local farmers along the way built taverns, called "stands," to serve the drovers, with many bedrooms and large pens and corncribs for the livestock." [. . .]

"What became known as the Drovers Road, or 'Old Stock Road,' comprised a wagon trail from Tennessee rising up over the Blue Ridge at Hickory Nut Gap and down the Fairview Valley into Asheville and points southward. Buncombe County lawyer, historian, bibliophile and author Forster Alexander Sondley (1857-1931) wrote that large-scale droving efforts from Tennessee passed through western North Carolina to South Carolina and Georgia markets as early as the late 1700s. The most onerous leg of the journey included the rugged terrain dividing Tennessee and Asheville. Before laborers constructed the Buncombe Turnpike,

---

[218] https://www.ancestraljourneys.com/swagerty/allen_inn_wolf_creek_story.htm, accessed on 24 Mar 2020
[219] *A History of Transportation in Western North Carolina: Trails, Roads, Rails, and Air* by Terry Ruscin, 2016 by Terry Ruscin, accessed on 24 Mar 2020, reprinted here with permission from Arcadia Publishing and The History Press. https://tinyurl.com/sj9jdwxf

drovers ventured along the banks of the French Broad River on their southbound journeys, as this course proved the route of least resistance. From the north, turnpikes led to the Old Drovers Road – the southern 'turnpike' – essentially a footpath and provisional wagon road. 'Rivers of hogs' and their drovers and drivers flowed almost nonstop from mid-October through mid-December from stockyards in Tennessee (Greeneville, Rogersville, Dandridge and Knoxville) through Warm Springs, Marshall, Woodfin, Asheville, Flat Rock and Pace's Gap (Saluda), North Carolina, and funneled through Travelers Rest, South Carolina, and into the market delta of Greeneville and Spartanburg, where livestock was slaughtered, butchered, rendered and smoked and much of it hence conveyed on to Augusta and the seaports of Savannah and Charleston." [. . .]

"A steady stream of drivers and their herds created the need for 'stands' along the way to serve as stopping points for rest and sustenance. Because of their short legs, swine could travel only six to ten miles each day. Accordingly, stock stands or taverns grew up along the Drovers Road to service hogs and other livestock as well as their drivers. Stands, located at intervals of every five or ten miles, provided not only meals and lodging for drovers but also pens, fenced-in lots and fodder for the livestock." [. . .]

Tollgate records suggest that from 150,000 to 200,000 hogs traveled on the turnpike each year in droves of from 300 to 3,000 head each. David Vance (1792-1844) of the Vance Inn claimed to have fed 110,000 hogs during one especially busy month. Innkeeper Hezekiah Alexander Carr Barnard (circa 1780-1882) made a similar claim." [. . .]

"Lodgers shared quarters with several to a room, generally sleeping on floors overlaid with blankets or on pallets in spaces heated with log-heap fires. Before bedtime, an average table would be laden with sliced meat and boiled root vegetables or a whole roasted ox and platters of spare ribs and sausages with sides such as boiled cabbage or sauerkraut, baked beans, sweet potatoes, biscuits, cornbread, cracklin' bread and cornpone. Beverages included buttermilk, sweet milk and coffee. Innkeepers included the price of repast in the lodging fee – one dollar – or charged on average from twenty to twenty-five cents per meal. Certain innkeepers sold whiskey or brandy or applejack for an additional fee. While all of that might sound appetizing, travelers at times complained about filthy conditions, rude service and unpalatable food, including 'chicken swimming in black grease served with lumps of soggy dough.' Sleeping arrangements proved crowded with privacy nil. In some cases, the livestock likely ate better than their drivers.

Figure 122 - Wolf Creek Train Depot, within walking distance of the Wolf Creek Inn. Photo circa 1905, with passengers prepared to board the train.

Figure 123 - Photo of Wolf Creek Inn, hanging in the home of Ms Betty Walker, photo digitized by the author. With appreciation to the Walker Family.

Said not to travel well on full stomachs, the animals were fed only once daily, in the evening during the overnight stays, with livestock being slopped in order of their arrival. Innkeepers bought corn at approximately fifty cents per bushel and sold it for seventy-five to eight cents per bushel. Local farmers and Indians provided fodder. Eight bushels of corn were stipulated for every one hundred hogs. Drovers many times purchased this feed on credit and reimbursed innkeepers on return junkets after having sold their livestock. At times, an innkeeper would take payment in lame animals.

Four-legged creatures slept in stockades, and turkeys roosted in the trees. Old accounts noted that it was with great difficulty each morning for drivers to coax the fowl down from their roosts.

The numbers of droves along this route peaked between 1830 and 1840. The state added gravel surfacing by the 1920s, and the federal government paved it in 1931. Eventually, railroads would provide more expeditious and cost-effective means of transporting livestock, with rail systems expanding briskly after the Civil War. By the late 1800s, most stock stands fell into disrepair or reverted to farmhouses or tourist inns. Others were torn down or left to rot."

Wash must have had hundreds of people coming through the "Wolf Creek Stagecoach Inn" every month, and his family needed to be churning out hundreds of meals for people and thousands of meals for the livestock. Isham and Emma likely spent their time at the Inn visiting and talking politics or otherwise with all who passed that way. **Scan the QR Code to the right to experience CMB LIVE: Walk around the grounds of the Wolf Creek Inn, see the ruins of the two chimneys, and learn from Ann Peck and Betty Walker.**

After some photos from the modern-day property, and a beautifully written 1877 article describing the Wolf Creek Inn, we will move on to the next mention of Sawbones, in the Personal section of *The Gazette…*

Figure 124 - Tour the Wolf Creek Inn with author Andy Peck, https://youtu.be/B15Jx FWPoEw

Figure 127- Painting of the Wolf Creek Inn (Front)- Hangs in the home of Ms Betty Walker of Wolf Creek, photo by author 29 Oct 2020. With appreciation to the Walker Family.

Figure 126 - Painting of the Wolf Creek Inn (Back)- Hangs in the home of Ms Betty Walker of Wolf Creek, photo by author 29 Oct 2020. With appreciation to the Walker Family.

Figure 125 - Albert Walker (son) with mother Betty Walker, photo by the author 29 Oct 2020. With appreciation to the Walker Family. Used with permission.

Wolf Creek Inn Visit by an 1877 Texas Traveler[220]

At seven next morning we took the train for Wolf's creek (the terminus of the road), steaming away at the wonderful rate of ten miles an hour. A part of the way lay through such magnificent scenery that we had reason to rejoice at the slow pace that enabled us to enjoy it. We crossed the French Broad, and our track was along its banks—the mountains towering above us, the rocks, the river with its rapids and addies (eddies), the rhododendrons blooming by the wayside, and the ferns clinging to the cliffs, form a picture you must see. I can only feel, not describe it. We were on an accommodation train, so well deserving its name that the conductor passed through the cars to say there was a spring by the road, and if the passengers wanted sulphur water he would stop and give them some. We wanted it, and he stopped accordingly.

At Wolf's creek was the dinner station; there, leaving the cars and bidding good-bye to railroads for this summer, we crossed a rustic bridge, and walking for a short distance along the shaded banks of a brawling creek, came to an old-fashioned country house. It looked so deliciously cool and clean, so far removed from the dust and heat of travel, that I felt I had caught a glimpse of Arcadia, and exclaimed involuntarily, "people who live here ought to be very good." The house was low and broad, with queer little windows blinking at us from the roof; a gallery in front, and a wide, open hospitable hall connecting the rooms, giving an air of welcome that was irresistible. At the back door was a garden, quaint and prim, with clean-swept walks, and fanciful beds ornamented with box(wood); in one of these shrubs is shown the place where, concealed by the foliage, the family hid their little store of silver from the "jayhawkers" during the war. We were ravenously hungry, when at noon we were called from gathering cherries in the orchard, to a dinner in keeping with the house-plain, palatable and plentiful. The dining-room floor was sanded, and the table ornamented with vases of flowers. The thermometer stood at 70 degrees here at noon. At 2 o'clock the stage rattled to the door and we started off in grand style, with the children inside and the "grown folks" on top. I confess I left Wolf's Creek with a tiny pang of regret, and the little ones seemed to sympathize with my feelings. They had been wild with delight, jumping over the rocks and throwing pebbles in the creek until called to the house to dry their shoes by the kitchen fire and prepare for the stage.

Figure 128 - Wolf Creek Depot Area behind Wolf Creek Inn Photo by author behind Wolf Creek Inn with permission from land owner, 29 Oct 2020

---

[220] M.C.K in "Chatty Letter From A Lady," *The Galveston Daily News*, Galveston, TX, 12 Jul 1877, 2.

7 JUL 1875 Personal. Wash Allen Detained[221] […]

Col. Wash. Allen, of the Warm Springs Hotel, junior, Riverside, Tennessee, was captured and detained one night last week, the guest of Maj. Guthrie of the Turley House. By the way, strange reports are current touching the probability of an early change in the domestic and social relations of Col. Washington. But whether it is a wife or a church he is to have charge of, 'Sawbones' must advise us."

It seems Isham was looked to as a man who knew what was happening in the social lives of prominent members of the East Tennessee community, especially his friends of course. This author did not find a written response by Sawbones to this inquiry by *The Gazette* editor.

Figure 129 - Mist over the Mountains in Wolf Creek, photo by author behind Wolf Creek Inn with permission from land owner. The Wolf Creek Inn originally stood to this right of the land displayed in this photo.

---

[221] Editors, "Personal", "Wash Allen Detained" added by Andy Peck, *The Morristown Gazette*, 7 Jul 1875, 3.

"SAWBONES" WANTS NO THEOLOGICAL WRANGLING.

To the Editor of the Morristown Gazette:

Every peaceable man in the country will thank you for protesting against the religious wrangle. We have all seen the bad effects of such contests. Two preachers, with a predominant object of attracting the public attention to themselves, will get up one of these wrangles and at once set an otherwise peaceable community by the ears. We recollect how Christians of different denominations used to slaughter each other at the tomb of Jesus, until a Turkish guard was placed there to stop the shameful slaughter. Every lover of peace should do everything in his power to frown down and discountenance this wrangle. Smother it in its incipiency. The question involved seems to be whether a man should be immersed or sprinkled to insure his salvation. I have read the Bible myself, and under our present form of government I am entitled to an opinion. I always thought that Christ, in being baptized, was only showing his disciples an example of cleanliness. He told them that cleanliness was next to godliness. Mahomet, who was an imitator of Christ, made it incumbent on his followers to wash three times a day. which may account for there being so many more Mahomedans than Christians. But if this immersion or sprinkling is necessary, then, from recent developments, it will require a ten horse power steam washer to operate on some eminent divines, before they will be in condition to promenade the streets of the New Jerusalem!　　SAWBONES.

16 FEB 1876 "SAWBONES" WANTS NO THEOLOGICAL WRANGLING.[222]

To the Editor of the Morristown Gazette:

Every peaceable man in the country will thank you for protesting against the religious wrangle. We have all seen the bad effects of such contests. Two preachers, with a predominant object of attracting the public attention to themselves, will get up one of these wrangles and at once set an otherwise peaceable community by the ears. We recollect how Christians of different denominations used to slaughter each other at the tomb of Jesus, until a Turkish guard was placed there to stop the shameful slaughter. Every lover of peace should do everything in his power to frown down and discountenance this wrangle. Smother it in its incipiency. The question involved seems to be whether a man should be immersed or sprinkled to insure his salvation. I have read the Bible myself, and under our present form of government I am entitled to an opinion. I always thought that Christ, in being baptized, was only showing his disciples an example of cleanliness. He told them that cleanliness was next to godliness. Mahomet, who was an imitator of Christ, made it incumbent on his followers to wash three times a day. which may account for there being so many more Mahomedans than Christians. But if this immersion or sprinkling is necessary, then, from recent developments, it will require a ten horse power steam washer to operate on some eminent divines, before they will be in condition to promenade the streets of the New Jerusalem!

SAWBONES."

The religious controversy referred to above, regarding which type of baptism is necessary, is discussed in detail on 9 Feb 1876 in the same *Morristown Gazette*. An advertisement for the actual debate appeared on 26 Jan 1876 in the same paper.[223] This article is entitled, "THEOLOGICAL PUGILISTS."

THEOLOGICAL PUGILISTS.

In an elaborate article in the last *Baptist Reflector*, commenting on a paragraph that appeared in a late issue of the GAZETTE about the misfortune that might attend the good citizens of the prosperous village of Mossy Creek, by making it the battle ground of a theological discussion on the subject of Baptism, brother Pope says:

'But we are told that these men are "wranglers." Turning to Webster, we find that wrangler means, 'An angry disputant; one who disputes with heat or peevishness.' What has Brother Boring done to merit such an epithet as this? He is known to the most of the citizens throughout this sections [sic], as a pleasant, agreeable gentleman, yet the GAZETTE thinks him an angry disputant. We think the Methodist community will look upon this as an unmerited compliment (?)' And he concludes his comments by announcing that,

'The GAZETTE is a good secular paper, but it makes bungling work of it when it touches theology. We shall have to revoke our letters patent, if we see any more such comments as the above.'

And so, we are to be shorn of our honors so lately won—our title to empty sounding words—and all for what? Why for this: in our first ecclesiastical effort, after the Pope had dubbed us

Figure 130 - The announcement below was carried in *The Morristown Gazette* on 26 Jan 1876, 2.

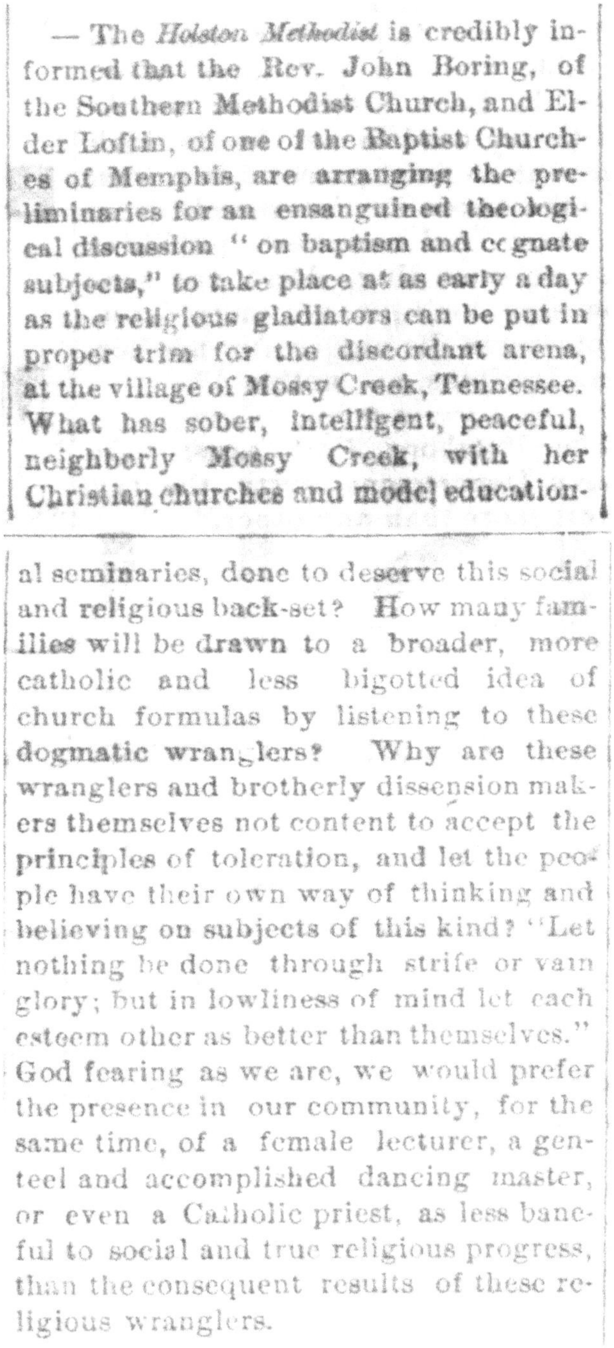

— The *Holston Methodist* is credibly informed that the Rev. John Boring, of the Southern Methodist Church, and Elder Loftin, of one of the Baptist Churches of Memphis, are arranging the preliminaries for an ensanguined theological discussion "on baptism and cognate subjects," to take place at as early a day as the religious gladiators can be put in proper trim for the discordant arena, at the village of Mossy Creek, Tennessee. What has sober, intelligent, peaceful, neighborly Mossy Creek, with her Christian churches and model education-

al seminaries, done to deserve this social and religious back-set? How many families will be drawn to a broader, more catholic and less bigotted idea of church formulas by listening to these dogmatic wranglers? Why are these wranglers and brotherly dissension makers themselves not content to accept the principles of toleration, and let the people have their own way of thinking and believing on subjects of this kind? "Let nothing be done through strife or vain glory; but in lowliness of mind let each esteem other as better than themselves." God fearing as we are, we would prefer the presence in our community, for the same time, of a female lecturer, a genteel and accomplished dancing master, or even a Catholic priest, as less baneful to social and true religious progress, than the consequent results of these religious wranglers.

---

[222] Dr. Isham Peck, "Sawbones Wants No Theological Wrangling," *The Morristown Gazette*, 16 Feb 1876, 2.
[223] https://chroniclingamerica.loc.gov/lccn/sn85033681/1876-01-26/ed-1/seq-2/, accessed on 24 May 2020

Figure 131 - Rev. John Boring - Methodist Episcopal Church, South (Photo from www.ourfamtree.org/records/ministers.php

D. D., in a paragraph deprecating the announcement of the *Holston Methodist* that a controversy on the subject of Baptism was being arranged to come off at Mossy Creek, between the Rev. Mr. Lofton, of the Baptist Church, and the Rev. John Boring, of the Methodist Episcopal Church, South, we dared to express the fear and belief that the proposed discussion would prove hurtful in a religious point of view to the community about Mossy Creek, and that the parties engaged in it as principals would appear as 'dogmatic wranglers.' This is the head and front of our offending. But the Pope, with the cuteness of a Cardinal and the subtlety of a lawyer, innocently asks: 'What has Brother Boring done to merit this epithet?' and gravely and ominously thinks 'that the Methodist community will look upon this as an unmerited *compliment*. (?) Go slow, Bro. Pope! Your *Reflector* doesn't mirror our appearance at all, and we cannot accept its reflections as true. We protest we gave no more censure to Mr. Boring than we did to Mr. Lofton, and that we did not pretend to hold the one less to blame than the other, whatever our private feelings on the matter may have been at the time. We don't propose to answer incorrect questions. But supposing it put in this shape: What have brothers Lofton and Boring done to merit this epithet? we very cheerfully and very frankly answer: we can accuse them of but one act whereby they should be styled 'dogmatic wranglers,' that is to say, common report has it that brother Lofton, at a time of profound religious peace and amity in the congregations of the Churches and amongst the patrons and teachers of the literary institutions at Mossy Creek, which are composed of almost every element of Protestant belief, *did challenge* brother Boring, of the Southern Methodist Church, to a public wrangle (or discussion, if you like the word better,) on the vexed subject of Baptism; and that brother Boring acceded (reluctantly we are told, and be it said to his credit,) *the challenge* from brother Lofton to engage in this wrangle (or controversy.) Up to the time of the sending of this *challenge* and its *acceptance*, the record of each gentleman, so far as we know, was clear; but this agreement now, alas! puts them each in the category of theological pugilists or 'dogmatic wranglers.'

Mr. Boring, and no doubt Mr. Lofton, too, are commissioned from high heaven to 'earnestly contend

Figure 132 - Rev. George A. Lofton, CSA https://tnsos.org/tsla/imagesearch/images/2495.jpg

for the faith once delivered to the saints.' For many years, Mr. Boring has been successfully doing this in the way his commission directs. No doubt the same may be said of Mr. Lofton. But in our humble Judgment they are outside their commissions now. They are soiling their robes. They have for the time ceased to 'preach the word'—ceased to 'call sinners to repentance' and have engaged in discussing the 'dogmas' of their respective denominations, or (as they no doubt believe,) each in exposing the dogmas of the other's denomination. With nothing but the kindliest personal feelings toward each gentleman, we have every reason to believe that this debate will be like all others of its class. It will be *earnest, heated*—perhaps *angry*—at least *heated*. It will therefore be (according to Webster.) a 'wrangle'— a 'wrangle' about 'dogmas.' The participants are therefore most unquestionably 'dogmatic wranglers'—with all that the words imply.

But we are told that we erred in supposing that religious [doctrinal] discussions are hurtful to true religious progress. In regard to this grave error, we have only to say, we have no way of judging the future but by the past; and judging the future by the past, we think we are warranted in predicting that for months and perhaps for years after this debate, there will be bickerings and heart burnings, among the good Christians about Mossy Creek, such as have never before existed. No Methodist will be made a Baptist by it, and no Baptist a Methodist. The denominational lines will be harshly drawn, and the children will learn to throw the phrases of the respective champions at each other in their juvenile wrangles. According to our observation, such have been the results of such discussions everywhere. We have the highest regard for each of the gentlemen, and believe them to be worthy Christian ministers. We know of Mr. Boring that he is a most acceptable and useful minister. A plain, unpretending, earnest man of kindly creed and gentle teachings, and when those speak of him who know him best, they speak with enthusiasm. We hope he may live long enough to preach thousands of gospel sermons, but not long enough to engage in another 'dogmatic wrangle.'

And now, Jo., thou imp of unsightly horns and serpent tale, put these sandals out of sight, hang this surplice in an outer room, give this Concordance to John Burts, this Theological Dictionary to John Brown, and if a Baptist or a Methodist should inquire for your theological editor, tell them he is absent at the Centennial. We will have peace."

Rev. John Boring was a well-known Methodist minister of the Mossy Creek Methodist Episcopal Church, South. The Christian Advocate, Volume 71 shares about his death in 1910 in this way, "In the death of Rev. John Boring on August 5, 1910, the Holston Conference has lost not only one of its oldest members, but one of its most saintly and useful

Christian Advocate

General Organ of the Methodist Episcopal Church, South.

THOS. N. IVEY, Editor.

Published Weekly by Smith & Lamar, Nashville, Tenn.

SUBSCRIPTION RATES: One year, $2; six months, $1; rate to all ministers, $1 per year. For information as to advertising, address J. Arthur Johnson, Advertising Manager, Nashville, Tenn.

Entered at post office, Nashville, Tenn., as second-class matter.

PERSONALS

characters. His was a life which will be for many years a sacred treasure to hundreds of men and women."[224]

Elder George A. Lofton (1839-1914) was on the ordination committee for an Elder W. C. McPherson at a Baptist Church in Holt's Corner, Marshall County, Tennessee in 1890.[225] His obituary reads, "***Obituary of George A. Lofton, Nashville, Tennessee.*** A most remarkable life came to its close in the death of Dr. George A. Lofton in Nashville, Tenn., on December 11, 1914, after an illness of several weeks. Born in Panola County, Miss., December 25, 1839, he had nearly completed his seventy-fifth year. Dr. Lofton enlisted in the Confederate army in 1861 as a private in the 1st Georgia Regiment and served to the close of the war. He was adjutant of the 9th Georgia Battalion in 1862-64 and commanded a battery in 1864-65. After the war he returned to Mercer University and graduated in 1872 with the degree of A. M. The degree of D. D. was conferred upon him by Baylor University in 1880, and the degree of L. L. D. by the University of Nashville, in 1910 and by Carson and Newman College in 1911. He was married to Miss Ella E. Martin, of Atlanta, Ga., in 1864. His wife, ever a true helpmate, survives him with one son. Dr. Lofton first studied law and practiced for a year in Americus, Ga.; but, feeling called to preach, he entered the ministry and became a prominent minister of the Baptist Church. His pastorate at Central Baptist Church, Nashville, was continuous from 1881 until his death. During that time he accomplished a wonderful work. As a preacher Dr. Lofton was strong, intense, and eloquent; as a pastor he was wise, sympathetic, loving and beloved. But he was even more widely known and admired as a writer. Chief among his books was "Character Sketches," of which some three hundred thousand copies have been sold throughout the country. SOURCE: Confederate Veteran Magazine, April, 1915."[226]

Sawbones expresses his theological position on the subject of baptism by quoting Jesus as saying, "cleanliness was next to godliness." Jesus never says this, but it is an oft quoted (mis-quoted) "verse" from the Bible, except for the fact that it is not in there. Before we jump on Isham too quickly for thinking that the phrase "cleanliness is next to godliness" is found in Scripture, and recognizing that he could have been saying it tongue in cheek anyway, check out the following info from JSTOR Daily:[227]

---

[224] *Christian Advocate.* United States: J.B. M'Ferrin for the Methodist Episcopal Church, South, 1910. 8, available free online at https://tinyurl.com/ChristianAdvocate1910, accessed on 24 Mar 2020

[225] *History of Middle Tennessee Baptists* by John Harvey Grime, 472.

[226] http://www.confederatevets.com/documents/lofton_tn_cv_04_15_ob.shtml, accessed 24 Mar 2020

[227] Livia Gershon, Using God to Sell Soap: Ivory Soap got its name from Psalm 45, JSTOR https://daily.jstor.org/using-god-to-sell-soap/, 20 Aug 2019.

"The phrase "cleanliness is next to godliness" goes back at least as far as a 1778 sermon by John Wesley. But, as religion and history scholars Richard J. Callahan, Jr., Kathryn Lofton, and Chad E. Seales explain, the phrase took on new meaning in the late nineteenth and early twentieth centuries as soap companies marketed their products in distinctly religious terms.

"Before the Civil War, the authors explain, a kind of "cleanliness" was important to Christian respectability, but this was as much about carefully ironed clothes and an upright self-presentation as the absence of dirt and body odor. Up until the 1870s, people typically used only hot water for cleaning. Soap was an optional accessory, not a staple. But, by the 1930s, Americans placed soap second only to food as the most important consumer product. This shift was one of the first victories for a concerted consumer marketing campaign, and it was also a victory for a particular view of Christianity.

In a nation where companies could comfortably assume they were selling their products to Protestant consumers, soap companies drew on religious language. Ivory Soap got its name from Psalm 45: "All thy garments smell of myrrh and aloes and cassia out of ivory palaces whereby they have made thee glad." The company placed the first ad for Ivory in a Christian weekly, and it kept up a close relationship with Protestant institutions. In 1896, social gospel theologian Washington Gladden spoke at a P&G dividend meeting, praising the relations "between employer and employees in Ivorydale, between the directing minds and helping hands."

Ivory wasn't alone. In the 1880s, the John H. Woodbury Company began a "Facial Purity League" for face-cleaning products. Callahan, Lofton, and Seales describe a marketing campaign that included "campaign buttons and membership contracts describing in vivid Christian language the connection between soap and moral worth, between purchase and regeneration." Another soap company, Wool Soap, promised to donate a penny to the Women's Christian Temperance Union for every Wool Soap wrapper returned to the company.

Soap markers also borrowed tactics from religious proselytizers. The Cleanliness Institute, founded in 1927 by a soap industry association, produced pamphlets designed to teach Americans new cleanliness rituals. The "Book About Baths," for example, took 24 pages to explain correct methods for morning bathing, after-work baths, bathing for children, and baths of different temperatures. Newspapers were enthusiastic about the Institute.

"As it is with godliness, so with cleanliness, there are many millions without the desire to repent and be laved," the *Detroit Free Press* punned. "We must continue to 'sell' the world on cleanliness."

Callahan, Lofton, and Seales explain how the push to sell soap depended on, and contributed to, a larger ideology. It brought together ideas of progress, the fight against prostitution and alcohol, and an optimistic, self-improving Protestant theology under the rubric of cleanliness. In an early example of the growing importance of marketing in a consumer capitalist economy, companies were selling much more than soap."

A link from the JSTOR blog routes to *Allegories of Progress: Industrial Religion in the United States* by Richard Callahan, Jr., Kathryn Lofton and Chad E. Seales. Page 20 and following address this use of religion to sell soap and how it began in America in the 1870s.[228] It is available for free online if you are interested in further reading on the subject. Isham ends his comments by saying in effect that the ministers will be so "dirty" from participating in this baptism debate that neither sprinkling nor immersion will be effectual enough, and that it will take a "ten horse power steam washer" to clean them well enough for them to be ready for heaven!

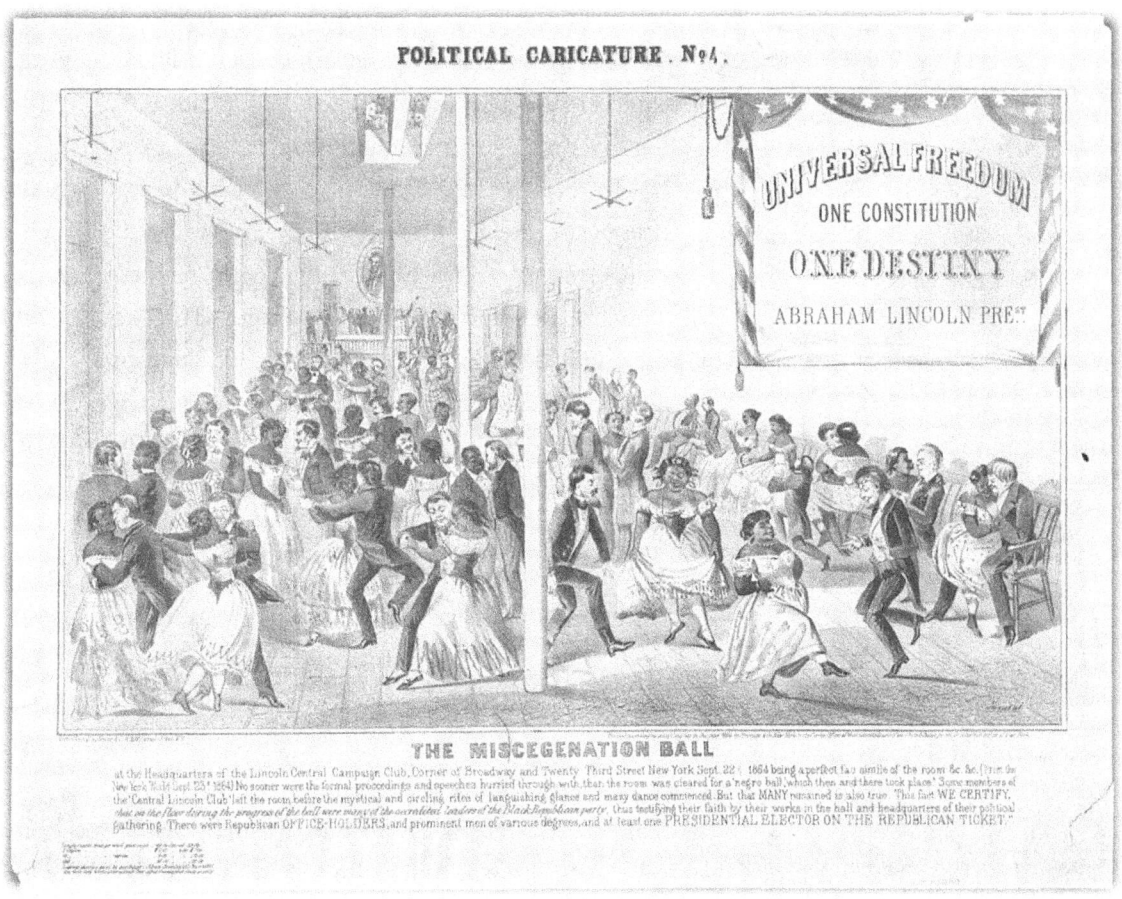

Figure 133 - G.W. Bromley & Co, and Kimmel & Forster. Political caricature. No. 4, The miscegenation ball. New York City New York, 1864. Photograph. https://www.loc.gov/item/2008661682/.
See 15 Nov 1875 OLD FLINT article in this volume and comments there regarding miscegenation on page 150.

In 1876, a person identifying themselves as "Whitehead" writes "AN OPEN NOTE TO 'SAWBONES'" and mentions Isham's brothers Bill (William Raine Peck) and Adam Clayton Peck.

---

228 Callahan, Richard J., et al. "Allegories of Progress: Industrial Religion in the United States." *Journal of the American Academy of Religion*, vol. 78, no. 1, 2010, pp. 1–39. *JSTOR*, www.jstor.org/stable/40666460. Accessed 24 Mar. 2020.

6 SEP 1876 AN OPEN NOTE TO "SAWBONES"[229]

AN OPEN NOTE TO "SAWBONES."

To the Editor of the Morristown Gazette:

To the Editor of the Morristown Gazette:

Your worthy correspondent, 'Sawbones,' wields a most graceful pen, cannot we prevail on him to favor us more frequently with his interesting articles from his home in the mountains of Cocke? If I mistake not his identity, I recognize a favorite correspondent of the old *Spirit of the Times*, who at that day hailed from 'Millikin's Bend,' the distant land to which he strayed off; and where he throve. East Tennesseans generally thrive when transplanted.

In November, 1825, the writer, then a stripling of fifteen summer's, entered the classic walls of Greeneville college-then a flourishing institution, presided over by the venerable, learned and good Doctor Coffin, who way prone to bring up, 'just in this connection,' certain unpleasant facts of dereliction, the relavency [sic] of which we could not appreciate. You, Sawbones, and your excellent brothers, Adam and Bill, were also students. By the bye, I don't think any one of us were student enough to impair his physical vigor. Jim Vance, too, who now saws bones in the good county of Sullivan, was another of the boys—and his brother Pat. So was Bill Morgan—gone long since to 'that bourne whence traveler returns'—and Mont Patton, then and now of Asheville, N.C., and the Coffins, *primus, secundus,* etc., down to *quintus,* all gone now but John. There are not many of us left. Adam fills a gallant soldier's grave, in the Valley of Virginia, where he fell in the battle of Piedmont, manfully contending for that which he believed to be right.

I remember in one of your communications to the old *Spirit,* (a very different paper from the present *Spirit,*) in giving an account of Bill's sport with hound and horn, he was called Col Bill; but you said, he was no Colonel. Well, if he was not then, he was afterwards one of the most gallant among that galaxy of Confederate Generals whose deeds of valor shed additional luster on Southern arms. He, too, has gone from among us. I am told it was a magnificent sight, when mounted on his splendid thoroughbred, of capacity

229 Dr. Isham Peck, "An Open Note To Sawbones," *The Morristown Gazette,* 6 Sep 1876, 2.

fully equal to his weight of eighteen stone, he led his command into the thickest of the fight.

WHITEHEAD."

Tusculum / Greeneville College

In discovering Whitehead's contribution to *The Morristown Gazette*, this author discovered the source of Isham's formal education. Let us now turn to information about Greeneville College. The author was able to visit Tusculum in October 2022, and the following are photos and a video from the trip. **CMB LIVE: Scan the QR**

Figure 134 - **CMB LIVE**: Scan for visit to Tusculum University, https://youtu.be/FJoaB An4vbk

Code to the right for a video visit with the author to Tusculum. Also see the house of Samuel Doak, co-founder of Tusculum Academy in 1818. He is best known for preaching to the Overmountain Men, including Isham's grandfather, Adam Peck, Sr. at Sycamore Shoals in 1780 as they assembled on their way to the Battle of Kings Mountain. What a treat for Isham to study under the minister who spiritually encouraged his grandpa on the way to such a major Revolutionary War battle.[230]

Figure 135 - Tusculum College history sign on campus, text to the bottom-right reads: "The oldest college in Tennessee, Tusculum College is a significant part of the state's Civil War occupation story. Old College, the only building remaining from that era, was built in 1841. Greeneville resident Andrew Johnson donated to the building's construction. He served as Tennessee's military governor during the war and as President of the United States after President Abraham Lincoln's assassination in April 1865. The Old College, listed on the National Register of Historic Places, now houses the President Andrew Johnson Museum and Library." Photo by the author.

---

[230] Samuel Doak, in the Tennessee Encyclopedia, https://tennesseeencyclopedia.net/entries/samuel-doak/.

Dr. Charles Coffin

Doctor Coffin is mentioned and it behooves us to learn about him, and in so doing, we will learn about Greeneville College. A thorough biography can be found in *Annals of the American Pulpit: Presbyterian. 1859, Vol IV* by William Buell Sprague.[231] The University of Tennessee Libraries give this short bio:

"Dr. Charles Coffin was the third president of the university (as East Tennessee College) from 1827 to 1832. Dr. Coffin was president of Greeneville College in 1826 when the trustees of East Tennessee College severed ties with Hampden-Sydney Academy. Coffin was a Massachusetts native and a Presbyterian minister with a DD from Williams College. He was also a Harvard graduate and held the MD degree. He came to Tennessee in 1800 to join the faculty of Greeneville College.

To entice him to relocate and head up East Tennessee College in its new campus home on "the Hill," the trustees purchased the adjacent property and house from Charles McClung Jr. as the president's residence and offered Coffin a salary of $1,500 per year.

Coffin married Susan Woodbridge Ayer (daughter of James and Mary [Woodbridge] Ayer) of New Milford, Maine, on April 19, 1802. Their eldest son (of 12 children, 10 of whom survived infancy) died on a visit to Columbia, Tennessee, in June 1855, and his body was returned to Knoxville on the first railroad train to enter the town."[232]

Figure 136 - Dr. Charles Coffin, D.D. President of Greenville College from 1810-1827
https://web.tusculum.edu/president/charles-coffin/

Searching for information about Isham, William, and Adam's attendance at Greeneville College proved quite difficult. The *Alumni catalogue, 1794-1918* by Tusculum College, gives important information that helps explain the difficulty. "The incompleteness of the lists of early graduates and the confusion and uncertainty of details before the Civil War are explained in the following extract from the preface of Dr. Jere Moore, '71, to the 'General Catalogue' of 1901: 'Strange as it may seem, in the early history of Greeneville College no effort was made to preserve even the names of the graduates. In a period of sixty years, not more than ten names appear on the records of the trustees. For many years no annual catalogue was issued. It being over one hundred and six years, all the early

---

[231] *Annals of the American Pulpit: Presbyterian Vol IV. 1859* – William Buell Sprague, Published 31 Dec 1858 by R. Carter and brothers, Pgs 246-256, https://archive.org/details/00839292.1350.emory.edu/page/245/mode/2up
[232] https://volopedia.lib.utk.edu/entries/charles-coffin/, accessed 3 Jan 2022.

graduates have long since passed away, and even the names of the most of them are no longer in memory. In case of Tusculum, all records prior to 1860 are lost."[233]

The book proceeds to give a "HISTORICAL SKETCH. Tusculum College traces its origin to two historic schools, Greeneville College and Tusculum Academy, the former being the oldest chartered college west of the Alleghany Mountains.

Hezekiah Balch, D.D. (B.A. Princeton, 1762), began preaching and teaching in Greeneville. Realizing the necessity for a college in the vast pioneer territory where the nearest higher institution of learning was beyond the mountains 175 miles away, Dr. Balch became

TUSCULUM ACADEMY (1818).
Erected when Dr. Doak came to Tusculum.
Figure 137 - Photo from College Alumni Catalogue 1794-1918 by Tusculum University

interested in starting a college near Greeneville. Through his influence, the General Assembly of the Territory of the United States south of the Ohio River granted a charter for Greeneville College on September 3. 1794.

"To an enlightened Representative from Davidson County is due the immortal honor of having made the first legislative effort, in the Territorial Assembly, in behalf of learning. On the 29th of August, 'Mr. White moved for leave, and presented a bill to establish a University in Greene County ; read for the first time, passed, and sent to the Council.' Four days later the bill became a law, creating a Literary Institution, though under a less imposing name, Greeneville College. The preamble to the act of incorporation follows:

'Whereas, in all well-regulated governments, it is the incumbent duty of the Legislature to consult the happiness of the rising generation, and endeavor to fit them for an honorable discharge of the social duties of life, by paying the strictest attention to their education, Be it enacted by the Governor,' etc." * (*See Hale's "History of Tennessee and Tennesseeans.")

Dr. Balch was made President, and the college located on his farm three miles south of Greeneville. The Trustees were : Hezekiah Balch, Samuel Doak, James Balch, Samuel Carrick, Robert Henderson, Gideon Blackburn, Archibald Roane, Joseph Hamilton, William Cocke, Daniel Kennedy, Landon Carter, Joseph Hardin, Sr., John Rhea and John Sevier.

In 1800, Rev. Charles Coffin, D.D. (Harvard, 1793), became associated with Dr. Balch as financial agent of the college ; through his efforts nearly all the books for the library and the greater part of the money for the first forty years were obtained. In 1839 the college was moved

_____

[233] Alumni catalogue, 1794-1918 by Tusculum College, 1918, 3-4.

to Greeneville and a new building erected. There was a vacancy in the office of President from 1847 to 1854, but interest revived under Rev. William B. Rankin, 1854-1858.

In 1818, Rev. Samuel Doak, D.D. (B.A. Princeton, 1775), after founding Washington College in 1795, and preaching and teaching there for twenty-three years, came to Tusculum, where he opened a private school near the present site of the college, called Tusculum Academy. He continued the work at Tusculum until his death in 1832. In 1835, Rev. Samuel W. Doak, D.D., second son of Dr. Samuel Doak, took up the work ; he obtained a charter for the Academy in 1842, and in 1844 the name was changed to Tusculum College. During the Civil War, the work of both colleges was interrupted. Students and professors became engaged in the conflict, the buildings were used as barracks for soldiers, the apparatus destroyed, and the libraries scattered. When the war closed and the period of reconstruction began, the property of each school was practically in ruins.

Tusculum College was reopened after the war by Samuel Smith Doak (B.A. Tusculum. 1852), and through his efforts the two colleges were united in 1868 under the name of Greeneville and Tusculum College, attempts toward this union having been made previous to the war. Women were first admitted to the institution about 1875. [. . .]

TUSCULUM COLLEGE: Founded as Tusculum Academy in 1818; chartered as Tusculum College in 1844; united in 1868 with Greeneville College under the name of Greeneville and Tusculum College."[234]

The Alumni Catalogue gives some wonderful corroborating evidence regarding other figures mentioned in Whitehead's article, though it does not mention any of the Peck boys unfortunately. Before 1802 it mentions numerous men graduating with B.A.s and M.As who become lawyers, senators, judges, ministers and one physician. Here are others mentioned who graduated approximately between 1820 and 1830:

"*BOWIE, JAMES, B.A - Graduated about 1829. Wholesale merchant in Charleston, S. C. m.(arried) a daughter of Dr. Charles Coffin, who was second President of Greeneville College.

*BOWIE, LANGDON. B.A - Graduated about 1827. Wholesale merchant in Charleston, S. C. m.(arried) a daughter of President Charles Coffin.

*COFFIN, CHARLES, B.A - Graduated about 1827. Eldest son of President Charles Coffin. Merchant ; lived in Knoxville.

*COFFIN, JAMES A., B.A - Graduated about 1827. Was located at Madisonville, Tenn., as early as 1834, where he lived and died. Lawyer, merchant, farmer.

---

[234] Ibid, 5-6, 12.

*HALE, PHILIP, B.A. – Physician

*MORGAN, FRANK, B.A.[235]

*VANCE, JAMES H., B.A[236] - b. January 4, 1811, Greeneville, Tenn. Academic course under Rev. Samuel Doak, D.D., Tusculum; graduated from Greeneville College about 1830. Practicing physician for many years. Member of Presbyterian Church. M.D., from Transylvania University, Ky. m. Miss Jane Sevier, August 26, 1832 ; six sons and five daughters, d. at his home at Kingsport, July 7, 1893.

*VANCE, NICHOLAS, B.A - Lived at Greeneville, Tenn., before graduation. Practicing physician."

Figure 138 - Burial at Oak Hill Memorial Park – Kingsport, Sullivan County, TN www.findagrave.com/memorial/88112226/james-harvey-vance

Dr. Jim Vance

The name that stands out in the above list and can help us get an idea for Isham's education is Jim Vance. From this short bio we learn that he was born just one month before Isham, graduates from Greeneville College in 1830, and becomes a practicing physician for many years. Also, he marries Miss Jane Sevier (Sevier being a very notable name in Tennessee, as John Sevier was the first governor of the state). Jane Sevier was daughter of Valentine Sevier, second son of Captain Robert Sevier and his wife, Keziah Robertson Sevier, who was a clerk of the Court at Greeneville for fifty-two years. Her mom was Nancy Dinwiddie and there were 12 brothers and sisters in all (born to Nancy). Here is Jane and Dr. James H. Vance's family info: "(1) **Jane Sevier, married about the year 1834, James H. Vance of Kingsport, Tennessee,** and had Charles Robertson Vance (who married Margaret Nelson and had James Isaac Vance, Joseph Anderson Vance, Charles Robertson Vance, Second, Margaret Jane Vance, and Rebecca M. Vance) ; Maria C. Vance (who married John R. King, of Leesburg, Virginia) ; Anna Elizabeth Vance (who died young); Keziah Vance; James N. Vance (who married Fannie Miller) ; Nannie Vance ; Joseph Vance (who married Mattie Fain and had Charles Rutledge Vance) ; and Johnnie Vance."[237]

Figure 139 –Burial at Oak Hill Memorial Park (Kingsport, Sullivan County, TN) www.findagrave.com/memorial/88112227/jane-vance

Captain Robert Sevier

Captain Robert Sevier, Jane's father, has a history that intersects with the Pecks at the Battle of Kings Mountain, where Isham's grandfather Adam Peck, Sr. fought.

---

[235] Ibid, Whitehead article mentions a Bill Morgan, possible relation (brother, etc…)

[236] Ibid, Whitehead article specifically mentions Jim Vance by name, also his brother Pat.

[237] *Notable Southern Families*, Vol 1. Compiled by Zella Armstrong. Published by The Lookout Publishing Co. Chattanooga, TN,183-184.

"Captain Robert Sevier, son of Valentine Sevier, Second and Joanna Goade Sevier was younger than his brothers, John and Valentine, Third, and was probably born about 1749, in Rockingham County, Virginia. He accompanied his father to the Mountains in 1772. **He was in the Battle of King's Mountain, October 7, 1780, and was there mortally wounded. He was thought to have been killed out right, but lived nine days.** Captain Robert Sevier married Keziah Robertson, daughter of Charles Robertson, one of the two famous brothers, Charles and James Robertson, and had two sons (I) Major Charles Sevier and **(II) Valentine Sevier.** (I) Major Charles Sevier married Elizabeth Witt. He served under General Andrew Jackson and had fourteen children, namely: (1) Robert Sevier whose family is all dead. **(2) Valentine Sevier married Anna Mourney.** (3) John Quinturf Sevier, who married three times, firstly a Henderson, secondly, a Bisckle, thirdly, Sarah Sangster and had at least two sons, John Bisckle Sevier and Dr. Charles Henry Sevier who married Cora E. Anderson and had two sons, Charles Anderson Sevier, of Jackson, Tennessee, and Dr. John Henry Sevier, of Brownsville, Tennessee. (4) Sevier, a daughter of Major Charles Sevier married a Russell and had a son Robert Russell, a soldier in the Mexican War and later in the Confederate Army.[238]

Another book chronicles the line on the Vance side, with extended information to show context and history.

"Charles Robertson was made one of the five judges of Watauga presided over by Col. John Carter. **He took part in the movement to establish the State of Franklin, and in 1787 he was Speaker of the Franklin Senate.** (William Cage was Speaker in 1785.) **As Captain of a company, Charles Robertson had already become distinguished in the performance of military service in the Revolutionary War under General Nathaniel Greene in the battle of Guildford Courthouse, who promoted him to the rank of Major. He was afterwards made Colonel. After the fall of the Franklin government he was a member of the General Assembly of North Carolina at Halifax.** Charles Robertson married Miss Susannah Nicholas. Their children were: 1. Charles Robertson II, born ——, married —— , died and was buried near Jonesboro, East Tennessee. They had a number of children. The will of Colonel Charles Robertson (Will Book of Davidson County, p. 68) mentions wife Susannah and children, Elijah, Mark, Claiborne, Rosamond, Rhoda, Susannah and Elizabeth Evans, who married Robert Evans, Sept. 21, 1797. Elsewhere the list is enlarged with the names of Charles Robertson II, William Robertson (William Blount?), Julius Caesar Robertson, Christopher Robertson, born in Wake County, North Carolina, about 1765 and

---

[238] Ibid, 183-184, emphasis added.

died in Tishomingo County, Mississippi, about 1855 (age 90), George and Kesiah. **Kesiah, daughter of Colonel Charles Robertson, married first Captain Robert Sevier. Robert Sevier, son of Colonel John Sevier, married Kesiah Robertson in 1777. He was mortally wounded in the battle of King's Mountain, dying on the way home, leaving a widow and two young sons.** She married second Mr. Tipton. Rosamond married Rev. Russell Bean, first white child born in Tennessee (son of "Good Mrs. Bean").

Figure 140 - Valentine Sevier (8 Jul 1780 - 24 Apr 1854) www.findagrave.com/memorial/20574894 /valentine-sevier

II - **One of the daughters of Charles Robertson II, of Jonesboro, was Kesiah Robertson, niece of Mrs. Kesiah (Robertson) Sevier. She married William K. Vance.** Her children were: Dr. James Harvey Vance, Patrick Vance, William Nicholas Vance, Caroline Vance, who married Cragmiles, and others. **Dr. James Harvey Vance lived at Kingsport, Tenn. He married his cousin, Miss Jane Sevier, daughter of Valentine Sevier, the son of Robert Sevier and his wife, Mrs. Kesiah (Robertson) Sevier.** Their children were: 1. Rev. Charles Robertson Vance of Bristol, Tenn., who married Miss Margaret Newland. Their issue was: a. Rev. Dr. James I. Vance, the distinguished pastor of the First Presbyterian Church in Nashville; Rev. James Isaac Vance, born — —, married in South Carolina Miss Mamie Stite Currell. Their children are: Margaret Vance, William Vance, Agnes Vance, Ruth Vance, who married George Killebrew, Jr., of Nashville, James W. Vance and Jane Vance. b. Maria Vance married King. c. William Vance, married ——. d. Kesiah Vance, married ——. e. Joseph Vance, married —— . f. Jane Vance, married ——. The second son of Rev. Charles Robertson Vance was Rev. Joseph Anderson Vance, a noted evangelist. The other children of Rev. Charles Robertson Vance were: Margaret Vance, and Rebecca Vance who married A. C. L. Hendrick, of Bristol, Tenn."[239]

Philip Hale

The list above also mentions a Philip Hale, who became a physician like Isham. *Sketches of Tennessee's Pioneer Baptist Preachers* by James Jehu Burnett shares this family history of Philip. Notable here is that their family is from New Market (next to where Isham lived in Mossy Creek), and Morristown (where *The Morristown Gazette* was published, and just up the road from New Market). The Hale family is full of ministers! "Jeremiah Hale had two sons, Henry and Jesse, who were able ministers of the Word; two nephews, Elder P. H. C. Hale (recently deceased), who was one of our best men and a great country pastor, and Elder J.

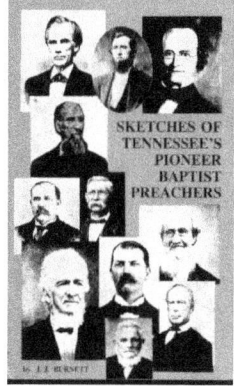

---

[239] The family chronicle and kinship book of Maclin, Clack, Cocke, Carter, Taylor, Cross, Gordon, and other related American lineages, published 1928 by Octavia Zollicoffer Bond, McDaniel Printing Co., 504-505, emphasis added.

F. Hale, of New Market, a successful pastor and evangelist. We also note the fact that W. C. Hale of Morristown, a useful pastor and many years the moderator of the Nolachucky Association, and Drs. Fred D. And P. T. Hale of Kentucky, sons of **Dr. Philip Hale, formerly of Warrensburg, Greene County, Tennessee**, are of the same stock and close of kin to the elder Hale, and are all able minsters of the New Testament. Jeremiah H. Hale of Eldorado Springs, Missouri, is the youngest son of Elder Jeremiah Hale, and the only member of the immediate family now living. W. H. Mullens, a money-making, public-spirited and liberal Baptist and citizen of Morristown, son of the only daughter (Martha) who lived to grow to womanhood, is a grandson of Elder Jeremiah Hale."[240]

Whitehead gives us info about other fellow students of Isham and their outcomes:

Coffin Children –	Whitehead says that at least 5 attended the school, and notably in the list given above, 4 are children of Dr. Coffin!
Mont Patton –	"then and now of Asheville, N.C."
Bill Morgan –	deceased at the time of the writing
Adam Clayton Peck –	Isham's brother – "fills a gallant soldier's grave, in the Valley of Virginia, where he fell in the battle of Piedmont"
Bill Peck –	William Raine Peck – Isham's brother – Bill apparently liked to play the sport of "hound and horn." He was called "Col. Bill" but Isham said "he was no Colonel." He ironically not only became a Colonel, but eventually a Brigadier General in the Confederate Army.

The author wrote to Tusculum University and contacted personnel in their History and Museum Studies Department. When asked about records from the time when Isham attended, Professor Peter Noll stated, "You're correct – there were no medical degrees. Greeneville College offered a BA degree - a liberal arts degree that was intended to teach the student how to think rather than train them for any specific profession. The curriculum was heavier in languages (Latin and Greek) than today, but otherwise a lot of the same (history, math, etc.). There are very few records that survive from Greeneville College. We have much of the original library, but student records have not survived. The alumni directory will give a bit of information on graduates. You can access that record online here: https://tinyurl.com/46m9w88s. You should be able to locate your relations in the link above. We don't have anything more than that in the archive."[241]

---

[240] *Sketches of Tennessee's Pioneer Baptist Preachers* by James Jehu Burnett, Copyright 1919, reprinted 1985 by The Overmountain Press, 55.

[241] Email correspondence between the author and Dr. Peter Noll, PhD, at Tusculum University, 26 Mar 20220.

Bill Porter's Spirit of the Times

Whitehead asks if Isham is the same person who had written for the *Spirit of the Times*.[242] He specifically says that Isham wrote for the "old" *Spirit* as opposed to the new *Spirit*. He must have written his articles between 1831 and 1856, because in 1856 the *Spirit of the Times* became *Porter's Spirit of the Times* and later *Wilkes' Spirit of the Times*. References to the "Old Spirit" refer to the original paper. Extended treatment of the paper, with its history, editor, and contributors can be found in *William T. Porter and the Spirit of the Times* by Norris Yates, 1957.

"The *Spirit of the Times* was the premier American sporting journal of the 19th century. It was founded in 1831 (the same year as *The Liberator*) by William T. Porter who edited it for 25 years. Porter lost financial control, so in 1856 he joined with George Wilkes to found *Porter's Spirit of the Times*. When Porter died in 1858, his share in the second *Spirit* fell into the hands of a New York lawyer.

Wilkes didn't get along with his new partner, so in September 1859 he established his own journal, *Wilkes' Spirit of the Times*. For a short time there were three *Spirits* being published simultaneously, but *Porter's Spirit* went out of business soon after. The original *Spirit* had a large portion of its subscribers in the South, so the Civil War sealed its fate, leaving Wilkes as the sole survivor after June 1861.

Published in New York City, the paper covered all kinds of sports: horseracing, hunting, billiards, baseball, boxing, skating, etc., as well as theater and other amusements. However, Wilkes was an exceptionally good writer himself and covered some Civil War battles (e.g., First Manassas) first hand. His coverage of the Civil War is personal and his opinions strong. An example from February 8, 1862:

---

[242] https://en.wikipedia.org/wiki/Spirit_of_the_Times, accessed 24 Mar 2020

"The Southern people who are in rebellion are our enemies. There is no description of property in their possessions, which it is not in our interest to destroy--even to the taking of their lives...These are the laws of war."

While the Union home front has more coverage here than in other publications, the war content and editorials--often in the form of letters--are worth noting as well. Wilkes was outraged by what he considered to be mismanagement of the War effort, and led the press effort to remove General George McClellan."[243]

After five years of searching, in Nov 2022, this author discovered that copies of *The Spirit of the Times* were digitized and available online (as of July 2021). Additionally, in further family research, an 1857 letter written by Isham's dad was located in the Knox County Archives that also references the newspaper. In it, Judge Peck says this, "Dear Sir, Having from age and inclination quit the practice of the Law _ and seeing from the many letters now[?] from you the deep interest you have taken, & are taking in my behalf _ I beg leave to refer you to my publication in the Spirit of the Times date Jan 3rd. No 47. p 554. head "See how the Lawyers differ" [.]"[244] This article has been found and will appear in a later book focused on Judge Jacob Peck.

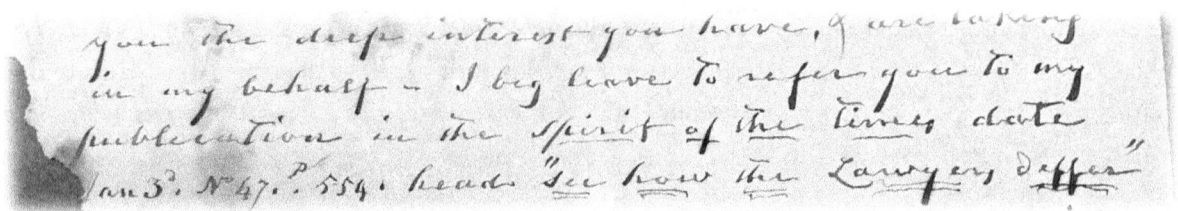

At this time, only one article written by "Sawbones" in the Spirit of the Times has been located. The paper lists at as being written from "S——, Tenn., Jan 23, 1852." If this was written by Isham, it was written 22 years before the first one found in *The Morristown Gazette*. In the next article, Isham claims to have written from the Swamp. And Whitehead says that "at that time" Isham hailed from "Millikin's Bend." But knowing that Isham was back and forth between Louisiana, Mississippi, and Tennessee, he is certainly capable of writing an article from Tennessee. Here is the 1852 article:

Figure 141 - Front Page Banner from Sawbones article newspaper, 21 Feb 1852, Public Domain

---

[243] https://www.lincolnandthecivilwar.com/SubLevelPages/WilkesSpirit.asp, accessed 24 Mar 2020

[244] Judge Jacob Peck, Knox County Archives, dated 14 or 19 March 1857, Oakland, Jefferson County, Tennessee

21 FEB 1852 SPIRIT OF THE TIMES "WHISPERING JOHN R——." [245]

Dear "Spirit." —I seldom *scribble* for my own amusement, or that of others, but the following is too good to be lost. In what is known as the "upper end" of my county there resides a man who has the *soubriquet*[246] of "Whispering John R——." This *title* he has gained form the fact that he always talks, (even in common conversation) like he was a major-general on parade, or, to use a more common expression, "like he was raised in a mill."

This gentleman, who, by-the-bye, is "one of them," mounted his horse one of our coldest mornings last week, before daylight, for the purpose of riding down to M——, in time to take the morning train of cars for N——. He rode up to the hotel just as the boarders and travellers were done breakfast, and were standing around the bar-room fire "picking their teeth."

He dismounted, and walking into the bar-room, spoke to the landlord in his usual *whispering* tone—

"Good morning, Mr. L——; how do you do this morning?"

"Very well, Mr. R——; how do you do?"

"Oh! I am well—but I'm so d—d cold I can't hardly talk."

Just then a *nervous* traveller, who was present, ran up to the landlord, and catching him by the coat, said—

"Mr. L——, for the Lord's sake have my horse caught as soon as possible!"

"What is the matter, my dear sir; has anything happened?"

"Nothing upon God's earth, only I want to get away from *here* before that man *thaws!*"

I left also for the *same* reason.   Yours truly,   SAWBONES

S——, Tenn., Jan. 23, 1852.

"Whitehead" is owed a great deal of gratitude for writing to the *Gazette,* as it gives great additional insights into the life of Isham, and his siblings as well. Fortunately, Isham was reading his paper, and he took the time to respond to Whitehead on 20 Sep 1876.

---

[245] Sawbones, 21 Feb 1852 The Spirit of the Times, Vol 22, Issue 1.
[246] Soubriquet: a descriptive name or epithet: nickname, Merriam Webster Online Dictionary

20 SEP 1876 "SAWBONES" REDIVIVUS: A Sketch of the Pulpit efforts Fifty Years ago.

To the Editor of the Morristown Gazette:

Who is my admirable friend and schoolmate, who calls himself 'Whitehead?' He has identified me as the individual who wrote for the old *Spirit of the Times* from a Southern swamp.

You remember when the officer carried a challenge to Harry Lorrequer? Harry said there was a mistake—he had never before heard of the challenging party; but when the officer told him that the challenger described him as the man who threw all Dublin into convulsions by playing Hamlet at private theatricals, Harry said that was sufficient—'I am your man!'

Poor Bill Porter! We will not see his like again! I knew him personally, and when he died they sent me a lock of his hair, which I have now.

Your excellent correspondent, Bascum, proposes that the preachers preach a crusade against the ladies' pull-back style of dress. Fifty years ago, there was a man who made these hills and valleys howl. He was a powerful man physically, and he could have preached a pull-back off of any woman in ten minutes. You read of him in a book called 'A History of Methodism in Tennessee.' He could make it rain by praying for it, or he could stop the rain in the same way. The book tells us he was on a certain occasion holding a revival in the woods. A great rain storm would be kept off until he could put through the few remaining sinners. It rained hard all around that crowed, but not a drop fell on them. I heard much of his preaching, and I have had a prejudice against the devil ever since. He did not fear the devil an iota, and I have heard him bully-rag and abuse the old fellow at a terrible rate. Store-clothes, ribbons and finery were very scarce fifty years ago. Women made the cloth and clothes for themselves. Each one had a fashion of her own—and such a fashion! The Lord would not have known some of them without stripping them. On one occasion, a young lady attended his preaching with a ribbon on her bonnet. He first told his hearers all about Heaven, and what a desirable place it was. He then described Hell. Told of the facilities for scorching sinners—Sulphur, coal, pitch, and turpentine. The furnaces lined with fire brick, drawing beautifully. Then the husbands were separated from their wives, the mother from her children, and pitched into eternal burning. By this time, old women

"SAWBONES" REDIVIVUS.

A Sketch of the Pulpit efforts Fifty Years ago.

To the Editor of the Morristown Gazette:

Who is my admirable friend and schoolmate, who calls himself "Whitehead?" He has identified me as the individual who wrote for the old *Spirit of the Times* from a Southern swamp.

You remember when the officer carried a challenge to Harry Lorrequer? Harry said there was a mistake—he had never before heard of the challenging party; but when the officer told him that the challenger described him as the man who threw all Dublin into convulsions by playing Hamlet at private theatricals, Harry said that was sufficient—"I am your man!"

Poor Bill Porter! We will not see his like again! I knew him personally, and when he died they sent me a lock of his hair, which I have now.

Your excellent correspondent, Bascum, proposes that the preachers preach a crusade against the ladies' pull-back style of dress. Fifty years ago, there was a man who made these hills and valleys howl. He was a powerful man physically, and he could have preached a pull-back off of any woman in ten minutes. You read of him in a book called a "History of Methodism in Tennessee." He could make it rain by praying for it, or he could stop the rain in the same way. The book tells us he was on a certain occasion holding a revival in the woods. A great rain storm approaching, he prayed that the storm would be kept off until he could put through the few remaining sinners. It rained hard all around that crowd, but not a drop fell on them. I heard much of his preaching, and I have had a prejudice against the devil ever since. He did not fear the devil an iota, and I have heard him bully-rag and abuse the old fellow at a terrible rate. Store-clothes, ribbons and finery were very scarce fifty years ago. Women made the cloth and clothes for themselves. Each one had a fashion of her own—and such a fashion! The Lord would not have known some of them without stripping them. On one occasion, a young lady attended his preaching with a ribbon on her bonnet. He first told his hearers all about Heaven, and what a desirable place it was. He then described Hell. Told of the facilities for scorching sinners—sulphur, coal, pitch and turpentine. The furnaces lined with fire brick, drawing beautifully. Then the husbands were separated from their wives, the mother from her children, and pitched into eternal burning. By this time, old women were in convulsions, kicking over benches, some of them sprawling on the floor, drumming with their heels. Children frightened and crying. The men yelling for mercy, and begging the Lord to come quickly and at once. The niggers in the corner doing their part to keep up the noise. An old brother on the outskirts dragging up an unrepentant cuss to the mourner's bench. Preacher storming through the crowd, defying the devil and his angels. About this time he noticed the young lady with the ribbon in her bonnet, and pointing his finger at her, he bawled out: "That gal will find no ribbons in hell!" The lady left the church, and when she returned the ribbon was gone.

SAWBONES.

were in convulsions, kicking over benches, some of them sprawling on the floor, drumming with their heels. Children frightened and crying. The men yelling for mercy and begging the Lord to come quickly and at once. The niggers in the corner doing their part to keep up the noise. An old brother on the outskirts dragging up an unrepentant cuss to the mourner's bench. Preacher storming through the crowd, defying the devil and his angels. About this time he noticed the young lady with the ribbon in her bonnet, and pointing his finger at her, he bawled out: 'That gal will find no ribbons in hell!' The lady left the church, and when returned the ribbon was gone.

SAWBONES."[247]

Harry Lorrequer

Harry Lorrequer refers to a character in a novel by Charles Jeames Lever, who wrote *The Confessions of Harry Lorrequer*. Notably, Isham's Vicksburg friend Dr. Hagan, newspaper editor, travelled to Ireland and dined with Charles Lever. He returned and told Isham about it. It is mentioned in the 8 Jul 1877 article by Sawbones. *Four Centuries of Geological Travel: The Search for Knowledge on Foot* edited by Patrick Wyse Jackson gives the following account, "Lever, 1839, *The Confessions of Harry Lorrequer*, p. 158. Chapter XX. Giesecke appears in chapter XX entitled 'A day in Dublin'. Harry Lorrequer is a Subaltern in a marching regiment (infantry). He is aged 20 something and the book starts in the year 181-. The story is appropriately a comedy, riotous in places, verging on slapstick. Reminiscent of Giesecke who played Hamlet on the stage, Lorrequer played the role of Shakespeare's Othello in private performances in Cork, and a small troupe from the regiment played at garrison balls, where the players were known as the 'corps dramatique'. Amongst these extremely amusing adventures figure the Mozart operas '*Don Giovanni*' and '*Figaro*'. Interestingly, Lorrequer is also the leader of the orchestra. Lady Morgan (Sydney Owenson) also featured in the novel and is mentioned in a poem about Dublin on page 87. Lady Morgan was a novelist from a theatrical family background and well-known member of Dublin society."[248]

In the actual novel about Harry Lorrequer, Harry says " 'Oh,' thought I, at last, 'his lordship is about to get up private theatricals, and has seen my Captain Absolute, or perhaps my Hamlet'—I could not say 'Othello' even to myself—'and is anxious to get "such unrivaled talent" even "for one night only.'" After many guesses this seemed the nearest I could think of; and by the time I had finished my dressing for dinner, it was quite clear to me I had solved all the secret of his lordship's attentions."[249]

---

[247] Author's note: Isham uses the "n" word, and this author objects to its usage…but includes it for historical accuracy

[248] Four Centuries of Geological Travel: The Search for Knowledge on Foot, Bicycle, Sledge and Camel *Issue 287 of Geological Society special publication*, 159.

[249] Harry Lorrequer by Charles Lever. London, Chapman and Hall, 193, Piccadilly. 1857. Digitized by Google, 19.

Later in the story, though, Lorrequer learns that Lord Callonby actually recognizes him not from his performances in Hamlet, but rather because Lorrequer is the nephew of his old friend, Sir Guy Lorrequer of Elton. So he was recognized, but not because of the reasons he thought (his outward performances)…but it was actually a closer, more friendly, familial connection.[250] It seems all of this is a complicated, allusionary[251] way to tell the readers that Whitehead was thinking of the right guy! AND that he felt a close connection with him as well.

Bill Porter and The Spirit of the Times - Bill Porter is William T. Porter, the editor for *The Spirit of the Times*. It is interesting that Isham was close enough to him that they sent him a lock of his hair. Porter's newspaper was very well known in the day. It is credited with fostering a new genre of literature called "Southwestern Humor." A popular book called *Odd Leaves from the Life of a Louisiana Swamp Doctor* was created from individual articles which originally appeared in *The Spirit of the Times*. This author thought for a time that *Odd Leaves* was written by Isham, but there appears to be sufficient evidence proving Henry Clay Lewis authored the work. Bill Porter "was a Whig with an even temper."[252] Though Isham seemed to be democratic politically, and a Whig during his time in Vicksburg, he clearly kept a wide circle of friends, who did not necessarily share his viewpoints. Isham would have corresponded with Bill when he mailed in his articles for the *Spirit*.

Bascum…who is this? We know Sawbones is Isham, we know Whitehead attended Greeneville College with Isham, but Bascum must be another contributor to the *Gazette*. A quick search on the University of Tennessee's Chronicling America website turned up an article written in the 13 Sep 1876 edition page 1 (one week prior to Isham's article) by one Thomas Bascum and the title of the article is "JURORS AND POLITICS. Bascum as a Lawyer— The Jurors of the Present Day Mixed with Politics— 'Good Lord, Deliver Us.'" Another article on the page is called "THOUGHTS FOR THE PEOPLE" by "Greybeard." In the 27 Sep 1876 issue, another contributor who goes by "Clinch" writes and references "our talented friend 'Bascum'" and another named "Big Ike."

For more context on the Bascum situation and the issue of a ladies' "pull-back style of dress," here is an article written 26 July 1876 front page by a person going by the nickname Bric-A-Brac.[253]

Figure 142 - Jules David (French, 1808–1892). Le Moniteur de la mode, January 4, 1876. Hand-painted etching. Düsseldorf: Universität Düsseldorf. Source: Universität Düsseldorf

---

[250] Ibid, 20-21.
[251] Author's word.
[252] *William T. Porter and the Spirit of the Times* by Norris Yates, 1957, 43.
[253] *The Morristown Gazette* 26 July 1876 https://chroniclingamerica.loc.gov/lccn/sn85033681/1876-07-26/ed-1/seq-1/

26 JUL 1876 "DISCURSORY." "Bric-a-Brac" Pleases His Brother—and Writes up 4th of July at Tazewell—a Capital Sketch.[254]

To The Editor of the Morristown Gazette:

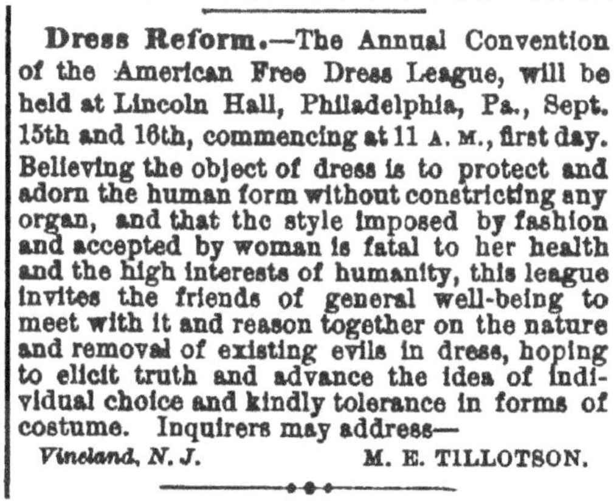

Dress Reform.—The Annual Convention of the American Free Dress League, will be held at Lincoln Hall, Philadelphia, Pa., Sept. 15th and 16th, commencing at 11 A. M., first day. Believing the object of dress is to protect and adorn the human form without constricting any organ, and that the style imposed by fashion and accepted by woman is fatal to her health and the high interests of humanity, this league invites the friends of general well-being to meet with it and reason together on the nature and removal of existing evils in dress, hoping to elicit truth and advance the idea of individual choice and kindly tolerance in forms of costume. Inquirers may address—

Vineland, N. J.   M. E. TILLOTSON.

Figure 143 - Dress Reform Convention Ad, 1875 The Cultivator and Country Gentleman, 557.

A few calmy eves agone, my brother-in-law, "Wilberforce," came to me, as I was seated upon my front stoop, enjoying an extended view of old Cumberland—that grand old range that, bathed in purple haze, lay sleeping before me—and touching me on the shoulder, remarked, "Bric, my mother has sent a servant girl and an umbrella for me." Wrapt in thought, I replied, "well, leave the servant girl and take the umbrella." My kinsman simply replied "can't." A little out of the fog, I suggested: Well, leave the umbrella, and take the servant girl." "Impracticable," returned Wilberforce. By this time I had emerged from my reverie and suggested to W. that I didn't care a *blank* what he did.

Approaching me in a suave manner, this mortal relation suggested he would esteem it a favor, as he was going home, if I would write something for him to the MORRISTOWN GAZETTE.

To comprehend the field, I obtained a copy of your valued journal, to study my chances.

The first article I noticed was the maceration of the **Revd. Bascum**, by "sweet sixteen." If I were **Bascum** I'd quit. The question of the "pull-back" has been one demanding the attention of our ablest humanitarians and Dr. **Bascum** should never have engaged in his crusade. In these days of women's rights, female suffrage and feminine assertion, any "pull-back" may be desirable; and, it is a matter of surprise to your correspondent that Bascum has got himself into business.

The glorious Fourth has waltzed into the past pleasantly and quietly. A celebration of the same was held in Tazewell, the county seat of this county. The ceremonies embraced an opening prayer; the reading of Washington's farewell address; and addresses from Maj. A. H. Pettibone and the Hon. H. T. Patton. The interest (or rather pleasure) of the occasion was enhanced by some excellent music from Prof. Austin's cornet Band. Chance threw Prof. Austin in our midst; his courtesy and the liberality of our county court secured us the services of himself and his corps.

It had been one of the problems of our "Centennial" to secure music for the occasion. Knoxville skill had been already secured, and while we could obtain the services of Prof. Shipley, and his associates, it was doubted whether string music was strong enough for the open air. Happily the colossal aggregation of Maxwell and Smith, embracing ten Warm Spring Indians, drifted hitherward, and the chance to secure a good band was not lost upon the Centennial management.

Thanks to the winning ways of your correspondent, the matter was arranged thusly: In return for the free services of the band, upon the Centennial occasion, the county court agreed to remit the county license; and one and all dissolved in mutual admiration we celebrated the Centennial of our national existence. The addresses were excellent and apt; the music eloquent and inspiring; the sun

---

[254] Bric-A-Brac, *The Morristown Gazette*, 26 Jul 1876, 1, emphasis added.

hot as blazes; and everything went merry as a marriage bell. Did the spirits of Washington and Lord Cornwallis look down upon the little town of Tazewell bereft of cows and hogs, and ablaze with flags and people asking each other to take dinner? They must have gathered a boquet [sic] of dog-fennel and wished the hamlet God-speed. The celebration over, we all repaired to the show tent erected in that Belgravia of Tazewell called Rabbit-town, and, furnishing the currency, passed in.

Every one knows what a show is, and 'twould be painting the lily to depict the same. 'Twas the usual 'blareing band;' the encircling seats, party-colored occupants and wilderness of flitting fans; the sprawling natives upon the sward, at intervals outside the ropes; and the tinsel, spangles, tights, clowns and somersaults, within the ring. Music, murmur; sweat, effluvia. Trapeze, carpet; India-rubber man and trained horse, and soforth, et cetera. Lemonade (of a ruby color) and candy. As the crowd is to your correspondent almost of equal interest with the trained performers, I amused myself looking around, observing; who was there: the play of expression induced by the performance, and the wonderful care exercised that there should be no break in the performances.

'Twas pleasant to look upon the faces around me; the little child; the chubby boy; the shy little girl; the aspiring young man; the coquetish young lady; the middle aged and the old; the Caucasian and the African; and, the county court, they were there, *a noble body of men*. Let me cast the shoes from off my feet, for I stand on hallowed ground.

The Spencerian Billingsly; the stately Robinson; the smiling Davis; the stern Cadle; the quiet Brown; the cassaba Buis; the dark-eyed Johnson ; the military Ellis; the two barreled Jennings; the courtly Lynch; the suave Mink were there; and last not least, that noblest Roman of them all, the Hatfield. Verily no other county could have presented such a galaxy. As the lily of the valley, the timid violet, the reserved hollyhock, the revolving sun flower, the ripening casaba melon, are dotted through nature; so were these guardians of their county's treasure and welfare scattered through the throng— a pleasant sight for sore eyes.

The ancient Egyptians had a grim custom of seating at their unrivalled feasts a corpse from the catacombs, shrivelled, weird, pungent with bitumin and rank with the odor of the grave, amid the crash and revel; the wine and the flowers; this stilly index of mortality reminded them of the common fate. As amid the coptic orgies this messenger from the dead reminded the pleasure seeker and the reckless of the mortality common to all; so did, in the gay assemblage gathered at Maxwell and Smith's colossal aggregation, the county court suggest that amid our financial embarrassment and political shuffle-board we had at the helm good men and true. To a friend, bound to me with hooks and steel and smuggled in on a check, I murmured, 'verily these Dogberry's are men of means, homoes of grasp. To which my friend replied, 'Dead heads! every man jack of them, except the county court clerk;' 'and he, with his usual perversity, has paid his own way although he could have dead-headed.' 'Expound, says I.' 'Well you know, you know, you arranged that as the band played for nothing the county license was to be cancelled.'

Yes, says I. 'Well, after you had made this arrangement, the casabaman, the man with the hemispheric abdomen, added that the County Court and their clerk should pass in free.' Well ; I'll be reconstructed! I exclaimed, did all dead-head? No; the dead-heads are all before you. I glanced athwart these chosen of their country and cried: Can these things be thusly? Yea, 'exclaimed my comrade,' 'tis so, and wherefore should it be otherwise? I have for my country fallen, and 'tis the last chance of some of us.' The clown threatened the impact of the stuffing; Pocahontas rushed in, and the bull-dog clung to the coon skin. The show was over. A century of American progress ebbed forth; an American citizen was hit: on the head with a candle-stick; Tazewell slumbered; the moon came out and peeped through the curtains at Bric-a-Brac's nose; the United States of America entered upon the second Centennial of our nation's history; the cricket and the katydid took up their nightly song; the pinch-bug buzzed and zipped around the room; the cats contested elections upon the balconies; the dogs yowled and barked at the stellar host; night had fallen upon Tazewell. Bric-a-Brac lay and thought everything must have an end. Men are born, live, struggle and die, but the world moves on. No matter how momentous may be political issues; no matter whether inflation or contraction convulses the commercial world, the glorious sun sets; the modest man will rise; the evening star glitters and skimmers upon the western horizon, a type of purity and constancy. Let the world be racked with internal commotions and bloody wars, the fact exists that Noah went into the ark; the whale swallowed Jonah; Joshua made the sun stand still; Sampson killed his thousands with the jaw-bone of an ass; the recollection will always be precious to the town of Tazewell that when upon the Centennial anniversary of our nation's life Maxwell & Smith's colossal aggregation appeared in Tazewell, twelve members of her County Court gained admission as dead-heads. Bric-a-Brac."

Figure 144 – The Battle of Little Bighorn, Charles Marion Russell - United States Library of Congress's Prints and Photographs division under the digital ID cph.3g07160
https://en.wikipedia.org/wiki/Battle_of_the_Little_Bighorn#/media/File:Charles_Marion_Russell_-_The_Custer_Fight_(1903).jpg

What a time this was in American history! It had been 100 years since the American founders had signed the Declaration of Independence. To add some historical perspective, not only was July 4, 1876 the Nation's Centennial, but another major U.S. Battle had just occurred. The Battle of Little Bighorn, also known as Custer's Last Stand, had just taken place in southeastern Montana Territory between 25-26 Jun 1876. History.com gives the following historical significance of the battle, "The Battle of the Little Bighorn, also called Custer's Last Stand, marked the most decisive Native American victory and the worst U.S. Army defeat in the long Plains Indian War. The demise of Custer and his men outraged many white Americans and confirmed their image of the Indians as wild and bloodthirsty. Meanwhile, the U.S. government increased its efforts to subdue the tribes. Within five years, almost all of the Sioux and Cheyenne would be confined to reservations."[255]

Women's Fashion in 1876 - *Fashion History Timeline* provides the following description of women's dress in 1876, "In 1876, the popular silhouette was straight in the front with volume distributed to the back. A typical dress of this year would be comprised of a long cuirass, which is a tight-fitting bodice often reaching down to the hips and upper thighs, over a skirt. The polonaise princess dress was also one of the most significant styles of the year. This refers to a dress with a very long overskirt with ample fabric in the back, often draped in interesting ways to show a bit of the underskirt beneath ("Chitchat on Fashions for March" 293). This year was devoted to making the female figure appear slender and, as described in *Godey's Lady's Book and Magazine*:

"Dresses are made more and more scant in front. Present beau ideal of fashion is for the figure to present a perfectly straight line all the way down in front while the skirt describes a well-supported train at the back... Cuirass bodices are made longer, waists elongated – the figure is not compressed but the outlines are clearly defined." (294)"[256]

Figure 145 - Designer unknown. Écru evening dress, 1876. Silk, lace. Bath: Fashion Museum of Bath. Source: Twitter

The University of Vermont also has a well-done article which chronicles the dresses of the 1870s.[257] Now Bric-A-Brac references "Sweet Sixteen" and her article in his article, let's keep chasing this rabbit a little longer...

---

[255] https://www.history.com/topics/native-american-history/battle-of-the-little-bighorn, accessed 26 Mar 2020
[256] https://fashionhistory.fitnyc.edu/1876-2/, accessed 26 Mar 2020, referenced inside the article are: "Chitchat on Fashions for December." *Godey's Lady Book and Magazine*, no. XCII (December 1876): 577–78. https://babel.hathitrust.org/cgi/pt?id=mdp.39015034639941;view=1up;seq=562. And "Chitchat on Fashions for March." *Godey's Lady Book and Magazine* XCII (June 1876): 293–94. https://babel.hathitrust.org/cgi/pt?id=mdp.39015014112935;view=1up;seq=293.
[257] https://www.uvm.edu/landscape/dating/clothing_and_hair/1870s_clothing_women.php, accessed 26 Mar 2020

28 JUN 1876 "FROM SWEET SIXTEEN: AFTER BASCUM WITH A SHARP STICK."[258]

To the editor of the Morristown Gazette:

May I be permitted to say a word in answer to your very sarcastic correspondent Bascum? I know it is only wasting time to notice his eloquent piece in your paper, for it is only a drop (and a very insignificant drop) in the ocean of stale criticism on fashion, which your sex have for some time been pouring on our unoffensive heads. Yet I am a woman, and shall feel relieved when I have had my say.

Now, Mr. Bascum, if you go to Church to worship God, as you say you do, why don't you do it, without staring out of countenance those awful "pin-back worshippers?" If you go to Church to pray, you go home to criticize those pin-backed women, whose dress you can describe much more minutely than can your wife or daughter. You think it impossible for a woman to go to Church to pray.

"How oft we give to thoughts and things our tone, And judge of others feelings by our own."

For what purpose do those "curled darlings" of society go to Church? Those noble men who line each side of the Church door till every "pin-back" has passed through, then saunter in just in time to hear the last part of the sermon, I ask you, why do they go to Church? "To pray, of course," you say. Then appearances are deceitful, indeed. Glance back, if you please, Mr. Bascum, over the history of the world, as far as your limited gaze will permit, and take the experience of our forefathers for the rest, and you will find that it has ever been so. Your noble sex, made in God's image, cork-toe boots and stove-pipe hats included, have criticized and condemned in vain. Women always have and always will dress just as it suits them.

Time has proved that fashion is very capricious and fleeting.

"Like a snow flake on the river, A moment seen, then gone forever."

So just let us alone, and this much-abused pin-back will soon be abandoned and replaced by other fashions. It is needless to hope the next style will find favor in your lordship's eyes, for the "lords of creation" will 'pitch into' the next fashion as violently as they have hitherto done. "If you were a preacher," a very wide supposition, it requires a tremendous leap of my vivid imagination to conceive of such an idea; you say you would follow the laudable example of John the Baptist in preaching and eating. Why don't you imitate him in dress? You have our full and free permission to do so. It would insure attention towards yourself, which is all you men desire after all. But you say 'it would be so odd.' Precisely; and 'it would be so odd' for some women to dress in the fashions of their grandmothers, while others wear the beautiful, bewitching *pin-back*. As you seem anxious to imitate some of the ancient saints, why not follow St. Paul, where he says, 'Charity thinketh no evil, but endureth *all* things.' Now, I think I hear you say: 'Pshaw! what is the use to try to argue with a woman?" But that is exactly what you of the masculine gender always say, when a woman gets the best of you in an argument; so you may say it just as frequently as you please.

M———."

In the original article by Sawbones, Isham points his readers to the book "History of Methodism in Tennessee 1818-1840" by John M'Ferrin. He shares about a preacher who "could have preached a

---

258 28 Jun 1876, *The Morristown Gazette*, 2.

pull-back off any woman in ten minutes." This author cannot find any reference to the account of the preacher holding off the rain, and the story about the lady returning with no ribbon is absent, but believes the preacher Isham is referring to is John Johnson. The following is a lengthy account of John's life and ministry, found in the aforementioned book.

Rev. John Johnson: Methodist Circuit Riding Preacher

In the year 1818 Nashville was first made a separate station. John Johnson was the preacher and William McMahon was the Presiding Elder. Mr. Johnson continued two years in this work, and was eminently useful and very highly esteemed. Indeed, he was no ordinary man. He was born in Louisa county, Virginia, Jan. 7th, 1783. His mother was left a widow with a large family when John was an infant. Her circumstances were straitened; in fact, she was reduced to poverty, and had no means of educating her son. When he had grown to be a young man, his mother, with some friends, made her way to Tennessee in an ox cart, and stopped near to where the town of Gallatin now stands, on the land of Mr. Douglass. This was about the year 1803. Here, young Johnson took his first lessons in the alphabet. It is stated in this wise:

"Mr. Douglass had an old negro man, who lived in a cabin nearby, and this negro knew the alphabet, but could go no farther. To him John applied for help. He resorted to his cabin night after night, and, with no other light than that of the fire, they pored over an old piece of a spelling- book which the negro owned, till the alphabet was completely mastered.

"There was still a wide gap between this and being able to read; but he had learned several hymns 'by heart' from hearing them sung; so he would have some one show him a hymn that he knew, in a piece of an old hymn-book — all that he had — and he would sometimes sit up till mid night trying to decipher the words and learn to spell, with no light but that of a fire. Yet he progressed so well that in two or three months he could 'make out' any hymn in his book by going over it two or three times, and in six months he could read in the New Testament so as to be understood tolerably well.

"For learning to write he had two copies. Each one was a song-ballad, written by some of his friends. These ballads he copied, or tried to copy, time after time, and until they were absolutely worn into shreds. By continued cultivation he improved the start thus obtained, till he wrote a pretty good plain hand."

In 1807, he was powerfully converted, and received into the Church by Jacob Young. He was admitted into the old "Western Conference on trial as a traveling preacher, at Liberty Hill, in 1808, and was sent to Hockhocking Circuit, Ohio. Up to this time he had made rapid improvements in study, and gave promise of future useful ness.

His second circuit was White Oak, Ohio. Here he had success. One sermon in particular made a profound impression.

"At one appointment — a rude hut in the woods called a meeting-house — by some mistake his intention to preach had not been duly announced. He started before day, and rode about twenty-five miles to reach the place. He waited till after the hour, and nobody came. At last, as he was about to despair of having a congregation, and depart, he saw a woman coming, carrying a child in her arms — or rather, as the custom was, when a child was two or three years old, upon her hip, with its feet astride. She came in and sat down. He looked at her; she seemed weary and sad. He thought of preaching; but no one else came, and his solitary auditor was evidently poor, as her dress, though clean, was faded and worn. She looked downcast and disappointed, as if she divined at once that there would be no service.

"At length he said to himself, 'I came here to preach, and by the help of God I'll do it!' He did. His soul grew happy; the poor woman's heart rejoiced, and she shouted the praises of God aloud, and, as he used to say, 'There was one universal shout all over the congregation.' He bade her good-bye, with a word of exhortation; and as she went away, trudging along the path by which she came, he could hear her every few steps, in a low voice, but one full of emotion, say, 'Glory!' The next time he came around, the little cabin was filled to overflowing; and on expressing his surprise at the fact, after sermon, he found that the woman had given a glowing account of the previous meeting, which had drawn out the whole settlement. And he was still more surprised when told that the woman, at his first appointment, had walked and carried her child ten miles on that occasion, as her husband persecuted her, and would not allow her to ride his horse to meeting. What a sad disappointment would that have been had Mr. Johnson failed to preach!

"But the effect of this sermon to a single hearer stopped not here. When she returned home, her husband growled out, 'Well, what kind of a fool did you have to preach out yonder to-day?' She mildly answered, 'He was a strange-looking man, but I never heard a man talk like he did in my life.' His curiosity was a little excited, and he asked, 'Why, what did he look like?' 'He was a stout sort of a man, with very dark face, and his hair was very black, and about half a yard long. I was afraid to look at him, he looked so solemn.' 'The d — ll!' grunted he; 'and what did he talk like?' 'Well, I don't know: he talked just like heaven and earth were coming together!' The man, whose name I believe was Baker, did not deign to make any remarks, but wondered in himself what kind of a man and what kind of talking that could be. In a few days he found that the curiosity to hear the new preacher was common; and before the next preaching-day came round, he had made up his mind to 'turn out with all the rest of the fools.'

"To the utter astonishment of Mrs. Baker, her husband told her to ride to meeting; he was going 'to see and hear the old cuss,' but he would walk. So he was one of the crowd that filled the little cabin when Mr. Johnson came on the second time. He was deeply convicted, but concealed his emotions till he got away from the crowd. He then frankly told his wife that she was right, and he was wrong. She knew not what to say to this, and said nothing. He walked on about a mile in silence, and then said, 'Wife, there's something the matter with me!' She answered, kindly, 'What do you think it is, Mr. Baker?' 'Dogged if I know; but I'm sick — heart-sick.' 'Get up and ride,' said she, 'and I'll walk.' 'No,' said he; and he walked more rapidly and uneasily along. No more was said about it; and Mrs. Baker thought the 'sick brash' had passed off. But after supper, he went out to feed his horse, and was gone rather long; she went to the door as it grew dark, and was greatly alarmed to hear cries and groans of distress at the stable.

She flew to the spot, and there was the hardened persecutor upon his knees, pleading in deepest agony for mercy. The 'sick brash' had not passed off! She shouted awhile, and then prayed awhile, then tried to instruct him in the way of salvation; and after a terrible struggle of two or three hours, he was enabled to embrace Christ as his Saviour, and raised a shout that made the hills around ring again. The devout but somewhat exaggerating wife declared that 'he raised a shout that was enough to wake the dead.'"

From this event there sprang up a glorious revival of religion; and Methodism was planted on so firm a basis here, that it has always since been the ruling faith in all that section of country. Baker's house became a preaching-place, a class was organized there, Baker was appointed leader, and faithfully and zealously did he act up to his profession down to the day of his death. So it may be safe to say, that that sermon to but one hearer was productive of more fruit than any other twenty sermons that Mr. Johnson preached during his ministry on this circuit."

Having finished his year, he was next sent to the Sandy Circuit, in Western Virginia.

"Toward the close of his labors on this circuit, he procured the services of a young licentiate for two or three weeks, and went over into Virginia to attend a camp-meeting held perhaps not far from Barboursville. He thought it would be a means of improvement to hear the

Figure 146 - From "The Circuit Rider" Blog by Michael Williams
https://michaelwilliamsstories.wordpress.com/2014/08/29/the-circuit-rider/

The Methodist circuit rider often travelled as many as forty or fifty miles between appointments, enduring hardships that now seem incredible. Travelling in all manner of weather through forests and fording streams and rivers, these riders frequently carried their few worldly possessions in saddle-bags. When they finally arrived at a community, the place of worship was often a house, a barn, a school - and in rare cases, a church. Many a circuit rider was responsible for the religious welfare of communities scattered throughout hundreds of square miles of territory.

educated preachers of the Old Dominion, and he hoped to have his spiritual strength renewed: he might assist in the labors at the altar, if need be; but he had little expectation of being called upon to preach. It never once occurred to him, however, that there was anything peculiar about his dress, or that that would influence his reception there. He wore a full suit of the coarsest quality of tow; and this, by a dozen wettings in the rain, and twice as many in the Big Sandy and its tributaries, had been brought to a dingy hue which it is easier to imagine than to name. He wore a broad-brimmed white wool hat, which he had worn every day since his conversion in 1807 — four years. His shoes were just such as the people of Virginia usually bought for their negroes; his pants were pinned over perfectly tight at the ankles; and his hair, parted in the middle, hung down loose and long around his shoulders. His very dark complexion, and his long, jet-black hair, were in striking contrast with the dingy white of his dress."

Figure 147 - Engraving of a Methodist Camp Meeting 1 Mar 1819 by Jacques Gérard Milbert (1766-1840) Library of Congress, Prints and Photographs Division (LC-USZC4-772) http://hdl.loc.gov/loc.pnp/cph.3b52282

Some inquisitive person about the camp where he lodged had managed to find out his vocation, and it was soon noised around that the strange-looking man was a preacher. The ministers were very much perplexed when they heard it; for it would not do to slight a brother, nor would it by any means do to put him up to preach. They, however, agreed to send one of their number to wait on him with an apology. He came to Mr. Johnson and said, 'My friend, I understand that you are a Methodist preacher.' 'I am, and a poor one at that,' was the response. 'Well, the people of this vicinity are proud and aristocratic,' our apologist proceeded; 'and we are afraid that if we have you to preach for us, they will take offense on account of your dress and appearance, and harm may in some way be the result. Be assured that it grieves us to manifest even the appearance of disrespect for one of our brethren. We entreat you, therefore, to take no offense at our not inviting you to preach.' 'I shall take no offense, brother,' Mr. Johnson meekly replied; 'I came not to preach, but in some humble way to do and to get good. Go on with your meeting, and suffer no uneasiness on my account.'

"They did 'go on with their meeting.' Sabbath came, and wore away; and still all was cold, formal, and lifeless. Not a shout nor a groan had been heard — except now and then a half-audible groan from Mr. Johnson, a little distance in rear of the stand — not a mourner answered to the calls and entreaties of the minister. Monday morning came. The crowd mostly dispersed, and all was bustle and activity on the part of the camp-holders, packing up their goods, and hastening to get away. The preachers had a little unfinished business to attend to, and they thought that, as it could now do no harm, Mr. Johnson might now preach at 11 o'clock, while they completed their business; and they retired to the most distant camp on the ground, that they might escape the mortification of witnessing his effort. It was bad enough for such a man to preach, and too bad for them to have both to hear the sermon and to see how the people treated a strange brother.

"At the appointed hour the horn sounded, and Mr. Johnson came solemnly and slowly along to the pulpit. He had spent an hour in the grove in prayer, and came with a broken, an humbled, and an overflowing heart. There were sitting listlessly under the vast 'shed,' a woman, three men, and three or four boys. Not disheartened, but strong in faith, he began the song,

'Come, ye sinners, poor and needy,'

and his stentorian voice made the forest ring. He sang with such spirit and power that many paused a moment to listen; and one after another joined the little assembly. He read, sang, and prayed; and there was something in his prayer which silenced in a great measure the confusion that had reigned around, and threw a deep solemnity over the place.

"By the time the preachers had concluded their business, Mr. Johnson was more than half through his subject, and his feelings and his voice were fast rising to the highest pitch. His voice became distinctly audible even to the ministers, and they began to listen and to catch his words. Finding he was not 'murdering the king's English,' as they had feared he would, they ventured to step outside their tent; and, behold, the bustle of preparation to leave had ceased, and every soul on the camp-ground was gathered into the congregation!

"Mr. Johnson was dwelling upon the consolations of religion. Soon an old sister raised a shout of joy. The effect was electric. It added a large drop to many a brimming cup; and more than twenty voices joined the shout at once. Our fugitive preachers crept stealthily to the 'shed,' glided almost involuntarily down the aisle to seats in the altar, where they sat with heads thrown back and streaming eyes, one excitable fellow among them ever and anon laughing out, 'Oh, ho-ho-ho-ho, glory!'

Figure 148 – *Religious Camp Meeting*. Watercolor by J. Maze Burbank, c. 1839. Old Dartmouth Historical Society-New Bedford Whaling Museum, New Bedford, Massachusetts. Gift of William F. Havemeyer (187)
http://www.loc.gov/exhibits/religion/rel07.html#obj186

"Mr. Johnson now turned to the contrast, the terrible doom of the wicked; and in a few minutes groans and screams were everywhere mingled with the praises, till the uproar would have drowned almost any other human voice but his. He now gave the usual invitation to mourners, and descended from the stand. The ministers rushed forward to meet him, implored his pardon, embraced him convulsively, and burst forth into shouts a little louder if possible than the rest. The altar was crowded by about forty mourners; and it was nearly five o'clock in the evening when the congregation 'broke up.'

"The campers unpacked their goods; those who had left returned; the meeting was resumed; it continued for two weeks, and resulted in the conversion of more than two hundred souls. So much more power has the man of warm emotions than the mere scholar, over the human heart."

After closing his labors on Sandy Circuit, he was appointed to the Natchez Circuit, Mississippi. The distance was some twelve hundred miles, and had to be made on horseback through the Indian nations. But he went promptly to his new field, and labored faithfully through the year.

In 1812, he was appointed to the Nashville Circuit. The following were his appointments, with the amounts paid him during the year:

COLLECTIONS ON NASHVILLE CIRCUIT.

Nashville	$8 43f		....	$1 25	$13 50
Tate's	1 25		$3 56£	....	....
Blair's	50		2 25	....	1 25
Carried forward	$10 18¾	$5 81¼	$1 25		$14 75

[…]

He traveled successively the Livingston and Christian Circuits, Kentucky, the Goose Creek Circuit, Tennessee, and then back to Livingston. As has been seen, he was stationed in Nashville, Oct., 1818. This was a great trial to him. He had never filled a city station, and feared the consequence of such appointment. He at first positively declined, but afterwards repented and went, where he remained two years. Here are extracts from Mrs. Johnson's account of his work in this station:

"William McMahon was the Presiding Elder; yet from some cause we were much more intimate with Brother T. L. Douglass, then superannuated in our vicinity. He was somewhat under the medium height, considerably inclined to corpulency, but very erect in his carriage. His demeanor was grave and dignified, his features handsome, and his countenance full of benevolence. His voice was full, round, and melodious, and his articulation unusually distinct. He did not look to be so much as forty years of age, yet I was told that he had been preaching for nearly twenty years. He had been Presiding Elder at Nashville four years, and after an interval of one year he again served a like period in the same place. I could not have thought that my poor body would outlive his vigorous frame — as I suppose I have — twenty-five years.

"At Nashville we found a comfortable home. We rented a house belonging to a young man whose name I do not now remember: it was situated in a suburb of the city which was known as Scuffletown, near Bass's tan-yard and West's spinning-factory. I had never been in so large a town before, and, as we first approached it, there seemed to me to be a myriad of chimneys; and even after a long stay — for we were there nearly three years — I did not know, or greatly care to know, much about the town. I suppose the population was then about 3,000. It was an incorporated city, and contained a bank, a market-house, a college, an academy for young ladies, a rope-walk, two distilleries, and three churches — Methodist, Presbyterian, and Baptist.

"I never met with as kind and generous a people as we found at Nashville. Few days, indeed, passed without some manifestation of this kindness. An article of dress for some of the family, some rarity for the table, some delicacy suited to the season, came with every week, and almost every day. It tried my very heart to give up every thing to be sold on leaving our home in Kentucky, but I believe our friends in Nashville, by gifts alone, more than replaced all that I then gave up. And O what a contrast between our pleasant home in the busy city and that of last year — a lonely cabin in the wilderness!

"I wish particularly to mention among our friends Jo. Elliston and his family, Matthew Quinn and family, Drs. Roane and Newnan, E. H. Foster, Mrs. Harrison, Parson'-Hume, Principal of the Academy, Mr. Southard, or Suthard, Mrs. Ewing — but time fails. I might mention as kind friends nearly every person whose acquaintance we formed in the city. "Mr. Johnson kept an account of every thing that we bought for the table, and the Church made good this amount, and paid him the disciplinary allowance — which was then one hundred dollars to the preacher, the same for the support of his wife, and sixteen dollars for each child under seven years of age. So our salary, besides table expenses, was about $232.

"This was an ample allowance, and far more than we had ever received before; yet I felt that, though rid of many of the difficulties and hardships with which I had had to contend heretofore, I was still bound to do what I could to aid in gaining a competency, and, if possible, 'something for a rainy day.' So, as soon as we were settled in our new home, I set out to find work to do. I soon found a hatter, a quiet little Methodist, whose shop was only a few rods from our door, and readily made an arrangement to trim hats for him at so much apiece. This kind of work was done in that day, I suppose, exclusively by hand, and chiefly by females. I allotted myself the task of earning 75 cents per day, and so zealously did I apply myself to the work, and so regularly did he furnish me work to do, that I think there were not a dozen days in the year that I fell short of that amount, except when sick.

"Mr. Johnson preached twice a week, and held prayer-meeting once a week, besides attending the class-meetings every Sabbath. His preaching was with power, was very acceptable to the Church, and attended with the best results. Hardly one Sabbath passed without a shout being heard in our church, and I think he preached no sermon that was not heard by many with tears, or other manifestations of deep emotion. The Church seemed to be rather in a state of constant and vigorous growth than of frequent revivals. A great number both of infants and adults were baptized. I remember that a widow lady of the name of Snow, the mother of five or six children, had them all baptized at her house at the same time. It was a very pretty sight to see them all so neat and orderly, standing in a line in the order of their ages, as Mr. Johnson for their mother dedicated them to God."

His second year is thus noted:

"Mr. Johnson was again sent to Nashville by the Conference — the Tennessee Conference, for the Kentucky Conference was not yet formed — which met at Nashville, in October, 1819. He now proposed that the society pay him a fixed salary, and dispense with the necessity for keeping accounts. Brother Jo. Elliston and Dr. Roane declared that less than a thousand dollars would not support a family in Nashville — at least, it would not support either of theirs; but Mr. Johnson said six hundred dollars would be enough to support his family, and that was all he desired. At his request it was fixed at that amount[.]

"By this time the young man in whose house we had been living, was married, and had need of his house. Mr. Johnson now rented one from E. H. Foster, who, as before stated, was a relative; though after the contract was made, and we were comfortably quartered in the house, he told Mr. Johnson that we should pay no rent, and besides, if we would remain in Nashville, we should have a lease on the house and lot for ninety- nine years on the same terms. I do not remember the street, or number of the house — if it was numbered — but it was near the residence of General Carroll. I went out but little. I can never forget, however, the dignified politeness and affability of General Carroll, as he almost every day passed our door."

It was in Nashville that Mr. Johnson had a debate with Mr. Vardiman, a celebrated Baptist minister from Kentucky, on the mode and subjects of baptism. Mr. Johnson's victory was complete, and the cause of Pedobaptism triumphantly sustained. He followed Mr. Vardiman to Clarksville, and thence to Hopkinsville, Kentucky, and so demolished this champion of immersion, that he returned to Northern Kentucky under the impression that there were giants in the South.

Mr. Johnson continued in the work of the ministry, filling many important appointments, as his health would permit, till 1857, when he died in peace, in the town of Mount Vernon, Illinois.

Mr. Johnson attained to high position in the Church. He acquired considerable learning, and was a profound theologian. He was an able and very interesting preacher, and greatly devoted to the cause of Christ. His personal appearance was not commanding, and yet he bore the marks of intelligence and great humility. The author had the pleasure of hearing him, and the sermon made a profound impression on the audience; it was preached in Russellville, Kentucky, in the year 1832.[259]

In 1918, people were still testifying to the power and effectiveness of the preaching ministry of Rev. John Johnson. The *Christian Advocate* shares:

One hundred years ago Methodism made a venture to make a station out of a Church that had paid only $23.18 ¾ toward the support of a pastor. The law of the Church made the salaries of all the preachers the same; and at the time Nashville was formed into a station the preacher and wife were entitled to $100 each and each child under seven years $16; so that the salary of the first stationed preacher was $232. Along with this salary the Church could and was expected to pay house rent, cost of feed, fuel, and grocery expenses.

The first station preacher was Rev. John Johnson. He was born in Louisa County, Va., January 7, 1783—one hundred and thirty-five years ago. When he was an infant, his father died and shortly afterwards his mother. In an Oxcart he moved to Sumner County, Tenn. An Old Negro man belonging to Mr. Douglass taught young John his alphabet, having learned a few hymns "by heart." Through the use of these he learned to read. Perhaps at a camp meeting in Sumner County

Figure 149 - *The History of Methodism* (1902) by John Fletcher Hurst, 28.
https://www.flickr.com/photos/internetarchivebookimages/14598130197/

in 1807 he was converted. While the glow of this new experience was in his heart, he at tended Conference at Liberty Hill, in Williamson County, and connected himself with that heroic brotherhood of early itinerants. His first appointment, announced at Liberty Hill, in Williamson County, Tenn., was a circuit in the State of Ohio.

---

[259] *History of Methodism in Tennessee: 1818 to 1840* – John Berry M'Ferrin, 46-63, Southern Methodist Publishing House, Nashville, TN 1873. Digitized by Google

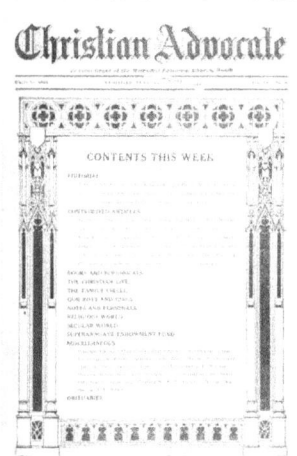

Nashville has had many remarkable men as pastors in the long century that has crept on, a day at a time, but none more remarkable in their day than Rev. John Johnson, who was the first stationed preacher. His third circuit was in Virginia; his fourth, in Natchez, Miss. It seems incredible to think of this poor, illiterate, country backwoods man searching out and forming pastoral charges in Ohio, Virginia, and Mississippi in the first five years of his itinerant ministry, and in eight or nine years coming to the capital of Tennessee to establish the first separate pastoral charge. He could not have even dreamed what has followed. As he wrought for the salvation of men one hundred years ago in Nashville, it never in the smallest sense occurred to him that he was a part, an integral part, in a great system and movement which in One hundred years should see a growth in the membership of from 75 to 11,000 and in the town from a population of between two and three thousand to over one hundred thousand. And when he preached in the little square church with three galleries located far down the hill on Church Street, he little dreamed of the twenty-four handsome churches in which as many thoroughly furnished Methodist preachers minister in holy service as it is to-day.

It is true that if Rev. John Johnson were to appear now in the pulpits of the Methodist churches of Nashville, with his long black hair parted in the middle, dressed in the plain homespun clothes, and wearing the coarse shoes, as he did one hundred years ago, he could not be expected to succeed. But in his day he ministered to the Ellistons, the Fosters, the Carrolls, and to the people of Nashville. There was in his ministries more than the eccentricities, more than the crudeness of his outward appearance. He was a great preacher of righteousness and brought the "good news" to Nashville a century ago. He believed where he could not see. He leaned on God. His successors need to do likewise. NEW ORLEANs, LA.[260]

In 1869 Rev. John Johnson's wife, Susannah Brooks Johnson wrote *Recollections of the Rev. John Johnson and His Home: An Autobiography*. This 348-page volume is available for free online.[261] Most of the story in *History of Methodism in Tennessee* is taken from his wife's account as her book was published in 1869, four years before the *History* was published. In addition, the United Methodist Church has a webpage devoted to circuit riding preachers, of which Rev. Johnson was one. It includes a 3:52 YouTube video that includes photos, museum exhibits, and more.[262]

---

[260] *Christian Advocate*, Volume 79, Issues 1-26, 1 Feb 1918, 18 (114).
[261] *Recollections of the Rev. John Johnson and His Home: An Autobiography*, Jan 1869, https://tinyurl.com/revjohnjohnson
[262] https://www.umc.org/en/content/the-hard-road-of-a-methodist-circuit-rider, Accessed 27 Mar 2020. Video can be found separately here: https://youtu.be/5zRXChPJOFE

Isham says that he "heard much of his preaching, and I have had a prejudice against the devil ever since." Rev. Johnson had a big impact on Isham, which is one of the reasons we have devoted so much coverage to this particular man. The other reason is that this author is a Baptist Pastor / Military Chaplain, and so writings by Isham that speak to religion are of particular interest. In summary, Isham seemed to appreciate the "hell-fire and brimstone" preaching of folks like Rev. Johnson. He also addressed the issue of "pull-back dresses" by spending considerable time sharing about Rev. Johnson's famous sermon at the camp meeting in Virginia, and the rest is probably from firsthand testimony of meetings he attended. It would appear that Isham is in agreement with Bascum in his disdain for the pull-back dresses, but his message is to focus on the gospel, preaching on heaven and hell, and if a preacher does that, he will only have to scant mention excessive fashion and it will be enough.

The image below is an advertisement for a special event held in Morristown in Oct 1876.

The next article comes in December of 1876 when Isham comments on news from a Knoxville paper.

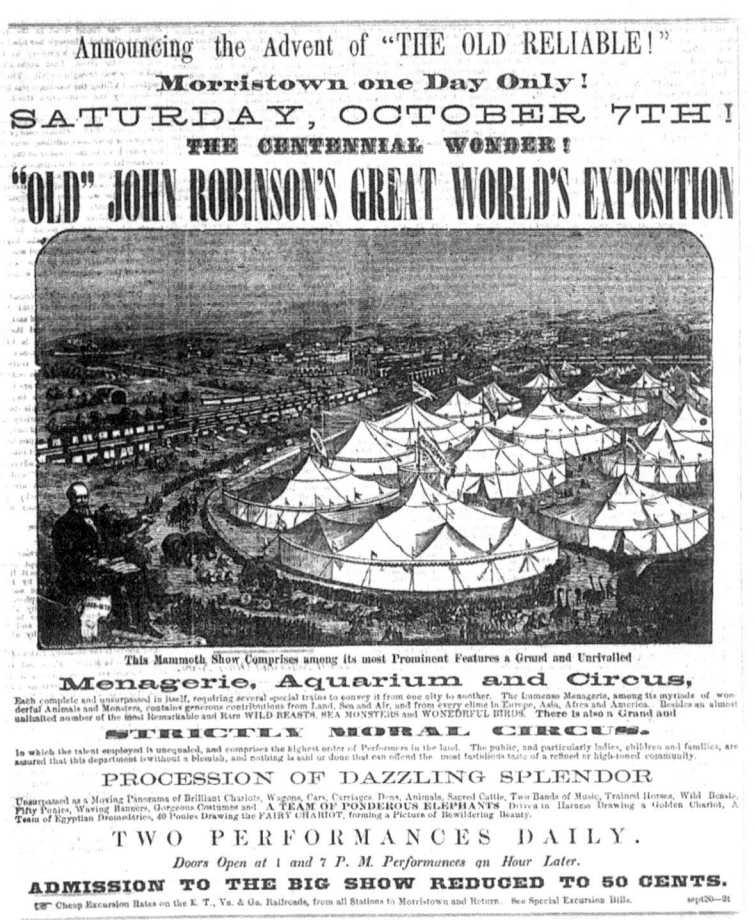

Figure 150 - Front page advertisement for "Old John Robinson's Great World's Exposition," in Morristown, Tennessee, to be held on 7 Oct 1876. Excerpts read, "The Centennial Wonder!" "This Mammoth Show Comprises among its most Prominent Features a Grand and Unrivaled Menagerie, Aquarium and Circus." "The immense menagerie, among its myriads of wonderful Animals and Monsters, contains generous contributions from Land, Sea, and Air, and from every clime in Europe, Asia, Africa and America. Besides an almost unlimited number of the most Remarkable and Rare WILD BEASTS, SEA MONSTERS AND WONDERFUL BIRDS. There is also a Grand and "STRICTLY MORAL CIRCUS" In which the talent employed is unequaled and comprises the highest order of Performers in the land…" "PROCESSION OF DAZZLING SPLENDOR" "TWO PERFORMANCES DAILY" "ADMISSION TO THE BIG SHOW REDUCED TO 50 CENTS" "Cheap Excursion Rates on the E. T., Va. & Ga Railroads, from all Stations to Morristown and Return. See Special Excursion Bills."

The Morristown Gazette, 20 Sep 1876, 1.

6 DEC 1876 ADVANCED CIVILIZATION AND SAW-MILLS.[263]

"To the Editor of the Morristown Gazette:

I read in a Knoxville paper, a short time since, a letter from a gentleman in New Jersey wishing to know if he could express his political opinions, without danger to himself, in Tennessee! He proposed to bring with him advanced Christian civilization and—saw mills!

Advanced Christian civilization is good!

I had thought all along that we had advanced to the extreme point in that direction!

About once a week we are treated to a dish of this gruel from some one of the Tennessee papers!

In view of the fact that no Northern man has been molested in Tennessee on account of his politics, it has become nauseating!

If the gentleman, Mr. Paulison, will come to Tennessee I will guarantee him safe from danger—except from lightning and bed-bugs!

Come on with the advanced Christianity and saw-mills, but I warn you that you will find an over-stock of both in Tennessee!   SAWBONES."

Figure 151 - John R. Paulison, Richard Romaine, Saddle River, Ridgefield Park, Bergen Co., NJ. Created 1876 by A.H. Walker (Image from Art Source Int'l)

Without a first name, it is difficult to narrow down exactly who Isham is referring to . . . but there is a prominent man named John Paul Paulison from Bergen, NJ who was active in business in 1876.

"John Paul Paulison, the subject of this sketch, was born at Hackensack, N. J., on the 19th of November, 1822.

On the death of his father, which occurred when he was little more than nine years of age, his widowed mother removed with the family to New York, where Mr. Paulison, at the early age of twelve, began his business career as a clerk in a mercantile house.

In 1848 he entered the office of the Atlantic Mutual Marine Insurance Company, and was accountant to that company until 1852, when he was elected secretary.

---

263 Dr. Isham Peck, "Advanced Civilization and Saw-Mills," *The Morristown Gazette*, 6 Dec 1876, 2.

In 1855 he was promoted to a vice-presidency in that company. Declining the latter office, however, he accepted the vice-presidency of the Astor Mutual Marine Insurance Company, and continued in the latter office until 1856, when he relinquished it to embark in business on his own account, as an average- adjuster, notary, insurance broker, and agent and underwriter for several insurance companies located out of the State.

In 1867 he was called to the position of vice-president of the Sun Mutual Marine Insurance Company, of which the late Hon. Moses H. Grinnell was then president. He relinquished his private business to accept that office, and in 1869, on Mr. Grinnell being appointed by President Grant collector for the port of New York, Mr. Paulison was elected president of the company, which position he still holds, as well as those of vice-president of the New York Board of Marine Underwriters, and vice-president of the American Shipmasters' Association [….] Mr. Paulison is descended from Dutch and English ancestors. His father was Paul Paulison, born in 1770, graduated from Princeton College in 1794, and only and elder

brother to Richard Paulison, who died at Hackensack in 1873, in the one hundredth year of his age…

The genealogy of Mr. Paulison is interesting in that it illustrates the manner of naming the children of the early Dutch settlers. For instance, we have, — 1st. Paulus Pieterse, meaning Paulus, Pieter's son. 2d. Martin Paulisse, meaning Martin, Paulus's son. 3d. Paulus Martense, meaning Paulus, Martin's son. 4th. John Paulison, meaning John, Paulus's son. 5th. Paul Paulison. 6th. John Paul Paulison. The baptismal name of the subject of this sketch is John Paulison (after his grandfather), but to distinguish himself from his cousin, John Richard Paulison, the son of his father's brother Richard, he adopted the name of his father, Paul, hence, John Paul Paulison.

In 1873, Mr. Paulison removed from New York to Tenafly, N. J., where he now resides. He is a great lover of astronomy, and has erected on his grounds at Tenafly an astronomical observatory containing a powerful telescope and other accessories for the examination and study of the heavenly bodies. In the erection of this observatory he has invented and put in operation appliances which are great improvements upon old methods."[264]

---

[264] *History of Bergen and Passaic Counties, New Jersey, With Biographical Sketches of Many of Its Pioneers and Prominent Men*, 293-294. Compiled by W. Woodford Clayton. Philadelphia: Everts and Peck, 1882.

"To the Editor of the Morristown Gazette:

I see by your last paper that the preachers are quarreling again, and what infamous language they use. It has been thus ever since christianity was introduced. I think I could suggest a plan by which they could settle their difficulties without involving the whole community. I spent the summer of 1867 on a large Louisiana plantation, all the negroes in the South had quit work and turned their attention to religion; about one-third of the men were preachers; boys of fifteen and many of the women were hard at it. At all times of

Figure 153 – "Picking Cotton on a Southern Plantation" by Getty Images

Figure 154 - "The Lost Cause," W. E. Omsley, 1868. (Courtesy of the Special Collections, Tulane University Library) http://www.digitalhistory.uh.edu/exhibits/reconstruction/section2/section 2_28b.html

the day or night, you could hear them on all the plantations on both sides of the river. One moonlight night about eight o'clock, I was sitting on my gallery, when a half dozen negro men came through the yard and to where I was sitting. At their head was a prominent preacher on the place. They came to tell me that they were going to kill another prominent preacher on the place, and wished to know what I thought of it. I asked what the man had been doing? What they were going to kill for? They said he is preaching *false doctrine*. I told them that thing of false and true doctrine had deluged the earth with blood, and the question was no nearer settled now then eighteen hundred years ago. I told them that the government allowed every man to hold and express an opinion on the subject, and that if they killed the man I would have them punished. They said they thought I was mistaken. That they had been to see the clerk of the parish court and he had told them that if the man was preaching false doctrine to kill him. I assured them that I would have them punished if they killed him, if I had to send to New Orleans for troops to do it. I advised them to get

[265] Dr. Isham Peck, "How 'Sawbones' would Settle Theological Differences," *The Morristown Gazette*, 6 Jun 1877, 2.

on their all-fours and butt it out with their heads. They left me in disgust. They did not kill the man, but drove him from the plantation. This would be an excellent way to settle such difficulties. It would insure a large number of spectators and a large collection of dimes, and the whole community would be delighted. This mode of settling difficulties is not original with me. About fifteen years ago, a difficulty was settled in this way on Beaver Creek, a few miles below New Market. The combattants [sic] were old A. and old B., (I could give names) Old A. put a flat rock in his hat to be very smart. They took a running start on their all fours, and when their heads met they bounced off the ground and lay for sometime as if dead.

The man who wrote the article in the *Tribune and Age* of May 24th, entitled "The Social Element of German Character," is a friend of the human race.

SAWBONES."

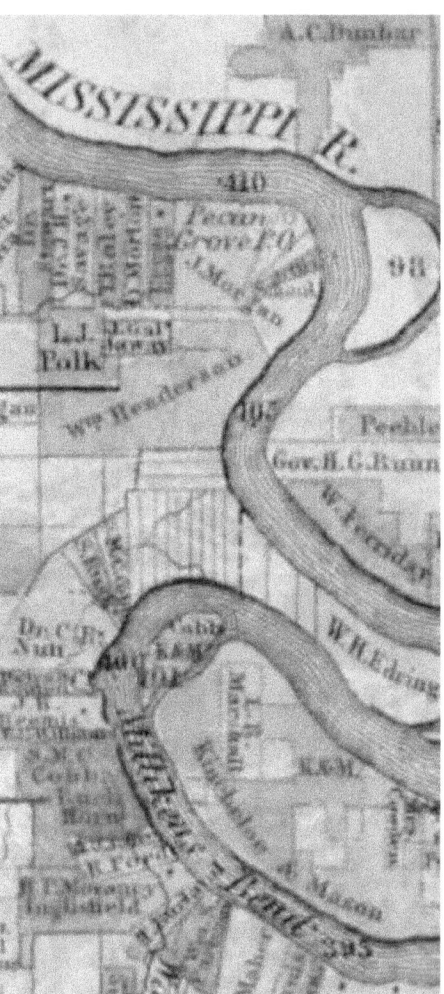

Figure 155 - Tourette Map 1853 - USGW Archives - Carroll Parish, LA (Henderson Plantation in Pink North of Milliken's Bend)

Isham was married to Emma and had already partially raised 6 children by the "summer of 1867" to which he refers here. His brother "Bill," General William Raine Peck had a large plantation in Madison Parish called "The Mountain," and Emma's family, William and Louise Henderson, had a large plantation in East Carroll County that ran along the Mississippi close to Milliken's Bend, called Henderson Plantation. *Ada's Journal* makes clear that they spent time on each plantation, but in this one he says "At all times of the day or night, you could hear them [preaching] on all the plantations on both sides of the river. It would seem most likely then, that he was at the Henderson Plantation. He is to be commended for stopping the murder from taking place, though the author cannot vouch for the method he suggested for resolving differences. The fact that these likely former slaves were turning to Isham, probably referred to as "Dr. Peck" by most, is notable. The fact that they were about to commit a murder in the name of religion, which could put them in prison, after they were so recently bound as slaves (just two years before) should have given them pause to think and seek out authorities in the area.

Figure 156 - The Texas African-American History Memorial in Austin, Texas.
(Credit: Elaine Thompson/AP Photo)

President Abraham Lincoln signed the Emancipation Proclamation on 1 Jan 1863, and Gen. Robert E. Lee surrendered to Ulysses S. Grant at Appomattox Courthouse on 9 Apr 1865, but President Andrew Johnson did not declare a formal end to the Civil War until August 1866. The final land battle was the Battle of Palmito Ranch where 350 Confederates defeated 800 Union troops. The CSS Shenandoah continued terrorizing Union commercial ships in the Bering Sea long after the land battles were finished. It wasn't until August 1865 that the Shenandoah stowed its guns and made a covert escape for England. Even then, it wasn't until 20 Aug 1866, in acknowledgement of Texas' new state government, that President Johnson was finally able to proclaim, "said insurrection is at an end and that peace, order, tranquility, and civil authority now exist in and throughout the whole United States of America."[266]

Isham and most of his family were supporters of the Confederacy, and 1867 was a time when everyone in our nation, especially Southerners, were trying to figure out what life was going to look like. This is the era commonly referred to by the term Reconstruction. "Reconstruction (1865-1877), the turbulent era following the Civil War, was the effort to reintegrate Southern states from the Confederacy and 4 million newly-freed slaves into the United States."[267] Along with political and legal transformations, there were many changes to religious life in the South. The religious life of slaves on many plantations had been repressed. Many were either not allowed to assemble, or they had white preachers who sometimes included propaganda in their messages, encouraging slaves to quietly obey their masters and not revolt. After Emancipation and at the close of the Civil War, freed slaves now had a new found freedom in worship, and there are other testimonies (besides Isham's) that many of the young men were "called to preach."

Nancy Bullock Woolridge gives a scholarly look at the religious life of slaves in her journal article "The Slave Preacher—Portrait of a Leader." She says, "From the available records it is clear that the old slave exhorter on the plantation was, first of all, a slave of an appreciable degree of native ability and force. To an impartial stranger who visited the community, he was a striking figure because of his impressive personality. Something about him might attract the attention of the visitor who would ask the master about the particular slave, and elicit the information that it was "Uncle ———," the

[266] Sarah Pruitt, *Why the Civil War Actually Ended 16 Months After Lee Surrendered, For one thing, things were a little confusing in Texas.* https://www.history.com/news/why-the-civil-war-actually-ended-16-months-after-lee-surrendered, 5 Mar 2018.
[267] History.com, *Reconstruction,* https://www.history.com/topics/american-civil-war/reconstruction, 29 Oct 2009.

religious leader of the plantation. In most cases the old preacher would be in reality a mature person, a man who was at least in middle life, one who had worked hard and well, one who apparently exerted some control over the slaves. From the point of view of the slave owner, the teachings of Christianity suited the situation admirably, for usually the exhorter taught principles of honesty, piety, and love. From the view point of the slave population the preacher served as arbiter, general counsellor, and mediator, even at times between master and slave. His advice was often proved to be sound, and his shrewdness in handling a delicate situation, on occasion worked to the advantage of the slave.

In the early days, usually the slave preacher was one of the slaves who had learned to read. The Bible was his text—his history, geography, and spelling book. He believed it implicitly and literally. Possessing remarkable powers of memory and imagination, he could recite whole passages verbatim—even when he had merely listened to the reading by some kindly disposed member of the master's family. As teacher and biblical interpreter to the young and old slaves, the preacher touched the lives of all in a most unique way. In most cases held in high respect by the other slaves, he wielded the most powerful influence of any other figure among Negroes. While his errors of ignorance in interpreting the scriptures have served as source for comic entertainment, as an individual the preacher was rarely amusing to his own folk. Even to the white persons who knew him intimately, he was seldom the comic character which later writers, especially writers of fiction, have made him."[268] The journal article goes on to quote a snippet of one slave preacher sermon, "Tain't no dream nor no joke," cried one of them (a preacher in thrilling eloquence); "de time's a'most yere. Der wont be no mo' whippin', no gwine to pay 'em for der work. O, my drudders! De bressed time's a knockin' at de door! De good Lord'll ramshackle de devil, and all de people in dis yere world, bof white and black, is a swine to live to gedder in peace." (Quoted from *Authentic Narrative of James Williams*. New York: The American Anti-Slavery Society, 1838. p. 26.).

Isham's grandpa, Adam Peck, Sr. arrived at Mossy Creek in 1792 and founded Mossy Creek, establishing his grist mill along the fast-running waters of the creek. In addition, he founded a church he named after his wife, Elizabeth, called Elizabeth Chapel. They had a slave, who went by Uncle John, whom Elizabeth had taught to read. Uncle John was installed as the preacher for Elizabeth Chapel. In the image here, please see the original grave stone of red color, then the larger concrete gravestone with plaque attached, and the

[268] Woolridge, Nancy Bullock. "The Slave Preacher--Portrait of a Leader." *The Journal of Negro Education* 14, no. 1 (1945): 28-37. Accessed March 28, 2020. doi:10.2307/2292771.

bronze plate as well. All three sections indicate the same information, that Adam and his son Judge Jacob Peck had a slave named Uncle John, whose wife was Sylvia.

Uncle John became the first preacher in Mossy Creek and people from a number of religious denominations would come to hear him preach. The first building they used was a simple log chapel, and the place where it stood is still marked by a brick monument and plaque in the Westview Cemetery, Jefferson City, TN.

Figure 157 - Monument to "A Log Chapel," First in Mossy Creek - Westview Cemetery, Jefferson City, TN Author's son Hudson Peck behind monument and local Jefferson City Historian Linda Gass to the right, photo taken by the author on 12 Jul 2017

The plaque reads, "A LOG CHAPEL STOOD HERE, ERECTED BY ADAM PECK FAMILY IN 1790. SITE OF EARLIEST CHRISTIAN ORIGINS AT MOSSY CREEK. CHARTERED METHODIST EPISCOPAL IN 1817, BAPTIST, PRESBYTERIAN, BLACK METHODISTS FORMED OWN GROUPS FROM THIS BEGINNING.

ELIZABETH CHAPEL M.E. ERECTED HERE IN 1850. USED BY FEDERAL TROOPS AT BATTLE OF MOSSY CREEK, DEC. 29, 1863. **Scan the QR Code below to experience CMB LIVE and join Linda Gass and the author's sons at the Elizabeth Chapel Monument.**

The log chapel stood until 1850 when a new "Elizabeth Chapel" was erected in the same location. The timbers used to build Elizabeth's Chapel still support the main sanctuary of the First United Methodist Church in Jefferson City, TN. By divine providence, the author was able to visit Jefferson City, stop by the First United Methodist Church when it was open, and a church secretary took him and his family to see the church building's foundations, so they could touch the logs that had supported the Elizabeth Chapel, and potentially supported the original

Figure 158 - **CMB Live** - Westview Cemetery and Pecks of Mossy Creek Origins https://youtu.be/uR8Sr XG8Zgs

Figure 159 - Foundation of First United Methodist Church Jefferson City, TN - Timbers originally used in Log Chapel, then Elizabeth Chapel, now supporting the sanctuary, Photo by the author 12 Jul 2017

log chapel as well. **Experience CMB LIVE: Scan the QR code below to join the Peck family as they touch and feel the original Elizabeth Chapel logs**.

Religion played a large part in Isham's upbringing. His family was known as the spiritual forebearers of the region. His grandpa Adam had settled Mossy Creek and erected the first church. His Uncle Moses Looney Peck

Figure 160 - CMB Live - Elizabeth Chapel Foundations found under the First United Methodist Church in Jefferson City, TN https://youtu.be/c7S2D 68Ymds

was a pastor, and numerous other relatives were active in the religious landscape of Eastern Tennessee. Moses was even listed as one of the prominent Union leaders in Jefferson County, TN.[269] More information about the Peck Family Spiritual Legacy and the Christian beginnings in Mossy Creek is available in *Salt and Light – A History*: FIRST UNITED METHODIST CHURCH, Jefferson City, Tennessee.

This concludes comments regarding Isham's 6 June 1877 article regarding his time on the plantation just after the Civil War ended.

Figure 161 – Scan this QR code or visit https://www.crossmountainbooks.com/sawbones-resources to watch videos and see photos of East Carroll Parish, LA and the land where Henderson Plantation used to be located.

A Sawbones article was published in *The Morristown Gazette* on 4 July 1877 and picked up by *The Daily Memphis Avalanche* on 8 July 1877. In this intriguing article, Isham relates his memories of duels and fighting between Vicksburg, Mississippi newspaper editors.

---

[269] Oliver Temple, *Notable Men of Tennessee: From 1833 to 1875, Their Times and Their Contemporaries*, New York, Cosmopolitan Press, 1912, 50, 52.

8 JUL 1877 FIGHTING EDITORS. Vicksburg Quill-Drivers of the Olden Time who Patronized the Coroner.[270]

Morristown (Tenn.) Gazette, 4th.

If your account in the last number of your paper of the fighting at Vicksburg was to be taken as evidence at the Day of Judgment, it would be rather hard on some of the boys. As I lived at Vicksburg at the time of these occurrences, and was personally acquainted with all the parties, I will try to set you right. In the first place, you call my old friend Dr. Hagan Hogan, and you say he was from the North. Dr. Hagan was an Irishman, and came to the United States after he was grown. I owned the building in which his paper was published for many years. While publishing his paper at Vicksburg he made a visit to Ireland. On his return he gave me a very amusing account of his interview and dining with Dr. Lever, the novelist. He said Lever was just the kind of a man I would expect to see after reading his writings. Now, after your blood-and-thunder account of Dr. Hagan, you will be surprised when I tell you that he never killed a man. The Doctor did do some rough-and-tumble fighting in which there was some shooting, and he fought two duels: one was with Flagg, the editor of the opposition paper. It was understood that they were to meet on the street opposite the Courthouse, armed with double barreled shotguns, and to blaze away. My brother loaded Hagan's gun at H.'s request, and as he handed it to him he said, "Hagan, you can't shoot worth a dam, but I have put a charge in that gun that will kick you out of range of the other man's shot." Flagg was slightly wounded. His other duel was with my old friend, Col. McCardle. Mc. was wounded in the hip. Col. McCardle is still living, and has edited a paper at Vicksburg, except at short intervans [sic], since 1838[.] Dr. Hagan was killed by Dan. Adams, who was the Gen. Dan. Adams left for dead at the battle of Shiloh. He recovered with the loss of an eye. After the war was law partner of Gen. Harry Hays at New Orleans. He then went to New York and practiced law—now dead. Hagan had said something in his paper about Judge Adams, Dan's father, who lived at Jackson, Miss. Dan went to Vicksburg and asked some one to point out Hagan to him. Hagan was crossing the street when A.[dams] attacked him; both were armed. They clinched and fell, and while both were down A.[dams] shot him in the head. Dr. H[agan] had a very reckless way of expressing himself in his paper. I have often told him that I would not insure his life 24 hours for 99 cents on the dollar. He was a small, quiet mannered gentleman—was never married. James Fall fought two duels with Tom Robbins. In the first fight neither was hurt. The next time a ditch was dug, and they fought in the ditch. Fall was shot in the knee. Tom Robbins married a niece of Jeff Davis [Jefferson Davis, President of the Confederate States of America from 1861-1865]. He died in a lunatic asylum at New York. I saw Robbins after the fight, and asked him why he fought in a ditch. He said: You know I cannot shoot on the wing, and Fall would not stand still. In the spring of 1867, I met Mr. Fall at the St. Charles, in New Orleans. I had not seen him for many years. He told me he had been in South America. I noticed that he walked lame, and I asked how he got hurt. He looked surprised, and said, don't you remember; this is Tom Robbins' work. James Downs, a law student of S[eargent]. S[mith]. Prentiss, was wounded in a duel with Tom Robbins. They fought with rifles. D.[owns] was shot in the breast, but recovered. Walter Hickey had a street fight with Dr. McLin. I witnessed it. McLin was killed. James Rian was killed in a duel by Dick

---

[270] Dr. Isham Peck, "Fighting Editors," *The Daily Memphis Avalanche*, 8 Jul 1877, 1.

Hammett (Rian, editor Sentinel; Hammett, editor Whig); they fought with pistols—fired three times—Rian would use a short eight-inch barrel pistol that he was used to; he cut Hammett's coat at the small of his back every fire. At the third fire Rian was shot through the heart. Geo[rge]. Jenkins was killed by Henry Crabb, a young lawyer, son of Judge Crabb, of Tennessee, with a bowieknife. Crabb went to California and headed a filibustering party; went to Sonora; they were all captured; Crabb's head was cut off and stuck on a pole. I cannot remember the name of the next editor. I did not know him. He was killed by a dry goods clerk on the street. But while the editors were fighting, the other boys were amusing themselves in the same way. I could tell you all about it, but enough.

SAWBONES.

In this article, Isham mentions 10 duels and a gruesome incident where Judge Crabb is decapitated and his head stuck on a pole. Here is a chart (broken into 3 parts) that attempts to organize the duels:

	Color Guide	Uninjured	Killed	Injured
		***See Sawbones	Resources Online For	Colorized Chart***
#	Date	Place	1st	1st's Position
1	3 Mar 1841	Vicksburg, MS	Dr. James Hagan	Editor for *Vicksburg Sentinel*
2		Vicksburg, MS	Dr. James Hagan	Editor for *Vicksburg Sentinel*
3	7 Jun 1843	Vicksburg, MS	Dr. James Hagan	Editor for *Vicksburg Sentinel*
4	18 Apr 1842	LA side of MS River	James S. Fall	Editor for *Vicksburg Sentinel*
5		Vicksburg, MS?	James S. Fall	Editor for *Vicksburg Sentinel*
6	5 May 1844	Vicksburg, MS?	Col. Thomas E. Robbins	Columnist for the *Sentinel* and Vicksburg Railroad Bank Trustee
7	6 May 1844	Vicksburg, MS?	Walter Hickey	Editor for *Vicksburg Sentinel*
8	29 Feb 1844	Vicksburg, MS?	James Ryan	Editor for *Vicksburg Sentinel*
9		Vicksburg, MS	John Jenkins	Editor for *Vicksburg Sentinel*
10	1857	Sonora	Judge Henry Crabb	Vicksburg Lawyer
11		Vicksburg, MS?	Editor of Paper	?

Figure 162 - Seargent Smith Prentiss (1808-1850) Prentiss moved to Vicksburg in 1832. Elected to Congress in 1837. Oil on Canvas. Photo by author. Original courtesy of Old Court House Museum in Vicksburg.

#	2nd	2nd's Position
1	Edmund Flagg	Editor for *Vicksburg Whig*
2	Col. Win H. McCardle	Editor for *Vicksburg Whig*
3	Gen. Daniel W. Adams	Son of Judge Adams (offended by *Sentinel* article)
4	Col. Thomas E. Robbins	Vicksburg Railroad Bank Trustee
5	Col. Thomas E. Robbins	Vicksburg Railroad Bank Trustee
6	James M. Downs	?
7	Dr. J. F. Macklin	?
8	Rick E. Hammett	Editor for *Vicksburg Whig*
9	Judge Henry A. Crabb (of TN)	Vicksburg Lawyer
10	Unknown	?
11	Dry Goods Clerk	

#	Outcome	Source
1	Flagg slightly wounded	Pistols, Politics and the Press: Dueling in 19th Century American Journalism
2	McCardle wounded in hip	Sawbones Article
3	Dr. Hagan shot in the head and died	Pistols, Politics and the Press: Dueling in 19th Century American Journalism
4	Neither man was hurt	Pistols, Politics and the Press: Dueling in 19th Century American Journalism
5	Fought in a ditch, Fall shot in knee	Sawbones Article
6	Downs shot in breast, but recovered	Sawbones Article
7	Dr. Macklin was killed	Sawbones Article
8	Ryan was shot through the heart	Pistols, Politics and the Press, 84
9	Jenkins stabbed Crabb several times, Crabb shot Jenkins in the heart, killing him	Sawbones Article
10	Crabb's head cutoff and stuck on a pole[271]	https://en.wikipedia.org/wiki/Henry_A._Crabb
11	Editor killed	Sawbones Article

Peck Family Connections

Isham says this "his brother" loaded the gun for Dr. Hagan in the first dual against Flagg. This was most likely his brother William Raine Peck, who years later would become a prominent civil war general known as "Big Peck", and the final commander of the famed Louisiana Tigers.

Additionally, Isham's brother, Colonel Wiley Hawkins Peck, was involved in a serious incident where he killed a man named Charles Harris at the St. Charles Hotel in New Orleans in January 1860. He was eventually acquitted, but the facts were established that he shot Harris multiple times and finished him off with a bowie knife. Isham travelled to New Orleans for the trial. There are two significant touch points here. One is that the events of the trial read like it was almost a duel between the men, both firing pistols at each other…except that it was in a crowded hotel rotunda. Second is that after his trial, Wiley offered Daniel W. Adams and Shepherd W. Brown (of New Orleans) as securities, and was released to be with his friends and return to his hotel. Brig. Gen. Daniel W. Adams (C.S.A.) is the man who eventually kills Dr. Hagan during incident #3 as described by Isham. Also, Shepherd W. Brown is the man referred to in *Ada's Journal*

Figure 163 - Brig. Gen. Daniel W. Adams, C.S.A., Commander of the Army of Tennessee's Louisiana Brigade, 1861, Library of Congress

---

[271] Highly Important from Sonora, Massacre of Henry A. Crabb, R. A. Woods, and Senator McCoun, Annihilation of the Party, Horrible Atrocities, California Digital Newspaper Collection, Daily Alta California, Volume 9, Number 133, 14 May 1857, https://tinyurl.com/massacreofhenrycrabb

and Emma's Letters as "Mr. Brown".[272] This Brown family's identity had been a mystery to the author until this discovery in *The Daily Delta.*[273]

The Duello: Dueling in Vicksburg

According to David Day of the *Vicksburg Daily News*, "Most of the local duels were held on a strip of land across the Yazoo River diversion canal called DeSoto Island. Dueling was illegal in Vicksburg and Warren County, and gentlemen wanted to avoid being arrested."[274] Describing one 1838 duel, Day quotes from an 1868 book by Joseph Barbière, "It was 1838, when, one bright morning, all Vicksburg was crossing the river to the 'battle ground,' as the encounters were all in one place and of frequent occurrence, as any stranger who visited Vicksburg, contemplating settlement, if a professional gentleman, had of necessity to fight a duel, to establish his claim to gentility. The river was covered with skiffs or canoes, (usually called dugouts,) as it was always a gala day, and witnessed with as much gusto as a 'bull-fight' in Spain, or the old English and French tournament of the good old day of legalized chivalry."[275]

Like Isham, Barbière had witnessed a number of duels in Vicksburg. He continues,

> "'Twas the case in the South, and particularly so in the State of Mississippi, from 1831 to 1842. Much of the effects of this epidemic that was called the "Duello," was witnessed by the author. Randolph and Tom Benton, had their opinion of the "code." Randolph changed his opinion three times in his life; once strongly advocated the principle, then condemned, then again became a supporter. During a latter stage of opinion, he fought Mr. Clay, Randolph's

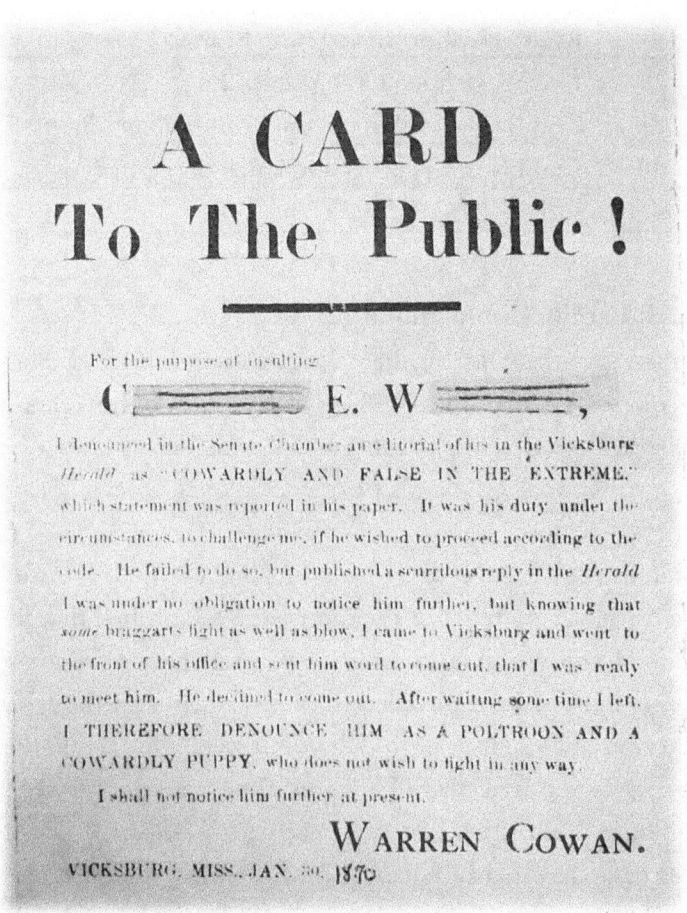

Figure 164 - A card meant to entice the subject to "the code," a duel, Vicksburg 30 Jan 1870.

---

[272] Emma Peck, *Ada's Journal and Emma's Letters*, Cross Mountain Books, 2021, see 107-111 for "When Peck Killed Harris" and 62-63 for the letter from Louisa N. Brown to Emma. At the end of the letter, Louisa says, "Say to your Brother, that Mr. Brown intends sending the gun the first person he meets with going to Greenville…" This may have been the gun that Wiley used to shoot Charles Harris…finally getting returned after the trial.

[273] The Case of Col. W. H. Peck, The Accused Committed for Manslaughter, Bail fixed at five thousand dollars, security furnished, *The Daily Delta*, New Orleans, Louisiana, 21 Jan 1860, 2.

[274] David Day, Dueling was a way of life, and death, in 1800s Vicksburg, https://vicksburgnews.com/dueling-was-a-way-of-life-and-death-in-1800s-vicksburg/, 1 Mar 2020.

[275] Joe Barbière, Lt. Col. Late C.S.A, *Scraps from the Prison Table at Camp Chase and Johnson's Island*, 1868, 244-245.

argument, was "Duelling" is individual war. I will give an instance of the feeling existing at that time in Vicksburg, Mississippi, the rendezvous, of such men as S. S. Prentiss, McClung, Robbins, and a host of others, gallant men, whose bravery was made the avenue to *mislead* them to (what is deemed by many) barbaric encounters. I was at the school of an old gentleman whom we all loved and feared, for he did not spare the ferule or the birch."

Barbière was a school-boy at the time of this particular event and had missed school to watch the duel, but then it was delayed for 3 hours and so he returned to school. When he returned, his professor scolded him and his friends for not sticking around to find out what happened at the delayed duel. The results were as follows: "Judge Lake's gun snapped, (they fought with double-barreled shot guns,) the latter lowered his gun magnanimously, and shot him in the knee. Sargeant [sic] S. Prentiss came from Portland, Maine, to Mississippi; a quaint, mild, gentlemanly master of the ferule. In five years he was the "Ney" of the State in the "code." " The notes in the book say that Judge Lake was "one of Mississippi's distinguished sons" and Tom Robbins "was a Pennsylvanian, and the soul of chivalry."[276]

Day writes, "Despite the forced chivalry of our past, people died in duels and did so in a violent way. Perhaps some of the most infamous duelists in Vicksburg were its newspaper editors, who tended to fight one another. This description from *After Sundown* by Monroe F. Cockrell, 1961, tells of the *Vicksburg Sentinel* editors, whose penchant for fighting brought the paper to its demise.[277]

"On January 31st, 1838, began the publication of the 'Vicksburg Tri-Weekly Sentinel' with James Hagan as its editor and publisher. The tragic history of this paper furnished one of the saddest chapters in the early story of the city. It was the organ of the Democratic party, an intensely partisan sheet, and though conducted with considerable ability, its vindictive and vituperative utterances constantly involved its editors in personal difficulties, five of whom on account of which met violent deaths, the first being James Hagan himself, the owner and proprietor, who was killed by Daniel Adams in a street encounter. The paper continued its precarious career until 1860, when Roy, its last editor was killed by Shepard at the corner of Washington and Clay Streets, shortly after which the 'Vicksburg Sentinel' breathed its last, leaving behind only a train of bloody memories."

  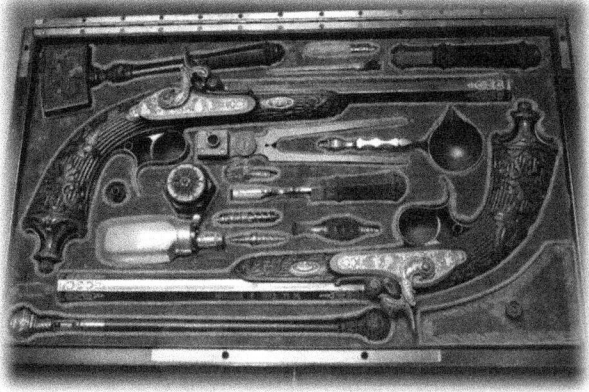

Figure 165 - Scan for the full text of "The Code of Honor" by John Lyde Wilson, originally printed in 1838, and reprinted in 1858. John Wilson was a former governor of South Carolina (1822-1824). The booklet was small enough to be carried in the dueling case, and listed the rules for duels.

---

[276] Ibid, 245.
[277] David Day, Dueling was a way of life, and death, in 1800s Vicksburg, 1 Mar 2020.

Anti-Dueling Society of Vicksburg

The third duel mentioned by Isham is that of Mr. Hagan, the editor of the Democratic *Vicksburg Sentinel*. In *Becoming Southern*, Christopher Morris shares:

Figure 167 - Scan for "A Very Violent Gentleman" by Terry Jones, an excellent article about Brig. Gen. Daniel W. Adams and the Hagan Affair

"Ever the irascible old man, Hagan had let his vituperative pen get him into dangerous scrapes before but had always managed to survive. In this instance he turned his poison on a Whiggish judge [Adams] and ruffled the feathers of the juror's son. The young man [Gen. Daniel W. Adams] came from Jackson armed and ready to fight. He met Hagan on the street around the corner from the editor's office, and there they quarreled and wrestled to the ground before the young man fired his pistol, sending a ball between Hagan's shoulders, up through his neck, and into his brain."[278]

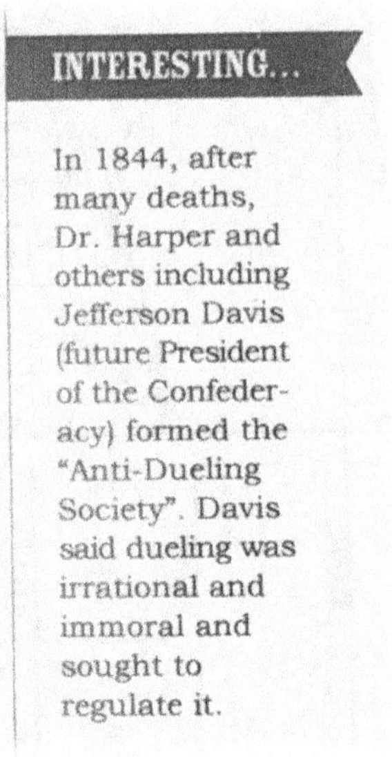

Morris shares that after this "bloody affair", a group led by Judge John Bodley got together and made it their goal to stop all gun battles in the streets of Vicksburg. This Anti-Dueling Society threatened to stop

Figure 166 - Note on "Anti-Dueling Society" Marker along the Vicksburg Heritage Walking Trail. Marker found on Crawford Street east of Adams Street, close to 1116 Crawford St, Vicksburg, MS 39180.

patronizing any newspaper that published inciting remarks, or challenges and responses. They even pressured the state legislature to forbid public officials from participating in the code. They also talked to the law in Louisiana, hoping they would arrest people who were engaging in dueling. Christopher Morris has a thorough treatment of this society in *Becoming Southern*, and for more details, including the involvement of Jefferson and Joe Davis, Thomas Robbins, Henry Vick, and more, see pages 129-131 in his excellent volume.[279]

Fall and Robbins Duels: Embezzlement and the Vicksburg Castle

Jordan Rushing, Assistant Director and Curator of the Old Court Museum, published an informative article that sheds much light on the two duels between Thomas Robbins and James Fall mentioned by Isham. Rushing states, "Robbins was a rather interesting man within the community of Vicksburg. Having arrived in the area around the mid-1830s, he began working as a cashier for the Commercial and Railroad Bank. By the end of the decade, the president of the bank pressed charges against Robbins in the amount of $125,000 for embezzlement, and pushed the news of his misconduct in the local newspapers. James S. Fall, the editor of one of the newspapers, became the target of Robbins after the story reached the public's hands resulting in a duel where Fall was injured. Despite his scarred reputation, he married Caroline Davis, the daughter of prominent planter Joseph Davis, in 1842. Dueling became a common remedy for Robbin's disputes. He crossed paths with both Judge William Lake and the famous orator, Seargent S. Prentiss, while many other challenges were averted after a public apology was made. His reputation as a duelist comes with a bit of irony seeing as he was also

---

[278] John Shannon, Jr., to Howard Morris, June 8, 1844, box 3, folder 28, Crutcher-Shannon Papers, MDAH. *Vicksburg Sentinel*, July 1 and 8, 1844. Williams, Dueling in the Old South, 32-33. A jury found Hagan's assailant not-guilty on grounds of self-defense.
[279] Christopher Morris, *Becoming Southern: The Evolution of a Way of Life, Warren County and Vicksburg, Mississippi, 1770-1860*, Oxford University Press, 1995, 129-131.

the founder of the Vicksburg Anti-dueling Society. On November 6, 1850, his life came to a conclusion in New York City. The Vicksburg Weekly Whig reported on his death saying "He was insane at the time of his death, as he had been for some time previous."[280]

Figure 168 - Robbins Castle on "Castle Hill" overlooking Vicksburg from the southern boundary of the city, circa 1840,
Courtesy of Jordan Rushing and the Old Court House Museum of Vicksburg, MS

DUEL BETWEEN BURR AND HAMILTON.

Figure 169 - 1901, Duel between Burr and Hamilton, from "Our Greater Country" by Henry Davenport Northrop, Philadelphia, PA, 506. Public Domain.

The next article is not written by Sawbones, but mentions him traveling to his plantations in Louisiana…

---

[280] Jordon Rushing, Lost Landmarks of Antebellum Vicksburg: The Castle, *Vicksburg Daily News*, https://vicksburgnews.com/lost-landmarks-of-antebellum-vicksburg-the-castle/, 14 Nov 2022.

28 NOV 1877 Personal. [ISHAM VISITING PLANTATIONS IN LOUISIANA][281]

"Th[omas]. Maloney, Esq., of Greeneville, one of the best newspaper men ever connected with the country press of this section, (at Greenville,) is at Newport.[282]

Dr. Peck, our inimitable contributor, "Sawbones," is visiting his plantations in Louisiana. He expects to call on Maj. And Mrs. Harry [and Mary G. Lusk] Heiss, of the *American*, as he returns. We make the announcement with the expectation of being paid in cusses—or gingseng [sic].

Judge Corbin, and family, departed last Friday morning for their home in Selma, Ala. The Judge and his interesting family have spent nearly two years in this vicinity, and made many warm friends who regret their departure. We trust they realized health and enjoyment while here, that their destination was safely reached, and they may again visit us in the future."

Personal.

Th. Maloney, Esq., of Greeneville, one of the best newspaper men ever connected with the country press of this section, (at Greenville,) is at Newport.

Dr. Peck, our inimitable contributor, "Sawbones," is visiting his plantations in Louisiana. He expects to call on Maj. and Mrs. Harry Heiss, of the *American*, as he returns We make the announcement with the expectation of being paid in cusses—or gingseng.

Judge Corbin, and family, departed last Friday morning for their home in Selma, Ala. The Judge and his interesting family have spent nearly two years in this vicinity, and made many warm friends who regret their departure. We trust they realized health and enjoyment while here, that their destination was safely reached, and they may again visit us in the future.

The middle paragraph of this article mentions a few things of note. First, it says that Isham was visiting his plantations in Louisiana. We know that Emma's family had the Henderson Plantation in East Carroll Parish, that his brother had his plantation called "The Mountain" in Madison Parish, but maybe Isham still owned the plantation he inherited from his second marriage with Helen (Rapalje) Glass from Vicksburg. This is an area for further research.

It mentions that Isham planned to call on Maj. and Mrs. Harry Heiss, of the *American*, on his way back from Louisiana. Maj. Heiss will come up more than once in the articles about Sawbones, especially later in the 26 and 29 April 1882 editions where some "reporters" spend the day with Isham, Maj. Heiss, and Wash Allen in Wolf Creek. Multiple periodicals of the day mention Heiss, and always in the context of him being an expert fisherman.

Figure 170 - Scan for Eddie Walker's "Page from the Past" about Maj. Harry Heiss in the *Newport Plain Talk*

[281] Editor, "Personal," [Isham Visiting Plantations in Louisiana] added by author, *The Morristown Gazette*, 28 Nov 1877, 2.
[282] "Thomas Maloney, grandson-in-law of President Andrew Johnson, published the *Greeneville Intelligencer*, a weekly newspaper in the mid-1870s." https://uncghistory.blogspot.com/2013/09/a-short-history-of-printing-press-at.html

Major Harry Heiss

An article titled *Tennessee—The Angler's Paradise* in *The American Angler*, reads this way, "Tennessee is wonderfully wellwatered, and singular to say not a single stream but what is tolerably well stocked with game fish. From Nashville as the center of the Middle division of the State, easy drives or rides on railroads land the angler at a creek, river or lake in which fish abound. The Western division is equally favored, while the Eastern and the section specially inquired about, may be classes as still more favored.

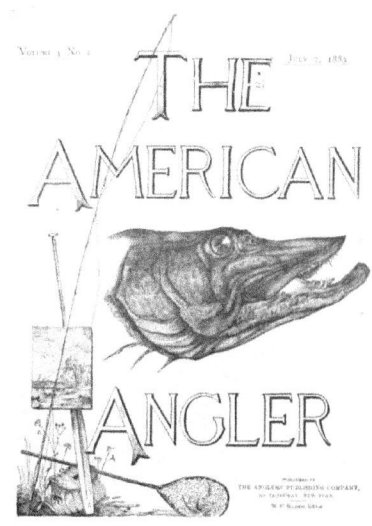

The mountain streams of East Tennessee, the Wautauga, Holston, and many smaller streams, teem with jack bass and black perch. Catfish, also classes in this State as among the familiar game fishes, are found there also. These are the few principal varieties of fish indigenous to our waters, though there are a number of varieties of perch, which are excellent for food, though affording but little sport to take with rod and reel. [. .]

I would suggest to 'Labrax,' if he desires good sport in a most beautiful country, and surrounded by the best of fellows—come to Nashville. Here he would meet Gen. Jones, **Maj. Harry Heiss**, Charley Furman, Charely Hillman, J. W. Allen, George Seay, and **Col. Geo. F. Akers**, each and all of whom are noted anglers, and enthusiastic for the sport. They know every stream in the State, and as sportsmen would only be too glad to impart their experience to him.   CLIMAX.   *Nashville, Tenn., Oct. 26, 1883.*"[283]

FOREST AND STREAM.

A WEEKLY JOURNAL OF THE ROD AND GUN.

TERMS, $4 A YEAR. 20 CTS. A COPY. }   NEW YORK, AUGUST 3, 1882.   { VOL. XIX.—No. 1.
SIX MONTHS, $2.   { Nos. 39 & 40 PARK ROW, NEW YORK.

In *Forest and Stream* from August 1882, a section called "TENNESSEE NOTES" reads this way, "There has been almost too much rain lately for good fishing in this portion of the State, although those who were fortunate enough to strike the streams before becoming too muddy had fine sport. Charlie Curry, who has just returned from the mountains of East Tennessee, gives glowing accounts of the speckled trout fishing up there. He was out several times with **Major Harry Heiss**, formerly of the Nashville American, which is of itself a guarantee of good sport, because a more scientific and industrious angler than the Major cannot be found anywhere. Charlie says that so abundant are these beautiful fish that hardly does the fly strike water than it is gobbled up by one of them. I hear of some superb fish being taken out of the Cumberland River at points in the mountains above navigation; these waters are entirely exempt from the evil of pot fishermen, and bass grow there to great size. Col. **Geo. F. Akers** and Col Griffith, President of the Kentucky Fish Commission, propose making these

---

[283] *The American Angler.* Angler's Publishing Company, 1883, emphasis added. [Akers and Heiss are friends with Isham]

secluded regions a visit shortly, and then we will hear of marvelous fish and still more marvelous adventures. **Col. Akers** has secured from a Scotch nobleman traveling in this country a novel reel, which, by the aid of a small electric battery carried upon the person, is said to denote the size and characters of the fish biting at the hook, which is attached to it. If this is really so, the days of fabulous fish stories and unhidden monsters of the deep are numbered.—J. D. H.”

Ginseng

Figure 171 - From
https://ag.tennessee.edu/plantsciences/Pages/Ginseng.aspx

The editor's reference to “being paid in cusses—or ginseng” is a funny one. The “cusses” are clearly a reference to the fact that they know Isham probably wouldn't want them spreading his “business” all over the paper, and they'll hear about it from him when he returns. And if you're curious about ginseng and its history in Tennessee, the University of Tennessee Institute of Agriculture has an interesting webpage devoted to its significance as one of the “ten plants that shaped Tennessee.”[284] Ginseng was probably such a prized item (that could be sold) that it would have been considered a real gift to receive ginseng from someone.

UTIA says, “In Appalachia, whether historically or in present day, there are few truer signs of trust and kinship than sharing the location of someone's personal or family 'sang patch. Part economy, part culture, part history, the tale of American ginseng (*Panax quinquefolius*) in East Tennessee and across the rest of the eastern deciduous forests where the plant is native is complex.

This native herbaceous perennial plant has been harvested and used or sold for hundreds of years. The North American species has long held a place in Native American medicine. When European settlers began arriving in the region, it didn't take long to connect the American *Panax* with related species highly valued in Asian medicine. Following this discovery early in the 1700s, ginseng became an export crop whose harvest was practiced or noted by historical figures from Daniel Boone to George Washington.

Figure 172 - Tillman E. Lee, A/C, (left) and Fred Markus, SCD Cooperator, observing seed pods on the ginseng plants on Markus' farm. Note the seed pods on the plants in the foreground. Lawrence County, Tenn. Soil Conservation District.
https://ag.tennessee.edu/plantsciences/Pages/Ginseng.aspx

---

[284] https://ag.tennessee.edu/plantsciences/Pages/Ginseng.aspx, accessed 2 Apr 2020

"King's cabin on Mt. Nebo," east Tennessee, 1886, photo credit: William Cox Cochran Great Smoky Mountains Photographic Collection, University of Tennessee Libraries. Mountain families such as this one depended heavily on the forest commons and forest products, particularly ginseng, for coffee, gunpowder, shot, and clothing.

Figure 173 - "Sangin' Io the Mountains, 41.

Wild harvest of American ginseng, known as "ginsenging" still exists in the Appalachians much as it has for generations. In the forest itself, the growth and productivity of ginseng offers confirmation of a healthy ecosystem. However, these slow-growing populations are constantly under pressure from harvesting for sale, as production of wild simulated ginseng has not been widely successful. Wild harvest is legal on private land, but illegal poaching is an ever-present issue on public lands, such as the Great Smoky Mountains National Park, where family ginseng patches may well pre-date the existence of the park itself. It is this intriguing mix of botany, ecology, history, culture, and medicine that place American ginseng on the list of the ten plants that shaped Tennessee."[285]

Figure 174- "Sangin' Io the Mountains, 40.

Popular image of Sang Digger, from Edgar Nye, "Nye's Little Story," *The State*, 18 November 1894. Newspaper reports of ginseng diggers in the Southern Appalachians contributed to the development of mountaineer stereotypes.

If one is into agriculture and history, please see the article called *Sangin' Io the Mountains: The Ginseng Economy of the Southern Appalachians, 1865-1900* by Luke Manget.[286] In his article, Manget says " 'Every storekeeper in the backwoods of the Cumberland Highland buys ginseng, and it readily passes for currency,' the *New York Sun* reported. 'Nearly all the mountain people in Kentucky and Tennessee dig ginseng and rely on it to furnish the food to tide them over the winter months.' The shift toward a more ginseng-dependent economy raised some concern about the possible depletion of the plant. The state of North Carolina began regulating the ginseng trade in 1867, prohibiting its harvest from April through August. Georgia followed with its own ginseng law in 1867, and West Virginia adopted a ginseng season in 1874. [. . .] One astonished writer from the *New York Herald* noted in 1867 that successful diggers could make as much as three

---

[285] Ibid.
[286] Luke Manget. "Sangin' Io the Mountains: The Ginseng Economy of the Southern Appalachians, 1865-1900." *Appalachian Journal* 40, no. 1/2 (2012): 28-56. Accessed April 3, 2020. www.jstor.org/stable/43489051.

dollars a day: 'They only make two [dollars] at the gold mines near Morganton; so it is better than gold digging, in North Carolina at least.' [. . .] A writer for the *Cincinnati Inquirer* called them [ginseng diggers] 'low-browed, stupid and sullen,' and a 'people who are as savage in instinct as those who roam the impenetrable wilds of Zululand.' [. . .] By the 1880s, reports like these helped solidify the sang digger in popular imagination as 'a race separate and apart, whom progress has left a full century behind.' [. . .] By the time these articles were published, at least some Southerners' perceptions of sang diggers had been already shaped by folklore that may have originated with slaves. 'I can remember when I was a boy in Virginia, years before the war, hearing the old negro mammies speak in almost whispers of the mysterious Sangers of the mountains,' one anonymous root dealer recalled. 'They were described as elfish beings, who lurked in the fastnesses, always on the watch for fat negro babies, which they would carry away to their inaccessible haunts, there to roast and eat them.' According to two sources published 15 years apart, children learned of this 'race of Tom Thumbs' that lived deep in the woods and commanded giant eagles to do their bidding. They were veritable 'bogy men,' who stood ready to do 'horrible things … to bad boys and girls.'

Manget has an entire section called "The Sang Digger Romanticized" and shares that a best-selling author named Amelie Rives even wrote a novel set in Warm Springs, Virginia, called *Tanis, the Sang-Digger* "which tells the story of a 'primitive-princess,' Tanis, who was proud to be a ginseng digger but turned to 'honest work' by helping a city couple form Massachusetts, the Gilmans, around their house."[287]

Though one could go deeper into the Ginseng economy and cover the article more extensively, the treatment here is sufficient to get an idea of what the editor was getting at. "Sangers" had a reputation for being rough, crude, and from a century before…so because Isham had his house in Wolf Creek, it is likely this was one more friendly "dig" into him being a "sanger" like some of the other mountain folks.

In April 1878 the editors of the *Gazette* once again mention Isham, sharing that "Sawbones" is giving a character reference in his own particular way for a man running for Governor of Tennessee.

---

[287] Ibid.

24 APR 1878 SWAGGERTY PANS OUT WELL.[288]

We learn that his many friends in Cocke county will present the name of James Swaggerty, Esq., of Newport, as their choice for Governor at the proper time. He is endorsed warmly by his neighbors, and a private note from our particularly critical and accurate friend, 'Sawbones,' assures us that 'he is a Christian gentleman, beyond the pale of any ring outside of Cocke county, and if elected would be a true friend to the gold washers of Wolf Creek and other people too. He pans out well."

In October 1872, James Swaggerty was listed in the Tennessee State Library and Archives as being age 72, having a son named William R. Swaggerty (of Newport), and James as a farmer. His son William fought for the Confederacy in Captain Edwin Allen's Co C, 26th Regiment, Tennessee Infantry, having enlisted on 26 Jun 1861. Their family filed a claim against the U.S. Government after the Civil War, saying that one of their mules had been taken during the War. Their claim was denied.[289] Six years later, James Swaggerty was close to 78 years old and running for Governor. In addition, Swaggerty was listed in the Congressional Serial Set as having been pardoned by President of the U.S. on 24 Oct 1865.[290] Not long before this pardon, in a letter from the Office of Provost-Marshal-General of East Tenn, on 5 Jan 1864 and writing from Knoxville, Brigadier General S. P. Carter says

Figure 175 – James Swagerty (21 Jul 1800 – 7 Feb 1885)
https://www.findagrave.com/memorial/87518498/james-swagerty

"General Alexander Smith and Esquire James Swaggerty, citizens of Cocke County, living 2 miles from Newport are the instigators of outrages committed by the rebels in that county."[291]

---

[288] Editor, "Swaggerty Pans Out Well," Title by Andy Peck, *The Morristown Gazette*, 24 Apr 1878, 2.
[289] https://www.tngenweb.org/cocke/cw/cwclaims.htm#wlmrswaggerty, accessed 2 Apr 2020
[290] Congressional Serial Set. United States: U.S. Government Printing Office, 1867.
[291] Cowles, Calvin Duvall., Kirkley, Joseph William., Davis, George Breckenridge., Scott, Robert Nicholson., Ainsworth, Frederick Caryton., Lazelle, Henry Martyn., Perry, Leslie J.. *The War of the Rebellion: A Compilation of the Official Records of the Union and Confederate Armies.* United States: U.S. Government Printing Office, 1891, 30.

Extensive history on James Swagerty, Jr. can be found on the Ancestral Journeys website.[292] It details his life, the Civil War service of his sons, the slaves at his farm, and his kind treatment of them.

A FindAGrave.com entry for Swaggerty's son, William Robinson Swagerty, says this, "He is the sixth of ten children of James and Nancy (Clark) Swagerty, natives of Cocke County. He [James] was for many years, justice of the peace, and was "High Constable" of the county for many years, and was a very successful farmer. He began life for himself a poor man, and before the Negroes were freed he was worth about $200,000, the fruit of his own industry and good management. Mr. and Mrs. Swagerty were of German descent. He was a son of James Swagerty, a native of Virginia, and was among the earliest settlers of Cocke County. He was for many years, justice of the peace. His first wife's name was Delilah, who died March 22, 1844, aged about seventy-one years. He was married again November 22, 1844, to Nancy H. Johnson. He was born in 1773 and died about 1868. Mr. James Swagerty, Jr. was born in 1800 and died 1885. Mr. W.R. Swagerty enlisted June 1861, in company C, Second Tennessee Infantry, Confederate States Army, and served until 1864, when after the battle of Mission ridge, he was captured and kept as a prisoner of war at Sevierville Jail until the close of the war. He was wounded at the battles of Murfreesboro and Chattanooga."[293] Regarding his son W. R., TN Gen Web says, "W.R. Swagerty, farmer and stock dealer at Newport, was born August 3, 1842, on the farm where he has since resided. He began life for himself when twenty-two years old and excepting some property received from his father, what he is now worth is mostly the fruit of his own industry and good management. He owns a fine farm of 396 acres near Newport. He was married in December, 1866, to Miss Lydia Allen, a daughter of James Allen, a native of Cocke County. He was a farmer, and served in the Mexican War. To Mr. and Mrs. Swagerty the following children have been born: Lora Anna, Fannie Dale, James M. (dead), Nannie Laura, Hattie Murray and Eunice. Mr. and Mrs. Swagerty's oldest and third daughters are members of the Missionary Baptist Church, and Mr. Swagerty is a Democrat in politics, and cast his first presidential vote for Horatio Seymour."[294]

Isham may have served with James' son William during the Mexican War, and both of their families had been in the area since the late 1700s. Isham was democratic and a supporter of the Confederacy, so he probably had no issues endorsing James in his run for Governor. Swaggerty was not elected for Governor, rather Albert S. Marks was elected Governor of Tennessee and served from 16 Feb 1879 to 17 Jan 1881. Marks was a Democrat from Kentucky.

Regarding Isham's comments that James would "pan out well," we are reminded that Isham makes a lot of "tongue in cheek" jokes. Multiple articles from the time period indicate that gold had been found in Wolf Creek and that there was even a Wolf Creek Gold "Bonanza"![295]

---

[292] Ancestral Journeys, James Swagerty, https://www.ancestraljourneys.website/swagerty4_clark.htm, accessed 8 Sep 23

[293] https://www.findagrave.com/memorial/87518316/william-robinson-swagerty, accessed 3 Apr 2020

[294] https://www.tngenweb.org/goodspeed/cocke/bios.html, accessed 3 Apr 2020

[295] See Sawbones Resources on the Cross Mountain Books website for the articles discussing Wolf Creek gold: https://www.crossmountainbooks.com/sawbones-resources

2 OCT 1878 NOT THAT SORT OF DOCTOR[296]
To the Editor of the Morristown Gazette:

I noticed in a Knoxville paper a few days since that Dr. Peck and others had been appointed to preside at a stock show to be held soon at Knoxville. If this refers to your correspondent, he most respectfully declines the honor. In fact, it would be impossible for him to be there, for at the time of the stock show the circus will be at Morristown—and that is the only kind of stock show he attends.

A short time since there was an assembly of eminent Presbyterian divines, from many states, at Knoxville. I saw in the newspapers that Dr. Peck was elected to preside. I was not surprised at this, knowing that I was eminently qualified to preside over a body of divines. I started immediately for Knoxville. At the depot I met a drummer.[297] He represented the fullness, cheapness and durability of the merchandise his house offered to the country trade. Rather curtly I explained the object of my visit. He told me I was not the man. I told him I certainly was, that there was no other Dr. Peck in Tennessee. He said the gentleman selected was a pious man. I said no man could excel me in that particular department, and referred him to my friend Captain Jim Swaggerty as the only man who knew me well. He said the Dr. Peck selected made a specialty of treating cases of chronic cussedness. I told him that I always carried the only safe remedy for that disease in my hip pocket. He said his man never used powder and ball, but preached to them. Then I gave up.

--I detest cruelty, and would not torture the Devil if he was in my power.

~SAWBONES."

As a pastor himself, this author appreciates the hilarity of the above article. Isham first turns down the opportunity to preside over a stock show in Knoxville, knowing that it is probably not really him personally who has been chosen to preside. Then he relays a story where he heard in the papers that "Dr. Peck" was to preside over many Presbyterian ministers in Knoxville. Not knowing that there were any other Dr. Pecks in Tennessee, he began his travels for Knoxville…only to find out along the way that there was a Dr. Peck who was a pastor and it was not really him they were seeking. Isham also lets us know that he was always "packing heat" and that he was ready to use it if necessary.

His final line, "I detest cruelty, and would not torture the Devil if he was in my power" is an interesting one. It also seems to be in high contrast to his comment just a couple sentences before regarding using his gun to treat "cussedness." Is Isham really saying that he detests cruelty? He is a physician so he must have a predisposition to helping people instead of hurting. All in all, though, this article is on the lighter side of Sawbones' contributions and seems to make light of his innocent thinking and possibly his pride.

---

[296] Dr. Isham Peck, "Not That Sort of Doctor," *The Morristown Gazette*, 2 Oct 1878, 2.
[297] Drummer = In the 19th century, "'drummer" was a popular name for traveling salesmen — think of the phrase 'drumming up' business. Drummers were also called commercial travelers, runners, or 'gripmen' ('grip' here referring to the trunk or suitcase carried by salesmen)." Bill Kemp, Historian for McLean County Museum of History, https://tinyurl.com/19thcenturydrummer. There were also "Christian Drummers", see the 1825 book called *The Christian Drummer* published by the American Tract Society: https://tinyurl.com/thechristiandrummer

"Our valued friend and correspondent. Dr. Peck, of Wolf Creek, spent last Sabbath in our town. We are pleased to add that owing to a severe attack of neuralgia in the face, the spreading of the yellow fever throughout Louisiana, and disappointment consequent upon not meeting Maj Heiss, of the *American*, as he expected, 'Sawbones' was in his usual devotional frame of mind."

Our valued friend and correspondent. Dr. Peck, of Wolf Creek, spent last Sabbath in our town. We are pleased to add that owing to a severe attack of neuralgia in the face, the spreading of the yellow fever throughout Louisiana, and disappointment consequent upon not meeting Maj Heiss, of the *American*, as he expected, "Sawbones" was in his usual devotional frame of mind.

Glen Ada and Wolf Creek, Tennessee - The article shown earlier, saying that Isham was visiting his plantations in Louisiana was written on 28 Nov 1877. This article was written 23 Oct 1878, nearly 11 months later. The mention of Maj Heiss would give reason to believe that he had been down in Louisiana for the majority of that time. There are many things of note in this short article – namely, that Dr. Peck is "of Wolf Creek," that he "spent last Sabbath in our town [Morristown], that he had a

Figure 176 - Google terrain map showing Wolf Creek and 2-mile radius
https://roadsidethoughts.com/tn/wolf-creek-xx-cocke-map.htm

"severe attack of neuralgia in the face," that there was a spreading of yellow fever throughout Louisiana, and that he was not able to meet with Maj Harry Heiss as originally planned. A question to consider is, what is meant by Isham being in "his usual devotional frame of mind"?

First of all, Isham had grown up in Mossy Creek. But by this time, he was "of Wolf Creek" meaning he made his residence there a substantial portion of the time. Wolf Creek is a small stream that comes off the French Broad River in Cocke County, TN. The creek runs along what is now Highway 25/70 and is located just west of the Tennessee / North Carolina state line. Del Rio, TN is just to the west of it, and Paint Rock, NC is just

to the east. The major towns on either side are Newport, TN on the west and Hot Springs, NC on

---

[298] Dr. Isham Peck, "Yellow Fever & Neuralgia In The Face," Title by Andy Peck, *The Morristown Gazette*, 23 Oct 1878, 2.

the east (Del Rio is a smaller town to the west). Wolf Creek sits in a valley between two lush and high mountain ridges. Isham was 42 years old and their first child Ada was 1 year and 1 month old when they picked out a homestead on their Wolf Creek land and called it Glen Ada in Aug 1854.

From *Ada's Journal*: "Father and Mother have picked out a pretty place, half a mile from here, on Wolf Creek, where we are going to have a Mountain home, and they have named it Glen_Ada." At the time the current article was written

Figure 177 - Wolf Creek, Glen Ada Property - Photo by Author 11 Jul 2017

(in 1878), they had owned the property for 24 years. **Experience CMB LIVE: Look around Glen Ada and view the French Broad River (QR Code on Left):** https://youtu.be/75xJBkWPW8s.

Figure 178 - CMB LIVE: Glen Ada and French Broad River in Wolf Creek, TN

Also watch as the author's family experiences Wolf Creek for the first time (Right): https://youtu.be/o9640ZTMJIc. A local Wolf Creek legend is that once you set your feet in Wolf Creek, it guarantees that you'll be back.

Morristown, Tennessee

Secondly, the article mentions that Isham had spent the last Sabbath in Morristown. Morristown, where the *Gazette* was published, is located 48 miles from Wolf Creek. It is located 10 miles from New Market. Wikipedia gives a good short history of the town, "The first European settler of what eventually became

Figure 179 - CMB LIVE: Peck Family Wading in Wolf Creek

Morristown was farmer Gideon Morris. It is recorded in Goodspeed's *History of Tennessee* that Gideon, along with an unspecified number of his siblings, arrived in the area of present-day Morristown from the Watauga Settlement, a short-lived semi-autonomous settlement located in northeast Tennessee that was originally leased from the resident Cherokee tribes during the 1770s.

Records in North Carolina indicate that a Morris family moved to the Watauga Settlement from North Carolina. According to Cora Davis Brooks, author of *History of Morristown 1787-1936*:

"Gideon Morris was listed as one of the signers of the petition to annex Watauga to North Carolina in 1775, and in the Fall of the same year he served in Colonel Christian's expedition against the Indians. (N. C. Colonial Records, Vol. 10, p. 708) (Kings Mountain Men by Miss Kate White.)"

In 1778 Gideon Morris appeared in court and swore allegiance ('History of South-west Virginia', by Summers). Lands were granted by the State of North Carolina to Gideon Morris in Washington,

Greene and Hawkins counties. He probably settled on portions of these grants either in 1787 or 1791, which was included in Jefferson county and now in Hamblen county.

The settlement founded by Gideon has, as far as is known, always been called Morristown. No known records exist demonstrating land grants in the area to anyone aside from Gideon and his extended family. Jefferson County, located southwest of Hamblen County, possesses a record in the Jefferson County Court House of the results of the execution of Gideon Morris' will, which includes property deeded to John Morris in 1817 for a 400-acre (160 ha) tract of land originally granted to Gideon by the state of North Carolina, and presumably comprising only a portion of the original grant due to the known size of the Morris family at that time. Gideon Morris lived on that tract of land until his death.

The famous pioneer and folk-hero David Crockett lived in present-day Morristown when his father, John Crockett, established a tavern there in 1794. The current-day Crockett Tavern Museum sits at the approximate location of the former tavern. The museum is also listed on the National Register of Historic Places." [299] The Wikipedia article goes on to share Morristown's Civil War history, demographics, and more.

Neuralgia - Thirdly, the article says that Isham had had a "severe attack of neuralgia in the face." WebMD says this regarding neuralgia, "Trigeminal neuralgia is an ongoing pain condition that affects certain nerves in your face. You might also hear it called 'tic douloureux.' People who have this condition say the pain might feel like an electric shock, and it can sometimes be intense. Doctors have treatments that can help, including medicine and surgery."[300] The article goes on to say that symptoms of neuralgia are: brief periods of stabbing or shooting pain, duration of a few seconds to several minutes, and it can be triggered by brushing your teeth, washing your face, or even a light breeze. Attacks can happen several times a day or week,

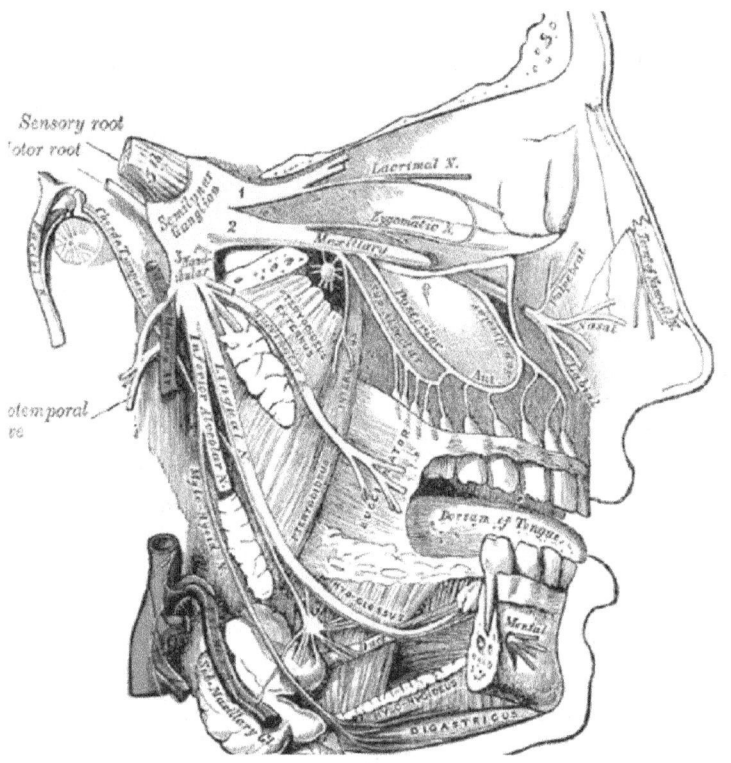

Figure 180 - http://face-facts.org/dxes/neuralgias/tn/, accessed 4 Apr 2020

followed by periods of none at all. The pain free periods are known as remission. The pain usually affects only one side of the face, and attacks and pain get worse over time. The pain is mostly in a person's cheek, jaw, teeth, gums, and lips, but not as much in the eyes or forehead. It can be caused

[299] https://en.wikipedia.org/wiki/Morristown,_Tennessee, accessed 4 Apr 2020
[300] https://www.webmd.com/pain-management/guide/trigeminal-neuralgia#1, accessed 4 Apr 2020

by diseases like multiple sclerosis, or a tumor in the face. In addition, if the trigeminal nerve is injured (i.e. by surgery, an accident, or a stroke), that [event] can trigger the neuralgia. It has also been linked to high blood pressure. It is also more common in people over age 50.[301]

Isham's Deer Attack and Broken Arm

One of the main injuries that Isham sustained in his life is recorded in *Ada's Journal and Emma's Letters: The Civil War Era Journal and Letters of Emma Peck*. It occurred on 2 April 1855 when Isham was 44 years old and staying on the Henderson Plantation in East Carroll Parish, Louisiana. A deer attacked him and broke his arm. In the tussle with the buck, his face could have easily received some trauma that triggered the neuralgia. There is no known cure for neuralgia, now referred to as Trigeminal Neuralgia (TN). Face Facts has a short video that does a good job of summarizing this condition: https://youtu.be/QtIfE1rfpbU (Scan QR Code to right). It says that it can even be triggered by talking. This condition may have contributed to Isham being in his "devotional" mood quite

Figure 181 - YouTube Video called "What is Trigeminal Neuralgia?"

often. Later articles say that he loved to be surrounded by his newspapers. Besides his desire to stay informed with the goings-on of the world, it may have been what caused him the least pain…sitting and reading.

Yellow Fever – The Saffron Scourge

Fourthly, the article says "that there was a spreading of yellow fever throughout Louisiana." History reveals that "between 1796 and 1905, sixty-seven yellow summers transpired in New Orleans, during which roughly fifty thousand people died." Christie Matherne Hall shares the following account, found in her article *The Saffron Scourge in New Orleans*. "Yellow fever went by many names in the nineteenth century: The Saffron Scourge, Yellow Jack, Stranger's Fever, Bronze John on his Saffron Steed. The virus earned all these names during its century-long stay in New Orleans, while doctors, governors, and generals argued over what it was and what to do about it. History paints tableaus of deeply haunted lives during this century—citizens fled the toxic summers, immigrants were buried or burned, and newspapers danced around the trenches for far too long. And finally, at the turn of the twentieth century, another war brought a concerted effort to

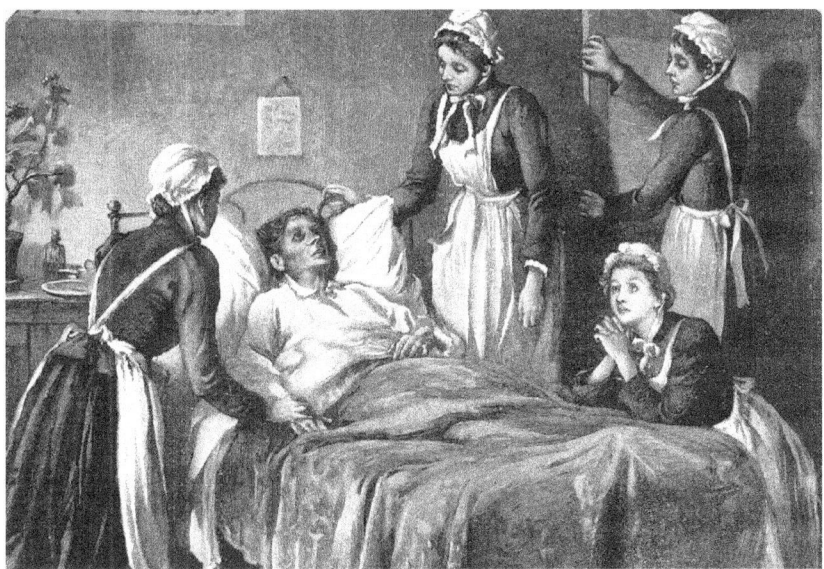

Figure 182 - Nurses seek to help man infected with Yellow Fever, from JSTOR, https://daily.jstor.org/19th-century-nurses-fight-to-battle-yellow-fever/

---

[301] https://www.webmd.com/pain-management/guide/trigeminal-neuralgia#2, accessed 4 Apr 2020

solve the mystery, banishing the fever from the city for good. But for that hundred years, no matter which government staked claim to it, Yellow Jack was the undisputed and unreported king of New Orleans."[302]

Wikipedia says, "The entire Mississippi River Valley from St. Louis south was affected, and tens of thousands fled the stricken cities of New Orleans, Vicksburg, and Memphis. An estimated 120,000 cases of yellow fever resulted in some 20,000 deaths.[24]

Memphis suffered several epidemics during the 1870s, culminating in the 1878 epidemic (called the Saffron Scourge of 1878), with more than 5,000 fatalities in the city. Some contemporary accounts said that commercial interests had prevented the rapid reporting of the outbreak of the epidemic, increasing the total number of deaths. People still did not understand how the disease developed or was transmitted, and did not know how to prevent it.[25]

The 1878 epidemic was the worst that occurred in the state of Mississippi. Sometimes known as "Yellow Jack", and "Bronze John", devastated Mississippi socially and economically. Entire families

Figure 183 - The Catholic Sisters of Charity tended the sick and dying in Memphis during the fever outbreaks of the 1870s. Owned by Tennessee State Library and Archives, archived here: https://cdm15138.contentdm.oclc.org/digital/collection/p15138coll18/id/78, accessed 4 Apr 2020

were killed, while others fled their homes for the presumed safety of other parts of the state. Quarantine regulations, passed to prevent the spread of the disease, brought trade to a stop. Some local economies never recovered. Beechland, near Vicksburg, became a ghost town because of the epidemic. By the end of the year, 3,227 people had died from the disease.[26]"[303]

---

[302] https://countryroadsmagazine.com/art-and-culture/history/yellow-fever/, accessed 4 Apr 2020

[303] https://en.wikipedia.org/wiki/History_of_yellow_fever#Lower_Mississippi_Valley:_1878, accessed 4 Apr 2020, end notes referred to are as follows: 24 Bloom, Khaled J. (1993), *The Mississippi Valley's Great Yellow Fever Epidemic of 1878*, Louisiana State University Press., 25 Crosby, M. C. (2006), *The American Plague: The Untold Story of Yellow Fever, the Epidemic That Shaped Our History.*, and 26 *Stephens Nuwer, Deanne (1999). "The 1878 Yellow Fever Epidemic along the Mississippi Gulf Coast". Gulf South Historical Review. 14 (2): 51–73.*

Figure 184 - Maj Harry Heiss, editor of Nashville American, as featured in the 18 Aug 2021 Newport Plain Talk article by Eddie Walker, Cocke County Historian

An article by JSTOR describes the heroic efforts by nearly 3,000 women who worked as nurses during the epidemic.[304] In the case of this outbreak, when Isham was travelling, he could not stop and visit his friend Harry Heiss due to either the yellow fever outbreak, or his neuralgia. Many years before, in May of 1854, the family could not stop on the way home from Louisiana because of a scarlet fever outbreak (see 3 May 1854 in *Ada's Journal*). It says, "We stayed three days, then took the cars for Loudon, and the Stage from there to Knoxville. The scarlet fever was bad at several places, so that we could not stop to rest." The Biennial Report from the Tennessee Department of Health chronicles some of these conditions that scourged various areas. It specifically says that "In 1854 epidemic cholera prevailed in and about Maynardville, Loudon, and Knoxville. . . In the past twenty-five years diphtheria has scourged some neighborhoods. While scarlet fever has not been malignant, a few localities have suffered severely from it. There has also been some cerebro-spinal meningitis, and during the last two years small-pox has appeared in Chattanooga, Knoxville, Mossy Creek, Morristown and Rogersville."[305] Regarding yellow fever, the same report says, "No case of yellow fever has occurred or been introduced into the State since the epidemic in Memphis in 1879. . . As a proper precaution against this much dreaded disease, the State Board cooperated with the Local Board of Memphis in calling upon the National Board of Health in the springs of 1880, '81, '82, and '83 to establish an inspection service on the Mississippi river and the railroads coming out of New Orleans. But very few cases occurred or were introduced into that city during these years. These were successfully controlled by the health authorities of Louisiana, and no great danger arose from or damage was done by them. It is hoped that a necessity may never arise for more rigid measures than these, and it is believed with proper vigilance along the Gulf coast all danger from yellow fever can be averted. The law creating the State Board of Health places upon it the obligation 'to declare quarantine whenever in their judgement the welfare of the public requires it, etc.'"[306]

Figure 185 - Info about Loudon, TN from Background Planet - https://backroadplanet. com/drive-loudon-county-tennessee

About one month later, Isham writes again to the *Gazette*. The same appeared in Nashville's *The Daily American* the following day. *The Daily American* was the paper where Heiss served as Editor.

---

[304] https://daily.jstor.org/19th-century-nurses-fight-to-battle-yellow-fever/, accessed 4 Apr 2020
[305] Biennial Report. United States: The State   Board of Health of Tennessee, 1885., 381.
[306] Ibid., 346.

20 NOV 1878 AN INQUIRY FROM "SAWBONES."[307]

To the Editor of the Morristown Gazette:

There is a gentleman and his wife here from Nashville. The wife says he is the best man in the world. That is exactly my opinion; but that is no reason why he should take all the fish out of the French Broad river. At the rate at which he is reeling out the bass there will not be one left in two weeks. Where is the Fish Commissioner or somebody?

SAWBONES

We know "the gentleman from Nashville." *He-iss* sportsman enough to beat *akers* of our present Commissioner when it comes to shoving suckers for salmon and cat fish for bass. Scare him this way, Doctor."

George Akers – Tennessee Fish Commissioner - This article is a tongue in cheek humor piece where Isham informs the public that Maj. Harry Heiss and his wife are currently staying with him in Wolf Creek and Harry is catching a ton of fish on the French Broad! The editor of the *Gazette* writes back in a punny way, saying "He is" but spelling it in Italics and adding an extra "s" to ensure that the readers understand it is HEISS who is the man referred to by Sawbones. The first hypothesis of this author was that "*akers*" referred to the last name of the Fish Commissioner in 1878 in *East* Tennessee, and was a play on the words "a curse." This theory proved nearly correct. The Bulletin of the United States Fish Commission, Volume 2, Page 430 indicates that since 1876, Col. George F. Akers was at least a man who studied "fish culture" and it is listed that he could be reached at the Nashville post office and is from the county of Davidson. It would seem that Col Akers is the Fish Commissioner, but for *Middle* Tennessee, and he is up with his friend Maj Harry Heiss and they are both catching a ton of fish! Sawbones' question at the end of the first paragraph, "Where is the Fish Commissioner or somebody?" is his way of joking about the fact that there is no *enforcement* of rules against catching too many fish going on, as Maj Heiss AND a Fish Commissioner are both on his land hauling in a great load.[308] Page 215 of the Bulletin from the year prior (1882) records a 21 May 1878 report from George F. Akers as follows, "George F. Akers, Nashville, Tenn., says: 'During present month quite a number of shad were taken near Nashville and sold in market.'"[309] Page 123 of another 1883 report

307 Dr. Isham Peck, "An Inquiry from Sawbones," *The Morristown Gazette*, 20 Nov 1878, 2.
308 Bulletin of the United States Fish Commission. United States: U.S. Government Printing Office, 1883, 430.
309 Bulletin of the United States Fish Commission. United States: U.S. Government Printing Office, 1882, 215.

clearly lists Col. George F. Akers as the Tennessee State Fish Commissioner from 1877-1882.[310] It may not be the same George Akers, but there is a "George Akers" listed as being a member of the 16th Regiment Opelousas 1814-1815 as a part of the 2nd Division under Maj Gen. Philemon Thomas in the Battle of New Orleans.[311] Col. Heiss's service in the Civil War is recorded earlier in this volume.

The two of them, Major Heiss and Colonel Akers must have travelled and fished together regularly. *The American Angler* from 19 July 1884 page 39 has an article called "Tennessee Angling" that includes reports about both of them and their fishing expeditions. Written by "Climax," same as the article listed earlier, it says,

> "Although I do not pretend to know one hundredth part of the anglers of Tennessee, yet I take the liberty of using the above wholesale caption, feeling authorized to do so by the fact that *The American Angler* reaches a great many of them, and should be in the hands of them all. My object is to tell where the anglers are (that I have the pleasure of knowing) and what they propose to do.
>
> General Ira P. Jones, State Fish and Game Commissioner E. D. Hicks, J.S. Demsville. . .
> **Colonel George F. Akers**. . . **Major Harry Heiss** (etc…)
>
> **Major Harry Heiss** and Alf. Horseley are up among the brooks and streams of East Tennessee, enjoying a long vacation in the woods [probably staying at Isham's home and fishing on the French Broad]. Both these gentlemen are expert enthusiasts after fish, and nothing surmountable bars them in their search for game. I expect ere long a leaf from the Major's notebook, then I will be able to furnish the readers of THE AMERICAN ANGLER much lively, interesting matter. [. . .]
>
> **Colonel George F. Akers** has just returned from Virginia and a cruise on board the Fish Hawk. He ways that the James River teems with the finest black bass, and that from the bridge in Lynchburg he has caught many a fine one. While the guest of Professor Baird, on the Fish Hawk, he had an opportunity for studying the *modus operandi* of artificially hatching shad. The Colonel has done a great deal for the advancement of fish culture in Tennessee, and is still a devotee to the cause and an enthusiastic angler. He tells me that it is his intention to return to Virginia in a short while for another bout with the finny tribe."[312]

Another article shares some additional background on Col. Akers, informing us that he hired a Mr. W. A. Clendenning of Nashville, to paint a camp scene on the banks of the Buffalo River near Molyneux's mill.[313] It says:

---

[310] Smiley, Charles Wesley. A List of the Published Reports of the Commissioners [of Fish and Fisheries] Appointed by Authority of the Various States of the United States: With Other Papers Relating to the Fish Commission. United States: n.p., 1883, 123.

[311] Troop Roster for Battle of New Orleans, 180, available at:
https://www.nps.gov/jela/learn/historyculture/upload/CHALTroopRoster.pdf, accessed 4 Apr 2020

[312] *The American Angler*. United States: Angler's Publishing Company, 1885. Article on Pg 39 (Vol 6) of 19 July 1884 issue, emphasis added.

[313] *The American Angler*. United States: Angler's Publishing Company, 1885. Article on Pgs 148-149 (Vol 6) in the 6 Sep 1884 edition, emphasis added. The author has not located any images of the painting. If found, please inform the author at info@crossmountainbooks.com.

ANGLING IN KENTUCKY.—We are permitted to publish the following letter from a former Fish Commissioner of Tennessee to our correspondent, "J. D. D.":
ROCKCASTLE SPRINGS, Ky., August 1, 1882.—I have reached the "climax" of fishing grounds. This place is certainly properly named. "Jim Crow's" letters in the *Courier-Journal* faintly portray the grandeur of these hills and streams; but read him of the 80th ult. I am sitting in the Grand Piazza, fronting the river, with a party of friends. My No. 8 reel at my side and the hook one hundred feet from me, extends into the deep water in full view. I have had some lively tugs, and have landed several fine fish. "Salmon," jack, bass, channel cat and other game fish fill the waters, and the angler is happy.—GEO. F. AKERS.

Figure 186 - Aug 1882 Report to Forest and Stream from Former Fish Commissioner George Akers about fishing in KY

ON "THE BANKS OF THE BUFFALO."— NASHVILLE ANGLERS. Walking into Charley Griffith's hardware and fishing tackle emporium this morning, I was shown a very handsomely executed oil painting, representing a camp scene on the banks of "Buffalo" near Molyneux's mill.

The picture was painted for its owner, **Colonel George F. Akers**, by Mr. W. A. Clendenning of this city, as a lasting reminder of the good old times, and to perpetuate during future generations the memories of the distinguished anglers then living in and around Nashville.

The artist visited the spot, and has been most happy in the exact reproduction of the lovely scenery, and at the same time selecting a point from which to show all its beauties. The period of the year is the beginning of autumn, when in this latitude nature seems to go wild in her fantastic display of color. Great oaks wear their stern green foliage, midst the golden tints of the maple and the silvery hues of the sycamore; the sumac has on its scarlet mantle as if to defy the sombre blackjack, and scrubs of other kinds. Broad fields of ripening corn, others of stubble, half green with a second crop which Jack Frost has disputed the rights of — all bear an air of triumph and satisfaction that denoted the fulfillment of a Divine will in this charming landscape the artist has done more than display his facility of blending colors, by surrounding them with a peculiar hazy atmosphere which carries the spectator's thoughts back to the very truth of Nature herself.

Figure 187 – Endorsement from George Akers in The American Angler. United States: Angler's Publishing Company, 1883, 364.

It is in such a place that the tents are pitched, and lolling about in the genial, warm, sunshine I could recognize the life-like pictures of the party. Old Uncle Nick Hobson[314], the veteran of the squad, is reclining against a stately ash, looking intently at "Die Winburn" (the cook) preparing the mid-day meal. In the center of the group are Rev. A. L. P. Green[315], Charles E. Hillman, Colonel A. W. Johnson, Frank Furman, General Ira P. Jones, and **Colonel Akers**. They are evidently in warm discussion over the morning's events, or perhaps speculating upon the doings of their comrade Captain W[illiam]. Stockell, who can be seen at some distance up the stream in a boat industriously battling with a good sized bass. How great a stock of provisions was in the larder, the artist did not make note of, though he did show in the entrance to one of the tents an *amphora* which was not of ancient times, nor did it appear to be an urn used for depositing the ashes of some departed hero. Notwithstanding it may have contained the spirit of either Lincoln or Robertson[316].

Every appliance known to make camp life comfortable was included in the outfit of this noted party; still, they could hardly be called, each and every one, industrious sportsmen. Once or twice every year they assembled and repaired first to one stream then to another, and then enjoyed a few days' angling, as no persons about here do at present.

The Rev. Fountain E. Pitts[317] should have been included in the picture, but unfortunately no portrait of him could be found to take his likeness from. He was a genuine fisherman and sportsman, and often boasted of his love of angling from the pulpit. He found no more delightful moments to reflect about and worship his Maker than when in the solitude of some rippling stream.

The anecdotes and experiences, as told by the gentlemen, were vividly brought to my mind as I gazed upon each picture. I had known them all, and more than once in my youth have I accompanied several of them on fishing excursions, and seeing them so naturally represented, my thoughts wandered back with delight.

---

[314] Hobson House: Oldest Home in the Edgefield Community, Audrey Creel, "How the Civil War led to the Subdivision of East Nashville," see https://bygone-nashville.mtsu.edu/items/show/41 for more info.

[315] "**Alexander Little Page Green** (a.k.a. "A.L.P. Green") (1806 or 1807 – July 15, 1874) was an American Methodist leader, slaveholder, and co-founder of Vanderbilt University. He was the founder of the Southern Methodist Publishing House. He was instrumental in moving the Methodist General Conference to Nashville, Tennessee, where he was the minister of McKendree United Methodist Church. He was an authority on fishing." https://en.wikipedia.org/wiki/Alexander_Little_Page_Green

[316] "Robertson" here likely refers to James Robertson (28 Jun 1742 – 1 Sep 1814), founder of Nashville & state senator.

[317] "**Fountain E. Pitts** (July 4, 1808 – May 22, 1874) was an American Methodist minister and Confederate chaplain. He established Methodist missions in Brazil and Argentina in 1835–1836. During the American Civil War, he was a chaplain and colonel in the Confederate States Army, and he became known as the "Fighting Parson". After the war, he was the first pastor of the McKendree Church (later known as the West End United Methodist Church) in Nashville, Tennessee, U.S. He also grew poppies to make opium." Source: https://en.wikipedia.org/wiki/Fountain_E._Pitts

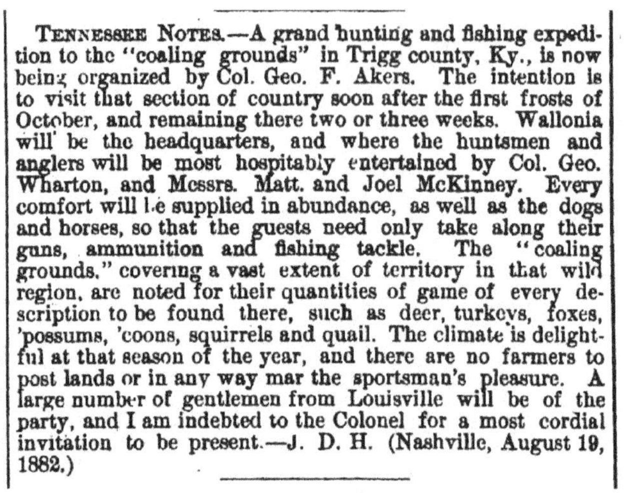

It is to be regretted that when **Colonel Akers** conceived the idea of having this historical work of art executed, he had not included in it the portraits of the late John Yeatman, Henry Yeatman[318], James A. McAlister, Colonel Otis, W. Armstead, Silas Macey, **Major Harry Heiss**, Alf. Horseley, and John Terrass. The souvenir would have then been complete, and the picture entitled to a post of honor in the library of our State capital.

TENNESSEE NOTES.—A grand hunting and fishing expedition to the "coaling grounds" in Trigg county, Ky., is now being organized by Col. Geo. F. Akers. The intention is to visit that section of country soon after the first frosts of October, and remaining there two or three weeks. Wallonia will be the headquarters, and where the huntsmen and anglers will be most hospitably entertained by Col. Geo. Wharton, and Messrs. Matt. and Joel McKinney. Every comfort will be supplied in abundance, as well as the dogs and horses, so that the guests need only take along their guns, ammunition and fishing tackle. The "coaling grounds," covering a vast extent of territory in that wild region, are noted for their quantities of game of every description to be found there, such as deer, turkeys, foxes, 'possums, 'coons, squirrels and quail. The climate is delightful at that season of the year, and there are no farmers to post lands or in any way mar the sportsman's pleasure. A large number of gentlemen from Louisville will be of the party, and I am indebted to the Colonel for a most cordial invitation to be present.—J. D. H. (Nashville, August 19, 1882.)

Figure 188 - 19 Aug 1882 George Akers is organizing a hunting and fishing expedition to KY - *Forest and Stream* 1883

At the time the older of these gentlemen lived, the fishing tackle in use was far more expensive, and infinitely inferior to that made to-day. These facts, however, gave rise to the practical application of their genius as sportsmen; they were compelled to make up their own inventions, and as a consequence, many of them became expert. I remember having seen lines, rods, seines, and landing nets of their handiwork, which would be recognized as excellent work even to-day; while knitting hooks on snoods no one could do more nicely than either Nick Hobson or Colonel Johnson. Except to do such rough work, and such jobs about the camp, as would interfere with their angling, these gentlemen did their own work, consequently there were no loafers permitted along, and when a candidate for membership showed a want of the sportsman's industry, he was dropped. The farmers along the various streams always hailed their appearance with pleasure; they would furnish them with poultry, eggs, milk, and butter, and be ever ready to serve them in any way. There was no bad faith, indecorous conduct, or infringement of rights practiced by the club, but, on the contrary, they made friends wherever they pitched their tents.

I hope that one of these days Colonel Akers will have the picture engraved or lithographed, certain as I am that every angler in the United States would gladly own a copy of it to hang up as a reminder to the rising generation. Not a single person represented in it but has the reverence (if dead) or the respect (if living) of every man, woman, and child who ever heard his name mentioned.

Nashville, August 27, 1884.   Climax.

---

[318] Henry Clay Yeatman at Petra and in the Levant, 1854 by David Kennedy, 24 Jun 2021, https://tinyurl.com/yeatmanatpetra

Still another article in the *Forest and Stream* written 11 July 1881 mentions both Heiss and Akers, "Several parties have been out fishing lately and had fair luck, though the present weather is entirely too hot for out-door sports. **Major Heiss**, of this city, is still in the mountains of East Tennessee, enjoying his angling tour. The "Major" is one of the most scientific and untiring disciples of "Sir Izaak" in this section, and, when he makes a raid on the fiery beauties, he never returns without his game. General Ira P. Jones is another of our noted fishermen, and a more genial and cultivated gentleman would be hard to find. As we say out here, "**George Akers** takes the cake." There is almost as much pleasure in listening to some of his fish stories as to catch them yourself, for in the former case you are sure to catch some big ones."[319]

The 1883 *Forest and Stream* Volume 19 includes an awesome exchange of letters regarding the new Fish Commissioner, Edward D. Hicks, and the Tennessee Governor. In the article it mentions that Col George F. Akers resigned his position at Fish Commissioner for Middle Tennessee "some time ago," and then includes a fun exchange. Hicks writes to the governor and sends him a new fishing rod claiming he learned that the governor's "highest aspiration" was to "yank out by main strength and awkwardness a slimy catfish from one of the sluggish muddy streams of West Tennessee" and claiming that once the governor lands a game black bass he will "emerge from the slime and become a respectable fisherman." Governor Alvin Hawkins (Republican) who served from 1881 to 1883, said the following, "I have 'cast' my line in some of the clear, rippling streams of the West 'peopled' with game fish moving through their crystal waters, or, anon, rushing as if on the wings of the wind to some deep, dark and shady pool, and the sight of which, as they darted hither and thither, has made my sport-man's heart to expand and glow with confident expectation that soon, perhaps, a half dozen or more, 'turning' one to five pounds each, would grace my basket. But the beautiful rod sent through your kindness would have been of little practical use then — it has no reel nor line; in fact, there is accompanying it but little of the paraphernalia which renders such rods so efficient in the hands of practical fishermen. **Again. I have made 'casts' in the pearly streams of East Tennessee — that secluded mountain land, the Italy of North America and the Eden of our sunny southland — where, truly to gladden the bounding heart of the disciple of Izaak**

Figure 189 - French Broad River, Wolf Creek, TN – Close to Weaver's Bend - Photo by the Author 23 Oct 2017

---

[319] *Forest and Stream*. United States: Forest and Stream Publishing Company, 1881. Vol 16, 494, emphasis added.

Walton[320], 'jocund day stands tiptoe on the misty mountain top,' and where, in drinking in the beauties of nature and the sublime and awe-inspiring grandeur which breaks upon the vision at every turn, one is constrained to exclaim, with a heart swelling with pride and every instinct of his being aglow with legitimate enthusiasm, 'This is my own beloved Tennessee.' I am sure the poet who wrote 'I would not stay alway,' etc., was not an East Tennessean and had never even visited that enchanted land, as I have done — never made incursions upon the denizens of her gloriously beautiful streams which reflect back to heaven the myriad rays of sunlight falling upon their rippling surfaces, as I have done. But I imagine no bass was ever taken from with a rod, however "aesthetic" the proportions, which was so sadly wanting in the appurtenances to a complete trout rod as the one sent. Permit me to again thank you for your highly appreciated gift — naked as it is. Very respectfully — Alvin Hawkins[321]." J. D. H."[322]

These are the men who Isham enjoyed spending time with, Maj Harry Heiss, and Col. George Akers. And from the description by the governor, and others – no wonder they wanted to spend as much time as they could with Isham, fishing on the French Broad in East Tennessee. **Scan the QR Code to the right to experience CMB LIVE: Stand with the author on the bank of the French Broad River in Wolf Creek, TN**.

Figure 190 - **CMB Live** - Bank of the French Broad River in Wolf Creek, TN https://youtu.be/udczc UeGAEQ

Sawbones articles from 1879-1886 are continued in…

Sawbones: The Life and Times of Dr. Isham Talbot Peck (1811-1887) Volume II

---

[320] "**Izaak Walton** (baptized 21 Sep 1593 – 15 Dec 1683) was an English writer. Best known as the author of *The Compleat Angler*, he also wrote a number of short biographies including one of his friend John Donne. They have been collected under the title of *Walton's Lives.*" https://en.wikipedia.org/wiki/Izaak_Walton

[321] "**Alvin Hawkins** (2 Dec 1821 – 27 Apr 1905) was an American jurist and politician. He served as the 22nd Governor of Tennessee from 1881 to 1883, one of just three Republicans to hold this position from the end of Reconstruction to the latter half of the 20th century. Hawkins was also a judge on the Tennessee Supreme Court in the late 1860s, and was briefly the U.S. consul to Havana, Cuba, in 1868." https://en.wikipedia.org/wiki/Alvin_Hawkins

[322] Forest and Stream. United States: Forest and Stream Publishing Company, 1883. 7 Sep 1882 issue. 110. Emphasis added.

CONCLUSION FOR SAWBONES ARTICLES

In total, I have found 25 articles written by Isham under the pen name Sawbones between 25 Mar 1874 and 13 Oct 1886, and one article written by him to *The Spirit of the Times* in 1852. In addition, during the same period, 17 articles were written addressed to him or about him, mostly in *The Morristown Gazette*, but also various other papers around the country.

In sharing his thoughts and opinions with the local paper and its editor John Helms, and after careful analysis, we have a compendium of life in East Tennessee during the Reconstruction Era and before.

In *Sawbones: Volume II*, the final 18 articles written between 12 Mar 1879 and 13 Oct 1886 are analyzed thoroughly. In addition, 7 appendices are added to *Volume II*. Subjects include Isham's Letters and a 40-page genealogical report which includes every descendant of Isham and Emma Peck.

PERSONAL NOTE FROM THE AUTHOR

How is it possible to get to know your ancestors in a meaningful way? So often in family research we are presented with a few photos, sometimes with no names on them. If we are lucky, we get our hands on some family documents with family charts, or perhaps some wills, birth/death certificates, and perhaps a mention in a book or newspaper.

Because Isham and his family took the time to write to the newspapers, and his sons published their own newspapers, and Charley wrote his book, and Emma kept Ada's Journal, and the Allen family hung on to the letters written between the families…we have LIFE recorded, poetry describing the difficulty of going through *Every Day* (see Charley's poem on pg 82 of *Charley's Novel*) in the 1800s, and a record of some of the lesser-known events, controversies, and debates of the day.

In the same way that my family before me took the time to write things down, and sometimes publish them, it brings me great joy to chronicle this information for everyone. It allows each of us to study the past, which informs our present and future. As the COVID-19 pandemic hit our world in the winter/spring of 2020, I was asked to remain home from work for a period of four months. My usual activity, visiting airmen in squadrons across the base, and counseling individuals and couples, grinded to a halt. My family kept their bedtime of 9 p.m., but my stored-up energy pushed me to research and write well into the night/early morning for weeks and months on end.

These volumes about Sawbones have been composed in bursts, and then slowly, and then more bursts over the past 3 years. I am forever indebted to the numerous family members, 1st, 2nd, 3rd, and 4th cousins included, who have helped me with my research. It has been great to get to know you!

A couple years ago I finally picked out a simple meerschaum pipe, and though I don't smoke, I still occasionally put it in my mouth. It sits next to me on my desk, which is surrounded by my research…newspapers and books relating to East Tennessee and family history especially. I think of Isham, and the newspaper men visiting him at his Wolf Creek estate, and them relating stories to each other of their life and times, and his friends, and the river, and the mountains. And I smile.

INDEX

Cross Mountain Books

In addition to *Sawbones Volume I*, please enjoy *Ada's Journal*, *Charley's Novel*, *Oblique City*, and forthcoming *He Loved the Folks* in The Pecks of Mossy Creek series.

Sawbones: The Life and Times of Dr. Isham Talbot Peck, Volume II

In the same style as Sawbones Volume I, author Andy Peck analyzes 18 additional Sawbones article published between 1879 and 1886. Topics covered include: Wolf Creek, Tennessee, the Buncombe Train, Mark Twain, extensive coverage of Mossy Creek / Jefferson City and its surrounding area, Carson-Newman University, 19th Century Medicine, Jesse James, the East Tennessee and Virigina Railroad, Hot Springs, North Carolina, President Andrew Jackson, Mississippi River Flooding, Bob Ingersoll, Plural-Marriage, Thomas Edison, Charles Darwin, Geology, Maj Harry Heiss, and D. L. Moody and Ira Sankey. Extensive appendices include: outline descendant reports for all children of Isham and Emma Peck to modern day, Isham's Letters, Early Plantation Life in Madison Parish, Louisiana, Peck land in the courts, and photos of Peck Family Gravestones.

ISBN 9781955121125 (pbk) | ISBN 9781955121132 (hardcover) | ISBN 9781955121149 (ebook)

Amazon Customer Review

Did you purchase Sawbones on Amazon? Please leave a review!

Reviews are a tremendous help in sharing the Pecks of Mossy Creek story with others!
Would you please take a moment and leave a review today?

Ordering Signed Copies

Would you like to order signed copies of a Cross Mountain Books title? To order, send an email to:
info@crossmountainbooks.com

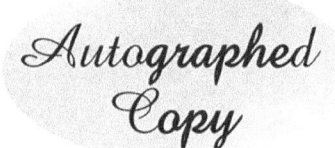

Copies may be secured for gift and personal use, or wholesale which includes a discount. Order copies for a friend, family member, or your business today!

Ada's Journal: The Civil War Era Journal and Letters of Emma Peck

Ada's Journal provides a window into history. Ada Louise Peck was a well-loved little girl (and Charley Peck's sister) who traveled back and forth between Mossy Creek, Tennessee and East Carroll Parish, Louisiana, starting in 1853. She experienced trials, health problems, and travel by railroad, steamboat, and stagecoach. This journal, recorded from Ada's perspective by her mom Emma, records the first two years of her short life. Edited by Andy Peck, over 70 photographs, maps, and historical references bring this true story to life in a powerful way. Journey with little Ada on a Mississippi River steamboat; keep your hands inside the train as you pass through the half-mile Cumberland Mountain Tunnel on the East Tennessee and Georgia Railroad; and enjoy the mountain hospitality at the Wolf Creek Inn as Ada visits with Mrs. Emma Allen, Peck family friend and hostess to hundreds along the French Broad River.

ISBN 9781955121002 (pbk) | ISBN 9781955121019 (hardcover)

ISBN 9781955121026 (ebook)

Amazon Customer Review

Experience Southern thoughts and fears of the American Civil War

Since I have always been fascinated by our tragic, American Civil War, the time frame of Ada's Journal & Emma's Letters naturally peaked my interest. I loved how Emma Peck wrote in the perspective of her beloved little daughter, Ada. Being from Dixie myself, I was able to understand and appreciate the Southern point of view Emma Peck and Emma Allen voiced concerning their thoughts and fears of the Civil War. Bring a descendant of Adam Peck, Sr., I was both surprised and delighted when this excellent book was published. I highly recommend this book.

Cross Mountain Books™

SCAN ME

amazon

Scan QR Code to purchase Ada's Journal from Amazon. To purchase signed copies, order directly from Cross Mountain Books.

www.crossmountainbooks.com/ada

Charley's Novel: Mary Anderson and Peacock the Mineralogist, the Bad Luck of a Young Southern Girl

Written in 1879, and set in Eastern Tennessee, North Carolina, Virginia, and West Virginia, this epic tale shares the compelling story of Mary Anderson, a wealthy young southern girl enchanted by the reputable and knowledgeable Mr. Peacock. Mary's father, Mr. Anderson, is eager to place his daughter and family in a better position with such a profitable union. But what if the allure of Peacock's beautiful feathers turns into a case of fatal attraction? Honeymoon excitement suddenly turns to tragedy in the mountains of North Carolina, and life will never be the same for Mary and her family. How will she handle her position as a refined young woman, wife, and mother, as she endures the abuse of the stranger, Mr. Peacock? Will Peacock fulfill his many promises? Will Mary fight her way to independence? Is there hope for her and her little boy?

ISBN 9781955121163 (pbk)
ISBN 9781955121170 (hardcover)
ISBN 9781955121187 (ebook)

Amazon Customer Review

★ ★ ★ ★ ★   **Charley's Novel causes a rollercoaster of emotions.**

Charley's Novel: Mary Anderson and Peacock the Mineralogist, The Bad Luck of a Young Southern Girl was a thrilling book to read because of the extreme diversity in its characters. The book had me hoping for the best possible outcome for the lead female character due to the scoundrel who tricked her into marrying him. I found myself experiencing incredible emotions of happiness, sadness, frustration, excitement and satisfaction. You will be happy you read this spellbinding novel.

Cross Mountain Books ™

SCAN ME

amazon

Scan QR Code to purchase Charley's Novel from Amazon. To purchase signed copies, order directly from Cross Mountain Books.

www.crossmountainbooks.com/charley

Oblique City: Wolf Creek, Tennessee

In 1893, Lewis W. Murch and his associates formed the American Oblique Manufacturing and City Development Company. In their attempt to entice investors from America and around the world, they developed this Prospectus. Though the hotel, manufacturing plants, and other dreams never materialized, Oblique City stands as a beautiful snapshot of what Wolf Creek, Tennessee (Cocke County) and the surrounding area looked like in the 1890s.

Oblique City contains references to: Minnehaha Cascade (Wolf Creek Falls); mountains, creeks and lakes; trout fishing, the Biltmore in Asheville, North Carolina; commerce in Newport, Tennessee; East Tennessee and North Carolina Railroad History, and visions of a temperance city where immorality would be unknown.

This first of its kind Historical Reprint contains original pages with 42 illustrations, engraved woodcuts from photographs, maps, and portraits. Index added.

Oblique City contains multiple images of Dr. Isham Peck's Wolf Creek home along with background information about the Peck family.

ISBN 9781955121200 (pbk) | ISBN 9781955121217 (hardcover)
ISBN 9781955121224 (ebook)

Amazon Customer Review

★ ★ ★ ★ ★ **It will transform you to the late 19th century**

I really enjoyed the descriptive details of Wolf Creek, TN and the beautiful French Broad River Valley in the late 19th Century. Some of my ancestors help settle this area and I have visited and explored Wolf Creek and the French Broad River and many other nearby places within Pisgah National Forrest. Oblique City gave me the chance to reexperience one of my favorite childhood vacations. It is too bad the American Oblique Manufacturing and City Development Company never came to fruition. What a fantastic place it would have been to both live and work. I strongly recommend this short book.

Scan QR Code to purchase Oblique City from Amazon. To purchase signed copies, order directly from Cross Mountain Books.
www.crossmountainbooks.com

*****Forthcoming Title*****

He Loved the Folks: Dr. Edward Jerome Peck
of Hot Springs, North Carolina by Andy Peck

In *He Loved the Folks*, learn how this doctor from Wolf Creek, Tennessee gently influenced the entire area around Hot Springs, North Carolina for good by his steady, faithful, medical care. Dr. Ed Peck (son of Dr. Isham Talbot Peck) was so loved at the time of his death, that the community came together and erected a monument to honor his life and love. He doctored Jane (Hicks) Gentry, the Appalachian folklorist and singer, and served important Hot Springs institutions including the Dorland Institute, Mountain Park Hotel, and the Southern Railway Surgeons Association. In *He Loved the Folks*, you will catch a glimpse as to why this man was so loved by the Hot Springs community, as he dedicated his life to them.

ISBN 9781955121040 (pbk)
ISBN 9781955121057 (hardcover)
ISBN 9781955121064 (ebook)

Peck Family visiting the Fairview Methodist Church, Hot Springs, NC memorial to Dr. Edward Peck (Top Left) Nette Peck (Top Right) Andy Peck with dad Drew Peck (Bottom Left) Andy with oldest son Justice Peck (Bottom Right) Andy with son Hudson Peck